MYSTICISM AFTER MODERNISM

CROWLEY, EVOLA, NEVILLE, WATTS, COLIN WILSON
& OTHER POPULIST GURUS

JAMES J. O'MEARA

MANTICORE PRESS

MYSTICISM AFTER MODERNISM: CROWLEY, EVOLA, NEVILLE, WATTS, COLIN WILSON AND OTHER POPULIST GURUS
James J. O'Meara
© Manticore Press, 2018. Second edition, 2020.
All rights reserved, no section of this book may be utilized without permission, including electronic reproductions without the permission of the author and publisher. Published in Australia.
Thema Classification:
QRYC (Esoteric Religions), VXMW (Magic), QDX (Popular Philosophy).
978-0-6487660-2-5
MANTICORE PRESS
WWW.MANTICORE.PRESS

Sacred to the Memory of
John N. Deck, PhD
Late Professor of Philosophy,
University of Windsor

"Πλωτῖνος ὁ καθ᾽ ἡμᾶς γεγονὼς φιλόσοφος …"

Porphyry,
Vita Plotini, 1

CONTENTS

Preface		7
1.	There & Then: *Personal & Memorial Reflections on Alan Watts*	9
2.	Alan Watts: The First Alt-Academic	29
3.	Re-Kindling Alan Watts	43
4.	"PC is for Squares, Man": *Alan Watts & the Game of Trump*	97
5.	Of Apes, Essence & The Afterlife	113
6.	Curses, Cut-Ups, & Contraptions: *The "Disastrous Success" of William Burroughs' Magick*	125
7.	"The Name is Crowley…Aleister Crowley": *Reflections on Enlightenment & Espionage*	141
8.	Two Orders: Evola and Hesse	153
9.	Battle of the Magicians: *Baron Evola between the Dancer & the Druid*	179
10.	Everything You Know Is Wrong! *Emericus Durden's Philosophical Fight Club*	197

11.	Lords of the Visible World: *A Modern Reconstruction of an Ancient Heresy*	215
12.	Ever Sacred, Ever Vexed: *Getting Down with the Lord of the Codes (Erik Davis)*	229
13.	Magick For Housewives: *The Not-so New Thought of Neville Goddard*	241
14.	Neville and the Rebel *(Colin Wilson's Religion and the Rebel)*	283
15.	The Secret of Trump's a Peale	315
16.	Lord Kek Commands! *A Look at the Origins of Meme Magic*	335

Index 349

PREFACE

> One can expect that one day religion, as well as theology itself, will become an *experimental science*, certainly an upheaval, not lacking interest, that leads us back to a proper view of mystical and traditional esotericism.[1]

A *specter is haunting Western culture: the specter of the populist guru.*

In the wake of the populist revolt against globalist tyranny, and its controversial tribunes like Trump, it's time for a look at what can now be discerned as an equally new development, on the fringes of Western civilization, among what came to be known as "popular culture," during the so-called pre- and post-war eras: a new kind of spiritual teacher or "guru," one more interested in methods, techniques and results than in dogmas, institutions, or—especially—followers.

Teachers like Alan Watts, Neville Goddard, Julius Evola, Aleister Crowley, and Colin Wilson; independent, critical, and above all, practical. Spiritual swashbucklers, taking no prisoners.

J. K. Krishnamurti was probably the first to be called an "anti-guru," and Alan Watts certainly recognized some affinities with him,[2] yet he was still too much in the guru mode—jet-setting around from Ojai to Gstaad, setting up retreat centers, counseling celibacy

---

[1] Julius Evola, "The New Spirit Movement"; originally published in *Bilychnis*, June, 1928.

[2] See *In My Own Way: An autobiography: 1915–1965* (New York: Pantheon, 1972).

while conducting adulterous affairs, etc.—to make the cut. All this has been exposed by the amusingly named U. G. Krishnamurti, yet the latter doesn't count either, since he seems to simply dismiss the spiritual quest altogether.[3]

Perhaps those who have looked in vain for a revival of traditional spirituality, and despaired, have been looking in the wrong place. Perhaps it has been here since the chaos that followed the First European Civil War,[4] but in a new form, more appropriate for the Kali Yuga.

"The tale grew in the telling," as Tolkien mused;[5] and so it was only when collecting and revising these essays and reviews for publication that the theme seemed to emerge. I would like to once again thank Dr. Gregory R. Johnson of Counter-Currents Publishing for his inspiration and support for their writing; John Morgan IV for directing his keen editorial eye and vast historical knowledge on them at the same publication; and Gwendolyn Taunton, stern editrix at Manticore Press, for welcoming the title essay therein and now shepherding the whole collection towards the light of day.

James J. O'Meara

Buda-Pest, 2018

---

[3] See *Courage to Stand Alone: Conversations with U.G. Krishnamurti* by Ellen J. Chrystal (Brooklyn, NY: Autonomedia, 1997).

[4] "Most of the writers and intellectuals during [the 20s and 30s] realized they were living between two explosions and between two wars. We [today] are living in the after effects of the Second European Civil War, which is really what the Second World War in Europe amounted to. And the First World War was the First European Civil War." Jonathan Bowden, "Revisionism: Left & Right, Hard & Soft" (speech at the 12th meeting of the New Right in London on November 3, 2007); Counter-Currents, May 12, 2015.

[5] See his Foreword to *The Lord of the Rings*.

THERE & THEN:
PERSONAL & MEMORIAL REFLECTIONS ON ALAN WATTS (1915-1973)

"It is the peculiar nature of my adolescent explorings of the Devon countryside...that made me what I am – and in many other ways besides writing...I have never gained any taste for what lies beyond the experience of solitary discovery...I have dabbled in many branches of natural and human history, and have a sound knowledge of none, and the same goes for countless other things besides. I like a kind of wandering wood acquaintance, and no more; a dilettante's, not a virtuoso's; always the green chaos rather than the printed map...I place all this entirely upon the original adolescent experience, for I do not think I was born so..." – John Fowles, *The Tree*

It all began with the FCC. "It" being my now some forty years of interest in *outré* subjects of metaphysics and general esoterica, as well as a perhaps poorly planned or executed lifelong indifference to the bourgeois way of life and the expectations of "success" therein.[6]

And "FCC" being the Federal Communications Commission, which, in those quaint days before Libertard ideologues fastened the "Demon of the Economy" on society (and when, curiously, the economy itself was performing like gangbusters, only to enter at that point a three-decade decline, at least for the White working man, if not the 0.01%), actually dared to regulate the activities of those licensed to use the "Public Airways."

---

[6] Or, as Watts would say, he had managed to live by "getting by, even successfully, without really deserving to do so" (*In My Own Way: An autobiography: 1915–1965*, New York: Pantheon, 1972, p. 262).

One thing the FCC did was to create and enforce something called the "Fairness Doctrine." Now, while I'm sure there were some problems, the general idea produced a situation in which, despite there being only three networks, extraordinary varieties of opinion could be heard.[7]

Another public benefit of this "regulatory straitjacket" was that every station had to present a certain amount of "religious" programming, preferably on Sunday morning. Well, you can imagine how this would set off today's Left, especially the Sunday part ("We're not ALL Christians now, you know!" Worse than wishing people "Merry Christmas.") But this was just after the reign of Eisenhower, falsely remembered as an era of conformity and repression, but actually one of the freedoms of bland indifference: "In other words, our form of government has no sense unless it is founded in a deeply felt religious faith, and *I don't care what it is*."[8]

As usual, so-called "repression" and "censorship" resulted in creativity and innovation. Thus it was that Detroit's WBAX, "the station that glows in the dark," one of the pioneers of "free-form" or "progressive" FM radio,[9] began Sunday morning broadcasts of

---

[7] I recall, for instance, even after the ascension of Reagan, which began the barbarian assault, seeing a debate between Arnaud de Borchgrave, reputed spook and editor of the Moonie-owned *Washington Times*, and Alexander Cockburn, Communist columnist and publisher. Today, while typically much is made of a superficial "diversity" of appearance, and even "conservative" networks talk about being "fair and balanced," opinion is rigidly held to the respective "talking points" (another typical term) of the Democrat and Republican parties. Voices like Cockburn or Chomsky are banished to the "publicly supported" radio hinterlands, being "old White men" unfit to appear next to the vibrant voices of the Left (admittedly, Cockburn is dead, but you get my point).

[8] See the full context and subsequent history here: en.wikipedia.org/wiki/And_I_don%27t_care_what_it_is

[9] "[Program Director Dave] Dixon had a "golden ear," introducing attentive listeners to cross-cultural music on a world scale. Only on his show could one be exposed to such gems as Paul Horn's *Inside the Taj Mahal*, *Gandharva* from Beaver & Krause, Richard Harris singing *MacArthur Park* and Harry Nilsson's *The Point* (a complete LP side). In between, he might have mixed in a cut from John Mayall's *Blues From Laurel Canyon*, some Savoy Brown (with original vocalist Chris Youlden), Cat Mother & the All-Night Newsboys and a track from Tim Buckley's *Happy Sad* release. Toss in some Brian Auger Trinity (featuring Julie Driscoll on vocals) and Laura Nyro singing *Eli's Coming* for good measure. Not to be overlooked, Detroit artists such as Frost (Dick Wagner), the Amboy Dukes (Ted Nugent), SRC and the Stooges (Iggy Pop) would also be integrated into the mix." — http://floydslips.blogspot.com/2009/07/freeform-radio-masterdave-dixon-on-wabx.html#0

the recorded lectures, and the one or two LPs, of Alan Watts. Thus began, when and for how long exactly, I know not, my acquaintance with the voice and ideas of Alan Watts, which were to have a singularly profound influence on subsequent thoughts and, indeed, subsequent life.[10]

I never had a chance to meet Watts, or even to see and hear him perform live—a rock idiom that seems appropriate—perhaps on one of his many lecture tours, or later at college;[11] He died quite soon after I first started reading him, suddenly in his sleep, and unexpectedly, being barely in his 50s and having just published his seemingly premature autobiography.[12] In those pre-internet days, I learned of his death while paging through an issue of *Playboy*; Watts having been a sometime contributor[13] and seen as a promoter of Hef's self-styled "Playboy Philosophy," his death merited a mention in the front matter.

He had simply, in the natural way of things (the Way of the Tao, the "Watercourse Way" as his last, posthumously published book calls it), passed into my life, exerted a heavy influence, and then simply disappeared, almost as if he had never existed in the first place, merely some books and lectures attributed, with more or less confidence, to one "Alan Watts," author.

Apparently, I didn't miss much, as Watts by this time was almost continuously drunk and pretty useless as an advisor. What I did learn at college was that a psychology instructor, in his youth, had tried to visit The Master and, having tracked him down to his Sausalito houseboat (remember, no internet or Google) found him, in the middle of the afternoon, passed out drunk on the deck.

---

[10] Nor was I alone: "His KPFA radio program fueled the 'San Francisco Renaissance.'" *Alan Watts–Here and Now: Contributions to Psychology, Philosophy, and Religion*; ed. Peter J. Columbus and Donadrian L. Rice (Albany, NY: SUNY Press, 2012), p. 4.

[11] As it turned out, the only big name I would ever see there was Martin Mull, who performed in the Second World War era gymnasium and opened with a song apparently, and appropriately, entitled "I've Played in Lots of Shitholes But This One Takes the Cake;" Marshall McLuhan and Joyce Carol Oates don't count, since they worked there.

[12] Although by the same age, Colin Wilson had published *three* autobiographies, with more to come.

[13] Several of the essays collected in *Does IT Matter? Essays on Man's Relation to Materiality* (New York: Pantheon, 1970) made their first appearance there.

Moreover, this prevented, by a kind of divine *force majeure*, the development of the kind of guru-disciple relationship that Watts always disparaged. In one of his most famous slogans, "When you get the message, you hang up the phone."[14]

Better, then, than any silly "guru/disciple" racket, I had his autobiography, which I would recommend to anyone as both an engagingly written account of a remarkable life, and as a compendium of Watts' philosophy, or at least his best thoughts and one-liners, legitimately recycled while narrating their origin in the course of the surprisingly eventful life of a "philosophical entertainer."[15]

I read it constantly, rather in the way boys of the same age and time were reading Tolkien;[16] and as many of them did, I eventually slowed down until I reached a point where I can't say I've so much as looked at it—although I did acquire a nice first edition to put on

---

[14] The sort of time-wasting or downright dangerous shenanigans of the "guru cult" that Watts opposed are well studied by Georg Feuerstein, both yoga scholar and cult victim, in his *Holy Madness: The Shock Tactics and Radical Teachings of Crazy-Wise Adepts, Holy Fools, and Rascal Gurus* (New York: Paragon House, 1991; rev. ed. *Holy Madness: Spirituality, Crazy-Wise Teachers, And Enlightenment,* Chino Valley, AZ: Hohm, 2006). For Traditionalists like Guénon and Evola, the guru is needed to pass on the spiritual energy of initiation, literally bringing about a "re-birth" without which all study and practice is futile. Later we'll look at criticisms of Watts' "non-practice" style of Zen and whether Watts himself fits into Feuerstein's "enlightened but psychologically non-transformed" diagnosis. Oddly enough I did have some later mild contacts with both of Feuerstein's main subjects, Chogyam Trungpa, at Naropa, and Da Free John (known today as Adi Da). Ironically, it was Watts' own gushing blurb on DFJ's first book ("I think we have an avatar here") that seemed to legitimize his "crazy wisdom" style as being "in the Way" of Watts; of course, he was probably just drunk when he wrote it.

[15] Although author of lots of books (including one bestseller modestly entitled *The Book*), Watts would not suggest using his books, or any books, as a guide: "Every Easter Sunday should be celebrated with a solemn and reverent burning of the Holy Scriptures, for the whole meaning of the resurrection and ascension of Christ into heaven (which is within you) is that God-man-hood is to be discovered here and now inwardly, not in the letter of the Bible." *Beyond Theology. The Art of Godmanship* (New York: Pantheon, 1964), pp. 164-165.

[16] As a result, I never did get around to reading Tolkien (as always, too much of a real outsider to be a geek), and to this day I have resisted the Tolkien Cult; my nodding acquaintance with the Mythos derived entirely from a reading of the National Lampoon's *Bored of the Rings* (Henry N. Beard and Douglas C. Kenney, 1969; reissued in 2011, the Guardian thinks it's still worth a read, and so do I: http://www.theguardian.com/books/booksblog/2011/feb/08/tolkien-bored-of-the-rings).

my shelf—in years. But then, "When you get the message, you hang up the phone."

Whether I could have become a disciple of Watts is doubtful; I was about 15 at this time, living in Detroit, not California, and lacked the kind of ambition, or gumption, or brutal necessity of poverty or abuse, that would have driven me out onto the road to join the kids running away to join the Summer of Love.[17]

While brushing aside any Freudian interpretations with scorn and derision, I might as well stipulate here that, as alluded to elsewhere, my father was poorly educated railroad conductor who worked double shifts and weekends so as to insure he had no contact with what we would have to designate as his "family," myself and my mother. As far as I know I inherited nothing from him other than a tendency to violent outbursts at the most inauspicious times, while enjoying the dubious benefits of being able to read, listen to or—within the limits of my wallet and the aforesaid lack of gumption—do anything I pleased.[18]

Was Watts, then, a (shudder) "father figure"? Perhaps. Further evidence might lie ahead.

For, after whimsically choosing to attend an unheralded college in provincial Ontario (again, remarkable lack of parental supervision, they being happy as long as it was a Catholic college), I had decided to major in Philosophy, since that seemed to be where Watts' ideas seemed to have led, and as noted, my parents had no interest in any practical results of my studies.[19] Fortunately, Windsor,

---

[17] You can find a mixture of both gumption and poverty in the 1933 film *Wild Boys on the Road*, in which nice, polite boys of the era decide the Depression has made them a burden to their families, and so take off to meet their fates on the road. Everyone was nice and polite then, even the kids and hobos! Today, they'd just move into the basement.

[18] See Greg Johnson's "Interview with James J. O'Meara" in *The Homo and the Negro* (San Francisco: Counter-Currents, 2012; Embiggened edition, 2017). As noted there, my mother, although an illiterate raised in the back country of the West Indies, did have, like many such primitive people, an unsuspected talent: something akin to astral projection, which could also account for my interests in the realms of the esoteric.

[19] "'Pheelosophy!' she exclaimed. 'Why you can't make a living out of phee*los*ophy!' The clouded crystal ball. But *then* I almost believed her." *In My Own Way*, p. 146. Well, I wasn't going to waste time like Watts, I'd plunge right into the contemplative life. That this perfectly suited my indolent nature was purely coincidental.

in its very backwardness, was more like the sort of seminaries Watts was familiar with, teaching Aristotle and St. Thomas, rather than the modern, analytic schools that Watts loathed, where one "does" philosophy from 9 to 5 and then home to martinis.[20] I did dabble a bit in Asian Studies, and Religious Studies, but not at all in Psychology, but they were clearly as limited to specialists as Watts would have thought.[21]

Besides, since Watts advocated a "no-practice" approach to spirituality, [22] there didn't seem to be any need, or much point, in undertaking anything but a theoretical path.[23]

And sure enough, though apparently wandering aimlessly and un-guided through the *venia legendi*, I found myself smack dab under the influence of another likely "father figure," Prof. John Norbert Deck, PhD.[24]

Now Deck, though apparently rather more anti-Zionist than even most of his generation,[25] did show a propensity to create what Kevin MacDonald has called the "Jewish Guru Effect," the creation of authoritarian study groups around charismatic figures, often involving the creation of private languages to keep outsiders at bay.[26]

---

[20] *In My Own Way*, p. 117, paraphrasing William Earle of Northwestern.

[21] Although, as noted, it was a Psychology professor who had actually developed an interest in Watts.

[22] According to Columbus & Rice, it's even known as "the Alan Watts fallacy." (p. 8)

[23] Deck, in fact, made quite a study of *theoria* among the Greeks; see his doctoral dissertation, *Nature, Contemplation and the One* (Toronto: University of Toronto Press, 1967; Burdett, NY: Larson, 1998; Toronto Heritage series, 2017 [Kindle iOS version], Appendix A; while the text of my Introduction to Philosophy class, Josef Pieper's *Leisure: The Basis of Culture* (New York: Pantheon, 1952; new translation by Gerald Malsbary, with an Introduction by Roger Scruton, South Bend, IN: St. Augustine's Press, 1998) promoted, based on St. Thomas if not Guénon, the need for a caste devoted to pure contemplation. This was an easy transition from Watts, whom a contemporary reviewer considered to be "one of the few contemporary [1953!] philosophers for whom contemplative reflection precedes action in the world." – Columbus and Rice, p. 7, quoting P. Wheelwright.

[24] It occurs to me that both Watts and Deck had huge families, with over 12 children and grandchildren, although Deck, the more traditional Catholic, had but one, obviously rather put-upon, wife.

[25] Unlike those romantic types who moved to Canada to join the RAF when America was still neutral, he had moved to Canada to escape the draft.

[26] See Kevin MacDonald, *The Culture of Critique* (2002)

Looking like Schopenhauer but dressed as a Trotskyite shop steward, Deck was easily the most oddly charismatic professor around, and I eagerly joined his Neoplatonic cult.[27] In an unprecedented burst of enthusiasm, I completed my coursework in little more two years, and eagerly entered the more private realms of the graduate seminar. Whereupon, the heavy-smoking, heavy-German-food-eating Deck dropped dead, in his mid-fifties.

That's right, dear readers, two mentors, both almost immediately dead. And I was barely twenty![28]

Though something of detour, I do fancy I picked up enough of the Greeks and the Scholastics to finally be able – after about another twenty years – to read and appreciate the "Big Shots" that Watts initially promoted, like Guénon[29] and Coomaraswamy, although I knew that Watts himself had come to find them a limited, and limiting, perspective.

So what, other than "Phee*los*ophy," did I learn or absorb from Watts? Although Watts insisted that metaphysics was always "rockily practical" itself—there, I picked that up!—it's mostly the practical matters that most readily come to mind, covered in the two aforesaid volumes, *In My Own Way* and *Does It Matter?* (the latter containing several of the aforesaid Playboy essays[30]); the first taking, of course, a more mouthwatering discursive approach, the former

---

[27] In what now seems a rather Straussian feature, all Western philosophy was secretly trying to emulate Plotinus. If you squinted hard enough.

[28] In all this, I fancied a remarkable similarity to the literally fatal influences Thomas Mann brought to bear on his character, Adrian Leverkuhn, in *Docktor Faustus*. That Leverkuhn was a stand-in for Nietzsche certainly warmed the old *amour-propre* if not *amor fati*. Prof. Schlepfuss was an obvious doppelganger for Deck, right down to his affectation of a "Jesuitical hood" accompanied by ironic bowing and hat-tipping to students (or, in Deck's case, a Franciscan cloak and designating his rather dim students as "Doctors" and fellow members of "the happy research team").

[29] The analogy I draw in "The Eldritch Evola" between Traditionalism and "weird fiction" lies in my inability to read Guénon's more apocalyptic writings without an actual feeling of dread overcoming myself. See *The Eldritch Evola…& Others* (San Francisco: Counter-Currents, 2012).

[30] And given a thoughtful review by Greg Johnson in his *Confessions of a Reluctant Hater* (2nd Ed., Revised and Expanded; San Francisco: Counter-Currents, 2016).

more thematic, if not really "scholarly" or academic, the sort of light touch that led some to sneeringly call him a "popularizer."[31]

Take "Murder in the Kitchen," a consideration of our confusion of "diet with medicine and cooking with pharmacology," trashing kitchens designed like laboratories ("molecular gastronomy," anyone?) and nasty plastic-ware made in Japan (now in China). In addition to inculcating a lifelong concern with what might be called bohemian gourmandizing, along the way Watts exposes vegetarians as philosophically inconsistent, ignoring the proven pain and emotions of plants simply because they lack faces and vocal chords. Not an argument likely to convince Savitri Devi,[32] but still useful at a time when the ethical pretensions of the trendy among us have moved beyond vegetarianism to veganism (collecting honey is exploitation, man!) and even raw food (cooked food being obviously fatal), seeking ever more rarified levels of moral and "scientific" one-upmanship over the proles.[33]

"Clothes – On and Off" take the same approach—"spiritual materialism"—to chart a sensible way between the false alternatives of asceticism (religious or "scientific") and senseless indulgence.[34] In

---

[31] Columbus and Rice, *op. cit.*, choose to press heavily on the "dreary" and "repressive" note when mentioning his upbringing in pre-War England, as did Watts himself, but he certainly benefited from the comparative richness of even a second-rate public school, learning enough to skip college and then later enter a seminary knowing more than the other students and even the instructors, eventually producing a translation of Dionysus' *Divine Names* (Deck would have approved!) Watts would point out that he could lard his books with Greek quotations and ponderous references, but what would be the point, other than to impress some stuffy academics?

[32] See *Impeachment of Man* (Costa Mesa, Cal.: The Noontide Press, 1991).

[33] Earlier (1955), James Bond found it useful as a pick-up line: "You wouldn't do that if you knew that flowers scream when they are picked," said Bond. …There's an Indian called Professor Bhose, who's written a treatise on the nervous system of flowers. He measured their reaction to pain. He even recorded the scream of a rose being picked. It must be one of the most heart-rending sounds in the world. I heard something like it as you picked that flower." "I don't believe it, "she said. "Anyway," she said maliciously, "I wouldn't have thought you were a person to get sentimental." – *Moonraker*, Chapter 16.

[34] Baron Evola took a similar approach in his magical and alchemical writing; abstaining from meat, for example, was a matter of spiritual hygiene, not sentimentality, and could be ruthlessly inverted in, say, Tantric rituals. Part of Watts' attraction to Da Free John likely derived from a similar practical approach; though endorsing a raw food diet, DFJ also sanctioned the strategic use of "dietary extras" as part of his "Crazy Wisdom" style.

this case, Watts abjured both the tightly laced-up, up-tight styles of "square" adults and the "aggressively slovenly and dowdy" (*In My Own Way*, p. 359) styles of the hippies. He wonders, sounding like a scold for once, how people could take all those drugs and then wear those awful, dreary hippie duds. Even when Watts still affected "normal" Western clothes, they were well-tailored (complete with walking stick 'for swagger' as he explained to a puzzled customs agent on his arrival in the States) enough to fit in at Sterling Cooper, and even in his Orientalist period they were replaced by immaculate, classical kimonos – with sword!

As the reference to *Mad Men*'s ad agency suggests, today we've sunk so far into sartorial slobbery that even those "stuffy" old White men (who share Watts' affection for mass quantities of vodka) seem swaggeringly stylish. Why, Alan would be right at home in Bert's Japonaiserie office, bow tie and all!

Perhaps Watts didn't quite get his own argument right; if he could have put aside a reflexive anti-Western, anti-businessman bias, and seen how low our clothing—especially the pants—would sink, he might have stuck with the Edwardian look. Perhaps, as Greg Johnson suggests, he just needed a better tailor?[35]

> Watts [actually] offers a defense of dandyism as a rebellion against modern democratic leveling and conformism, as well as uptight and aggressive relations to one another and the natural world. He

---

"While this strict diet and periodic fasting were being observed in San Francisco, the guru and his fluctuating, but small, inner circle appeared to be engaging in increasingly riotous, drunken parties. I was told by one of the guru's housekeepers that Da Free John and his "intimate associates" had somehow spent $18,000, *in one month*, on gourmet food items and booze! If true, this represents almost miraculous excess, given the power of the dollar in 1974." Scott Lowe, "The Strange Case of Franklin Jones," in *DA: The Strange Case of Franklin Jones* by Scott Lowe and David Lane (Walnut CA: Mt. San Antonio College, 1996). Rudolf Steiner, in response to a student struggling over his diet, advised that "It is better to eat ham than to think about ham."

[35] A not entirely facetious rebuttal; Watts may indeed not have been able to find a good tailor after leaving London. Paul Fussell, whose *Class: A Guide to the American Class System* (New York: Summit, 1983) served to expand and update Watts' careful sartorial observations, remarks therein that "It is possible to become incapable of being comfortable in anything *but* a Brooks Brothers suit." The actual fitting of a bespoke suit in London takes months, and includes an afternoon of crawling around on all fours.

might also add Puritanical Gnosticism. There is no reason why the playful and refined embrace of material existence should not allow some room for male vanity. "Human beings the whole world over need to relax, become *gentle*men, take themselves lightly, and 'come off it.' Easy, gracious, and colorful clothing might well be a beginning" (p. 68). But Watts also needs to "come off it" and admit that military uniforms, along with priestly vestments, are one of the great Western bastions of dandyism.[36]

More generally, Watts was certainly aware of, and opposed to, the way the need, as he perceived it, to "relax" was being perverted into "let it all hang out." As Columbus and Rice note, though he was one of the founders of Esalen and the "human potential movement" himself, he was by no means supporter of "Beat" culture. *In My Own Way* has a stunning rejoinder to all that hot tub chatter:

> In such situations people will invariably say to me, "Oh come on, Alan, we haven't yet seen *the real you*." To which I can only reply, "Well, look, I am right here, all of me, and if you can't see you must question your own sensitivity." (p. 209)

He goes on to point out that the "metaphysical assumptions" of such hot-tub chatter, superficially "friendly" but really aimed to tear down and re-build, are "ill-digested Darwin and Freud, with a touch of Jesus" and are, moreover, "demonstrably false."

As the references to Freud and Jesus show, Watts was, like many if not most intellectuals of his era, somewhat "Jew-wise." His opposition to the Businessman and Priest is implicitly Traditionalist, and so is his opposition to their fake alternative, the Slob.

And so it comes as no surprise that when he comes to consider "Wealth versus Money" in the opening essay of the book, the titular opposition is between the abstract financial chicanery of the capitalist, versus the concrete wealth of real, material production. Rather than be seduced by money, Watts urges us to "wake up" and realize that "money" is a system of measurement, and that the State

---

[36] *Op. cit.*

can no more "run out of" money than it can run out of inches or gallons.³⁷ As Greg Johnson points out,

> In fact, the foundation of his proposals is merely a version of C. H. Douglas' Social Credit theory. Of course Watts had good reason not to mention Douglas in the pages of *Playboy* in 1968: Social Credit was the economic system favored by Anglophone fascists like Ezra Pound.

And consider that other impudence, the Darwinist presumption. As always, it's presented as Just Fact, too well established to bother with proof, and any questioners are portrayed, as Alex Kurtagic said recently in another context,

> Primitive nincompoops whose company no self-respecting, cultured, intelligent person would ever seek or tolerate, equivalent to the stereotype of the White hillbilly from the American South, dysgenically inbred, gap-toothed, jug-eared, and of negligible cranial cubicage.³⁸

So I was pleased to find, on perusing a lovely first edition of Alan Watts' *Beyond Theology*, that the hip, Zen-read, LSD-expanded intelligentsia of 1965 were applying their psychedelic insights against dreary old Dad by advocating ... intelligent design:

> A universe which grows human beings is as much a human, or humaning, universe as a tree which grows apples is an apple tree. ...There is still much to be said for the old theistic argument that *the materialist-mechanistic atheist is declaring his own intelligence to be no more than a special form of unintelligence...*

---

[37] Thus, the State is perpetually strapped for "cash," needing to "balance its books like a family or business," as "conservatives" like to say; no money for health care or social security. But when the "conservatives" want something, like a war in Iraq, suddenly trillions of "dollars" appear out of nowhere! For more on this topic, see the works of Kerry Bolton, such as *The Banking Swindle: Money Creation and the State* (London, Black House, 2013).

[38] http://www.theoccidentalobserver.net/authors/Kurtagic-NotRacist.html.

> The real theological problem for today is that it is, first of all, utterly implausible to think of this Ground as having the monarchical and paternal character of the Biblical Lord God. But, secondly, *there is the much more serious difficulty of freeing oneself from the insidious plausibility of the mythology of nineteenth century scientism*, from the notion that the universe is *gyrating stupidity* in which the mind of man is nothing but a chemical fantasy doomed to frustration. It is insufficiently recognized that this is a vision of the world inspired by the revolt against the Lord God of those who had formerly held the role of his slaves. This reductionist view of the universe with its muscular claims to realism and facing-factuality is at root a proletarian and servile resentment against quality, genius, imagination, poetry, fantasy, inventiveness and gaiety. *Within twenty or thirty years it will seem as superstitious as flat-earthism.*

Well, he seems to have been a little off on that prediction; the argument is still valid, though.[39] I also love how Watts could see, even back then, that the argument was indeed about intelligence, and the phony opposition between Creationist Priests and Materialist Scientists; and what wonderful phrases he comes up with:

---

[39] Watts might also be taken to task for not citing Shaw, among others, who saw through the Darwinist presumption to "read off" a metaphysical presupposition ("gyrating stupidity") from "empirical evidence," (as Sir Peter Medawar said about the ridiculous "priest of evolution" Teilhard de Chardin) and exactly why they felt they needed to do so. But what else could they do? The "metaphysical" presupposition is actually absurd, and hence not metaphysical at all but "pseudo-metaphysical," and lacking both religion [which they rightly opposed] and metaphysical tradition [Watts' actually source, through Guénon, and which they were ignorant of, thanks to the same religion], only "science" is left to prop up their absurd claims. Those of us who have left the Father God behind find no such need, and hence can freely point out the impossibility of tornadoes assembling jet engines in junkyards "if given enough time," while, as Prof. Dennett himself admitted in an earlier, more intellectually honest period ("Why the Law of Effect Won't Go Away"; see Huston Smith's discussion of it in *Forgotten Truth* [New York: Harper & Row, 1977, pp. 135ff.]), the materialistic scientist is forced to swallow the absurdity, for fear of letting God in again. The real source of their dogma is their own psychological checkmate; hence their obsession with propagandizing and mocking their opponents.

"insidious plausibility," "gyrating stupidity." I vote we start using these ourselves; what else is the opponent of ID but an advocate of "gyrating stupidity;" any guesses as to how many "factuality-facing" fashionable atheists will have the intellectual courage to grasp the term as indeed articulating their view, or give the reason why not?

But isn't all this too specific, too small scale, to justify calling someone an 'influence', not just on oneself but on the culture in general? Maybe I should go back to the more general, more abstract level. Other than a vague, perhaps self-satisfying interest in philosophical contemplation, what *ideas* did Watts inculcate?

The problem here is the difficulty of turning one's mind inward, and ascertaining what the gears and setting of itself are. If his ideas have become a part of my intellectual apparatus, how do I discern that?

As it happens, I recently got around to reading a book from the Wattsian 70s that, despite no evidence of any overt influence, reminded me enough of his ideas to serve a kind of mirror, in which I could find myself recalling one or more of Watts' notions: *The Tree*, by John Fowles.

Fowles seems to have had a late-Victorian, middle-class father very similar to Watts' own (a pattern?), or indeed Watts himself (twice, or in Watts' case thrice, married, and leaving endless children to support), with two "private anomalies": a "fascination with philosophy" (though precisely of the analytical kind) and "his little sacred grove of fruit trees." To his father's frustration, Fowles did not grow up to share his love of pruning gardens and classifying reality, but "branched off" in quite another direction, deriving a different lesson:

> We feel or think we feel, nearest to a tree's "essence" when it chanced to stand like us, in isolation, but evolution did not intend trees to grow singly...they are social creatures, and no more natural as isolated specimens than man is as a marooned sailor or a hermit. Their society in turn creates or supports other societies of plants, insects, birds, mammals, micro-organisms; all of which we may choose to isolated and section off, but which remain no less the ideal entity, or whole experience of the wood...

> The true wood, the true place of any kind, is the sum of all its phenomena…a togetherness of beings. It is only because such a vast sum of interactions and coincidences in time and place is beyond science's calculations…that we so habitually ignore it, and treat the flight of the bird and the branch it flies from…as separate events, of riddles—what bird? Which branch? These question-boundaries (where do I file that?) are ours, not of reality.

That's it! That's Watts' most characteristic, most all-around, most important notion. As such he, unlike Fowles, coins a word for it: "goeswith."

> The individual may be understood neither as an isolated person nor as an expendable humanoid working machine. He may be seen, instead, as one particular focal point at which the whole universe expresses itself—as an incarnation of the Self, of the Godhead, or whatever one may choose to call IT…
>
> In the Nootka language, a church is "housing religiously a shop is" housing tradingly. …Does it really explain to say that a man is running? On the contrary, the only explanation would be a description of the field or situation in which "a manning goes-with running" "as distinct from a manning goes-with sitting" [remember that "the universe peoples" in the Intelligent Design quote above?]…"the cause" of the behavior is the situation as a whole, the organization/environment…[40]

Fowles also sees that this creating of relatively abstract objects by the imposing of boundaries for purposes of analysis, which objects are then mistaken for what's really there, is what leads to the dreary pseudo-material world Watts' *Playboy* essays were attacking:

> Brainwashed by most modern societies into believing that the act of acquisition is more enjoyable than the fact of having acquired, that getting beats having got, mere names and the

---

[40] *The Book: On the Taboo Against Knowing Who You Are* (New York: Pantheon, 1966; Vintage, 1989), pp. 78, 95.

objects they are tied to soon become stale. There is a constant need, or compulsion, to seek new objects and names – in the context of nature, new species and experiences.

Since mere names are ultimately unsatisfying, yet we have been brainwashed into believing that names are things, we seek more and more (quantity) rather than better and better (quality). Our "materialists" are actually gnostic spiritualists. We need "a thoroughgoing spiritual materialism."

> Our fallacy lies in supposing that the limiting nature of scientific method corresponds to the nature of ordinary experience. [Rather] *it is quintessentially 'wild'* – unphilosophical, irrational, uncontrollable, incalculable. In fact it corresponds very closely—despite our endless efforts to 'garden,' to invent disciplining social and intellectual systems—with wild nature.

Which, of course, not only affects our world but also affects our psychology, our spiritual state; as Fowles points out,

> We are all in a way *creating our future out of our present*; our 'published' outward behaviour out of our inner green being. [Bur] society does not want us to. Such random personal creativity is offensive to all machines.

> We lack trust in the present, this moment, this actual seeing, because our culture tells us *to trust only the reported back, the publicly framed, the edited, the thing set in the clearly artistic of the clearly scientific angle of perspective.* …Nature resists this. It waits to be seen otherwise, in its individual presentness and from our individual presentness.

This is why the West has turned to various Eastern spiritual techniques, such as meditation; yet like Watts (the "Watts Fallacy" of no-practice), Fowles is skeptical:

As we in the West have converted them to our use, which seems increasingly in a narcissistic way to make ourselves feel more positive, more meaningful, more dynamic.

Now, at this point, you may be asking, if you are still here, "So what? Who cares about you and your Watts stories? And who cares about some equally, though more recently, dead British novelist with a tree fixation?" Fair enough point. Although Watts often referred to himself as a "philosophical entertainer," he also considered himself a serious enough scholar, and would want to be evaluated as such. For this purpose, I suggest you consider the volume that Columbus and Rice have put together, which *Choice* says is "well conceived, well written, well edited, and accessible to undergraduates as well as scholars."[41]

More particularly, the book itself is a remarkable demonstration of the breadth and depth of Alan Watts' contributions to post-War culture. Chapters address perennial philosophy and psychology, psychedelic research and experience, phenomenological analysis, personal transformation, and, of course, gender and sexuality.

The opening chapter by Hood sets the framework for all this by laying out "Four Major Debates in the Psychology of Religion" and offering both Watts' considered opinions, based largely on his own experience, as well as contemporary empirical research supporting him, concluding that "academics whose disdain of popular works kept Alan from a broader appreciation among scholars nevertheless belatedly championed his views in the academy." (p. 26). As Schopenhauer said, new ideas are first ridiculed, then silently appropriated.

Of course, as the kids say, your mileage may vary, or, as we used to say in Philosophy class, one man's *modus ponens* is another man's *modus tollens*. Hood, for example, thinks, like many of today's academic counterparts of the ones who "disdained" Watts, that perennialism in religion (Guénon, Coomaraswamy[42]) or

---

[41] It's ridiculously expensive, but also, for some reason, available online as individual pdf files, so knock yourself out here: http://muse.jhu.edu/books/9781438442013.

[42] Watts seems to have known René Guénon by books and A. K. Coomaraswamy by acquaintance; I can find no evidence of any contact with Alain Daniélou, despite sharing both funding from Bollingen and consequently a publisher (Pantheon) and none with Evola.

psychology (William James) is somehow vitiated by "Cartesianism" and something he calls "objectivism;" as for me, I find my withers unrung,[43] and say hooray for Perennialism, then!

On the other hand, Miriam Levering ("Alan Watts on Nature, Gender, and Sexuality: A Contemporary View") thinks that Watt's "polar" idea of male and female is what Luce Irigaray would call a "premature delineation." And although using this as grist for the usual feminist mill, it also suggests to me Alain Daniélou's criticism of appeals by self-styled "Traditionalists" to male and female "principles" as if they were static archetypes, rather than poles that conjure up an infinity of sub-divisions and re-combinations, as in the gods of the Hindu pantheon.[44]

Speaking of Traditionalists, or even White Nationalists, or at least those who might be a tad *simpatico*, there's an interesting contribution from Ralph Metzner, who was one of the pioneers of drug experimentation at Harvard in the 60s. While Leary seemed to worship himself, and Richard Alpert, as MacDonald would expect, costumed himself as the "guru" Baba Ram Dass (or "Rammed Ass" as his brother liked to call him), Metzger, at least in recent years, has chosen to concentrate on his own Germanic roots.[45]

Metzner's essay is mainly devoted to Watts' personal and professional role in his life and career as a psychedelic researcher and spiritual adventurer; and while Editor Rice gives us an excellent account of "Alan Watts and the Neuroscience of Transcendence," no one really ties together Watts on psychedelics, transcendence, and spiritual methodology.

Rather than concentrating on "The Watts Fallacy" of "no-practice practice," as the representatives of various rival methodologies do,[46]

---

[43] "Let the galled jade winch; our withers are unrung." (*Hamlet*: 3.2., lines 281-284).

[44] See, for example, my "Tradition, Homosexuality and Really-Existing Tradition" in *The Homo and the Negro, op. cit.*

[45] See his *The Well of Remembrance: Rediscovering the Earth Wisdom Myths of Northern Europe* (Boston: Shambhala. 1994) and, more recently, "The (Nine) Doors of Perception: Ralph Metzner on the Sixties, Psychedelic Shamanism, and the Northern Tradition" by Carl Abrahamson and Joshua Buckley in *TYR* 4, pp. 237-260.

[46] For the Perennialist riposte, see "Anti-Theology and the Riddles of Alcyone" by Whitall N. Perry (*Studies in Comparative Religion*, Vol. 6, No. 3).

we should notice first, that psychedelics not only confirmed for Watts his most important, already-arrived at insight – the stumble into alienation from the world and from our own selves:

> The mistake which we have made—and this, if anything, is the fall of man—is to suppose that that extra circuit, that ability to take an attitude toward the rest of life as a whole, is the same as actually standing aside and being separate from what we see. We seem to feel that the ting which knows that it knows is one's essential self, that—in other words—or personal identity is entirely on the side of the commentator. We forget, because we learn to ignore so subtly, the larger organismic fact that self-consciousness is simply a subordinate part and an instrument of our whole being, a sort of mental counterpart of the finger-thumb opposition in the human hand. Now which is really you, the finger or the thumb?

> In short [writes Rice] transcendent experience for Alan Watts was a transcendence of dissociated ego consciousness. It is a vividly clear perception that "what we are talking about is ourselves, and ourselves in a sense far more basic and real that that extra circuit which knows knowing."[47]

But it also gave him the key to a no-method method: traditional spiritual practices are self-defeating, since they only strengthen the illusion that we are a separate thing (the extra circuit), which is able to control the ego itself.

But what if enlightenment is, itself, the giving up of control? How can increasing control end control?

Rather than concentrating on the "fallacy" of no-practice, as if it were just a matter of some heretical opinion based on linguistic maneuvers, concentrate on the inefficiency of traditional spiritual practices, such as the "aching legs" school of Zen meditation, versus psychedelic drugs.

---

[47] p. 136, quoting Watts, "The Water" in *Cloud Hidden, Whereabouts Unknown* (New York: Pantheon, 1973), pp.8-9.

This is the line that has been taken up by internet researcher Michael Hoffman. [48] On his website, Hoffman, who has said he regards Watts as the most important philosopher of the 20th century, writes:

> Alan Watts' genius was to understand Zen as insight into self-control cybernetics, a theme that I have followed through to completeness.[49]
>
> Alan Watts translated the eastern philosophies into words the Western mind could relate to. I admire Watts' style and goals of communication. He also proved his ability to write in the scholarly mode: *The Supreme Identity, Behold the Spirit.*
>
> Watts focuses on enlightenment *through* taking frustration (about poor control) to its full development. Then you understand the true nature of control, through wrestling with it. Underlying all this wrestling with self-control is a deeper source of control that trumps our control. You learn to mentally see this prior or deeper level of control: the ground of being, from which emanates our every thought, choice, and mental tension. The only way to "trust" and "stop controlling" is to discover and clearly conceptualize the nature of self-control, and its relationship with the ground of being, or "the great Tao that flows everywhere". Then you realize that all your controlling has always been, by its very nature, flowing from a source beyond your control. Then, you are logically, conceptually *forced* to see that trusting is the only possible action, because you have always been at the mercy of the Tao, that intrudes even into your decisions. This isn't the very clearest wording possible, but it's how Watts describes the essence of enlightenment in *The Way of Zen* and in the essay "Zen and the Problem of Control" in *This Is It*.[50]
>
> The Tao's control underlies all our sensation of lack of control and self-struggle, our inability to force and restrain our own

---

[48] Not, of course, the conspiracy-monger, who is, literally, Michael Hoffman II.

[49] http://www.egodeath.com/presetcontrolthoughts.htm

[50] Referring to *The Way of Zen.* New York: Pantheon, 1957; "Zen and the Problem of Control," in *This Is It and Other Essays.* New York: Vintage, 1973 (1958).

thoughts, and our inability to silence our own mind. Watts portrays the method of Zen as "enlightenment through the complete frustration of control". Watts' genius, in my view, is the discovery of the connection between self-control cybernetics and Zen. My philosophy fully highlights this connection and makes it central. Self-control cybernetics is the foundation of my system of philosophy. The way to escape ego and control is by pushing and magnifying ego and control to their utter limits, till they collapse of their own weight. Do not *reduce* and moderate ego and control. Rather, blow them up to make them fully visible in the light. The way to ego transcendence is to blow up ego.[51]

Columbus and Rice demonstrate the importance of Alan Watts to contemporary academic research; Hoffman's website shows his influence on cutting-edge work. Glancing through either should convince any reader who has been intrigued by these reflections and wants to make up his own mind, that Alan Watts remains, a hundred years after his birth, a central figure of Western culture.

As for myself, my Sunday morning routine remains the largely the same as was set to back in the WABX days. I still find it nearly impossible to sleep later than 6am, and while the local Pacifica outlet no longer seems to have any interest in Watts' old KPFA broadcasts, even as giveaways during their incessant fundraising campaigns,[52] a local college station, WKCR, broadcasts two hours of Indian classical music on the Sabbath, and then it's time for Chris Whent's early music program, "Here of a Sunday Morning," on Pacifica's WBAI. I think Watts would approve, and come to think of it, Whent does have a goatee and a British accent.

Counter-Currents/*North American New Right*

January 5, 2015

---

[51] http://www.egodeath.com/egodeath.htm

[52] The "Moorish Orthodox Radio Crusade" of fellow KPFA alumnus Peter Lamborn Wilson was a kind of Tuesday night substitute, though he seems to have disappeared somewhere upstate. For the importance of Wilson's show see the Greg Johnson interview referenced above.

ALAN WATTS: THE FIRST ALT-ACADEMIC

"I have a confession to make: I enjoy reading Alan Watts' books. This simple statement [is] a veritable coming out of the philosophical closet." – Philosophy professor Samir Chopra[53]

I t's no secret that I'm a Big Fan[54] of Alan Watts. If your image of Watts comes from the legacy media, or that hippie teacher in high school, then that may seem odd; but then, like most everything you got from the legacy media and the hippies, it's wrong.[55]

Editors Peter J. Columbus and Donadrian L. Rice previously gave us *Alan Watts–Here and Now: Contributions to Psychology, Philosophy, and Religion*, which presented contemporary evaluations of Watts' legacy. In what amounts to a companion volume,[56] they go back to the source, assembling a "much needed" collection of his scholarly works so as to facilitate an answer to the still-vexed question, just what was Alan Watts?

Despite its somewhat steep price tag (perhaps justified by the number of permissions required) and rather ghastly cover, this will

---

[53] From his online blog, September 24. 2014.

[54] Though not in the Patton Oswald sense.

[55] The hippies themselves were a creation of the (now) legacy media; see Miles Mathis, "The Hippie Matrix," here: http://mileswmathis.com/hippie.pdf.

[56] *Alan Watts - In the Academy; Essays and Lectures* (SUNY series in Transpersonal and Humanistic Psychology). Edited and with an introduction by Peter J. Columbus and Donadrian L. Rice (Albany: SUNY Press, 2017).

be a must-have volume for Watts' fans, as much of this material has never seen the light of day since publication, but is known to us through tantalizing hints given out in his autobiography, *In My Own Way* (Pantheon, 1972); while those who want to know what all the fuss is about will find more than enough here to show why serious people take Alan Watts seriously (although as we'll see he would have detested the word "serious").

The editors' Introduction, "Alan Watts and the Academic Enterprise," starts with a rehearsal of Watts' remarkably conventional and literally old-school background: "educated at elite Anglican preparatory academies" and Seabury-Western Theological Seminary, ordination as an Episcopal priest, chaplain and theologian at Northwestern University, professor of comparative philosophy at the American Academy of Asian Studies, visiting scholar at Harvard, an honorary doctorate from the University of Vermont.

And yet at each stage Watts eventually found some way to get expelled – or to free himself, as he saw it (though perhaps only later). Right from the start, his conventional academic career was scotched when he failed to get a scholarship to Cambridge, due to answering the essay question on Courage "in the style of Nietzsche, whose *Zarathustra* I had just read."

This section might be called Who Watts, and what follows could be said to add three more w's to Watts: Why Watts, What Watts and Which Watts.

WHY WATTS?

Ultimately, despite a formidable classical education, much of it self-taught,

> [He] dubbed himself a "philosophical entertainer" because, he wrote, "I have some difficulty in taking myself and my work seriously – or perhaps the right word is 'pompously.'"[57]

---

[57] Quoted by the editors from *In My Own Way* (New York: Pantheon, 1972), p. 252. For some reflections on Watts and his distinction between being serious and being sincere, see my "PC is for Squares, Man," *infra*. Reviewing *Amadeus*, Roger Ebert observed that

In approaching their formidable task of presenting Alan Watts as worthy of academic attention, the editors see it as involving three preliminary questions.

> First is the question of validity: Does Alan Watts have a body of work that could reasonably and justifiably be called academic or scholarly?

Based on the 30 papers gathered here—described by the editors as "contributions to professional journals," "papers presented at academic conferences," works produced under grants from various foundations, and writings and lectures during his tenure at various academic institutions—the answer to that question must be a resounding "Yes."[58]

A second question is: "Does Watts' thinking count as a dependable voice or relevant topic of conversation within contemporary academe?" Here too the editors marshal an impressive array of bibliographic evidence that

> There is in the second decade of the twenty-first century an identifiable renaissance of interest in Alan Watts. His work is garnering renewed attention from emerging scholars and established thinkers in psychology, philosophy, religion, history, art and literary theory.

A third question asks "Is there a clear and present need for a comprehensive assemblage of Watts' academic works? The editors locate that need in the "differing opinions concerning the degree

---

"True geniuses rarely take their own work seriously, because it comes so easily for them. Great writers (Nabokov, Dickens, Wodehouse) make it look like play. Almost-great writers (Mann, Galsworthy, Wolfe) make it look like Herculean triumph."The Great Movies II (New York: BroadwayBooks, 2005).

[58] The editors also point out that Watts' publications were reviewed in academic journals and other professional media. An appendix lists "Academic and Literary Reviews of Watts' Major Texts," which reveals that apart from the expected Anglican theological journals and, later, various psychedelic and religiously comparative reviews, it would appear that Anthony Flew reviewed *Beyond Theology: The Art of Godmanship* (an oddly dated title for probably his best book) in the *New York Review of Books* (under the title "Hip Homiletics," presumably panning it) and someone reviewed that ultimate work of guru/popularization, *The Book: On the Taboo Against Knowing Who You Are*, in the *Review of Metaphysics*.

of continuity versus change in...his earlier and later works," as well as determining what represented "the apex of Watts' thinking [and] when and how his philosophical vision was most vital and perceptive."

Rather than taking a stand on this here and now,[59] the editors have arranged the works thematically, and then chronologically therein. Thus, the collection "provides a database for readers to gauge comparisons and contrasts of Watts' developmental trajectories reflected in and across a range of topics, including language and mysticism (Part 1), Buddhism and Zen (Part 2), Christianity (Part 3), comparative religion (Part 4), psychedelics (Part 5), and psychology and psychotherapy (Part 6)."

WHAT WATTS?

Part I: Language and Mysticism, containing essays from the 1950s ("On the Meaning and Relation of Absolute and Relative," "The Negative Way," "The Language of Metaphysical Experience: The Sense of Non-Sense" and "On Philosophical Synthesis") as well as the posthumous 1975 "Philosophy Beyond Words" shows Watts "employing both apophatic *and* cataphatic languages toward expressing and talking about mystical experience," thus already engaging in the chief problematics of contemporary philosophy of religious experience: how does language structure or limit mystical experience, and whether mystical experience is universal or culturally determined.

"The Language of Metaphysical Experience: The Sense of Non-Sense" may seem like a rather rarified and la-de-da topic, but the context shows its continuing relevance. It was presented at a conference at Columbia University, and was organized by, among others, Franz Boas, in order to "create a framework for the preservation of democracy and intellectual freedom thought

---

[59] In their previous collection, editor Columbus said that "Watts' mature offerings were qualitatively and creatively different from his earlier output in terms of his approach to various topics, selection of content, methods of analysis, and modes of discussion."

he collaboration of scholars from a wide variety of disciplines." Apparently, Boas and the others "blamed the development of "value-free" scholarship for the rise of European fascism," according to a note in the archives of the conference, housed at the Jewish Theological Seminary in New York. Although the connection to Boas shows what kind of non-value-free scholarship was in mind, it's interesting to note that such a conference, seeking to "synthesize *traditional values* and academic scholarship," would today likely be protested as itself fascist.

The concluding essay here, "Philosophy Beyond Words," is also interesting for its context; it was published posthumously in *The Owl of Minerva: Philosophers on Philosophy*,[60] where Watts rubs shoulders, metaphorically at least, with the likes of Karl Popper, W.V.O. Quine, Herbert Marcuse and A. J. Ayer.

Part II: Buddhism and Zen, includes essays from 1941 "The Problem of Faith and Works in Buddhism"—Watts' first-ever academic journal article—to a "Prefatory Essay" to Suzuki's *Outlines of Mahayana Buddhism* from 1963, and even includes the famous *Beat Zen, Square Zen, and Zen* from 1958. At first the latter seems out of place; although technically an essay for *Chicago Review*, revised versions were published as a booklet (City Lights) and as a chapter in Watts' *This is It, and other Essays on Zen and Spiritual Experience* (Pantheon, 1960), both still in print. However, the editors point out that it "anticipates a genre of postmodern scholarship that deconstructs European and North American approaches to Asian cultures and histories toward uncovering hidden assumptions and biases," and thus also anticipates Watts' move from Traditionalism to hermeneutics, of which more anon.

"The Way of Liberation in Zen Buddhism" (1955) "is yet another example in which he was one step ahead of the cutting-edge thinkers of his era," as this discussion of the "double-bind" problem appeared "one year before Bateson, Jackson, Haley, and Weakland (1956) published their classic essay, "Toward a Theory of Schizophrenia."

---

[60] Not the "peer-reviewed academic journal focusing on the work and legacy of Georg Wilhelm Friedrich Hegel" (as Wikipedia calls it) but a collection edited by Charles J. Bontempo and S. Jack Odell (New York: McGraw Hill, 1976).

"Zen and Politics" (1962) has even more contemporary relevance. This is Watts' "brief rebuttal" to an article which argued that Zen's lack of moral concerns led to it supporting World War II atrocities. "The debate foreshadows later controversies concerning the role of Zen in Japan during World War II," but also the discussion of this topic in Jason Reza Jorjani's *Prometheus and Atlas* (London: Arktos, 2016). Although Watts seeks to defend Zen from this charge, it's ironic that the editors earlier note that rather than being a "popularizer" of Suzuki, "Watts challenged D. T. Suzuki's ahistorical narratives by locating Zen within a temporal-developmental trajectory," which is exactly the approach Jorjani takes in deriving the opposite conclusion.

Part III: Christianity, actually consists of material deriving from Watts' period as an Episcopal priest. The prize here is his 1944 translation, with brief introduction, of the *Theologia Mystica* of St. Dionysus (now considered "Pseudo-Dionysus" by the scholars), the *locus classicus* of Western ideas of apophatic theology. Prepared during his seminary training, the translation (thanks to the Greek hammered into him at those Anglican prep schools) and introduction (thanks to his own independent studies) would seem enough to settle the question of his scholarly equipment. It's been long out of print, except for a 1971 reprint from The Society for Comparative Philosophy (apparently Watts himself) that fetches high prices on Amazon.

The remaining essays—"The Case for God", "The Meaning of Priesthood", and "The Christian Doctrine of Marriage" (all from 1946)—seem to show Watts trying very hard to be a respectable Episcopal clergyman, turning out respectable pieces of mildly scholarly uplift, and succeeding all too well. It was his personal doubts about Christianity, and concerns over how respectable his personal views on "the doctrine of marriage" might be, that would lead him to resign from both Church and University.

Part IV: Comparative Religion, consists of four essays which are "excellent examples of Watts' hermeneutical turn in the 1960s and beyond," the meaning and significance of which we will return to in the next section, Which Watts.

Part V: Psychedelics contains four essays from the early 60s to early 70s. Despite later criticism, especially for "misinterpreting ego *regression* as ego *transcendence*," the editors conclude that "Watts' qualitative work on psychedelics nevertheless remains pertinent as archival data for theory, pedagogy, and in contemporary analyses of psychedelic experience in relation to psychospiritual narratives, Buddhist practice and postmodern thinking."

Since room was found for "Beat Zen, Square Zen, and Zen," despite its availability elsewhere, one wishes the editors could also have included "Zen and the Problem of Control," which was reprinted in the same *This Is It*, and is probably Watts' most important essay on psychedelic experience.[61]

Part VI: Psychology and Psychotherapy collects six essays and an interview, ranging from 1951 to 1973, establishing Watts as "a trailblazer in humanistic and transpersonal psychologies."[62]

In the final essay, "Psychotherapy and Eastern Religion: Metaphysical Bases of Psychiatry," Watts considers intellectual assumptions underlying Western psychotherapy affecting the understanding, fear and acceptance of death. Ironically, the essay was given as an invited address at Forest Hospital in Des Plains, Illinois, in January 1973. It was the month of his birth, in the year of his death."

WHICH WATTS?

It seems clear that Watts was a man of formidable though somewhat eccentric education, fully accepted as a co-worker in the academic world of his time, and he continues to have relevance there today.

---

[61] Michael Hoffman considers it the most important essay of the 20th century. "Breakthrough from applying Minkowski block universe with frozen future to Alan Watts' writings on Zen and the problem of control. More powerful ego death and transcendence came from this idea than from practice of (non-drug) meditation and idea of nonduality (current in late 80s)." See "Michael Hoffman Interview on Expanding Mind podcast with Erik Davis," here: https://cyberdisciple.wordpress.com/2016/01/29/michael-hoffman-interview-on-expanding-mind-podcast-with-erik-davis/.

[62] The conspiracy-minded might notice that "Watts' early psychological writings were inspired by the tutorage (1936–1938) of psychiatrist Eric Graham Howe (1896–1975), a cofounder of the famous Tavistock Clinic."

Why then has he continued to be dismissed as a "guru" or a mere "popularizer"?[63]

Mostly, the answer, if not the blame, lies with Watts himself. He rejected the spirit of seriousness and heaviness,[64] and deliberately set himself another task: a "philosophical entertainer."[65]

The editors suggest that their synoptic presentation of Watts' scholarly work leads to the possibility of a more thematic—if not more serious—reason: his rejection of the Traditionalist school of metaphysics and comparative religion.

As Greg Johnson describes it:

> Although Watts found Traditionalism useful in liberating his mind from Christianity, he ultimately rejected it. In the Preface to *Beyond Theology*, he explains his reason. Traditionalists claim that Christianity is just an exoteric expression of the one primordial tradition which is the inner truth of all religions. But Watts points out that there is no evidence that the founders of Christianity thought that way. Instead, Christianity has always insisted on what Jan Assmann calls the "Mosaic distinction" between true and false religions. Christianity is the one true religion, and all others are simply false. Thus in *The Supreme Identity*, Watts treats Christianity as an expression of primordial truth, but in *Beyond Theology*, he treats it as a mode of illusion.[66]

---

[63] It's somewhat ironic that academics dismiss "gurus," since many fashionable intellectual movements, such as Marxism, psychoanalysis, "critical theory," etc. are essentially cults. See Kevin MacDonald, *The Culture of Critique: An Evolutionary Analysis of Jewish Involvement in Twentieth-Century Intellectual and Political Movements* (Bloomington, IN: 1stBooks Library, 2002; originally published in 1998 by Praeger, Westport, CT).

[64] The word 'guru' actually means 'heavy' in Sanskrit.

[65] Ironically, Watts admired but rejected the method of Coomaraswamy, who demonstrated his unquestioned scholarly chops by writing papers and articles where the main text was swamped under footnotes that could go on for pages; the joke being, as Watts pointed out, that the "good stuff" was often hidden in that forest of notes. Watts attributed this to Coomaraswamy's adherence to the guru tradition, where students are expected to "work for it" rather than be spoon-fed. See *In My Own Way*, p. 227.

[66] "Alan Watts at 100," Reprinted in Greg Johnson. *Confessions of a Reluctant Hater*, 2nd Ed., Revised and Expanded (San Francisco: Counter-Currents, 2016).

The editors are scholarly and fair-minded enough to give us the Traditionalist riposte:

> *Beyond Theology, The Art of Godmanship*, [is] a *crazy pastiche* of esoteric insights and false deductions, yet typically symptomatic of the ills to which so much of the pseudo-spiritual flesh of our times is heir.[67]

Indeed, up until *The Supreme Identity*,[68] his most fully Traditionalist book, Watts' works were pretty "scholarly" and conventionally academic; indeed, most would consider it Watts' most scholarly work of all. The abandonment of Traditionalism and the adoption of the "philosophical entertainer" were all of a piece.

We can see a hint of what was at stake in Perry's scornful remark about "a crazy pastiche" and Watts' refusal of "all or nothing commitment" to a religious tradition. The editors call this Watts' "hermeneutical turn;" rather than seeking some supposed "transcendental unity" above, behind, or perhaps beneath the variety of religions and cultures,

> Watts...turned toward hermeneutical analyses exploring interconnections and disjunctions between localized narratives. Through this kind of interpretive study, one arrives at an expanded awareness and comprehension of perspectives via the dialectical rotation of differing vantage points.

---

[67] Whitall N. Perry, "Anti-Theology and the Riddles of Alcyone," *Studies in Comparative Religion*, vol. 6, no.3, here:http://www.studiesincomparativereligion.com/Public/articles/Anti-Theology_and_the_Riddles_of_Alcyone-by_Alan_Watts.aspx. Perry goes on to say that "He tells us he broke away from the *philosophia perennis* outlook because "there is not a scrap of evidence that the Christian hierarchy was ever aware of itself as one among several lines of transmission for a universal tradition", whereas "the so-called 'traditionalist school'... regards every orthodox spiritual tradition as a more-or-less deliberate adaptation of the *philosophia perennis* to the needs of different cultures." The truth is, exclusivity is not the prerogative of Christianity: there never has been a religion East or West that did not require what Watts calls "an all-or-nothing commitment", and certainly none of the above-named proponents of the perennial wisdom ever claimed otherwise."

[68] *The Supreme Identity: An Essay on Oriental Metaphysic and the Christian Religion*, (New York: Noonday Press/Farrar, Straus & Giroux, 1950).

For example, in what would be his last book, *Tao: The Watercourse Way*, Watts pursues

> a historical hermeneutic in that he seeks to understand what the "far-off echoes" of fifth and fourth-century B.C. Daoism mean to the contemporary state of affairs. The analysis is a cultural hermeneutic in that he seeks to "interpret and clarify the principles of Lao-tzu, Chuang-tzu, and Lieh-tzu" in relation to Euro-American thinking. The text also is a personal hermeneutic because, writes Watts, "I am…interested in how these ancient writings reverberate on the harp of my own brain, which has, of course, been tuned to the scales of Western culture."

Needless to say (although the editors do say it) this kind of position was not only a way to overcome the extreme specialization and isolation of the academy (fewer and fewer knowing more and more about less and less)[69] but was also an extremely valuable tool for navigating, or guiding others through, the increasingly inter-connected "global village" that McLuhan, another "popular" Trickster, was already predicting in the 1960s.

Navigating and guiding are indeed the roles of a somewhat more respected "entertainer," Hermes/Mercury.

> Greek folklore suggests that Hermes, often considered the etymological root of hermeneutics, was himself a kind of philosophical entertainer inhabiting and playing within the flux and flow of language and communicative processes. In this way it seems the epithet was Watts' lighthearted tactic for acknowledging his transition toward hermeneutical writing.

---

[69] Similar concern led Hermann Hesse to propose a similarly playful solution: a game. "They say it is a substitute of the arts, and that the players are *mere popularizers* … artistic dilettantes.… The strict scholars and scientists despise it." The resultant novel also explores the perils of seeking to become an "all or nothing" Chinese scholar, and the need to reject the role of "guru" (Knecht dies so that his student can, as Watts would say, "hang up the phone." When asked by Knecht "isn't' there some kind of dogma?" the wise old Music Master gives the Wattsian response: "There is truth, but no doctrine, absolute perfect dogma. Perfect yourself. The deity is within you." See my "Two Orders, Same Man: Hesse, Evola," *infra*.

Moreover, the editors locate Watts' reputation in a "a Sartrean triad in the semblance of *No Exit:*"

> Academic intellectuals reject Watts as a popularizer; popular audiences problematically idolize him as a guru; and gurus, that is to say, mystics, spiritual teachers, and religious practitioners criticize him as too intellectual. It seems plausible to suggest that Watts' philosophical entertainer moniker was his way of "exiting" the existential dilemma... in other words, an interpretive strategy intended (successfully or not) to disarm critics and fanatics alike.[70]

The editors also locate an influence from "the tutorage from 1934 to 1936 of Serbian philosopher Dimitrije Mitrinovic (1887–1953)," whom they identify as

> A formative thinker in the pre–World War I Young Bosnia movement and subsequent New Europe Group and New Britain Movement, Mitrinovic integrated mystical metaphysics and transformative political-social philosophy.

Readers of Counter-Currents may have a different view of the significance of Mitrinovic.[71]

Watts himself must have been slyly giving the game away when he said that "I have some difficulty in taking myself and my work seriously—or perhaps the right word is 'pompously.'"[72]

---

[70] McLuhan also attempted to disarm critics by insisting his pronouncements were not dogma or conclusions but "probes" meant to stimulate thought. Wikipedia says: "While some critics have taken issue with McLuhan's writing style and mode of argument, McLuhan himself urged readers to think of his work as "probes" or "*mosaics*" offering a toolkit approach to thinking about the media. His eclectic writing style has also been praised for its postmodern sensibilities and suitability for virtual space." See also Paul Grossweiler, *The Method is the Message: Rethinking McLuhan through Critical Theory* (Montreal: Black Rose, 1998), 155-81, and Paul Levinson, *Digital McLuhan: A Guide to the Information Millennium* (New York: Routledge,1999), 30.

[71] Greg Johnson writes that "Politically, Watts was a man of the right. In his youth, he was a follower of the mysterious Serbian guru and operator Dimitrije Mitrinovic, an advocate of such quasi-fascistic ideas as Guild Socialism, Social Credit, and European Unity (as long as it was not Hitler who was doing the unifying)." See "Remembering Alan Watts: January 6, 1915 to November 16, 1973," here: https://www.counter-currents.com/2014/01/remembering-alan-watts-january-6-1915-to-november-16-1973/.

[72] *Cloud-hidden, Whereabouts Unknown: A Mountain Journal*, (New York: Pantheon

The editors quote this and although they take it (I think) as the inspiration for entitling their biographical section "Pomp and Circumstance," they do not pick up on the other association of "pomp;" for one of the chief functions of Hermes was as *psychopomp* or guide to the soul, usually on the journey to the underworld.[73]

We may find a contemporary analogue of Watts the philosophical entertainer right here and now on the alt-right in the work of the aforementioned Jason Reza Jorjani, whose *Prometheus and Atlas* emphasizes the need for a "mercurial metaphysics" and a literally playful or childlike use of language in order to explore the liminal or "spectral" aspects of our globalized and globalizing Western *Weltanschauung*.

That Jorjani has recently published a denunciation of Traditionalism,[74] and that both authors are fascinated with the occult, Taoism, Zen and Japan (though perhaps reaching different evaluations of the latter) only adds to what both would likely call the synchronicity.

Of course, as a philosophical entertainer, Watts was unlikely to talk about such things as hermeneutics, at least as applied to himself. In *Beyond Theology* (the book of "crazy pastiche" that upset Perry so much) Watts describes his technique as the "Chinese Box method" (although it sounds more like the Russian Doll method): what happens when we fit, say, Christianity into Hinduism, and—if we can—vice versa?

All of these Eurasian boxes may remind one—or at least me—of *Mad Men*'s Bert Cooper, who, in perhaps the greatest moment of surprise in cable TV history, dismissed the revelation that Don

---

Books, 1973), p. 252.

[73] Perhaps most familiar to contemporary readers as a device in Mann's *Death in Venice*, where Aschenbach is "led on" by a series of mysterious male figures, finally culminating in the image of the beautiful boy waving at him from the sea as Aschenbach succumbs to the plague.

[74] Begin note with: See "Against Perennial Philosophy," reprinted in *Lovers of Sophia* (Arktos, 2020). His objections—the intellectually stultifying consequences of assuming pre-existing "perfect" body of knowledge, which can then only be acquired by attendance on a guru—parallel Watts' own.

Draper[75] was "a fraud, a liar, a criminal even" with the laconic Japanese proverb, "A man *is*, whatever *room* he is in."[76]

Bert Cooper in fact recalls the mid-century Watts, well-dressed and goatee'd in his midcentury modern office splashed with *Japonaiserie*, including a very Wattsian touch: a classic of tentacle porn.[77] He dies in the middle of the last season, but returns now and again to give Don advice, and in the finale Don receives enlightenment – or at least the inspiration for a Coke commercial – from a rather Wattsian dude at a rather Esalen-ish retreat.

Well, I guess it's time to leave this room; "when you get the message, you hang up the phone." Academic, priest, theologian, boarding school scholar, guru, popularizer, philosophical entertainer – on the evidence of the essays collected here with such scholarly devotion, I propose that Alan Watts was not so much "anti-academic" as he was *the first alt-academic*.

Counter-Currents/*North American New Right*

July 3, 2017

---

[75] Himself a Hermetic figure, who 'dons' and 'drapes' himself as the situation requires. The producers no doubt intended all this to be a bitter satire of the "fakeness" of WASP culture, their Semitic seriousness failing to grasp the value of Hermetic play. See my essays collected in *End of an Era: Mad Men and the Ordeal of Civility* (San Francisco: Counter-Currents, 2015).

[76] Watch it here: https://www.youtube.com/watch?v=OqkHPsY8p84.

[77] "What man imagined her ecstasy?" is his hermeneutical comment. The octopus print, from 1814 and usually known in the English-speaking world as *The Dream of the Fisherman's Wife*, is by Katsushika Hokusai, otherwise known for *The Great Wave*. "Not unlike the world of *Mad Men*, modern Japanese culture blends the button-down salaryman with the libidinous rake." See "Bert Cooper's Freaky Octopus Picture," here: http://blogs.artinfo.com/lacmonfire/2010/07/19/bert-cooper%E2%80%99s-freaky-octopus-picture/.

Watts however was rather censorious about modern Japan—"There's no square like a Japanese square"—and bemoaned how all the trappings of antique Zen he loved were regarded by young Japanese as hopelessly boring and rather creepy.

RE-KINDLING ALAN WATTS

"For God is not niggardly in his self-revelation; he exposes himself right before our eyes." – Alan Watts

"What was needed was not some new religious cult but some simple way of accessing religious or mystical experience, of the sort that must have been known to the monks and cathedral-builders of the Middle Ages." – Colin Wilson[78]

Praise be to Amazon! Thanks to their Kindle technology, I've been able to relocate here to Central Europe (a certain city beginning with "Buda" and ending with "Pest") and bring most of my library with me!

Contrary to the fears of the Luddites, new technologies do not—at least, not always—destroy or occlude the products of a previous technological stage; in fact, as McLuhan pointed out, the content of a new medium *is* the old medium.

Thus printing did not replace manuscripts but made them accessible (thereby eliminating the need for universities, as McLuhan also pointed out). Greedy record companies, desperate for content, issued collections of 78s on LPs (and later, LPs on CD); thus did Harry Smith's *Anthology of American Folk Music*, 3 double LP sets, rescue dozens of pre-War artists from obscurity, and sparked the "folk music revival."

---

[78] *The Angry Years: The Rise and Fall of the Angry Young Men* (London, Robson Books, 2007; Kindle, 2014), p. 66.

Speaking only for myself, I can say that the development of the epub technology, specifically Amazon's Kindle, has not only made whole libraries available for free or minimal cost, but has also made even books much easier to read, and thus *more read*.[79]

Case in point: Alan Watts, and the book under review.

After discovering the works of Alan Watts in the early 70s, in the form of Sunday morning radio broadcasts,[80] I proceeded to compulsively acquire and read his books, from the earliest—*The Spirit of Zen: A Way of Life, Work, and Art in the Far East* (1936, at the age of 21)—to his most recent, the posthumous collection *Cloud-hidden, Whereabouts Unknown: A Mountain Journal* (1973) and *Tao: The Watercourse Way* (1975), a collaboration with calligrapher Chungliang Al Huang who also finished the text after Watts' death in 1972. Eventually, I even acquired some obscure incunabula, such as his hand-written *The Art of Contemplation: A Facsimile Manuscript with Doodle* (1972), and even a reprint of his translation of the 1944 *Theologia Mystica: Being the Treatise of Saint Dionysius, Pseudo-Areopagite, on Mystical Theology, Together with the First and Fifth Epistles*.[81]

Among those works was, of course, *Behold the Spirit* (1947),

---

[79] For example, I only managed to actually read *Moby Dick* thanks to a kindle version that could be easily carried around and read on the train. To bring all these points together, the internet already made Yockey's *Imperium* available to me in a cheap mass-market paperback from the 60s (Noontide Press—Sausalito, just like Watts, I know notice!—1962) but it's still thick as a brick and sports a bright pink [!] nutzi cover, making it something to read behind closed doors. Scholars and collectors might appreciate Wermod's recent hardcover edition, but at $80 it's much less likely to produce a new generation of interested readers than any of the—admittedly, poorly produced—Kindles on Amazon (for now…).

[80] As explained elsewhere ("There & Then: Personal & Memorial Reflections on Alan Watts (1915-1973)", *supra*), back then the FCC's "Fairness Doctrine" required radio stations to broadcast a certain amount of "religious" content, which Detroit's pioneer "underground" FM station, WABX, fulfilled by re-broadcasting Alan Watts' lectures and other performances from KPFA San Francisco.

[81] This was a student exercise, republished in 1972 by the Society for Comparative Philosophy in Sausalito, apparently another Watts project that dissipated with his death— you can now find it in *Alan Watts—In the Academy: Essays and Lectures* (SUNY series in Transpersonal and Humanistic Psychology); edited and with an introduction by Peter J. Columbus and Donadrian L. Rice (Albany: State University of New York Press, 2017); see my discussion *supra*.

which had also been recently reprinted with a new, rather diffident, Preface from Watts. Like the similar preface to his later, Traditionalist work, *The Supreme Identity: An Essay on Oriental Metaphysic and the Christian Religion* (1950), it gave Watts' current views, while almost seeming to discourage anyone from reading the main text.[82]

That was fine with me; I was happy enough to read his latest thoughts, and keep the book proudly displayed with the others.[83] And so it remained, until the kindle went on sale for $1.99, and I decided to free up some space and maybe finally take a look-see.[84]

That rascal guru! That wily old shaman! He hid the best stuff in plain view!

Incredibly, I wager that most all of what would become his most characteristic themes, memes and crochets can be found here:

Union with Reality/God/Brahman etc. is and must be a present reality because it is timeless;

Therefore, any attempt to "get" or "become" it must fail, as such an attempt is based on the false assumption of its present lack; all such traditional "methods" (meditation, prayer, sacraments, etc.) must be understood rather as expressions of joy and gratitude for *what is*; in fact, the frenzied pursuit of anything—especially life itself—is the surest way to lose it.

---

[82] The reader will have noted the noticeable amount of works republished in the years close to his death, which were also his peak of popularity among the general public. No one can begrudge the man striking while the iron is hot, so to speak, but in Watts' case the irony is that this supposed spokesman for "free love" was supporting an entourage of three wives and eleven children and grandchildren, and it was his old-fashioned sense of personal responsibility that drove his overwork and over-production, resulting in charges of sliding into popularization, enabling his alcoholism, and likely his early death. For a personal account of Watts' last days, see Al Chuang's reflections in their posthumous collaboration *Tao: The Watercourse Way*.

[83] Another intellectual irrelevancy tendency obviated by the kindle; Evola, for instance, gave away any book he read, considering libraries to be bourgeois; Stephan George limited his followers to a personal collection of no more than 50 volumes. J. P. Donleavy, author of *The Ginger Man*, was reputed to keep "only one book in his house: *The Ginger Man*, and was usually found reading it." – Colin Wilson, *The Angry Years* (Robson Books, 2007), p. 81.

[84] *Behold the Spirit: A Study in the Necessity of Mystical Religion* (New York: Pantheon, 1947; reissued with a new Preface, 1971; Kindle, 2016).

Nature/Reality/the Universe cannot be "analyzed" from some position of supposed separation and superiority; the attempt to do so results in a model of reality as a meaningless machine or collection of disconnected bits, a distortion and even outright illusion, no matter how much scientists and others perversely insist on it being "the way things really are."

To avoid spiritual and perhaps historical catastrophe, Western Man must abandon the false alternatives of rugged materialism and prissy spiritualism and develop a thoroughgoing spiritual materialism.[85]

And so on; *but* expressed in the language of Christian theology—specifically, "the central principle of the Christian mythos, the mystery of the Incarnation, of the Word made flesh"[86]—and in the manner of 1940s-era Christian lay observers and popular theologians, a bit like C. S. Lewis or Fulton Sheen, but with a considerable amount of the formidable intellect and range of reference of an Etienne Gilson or Jacques Maritain.

Watts writes as a Thomist,[87] but one who's read at least Coomaraswamy, if not Guénon (but certainly not Evola[88]), although the book makes no references to Traditionalism and Traditionalists as such (unlike his next book, *The Supreme Identity*), and the text is the stronger, more compelling, and less dated, for that reason.

According to Wikipedia, where the book has its own mini-article,

---

[85] See Greg Johnson, "The Spiritual Materialism of Alan Watts: A Review of *Does it Matter?* in his *Confessions of a Reluctant Hater* (2nd Ed., Revised and Expanded; San Francisco: Counter-Currents, 2016).

[86] Interpreted in the manner of the Eastern Church, as a timeless act in which God, through Christ, takes on the nature of Man; not something to be achieved through good works (Roman Catholicism) or conditional on acceptance by faith (Lutherism).

[87] "To defend itself against the modern disintegration philosophy must return to the point from which it began to decay, to scholasticism, and the robust common sense of St. Thomas." (p. 47).

[88] Evola's book on Buddhism, *The Doctrine of Awakening*, was translated into English in 1948, just a year later; but I have never seen any indication that Watts ever read Evola, or vice versa.

This book is the most extensive example of his early effort to find a non-dualistic interpretation of Anglican theology in terms of *The Perennial Philosophy* as expounded in Aldous Huxley's contemporary work of that name and later made popular in the talks of Joseph Campbell. ...Its importance lies partly in its exposition of Watts' earliest attempt to reconcile traditional Anglican theology with a mystical, Buddhist based approach, but also as a personal expression of the mystical experience.

Incredibly, this was apparently written as a master's thesis (M. Div., Seabury Theological); which becomes even more amazing when you remember that this is the only earned degree Watts every acquired, even beforehand.[89] That's right, Watts never acquired a B.A., and pretty much never attended a college or university;[90] his ability to simply enter a theological seminary and master its contents within a few months might, with some modesty, be a tribute to the value of a British public school education as well as native ability.[91]

Impressive enough as a demonstration of academic pseudomorphism, and providing a bit of nostalgia for those of us who lived through similar environments, it does show the corresponding vices. In particular, one notes the tendency—academic, but itself a function of the Scholasticism that formed the modern academy—to spell everything out, hunt down every last detail and implication, and delight in restating positions in one new way after another. One is certainly glad that the post-academic Watts pruned back this sort of thing considerably.[92]

---

[89] Around the time of this reissue the University of Vermont awarded the later, famous Watts a D.D.

[90] He later learned that his failure to win a scholarship to Cambridge was due to writing a exam essay on Courage "in the style of Nietzsche's *Zarathustra*, which I had just read." The ever-dangerous Nietzsche! See Watts' autobiography, *In My Own Way*, p.102).

[91] Watts observes in his autobiography that while his classmates struggled with the Greek New Testament, Watts would prepare three or four possible translations of disputed passages and then guess—always correctly—that the instructor would choose the most banal.

[92] In the same way Watts recommends the Zen koan: "something of this kind would be a refreshing and invigorating relief from the interminable explanations of theologians... necessary as these may be." (p. 111).

The reader who lacks such a background may nevertheless be able to get a grip or find a foothold here, and may even be at an advantage, as Watts starts off rather boldly by dabbling in the idea of "world ages" *a la* Spengler or Joachim of Flores (the origin of the "Third Whatever" meme) or the (unknown and unmentioned) Yockey; a fairly brave choice, at a time when all things German were identified with Prussian martinets, and indicative of Watts' surprising (to some) Rightist sympathies[93] (of which more anon).

In his 1971 Preface Watts downplays his talk of world ages in the opening chapter, saying he no longer believes in historical timetables and "New Ages," but the reader may well find his discussion of Spengler of some interest today. Just as Yockey tried to re-tool Spengler's Caesarism into a revival of Imperium rather than a dead end, so Watts modifies Spengler's idea of the Second Religiosity.[94]

Due to what Watts calls an "exceedingly superficial philosophy" and "a certain emotional immaturity," Spengler

> Sees that the Second Religiousness employs the "Springtime" or infancy forms of religion, but does not seem to realize that they are understood in a new, interior and spiritually creative sense.

Where Spengler can only see regression to decadent or infantilized forms of a culture's original spirituality, a period of mush-minded mysticism, Watts observes that it is in such "decadent" periods that "the profoundest spirituality of the human race" appears (such Plotinus or Augustine).[95] Thus, for Watts, the Third Age is one of

---

[93] For more on Watts as "quite a man of the Right," see Greg Johnson, "Alan Watts at 100" in his *Confessions of a Reluctant Hater* (2nd Ed., Revised and Expanded; San Francisco: Counter-Currents, 2016).

[94] Discussing his follow-up to *The Outsider*, *Religion and the Rebel*, Colin Wilson notes that "Where history is concerned, it seemed clear that Spengler's conclusion—that the modern world is plunging into decadence and collapse was overly pessimistic...Civilizations can be revitalized by their 'creative minorities', that is, by Outsiders." *The Angry Years*, p. 98.

[95] Evola, reviewing *Imperium*, criticized Yockey for simply misreading Spengler in the American "can-do" spirit. Ironically, he would likely agree with Watts, that Spengler was a philistine in matters spiritual, given what he says in his own Introduction to the Italian edition of *Decline* as well as his autobiography: "Spengler lacked any understanding of metaphysics or transcendence;" see *The Path of Cinnabar* (London: Arktos, 2009), pp. 202-03.

maturity and wisdom, not sclerosis and senility; and he points out that Christianity itself is a product of the Second Religiousness of Judaism, "giving a mystical and interior interpretation to the primitive religion of the law and the sacrificial worship of the Temple."[96]

> In the stage of infancy, the church's moral teaching is of necessity authoritarian and legalistic.[97] In adolescence, intensely earnest and self-consciously heroic, following after extremely lofty ideals. In maturity, we return somewhat to earth, and find the source of morality neither in external authority, nor in remote ideals, but in the consciousness of God himself in the heart.[98]

Before unpacking the Third Age, and that "new, interior and spiritually creative sense," let's try to understand what Watts is doing here. First, it is necessary to grasp what he is *not* doing. He isn't trying to prune away from Catholic Christianity[99] some supposedly

---

[96] To anticipate a bit, and to make a point Watts would likely never make himself: when the Romans put an end to the childish Temple cult, Jews could have followed Christ in his new, Third Age religion of the Holy Spirit, but instead clung to the Pharisees.

[97] Cf. the prolonged infancy of Ignatius Reilly.

[98] The three (or more) stage model continues to find adherents. John Halstead observes that "In his book, *Crafting the Art of Magic*, Kelly [Aidan Kelly, the founder of the New Reformed Order of the Golden Dawn, a West Coast Neo-Pagan tradition organized in 1967] describes the same three stages in the development of an individual's religious maturity identified by Alan Watts." Later, Toronto academic James Fowler's book, *Stages of Faith*, [Harper, 1995] "describes this same process as Watts and Kelly…but in much more detail, drawing on the theories of psychologists Piaget, Kohlberg, Erickson, and others. Fowler describes 6 stages of spiritual development. Fowler's Stages 2/3, 4, and 5 correspond roughly to the three stages described by Watts and Kelly above: a mythologizing stage, a de-mythologizing stage, and a reconstructive stage. (Fowler's Stage 1 corresponds to early childhood, of which most of us have little memory, and Stage 6 essentially corresponds to what might be called "enlightenment", which few of us will ever experience.)" See John Halstead: "Stages of (My) Faith," here: https://humanisticpaganism.com/2014/01/26/stages-of-my-faith-development/.

[99] For Watts, "the Church" is what he calls—as others did then—"Catholic Christianity," meaning the common elements that are truly universally held and hence "catholic;" as opposed to one particular church arrogantly claiming the name "Catholic" and pretending that other confessions are simply heretical or schismatic. Anglicans of this sort would think of themselves as being Catholics who had simply sent the old man in Italy packing, without any significant change in doctrine, unlike those weird Dissenters and other breeds outside

man-made or "pagan" accretions, in order to arrive at a "primitive" gospel message, presumably all about Jesus, and thus both intensely personal and unique among world religions ("No man comes to the Father..."). Nor is he trying to interest secular adults, or "the kids," in a revamped Christianity more in tune with science or hip musical genres.

Watts has no problems with "pagan" elements (see next book, *Easter – Its Story and Meaning*[100])—Christianity has always welcomed wisdom wherever it may be found, and these are its strongest, most vital periods—nor any interest in proving the "uniqueness" of Christianity ("what is the interest in a reanimated corpse?" he asks).

The best approach might be to look at his subtitle and ask "why, or how, is mysticism *necessary*?" I would suggest it is necessary in two senses: it is a logically or psychologically necessary next step; and it is what is *needed* for religion to survive today.

Everyone knows (in 1947) the Church is dead or dying. There are plenty of remedies promoted, but they are all inadequate, because they are ad hoc, purely human solutions that take for granted that the Church is just another man-made institution that needs ongoing maintenance, like a bridge or subway. But if the Church is

---

the law. (Cf. the "No true Scotsman" fallacy). Today, the Episcopal Church describes itself as "Protestant, yet Catholic" ("What makes us Anglican? Hallmarks of the Episcopal Church"). Writing of the translation philosophy that produced the King James Bible, which tries to steer between Anglican Royalists and Puritan Separatists, Adam Nicolson says "avoidance of choice is, in the end, the heart of the King James Bible. It does not choose. It absorbs and includes. It is in that sense catholic, as Jacobean Englishmen consistently called their church: not Roman but catholic, embracing all. See his *God's Secretaries: The Making of the King James Bible* (Harper/Collins, 2003), loc. 3672. I suspect actual Roman Catholics thought otherwise. Nicolson describes the execution of the Jesuit Fr. Garnet, supposed accomplice of Guy Fawkes: "A man in the huge crowd shouted out, 'Mr Garnet, it is expected you should recant.' Garnet said, 'God forbid, I never had any such meaning, but ever meant to die a true and perfect Catholic.' The extraordinary Jacobean ability to dispute, to be witty on the brink of the precipice, at this of all moments, now came to the fore. John Overall, considering the claims of the Church of England to be the true primitive church, then said to the Jesuit, 'But Mr Garnet, we are all Catholics.'" (*op. cit.*, loc. 1796). Frederick Rolfe ("Baron Corvo"), although himself a convert, would refer to the Anglican Canon in Venice as "the heresiarch." In fact, one suspects he converted for the sheer joy of living in opposition to the masses of British people. Still, few went as far as devout Jews, who would spit when passing a Christian cemetery.

[100] Although admittedly Watts dismisses it as "a potboiler" (*Way*, p. 174)

understood as "part of a God-controlled design of history" it must be understood to be undergoing a necessary, organic development along with and promoting the development of human consciousness.

In other words, as consciousness develops, so does religion.

Watts' developmental model—Father, Son, Holy Spirit—is basically mapped onto Western[101] Church history: Roman Catholic, Protestant and...what? To see the needed, necessary next step let's first unpack the first two stages.

Roman Catholicism is the religion of man's childhood,[102] where the soul is satisfied with mere symbols, the assurance given by authorities that something happened somewhere that will make everything alright, if one just believes hard enough.

Protestantism[103] is the religion of adolescence: rebellious, rejecting authority, requiring that things be written down (*sola scriptura*) and exhaustively explained (daily four-hour sermons), like other honest business transactions (a religion of shopkeepers); and above all demanding the *inner meaning* of doctrine and dogma, not mere passive acceptance.

Protestantism goes along with modern science, and while both have provided us with much of values (hospitals, clean water, etc.),[104] the downside has been considerable.[105] The method of scientific

---

[101] Like most Westerners Watts in his outline seems to ignore the existence of the Greek or Eastern church, which arguably represents the true stream of Christian teaching. But in his discussion of mysticism Watts alludes to the Eastern traditions of *theodosis*, God becoming man so that man can become (or realize himself to be) God, so there is a kind of archeofuturism here, the new dispensation seeming to be a rebirth of Orthodox spirituality.

[102] Remember that Watts, like Spengler, sees the birth of Christianity to be part of the final stage of the previous civilization, and in that sense fully mature. The confusingly named "Middle Ages" hides the reality that Christianity as such is a product of the mature Classical period (Stoicism, etc.) while Roman Catholicism, characteristic of the "middle" ages, is actually the childish stage of the later, European civilization.

[103] By "Protestantism" Watts means Lutheranism and Calvinism, while Anglicanism remains within "Catholic Christianity."

[104] "All right... all right... but apart from better sanitation and medicine and education and irrigation and public health and roads and a freshwater system and baths and public order... what *have* the Romans done for *us*?" *Monty Python's Life of Brian* (Terry Jones, 1979). Cuckservative William F. Buckley demanded the film be prosecuted for blasphemy.

[105] Yeats, I believe, said that modern science gives us longer and longer lives, while

analysis (as the word would indeed seem to imply) leaves us with a "world" made up of random bits, producing nihilism—once you dissect the frog, it's not a frog anymore—while the obsessive examination of conscience produces an infinite regress or vicious circle of guilt and pride, leading to existential despair. [106]

Here we see what will be two of Watts' favorite memes, the "gyrating stupidity" (as he calls it in *Beyond Theology*) of modern materialism, and the "double bind dilemma" of trying to be good, trying to achieve enlightenment, trying to answer the Zen koan, etc., which can only be "solved" if "dissolved" by being pursued to exhaustion—like Sambo's tigers—and the subsequent giving up the futile struggle and just letting things be.[107]

But before exhausting ourselves as well, let's take a break, with a little something I call "Excursus on Cradle Catholics."

EXCURSUS: CRADLE CATHOLICS

"And stay away from Anglo-Catholics; they are all Sodomites with atrocious accents." – *Brideshead Revisited*

Despite Watts' repeated warnings that designating states of consciousness as pertaining to childhood or adolescence carries no intent to denigrate them[108]—children are not failed adults—some, particularly Catholics themselves, may find it insulting or perhaps just inaccurate to locate Roman Catholicism in the childhood category.

---

removing any reason to live.

[106] "It is a pet notion of mine that certain theological systems (like Calvinism) are inversion of the humility they profess, since they appeal to human vanity rather than deflate it. Poor man, that he needs the doctrine of the fall to invest him with a little glamour! Pitiful ego, that must sit in sackcloth and ashes and fancy itself the butt of Reprobation!" says the Rev. Mackerel of the People's Liberal Church of Avalon, Conn., in *The Mackerel Plaza* (1958) by Peter De Vries, himself a graduate of Calvin College. He has been described by the philosopher Daniel Dennett as "probably the funniest writer on religion ever."

[107] Evola prefers the rather painful metaphor of "a rupture of levels." See *Ride the Tiger*.

[108] Not that there's anything wrong with that…

It is interesting to note that some confirmation of this picture from a source contemporaneous with Watts and his book, and from the same "Catholic" (again, in Watt's sense of Roman Catholic – Anglican) *milieu*: Evelyn Waugh's *Brideshead Revisited*.[109] In particular, the main characters seem to embody Watts' notion of the Catholic state of mind.[110]

Take young Sebastian, here being interrogated by his new friend, Charles, exemplifying the mutual incomprehension of the Catholic child and Protestant adolescent:

'But my dear Sebastian, you can't seriously believe it all.'

'Can't I?'

'I mean about Christmas and the star and the three kings and the ox and the ass.'

'Oh yes, I believe that. It's a lovely idea.'

'But you can't believe things because they're a lovely idea.'

'But I do. That's how I believe.'

…

'Well,' I said, 'if you can believe all that and you don't want to be good, where's the difficulty about your religion?'

'If you can't see, you can't'

'Well, where?'

'Oh, don't be a bore, Charles. I want to read about a woman in Hull who's been using an instrument.' (p. 85)

Sebastian clearly has imbibed his religious ideas (if one can call them that) from his mother, Lady Marchmain:

---

[109] *Brideshead Revisited: The Sacred and Profane Memories of Captain Charles Ryder* (London: Chapman & Hall, 1945 [i.e. 1944]).

[110] I can find no mention of either Waugh or *Brideshead* in his *Collected Letters*.

I [Charles again] said something about a camel and the eye of a needle and she rose happily to the point.

'But of course,' she said, 'it's very unexpected for a camel to go through the eye of a needle, but the gospel is simply a catalogue of unexpected things. It's not to be expected that an ox and an ass should worship at the crib. Animals are always doing the oddest things in the lives of the saints. It's all part of the poetry, the Alice-in-Wonderland side, of religion.' (p. 123)

No surprise she entertains the family with evening readings of Chesterton.[111]

By contrast, the eldest son, "Bridey" (the Earl of Brideshead; no Christian name ever provided), manifests childhood in the nerd register – unworldly, self-absorbed, impolite and impolitic, yet so obsessed with dogma and ritual that the family feared he might become a priest. As Anthony Blanche tells us:

"There's Brideshead who's something archaic, out of a cave that's been sealed for centuries. He has the face as though an Aztec sculptor had attempted a portrait of Sebastian; he's a learned bigot, a ceremonious barbarian, a snow-bound lama...Well, anything you like."

This combination of the primitive and the learned perfectly instantiates what Watts describes as the Catholic attempt to emulate Protestant moral seriousness, resulting in the dreary Puritanism of the Irish or French Catholics. Indeed, it is Bridey who carelessly (in both senses) triggers off the moral climax of the novel when he smugly points out his new wife can't possibly share a roof with his adulterous sister Julia:

'You must understand that Beryl is a woman of strict Catholic principle fortified by the prejudices of the middle class. I couldn't

---

[111] Watts: "a Protestant Chesterton, not to mention a Protestant Rabelais, is well-nigh inconceivable." Watts also notes the creepy kind of cheerfulness put forward by the Protestant, reminding one of the Ned Flanders character on *The Simpsons*.

possibly bring her here. It is a matter of indifference whether you choose to live in sin with Rex or Charles or both—I have always avoided inquiry into the details of your *menage*—but in no case would Beryl consent to be your guest.' (p. 272)

Bridey's having "always avoided inquiry into the details" is a remnant of the moral laxity (from the Protestant viewpoint) of the traditional Catholic; his father's mistress, Cara, is an Italian who voices the more relaxed attitudes of the South:

'I know of these romantic friendships of the English and the Germans. They are not Latin. I think they are very good if they do not go on too long.'

'It is a kind of love that comes to children before they know its meaning. In England it comes when you are almost men; I think I like that. It is better to have that kind of love for another boy than for a girl. Alex [Lord Brideshead] you see had it for a girl, for his wife.' (p. 100)

And this brings us back to a celebrated passage at the start of the novel, as Charles describes his first summer with Sebastian, sounding both notes of childhood and moral laxity:

Descent or ascent? It seems to me that I grew younger daily with each adult habit that I acquired. I had lived a lonely childhood and a boyhood straitened by war and overshadowed by bereavement; to the hard bachelordom of English adolescence, the premature dignity and authority of the school system, I had added a sad and grim strain of my own. Now, that summer term with Sebastian, it seemed as though I was being given a brief spell of what I had never known, a happy childhood, and though its toys were silk shirts and liqueurs and cigars and *its naughtiness high in the catalogue of grave sins*, there was something of nursery freshness about us that fell little short of the joy of innocence. (p. 46)

Implicit here and in Cara's comments is the idea of an indulgence toward childhood romances that are expected to transition into a respectable adulthood, as illustrated by Charles' passage from Sebastian to his sister Julia.[112] Even this might be seen as analogous to Watts' model of consciousness maturing through several levels, each worthy in itself; what must be avoided is becoming stuck or even attempting to regress:

> 'Sebastian is in love with his own childhood. That will make him very unhappy. His teddy-bear, his nanny…and he is nineteen years old.' (p. 100)

The Catholic with his rosary, the Protestant with his rigid moral code; these are expired and unacceptable models for a truly modern mind. Rather than regressing to former modes, religion must rediscover the Spirit again, now at a higher level, thanks to the long pilgrimage through adolescence. Perhaps Waugh is making that point too, as Charles "revisits" Brideshead (the house, not the Earl) years later, having put aside both Sebastian and Julia:

> There was one part of the house I had not yet visited, and I went there now. *The chapel showed no ill-effects of its long neglect*; the art-nouveau paint was *as fresh and bright as ever*; the art-nouveau lamp burned once more before the altar. I said a prayer, *an ancient, newly-learned form of words*, and left, turning towards the camp; and *as I walked back*, and the cook-house bugle *sounded ahead of me*, I thought:

> 'The builders did not know the uses to which their work would descend; *they made a new house with the stones of the old castle*; year by year, generation after generation, they enriched and extended it; year by year the great harvest of timber in the park grew to ripeness; until, in sudden frost, came the age of Hooper [i.e., secular materialism]; the place was desolate and the work all brought to nothing; *Quomodo sedet sola civitas*. Vanity of

---

[112] Although the motif of the conveniently similar sister, like the girl who is only disguised as a boy for some reason, has not infrequently been used to covertly continue such relationships in fiction; see, for example, Baron Corvo's *Desire and Pursuit of the Whole*.

vanities, all is vanity.'

'And yet,' I thought…that is not the last word; it is not even an apt word; it is a dead word from ten years back.

> '*Something quite remote from anything the builders intended, has come out of their work*, and out of the fierce little human tragedy in which I played; something none of us thought about at the time; a small red flame—a beaten-copper lamp of deplorable design relit before the beaten-copper doors of a tabernacle; the flame which the old knights saw from their tombs, which they saw put out; that flame burns again for other soldiers, far from home, farther, in heart, than Acre or Jerusalem. *It could not have been lit but for the builders and the tragedians*, and there I found it this morning, *burning anew among the old stones*.'

★★★[113]

As a result of his more developed consciousness, modern man demands the meaning of the doctrine, not more or more sophisticated doctrine; and certainly not a "return to tradition." Modern man needs not dogma but what dogma *means*; the thing itself. This is the maturing of man's spiritual consciousness, a development to be encouraged as being the whole point of the enterprise, not a "deviation" to be fought against and turned aside."[114]

---

[113] "Asterisks, too serve to refresh the reader's eye and mind…I could not possibly have granted a chapter of its own to the foregoing excursus…" *Doctor Faustus: The Life of the German Composer Adrian Leverkühn as told by a Friend* by Thomas Mann, translated by John E. Woods (New York: Knopf, 1999), p. 189.

[114] As we'll see, this is the position of the so-called "traditionalist," of the Roman Catholic or Perennialist sort; "trends as the nineteenth-century Gothic revival and the reversion of the Roman Catholic Church at that time to an extreme traditionalism and obscurantism against the rise of liberalism." (p. 31). Gothic Revival was exemplified by Ralph Adams Cram, but Cram, like Watts, wanted to go back behind the Renaissance in order to move forward; he was as much a modernist as a medievalist. See my "Ralph Adams Cram: Wild Boy of American Architecture," reprinted in *The Eldritch Evola…& Others: Traditionalist Meditations on Literature, Art, & Culture*; ed. Greg Johnson (San Francisco: Counter-Currents, 2014). The architect of, among many other sites, the Episcopal Cathedral of St. John the Divine in New York, Cram is honored on December 16th in the Episcopalian calendar.

> The task of Protestantism was to break the shell, though because the Protestants did not fully realize this and did not know about the fruit inside, the job has been inexpertly and irreverently done.
>
> They have hammered away with gusto; they have cracked the entire surface; they have taken whole chunks of the shell right off, and, having thrown some of them away, have taken the rest into a corner and there tried to piece them together in a different form. But the fruit has not interested them. Protestantism has simply broken up the system of symbolism, reduced it and re-formed it, and, in these later times, has practically discarded the whole thing. The time has come for us to attend to the long-neglected fruit. (p. 41)

For Protestantism, misdirected though it has been, was nevertheless a necessary movement, needed in order that the "shell" of dogma, passively accepted by the Roman Catholic, be cracked, and the kernel obtained and brought to fruition within ourselves.[115]

> Truly, truly, I tell you, unless a kernel of wheat falls to the ground and dies, it remains only a seed; but if it dies, it bears much fruit. (John 12:24)

Hence, the periodic, now (as then) on the upswing interest in various "mystical" teachings, foreign and domestic; a legitimate but misconceived quest; Watts agrees with Spengler in discounting what today we would call "New Age" spirituality as immature,

---

[115] As Watts says several times, to get the nut you must break the shell; cf. Mann's *Dr. Faustus*: "He that would eat the kernel must crack the nut" is a German proverb favored by one of the protagonist's Protestant theology professors, and he recalls it several times throughout his subsequent rise and fall (pp. 95, 198, 509 in the Lowe-Porter translation; for some reason, John Woods' later translation renders this as "you must set pins if you would bowl", pp105, 526). In an embarrassing scene, the same professor tries to chase away the Devil by hurling a bread roll at him; Watts illustrates the Protestant attitude by alluding to the inspiration, Luther hurling an inkpot at Satan (p. 191). However, Watts apparently was interested in but did not see *Dr. Faustus* until he received it as a Christmas present in 1949 (Letter of January 10, 1949; *Letters*, p. 240). He would likely know the phrase in its Anglican context, from the Preface to the 1611 King James Bible, by Miles Smith: "Translation it is that openeth the window, to let in the light, that breaketh the shell, that we may eat the kernel."

unhistorical, and often implicitly if not explicitly Gnostic and hence retrograde.

Would that these seekers knew that the Catholic Christianity has its own, vastly more sophisticated spiritual techniques; but how can they find out, when even the Church itself, in the person of its ministers, doesn't know anymore?

To remedy this, Watts turns to the late stages of other cultures—including our own late Classical period, whose mature wisdom gave birth to early Christianity—to try to suggest the inner meaning of the Christian mythos, the actual experience of the Holy Spirit.

> In the great ages of Christian thought theology has always been able to embrace and absorb alien systems much to its own enrichment. In fact, every great advance in Christian theology has involved the absorption of an alien philosophy…It is not too much to predict that the next great step in Christian theology will be due, in part, to the absorption of Hinduism, Buddhism, Taoism, and, perhaps, Mohammedan Sufism, all of which are profoundly mystical religions. (p. 53)

For purposes of this review essay, I've tried to distill the logical outline of the book, but I have to say that apart from a superficial structure of chapters and topics, and local arguments on particular points, it doesn't really have an overall vector that marches the reader from Point A to Point B until the reader is forced to accept some predetermined conclusions; but rather drift from moment to moment, in which various themes, points of view and images are introduced and revisited as seems necessary; which, as we'll see, is appropriate to a number of those themes, such as the importance of living in the moment, and the freedom of man to accept God's offer of union or not.[116]

---

[116] It's also appropriate as being the method of Plotinus, who summed up what Watts considers the high, late wisdom of Classical culture (see the discussion of Spengler's "second religiosity" above), and was part of the same mid-century Thomistic academic world Watts is operating in, which I encountered at the University of Windsor, where John N. Deck held forth on Plotinus—who, in his own doctoral dissertation on Plotinus, says he does not so much prove his conclusions as accustom us to them by talking *around* them: "In many places he does not so much prove his propositions and notions as accustom his hearers

In any event, as I've said, the real fascination here is how early, and how well, Watts was able to formulate most of what would become his signature tropes or memes in the language of traditional Catholic Christianity.

But I certainly don't mean to suggest there is anything boring or repetitive here. Even at this early point in his career, Watts seems to be incapable of writing a dull page, or even paragraph.[117] As already suggested, the interest here is in how easily Watts expresses, in purely Christian language, most of the memes he would propagate during his career as a "New Age" or even "hippie" lecturer.

His use of the non-dualist school of the Hindu Vedanta to explain how the Christian God is a superior conception to any "pantheistic" deity, by being able to create real, "other" beings while still remaining indivisible, makes most of those smug claims about "what we can learn from the Hindus" look rather jejune; this is the best kind of Traditionalism, using the deepest insights of one culture (to return to Spengler's language) to illuminate the equal depths of another.

Throughout, Watts moves with ease from the Christian dogma of the Incarnation—union with God which is freely and already given, to the futility of methods—union with God something which we not only cannot fail to achieve but cannot even try to achieve, and, indeed, we cannot even refuse it if we wanted to (Hell being the sufferings of those who obstinately chose to refuse), to his more general and more familiar point that life can only be lived as what Coomaraswamy called "the perpetual uncalculated life in the present" rather than something we plan to *get*, someday, if we follow the right recipe.[118]

---

and readers to their truth. The result is that it often seems that he is proving conclusions by premises and premises by conclusion, when in fact he is elaborating an intuition…and rendering it plausible and acceptable." See John N. Deck, *Nature, Contemplation, and the One: A Study in the Philosophy of Plotinus* (University of Toronto Press, 1969; Toronto Heritage series, 2017 [Kindle iOS version]).

[117] *Unlike* Plotinus, whose collected discourses—*The Enneads*, produced late in life by a man who, unlike Watts, despises language and communication as he does the body and other mere matter—are written in the worst Greek of any surviving classic, yet contain passages where, as Yeats said of the translation by his fellow Irishman Stephan MacKenna, "one has the sense of great doors flung open."

[118] Watts justifies the move "for the reason that the reality of religion and the reality of life

At times Watts manages to both clarify the traditional language of Christian mysticism and express his own views more clearly than he would again:

> The consciousness of union with God thus realized is mystical, that is, veiled, rather than beatific; it is not an absolutely direct and full consciousness, but resembles to some extent the consciousness which we have of our own selves. For while we cannot perceive out own egos directly, we know that we exist… and this knowledge is present as an undertone in all other knowledge. Similarly, the mystical knowledge of God is a knowledge of God in the act of this presence and union with us, but is not immediate vision and apprehension of the divine essence. Presumably this is only possible when actual death has removed the ego from standing in its own light. (p. 100 and footnote 12)[119]

Indeed, even death can't escape Watts' expanding vision of the ever-present union:

> Abandoning all concepts and conventional feelings about Reality, letting go of all devices and methods for realizing union with god, we approach the Now just as it is.
>
> Looked at from an intellectual and emotional point of view, the Eternal Now certainly seems dry and empty. From this standpoint, entering into it seems a kind of death, and the surrender of cherished intellectual and emotional consolations is indeed a sharing in the death of the cross, from which the whole power of the Resurrection flows.
>
> Apparently there is nothing in God, and yet everything comes out of him. Sun, moon, stars, mountains, trees, men – all have

---

are one and the same." (p. 105)

[119] Again, there is something very Plotinian both in the idea mystical experience as operating alongside everyday consciousness, and in the process of freeing our notion of consciousness from one impediment after another, until finally even the ego itself drops out, leaving…a kind of "super" consciousness? See especially Deck, *op. cit.*

> their being in and emerge from the Now, from something which, when we try to think about it, instantly seems boundless and void.
>
> There seems no reason why creative life should come out of it, but it does because there is God himself. ...This fear of the Void is lack of faith in the reality of God.

This, along with some musing about how God occupied himself before Creation, remind me a bit of my own recent Wattsian reflections on the relation, if any, between the end of our existence and God's self-amusements;[120] as Watts says, "God is not niggardly in his self-revelation; he exposes himself right before our eyes." (p. 91).

When Watts comes to explicitly discuss the life of Action, the disparagement of methods and the Kantian reorientation of such tools as liturgy, sacraments, prayer etc. into expressions of joyous gratitude rather than desperate attempts to grasp at God or reality, naturally takes the form of tossing aside laws, commandments, regulations, and other Judaica.[121] Instead of vainly trying to "act morally" by hypocritically following rules,

> Delivered from the vicious circle of bad self-consciousness... [the] principle of action will no more be a moral code; it will be the indwelling Holy Spirit. (p. 212)
>
> Since the Reformation [viz, the adolescent stage of culture] we have largely regarded morality as an end in itself.... A morality which proceeds from the realization of union with God [the third, mature, stage] will see that its end is the perfection of this realization for all human beings. (p. 214)

Naturally, in an Incarnational religion, this union "extends to all his human functions, for no human function is incompatible with God" (p. 216), which are to be subject to "control and beautification." Here

---

[120] See "Of Apes, Essence, and the Afterlife," *infra*.

[121] Watts never disparages Jews and Judaism as such, but does says that "Christianity is different in principle from Judaism and other legalistic religions" (p.213).

we see the beginnings of Watts' call for a true "spiritual materialism."[122]

Of course, this includes sexuality, and here we can see how Watts' "bohemian lifestyle," as he calls it in his 1971 Preface, could raise some questions about his suitability as a university chaplain:

> For example, a person is not sexually controlled in any real sense by mere limitations of the frequency of intercourse or the number of his partners. To realize union with God in terms of sexual life, he must exercise control within the act of sex, and as this will require practice the act cannot be too infrequent. (p. 217)

Indeed.[123] Actually, some Traditionalists, such as Evola or Alain Danielou, would be just fine with this, but then their works raise some eyebrows as well.[124]

---

[122] See Greg Johnson's "The Spiritual Materialism of Alan Watts: A Review of *Does it Matter?*" in his *Confessions of a Reluctant Hater* (2nd Ed., Revised and Expanded; San Francisco: Counter-Currents, 2016).

[123] One, or at least myself, can't help but be reminded of Dr. Strangelove's plan for post-nuclear war survival:

> General "Buck" Turgidson: Doctor, you mentioned the ratio of ten women to each man. Now, wouldn't that necessitate the abandonment of the so-called monogamous sexual relationship, I mean, as far as men were concerned?
>
> Dr. Strangelove: Regrettably, yes. But it is, you know, a sacrifice required for the future of the human race. I hasten to add that since each man will be required to do prodigious... service along these lines, the women will have to be selected for their sexual characteristics which will have to be of a highly stimulating nature.
>
> Ambassador de Sadesky: I must confess, you have an astonishingly good idea there, Doctor.

See my essay "From Odd John to Strange Love," reprinted in *Green Nazis in Space! New Essays on Literature, Art, & Culture*; edited by Greg Johnson (San Francisco: Counter-Currents, 2015).

[124] For Evola, see *Eros and the Mysteries of Love: The Metaphysics of Sex* (New York: Inner Traditions, 1983; *Edizioni Mediterranee*, 1969) as well as "Beyond Prudery and Perversion: The Sexual Aesthetics and Metaphysics of Julius Evola" by Keith Preston (online here: https://attackthesystem.com/2012/07/19/beyond-prudery-and-perversion-the-sexual-aesthetics-and-metaphysics-of-julius-evola/): "Where Evola's thought is to be most sharply differentiated from that of modern leftists is not on the matter of sex-phobia, but on the question of sexual egalitarianism. Unlike the Christian puritans who regard deviants from the heterosexual, procreative sexual paradigm as criminals against the natural order, Evola apparently understood the existence of such "sexual identities" as a naturally occurring phenomenon. Unlike modern liberals, Evola opposed the elevation of such sexual identities or practices to the level of equivalence with "normal" procreative and kinship related forms

In any event, Watts has some interesting ideas about the nature of this control, and why it requires practice, which we will need to explore a bit later; we've also breached the topic of Traditionalism, or at least Traditionalists, and the suitability of Watts as an Episcopal chaplain, all of which deserve, and will now get, their own examinations.

PARTINGS I – WATTS AND TRADITIONALISM

Of course, all this needs to be read against his later works addressed to Christian theology, as he says in the 1971 Preface; in particular *Beyond Theology: The Art of Godmanship* (1964), where he settles his accounts with Traditionalism; as Greg Johnson describes it:

> Although Watts found Traditionalism useful in liberating his mind from Christianity, he ultimately rejected it. In the Preface to *Beyond Theology*, he explains his reason. Traditionalists claim that Christianity is just an exoteric expression of the one primordial tradition which is the inner truth of all religions. But Watts points out that there is no evidence that the founders of Christianity thought that way. Instead, Christianity has always insisted on what Jan Assmann calls the "Mosaic distinction" between true and false religions. Christianity is the one true religion, and all others are simply false.[125]

To Watts' heresy Whitall Perry, deputized as a sort of Pope of Tradition, replied:

---

of sexual expression and relationship." Daniélou—translator of the *Kama Sutra*—travelled rural India in the 30s in a trailer home with his longtime companion; in *The Way to the Labyrinth: Memories of East and West* (New Directions, 1987), Daniélou recounts his first sexual experience—with a twenty-year old, six-foot-seven baseball player—after which he "murmured: 'there must be a God for such happiness to be possible!' For a long time I had ceased to believe in the Christian God. ...Oddly enough, it was in that moment of intense pleasure that a god of sensuousness, happiness and light was reveal to me...all I need to do now was find him." (p. 63).

[125] "Alan Watts at 100," *loc.cit.*

He tells us he broke away from the *philosophia perennis* outlook because 'there is not a scrap of evidence that the Christian hierarchy was ever aware of itself as one among several lines of transmission for a universal tradition,' whereas 'the so-called "traditionalist school"...regards every orthodox spiritual tradition as a more-or-less deliberate adaptation of the *philosophia perennis* to the needs of different cultures.' The truth is, exclusivity is not the prerogative of Christianity: there never has been a religion East or West that did not require what Watts calls 'an all-or-nothing commitment,' and certainly none of the above named proponents of the perennial wisdom ever claimed otherwise.[126]

But this is really just a detail. The real issue that bugs Perry is Watts' seemingly cavalier attitude to dogmas and symbols. He's particularly outraged by Watts' suggestion that the Resurrection be celebrated at Easter by the ceremonial burning of a copy of the Bible – admittedly, a bit extreme.[127]

I've always thought that Perry somewhat missed the point, and here in his 1947 book we find Watts addressing Perry *avant le lettre*, and speaking in more detail on this than I think he ever did later.

Watts insists that our feeling is as valuable as our thinking, and that if we think otherwise it is only because we have, in fact, neglected to develop our feelings as we have our intellect. As it is, out outdated and in any event inadequate symbols of God, Christ, etc. make it impossible for modern man—or someone from a culture as aesthetically developed as the Chinese—to take the Christian message seriously. As he says in *Beyond Theology*, in a passage that Perry quotes with scorn:

---

[126] Whitall N. Perry, "Anti-Theology and the Riddles of Alcyone," *Studies in Comparative Religion*, vol. 6, no. 3, here: http://www.studiesincomparativereligion.com/Public/articles/Anti-Theology_and_the_Riddles_of_Alcyone-by_Alan_Watts.aspx.

[127] Wasn't there a Protestant pastor who wanted to deliberately provoke Moslems by burning the *Koran*? The affinity of Traditionalism for the mental atmosphere of militant Islam will be noted again soon.

> The general climate of twentieth-century knowledge and thought has made it [the existence of such a anthropomorphic God] thoroughly implausible and slightly comic. And so long as we are exhorted in church services to address ourselves (for example) 'with a pure heart and a humble voice unto the throne of the heavenly grace,' the very idea of God will be contaminated with this now ridiculous image. It is simply unimaginable that the universe of modern astronomy and physics, biology and chemistry, should be the creation of any such pompous potentate; our world is much too astonishing for any explanation of that kind to be meaningful.

In *Behold the Spirit*, he emphasizes that symbols, to be effective, must appeal to the whole man, and thus

> Because man is so powerfully controlled by [aesthetic perception and feeling], an image of God deficient in beauty is of small appeal to him, and this is especially true of that stratum of the modern mind which we been considering throughout this book – the educated, sincere, thoughtful and spiritually hungry pagan. He is repelled by the downright ugliness and joylessness of so much that passes for Christianity. This cannot be changed by mere external adjustments in ecclesiastical art and manners...it *must proceed from an inner experience* of the beauty and the joy of God.

Again, the necessity of mysticism, the need to crack the shell to reach the kernel. Traditionalists like Perry want to preserve it, intact, at all cost, and if you don't want to accept it as is, then hard cheese and great sucks to you.

In a sense, Watts never abandoned the Traditionalist sensibility, only its diagnosis and method.[128] Both agreed that modern man had met an impasse, and that a spiritual renewal was needed. For Traditionalists like Guénon or Schuon, the religious Reformation and the artistic and scientific Renaissance were twin cataclysms,

---

[128] In *The Same Man: George Orwell and Evelyn Waugh in Love and War* (New York: Random House, 2008), David Lebedoff attempts to argue that George Orwell and Evelyn Waugh, apparently polar opposites, were in fact soul mates; each despised the modern world, but their solutions—return to Mediaevalism, progress to the Socialist utopia—were polar opposites

global catastrophes, no doubt Satanically inspired; they have brought us to despair and must be renounced.

In such works as *The Crisis of the Modern World*, Guénon heaps scorn on the petty toys of modern technology, which previous, "integral" civilizations would have disdained, and mocks modern man who has worn himself out exploring the paltry "horizontal" dimensions of the material world while ignoring or denying the "vertical" dimension of spiritual transcendence.

Schuon, for his part, in his *Logic and Transcendence*, calls critical analysis "a contradiction in itself and thus a pure absurdity" and denounces those who, with "arrogant unconsciousness" would "kill with their petty vitriolic thoughts" the "great spokesmen of metaphysics." As for Beethoven, well, "there is some music that ought not to have been made."[129]

As we've seen, Watts wanted no part of such obscurantism.[130] The transition from childhood belief to adolescent doubt is necessary and valuable; rather than abandoning this achievement it must be completed, brought to fruition by a rediscovery of the inner meaning of the symbols.

As for method, since Watts did not want to abandon the phenomena, he could not pretend to escape to some "higher" viewpoint. Rather than seeking some supposed "transcendental unity" above, behind, or perhaps beneath the variety of religions and cultures,

---

[129] *Logic and Transcendence*, by Frithjof Schuon (New York: Harper & Row, 1975); in his review, Perry calls it his "masterwork [which] in its textual magnitude and multifaceted precision—logical, intellectual, and spiritual—offers a veritable panoply of what might be called the Schuonian cosmorama." *Studies in Comparative Religion*, Vol. 9, No. 4. (Autumn, 1975).

[130] Although Traditionalists may make token gestures against modernity, no doubt eschewing video games and shopping for "organic" produce, etc., they by and large seem happy enough to make use of the "toys" of modern technology – cars, planes, modern publishing methods (even a hand-cranked press is a "modern" invention). They no doubt justify this to themselves the same way Islamic militants use modern explosives, guns, and the Internet while attempting to impose a Mediaeval Caliphate; the attraction of Traditionalists to Islam—which never had a Reformation—is note-worthy.

> Watts…turned toward hermeneutical analyses exploring interconnections and disjunctions between localized narratives. Through this kind of interpretive study, one arrives at an expanded awareness and comprehension of perspectives via the dialectical rotation of differing vantage points.[131]

At least implicitly, this was a move from foundationalism if not fundamentalism to perspectivism. As Watts introduces his topic in *Behold the Spirit*, he argues that for our lives to have meaning, we must know how things are, and fortunately there is a way things are that can be known.

But what if this world is a will to power, and nothing else besides? What if meaning, if it exists, can only arise out of a battle of worldviews? Here, in his hermeneutic turn, we see Watts adumbrating themes that would be brought to a climax in the work of Jason Jorjani, of which more anon.

PARTINGS II – WATTS AND THE CHURCH TODAY: REAL PRESENCE OR REAL ESTATE?

Watts was quite successful in his attempt to express the *religio perennis* in the language of Christian theology; not just in my opinion today, but among his Episcopal peers at the time (one fellow university chaplain even called it "the most important book on religion in this century"[132]), yet within four years he resigned his position, left the Church and embarked on his more characteristic career as an alt-academic and, eventually, something of a counter-cultural guru. What happened?

According to his letter of resignation,[133] it was what he later called the Church's dogmatic imperialism:

---

[131] *Alan Watts – In the Academy: Essays and Lectures* (SUNY series in Transpersonal and Humanistic Psychology); edited and with an introduction by Peter J. Columbus and Donadrian L. Rice (Albany: SUNY Press, 2017), kindle loc. 560-566; see my review *supra*.

[132] *In My Own Way*, p. 198.

[133] Online here: http://www.wisdom2be.com/files/b0f09249af99a337e7264d8fc826a694-129.html.

"During the past years I have continued my studies of the spiritual teachings of the Orient, alongside with Catholic theology, and, though I have sometimes doubted it, I am now fully persuaded that the Church's claim to be the best of all ways to God is not only a mistake, but also a symptom of anxiety. Obviously, one who has found a great truth is eager to share it with others. But to insist—often in ignorance of other revelations—that one's own is supreme argues a certain inferiority complex characteristic of all imperialisms. "Me thinks thou doth protest too much." This claim of supremacy is, for me, the chiefest sign of how deeply the Church is committed to this self-strangulation, this anxiety for certainty, and I cannot support the proselytism in which it issues."

In an interview in *LIFE* magazine in 1961 Watts said that he left the church "not because it doesn't practice what it preaches, but because it preaches."[134]

In 1964's *Beyond Theology* he concluded:

My previous discussions did not take proper account of that whole aspect of Christianity which is uncompromising, ornery, militant, rigorous, imperious, and invincibly self-righteous.

Of course, forcing his hand would have been concern over his somewhat irregular lifestyle, which would ultimately include divorcing his first wife, Eleanor (who was, at the time, having an affair with the choirmaster), and marrying a former student. A bit tame compared to a Weinstein, but not really the done thing for an Episcopalian chaplain in the 1940s.

One can't help but wonder if Watts would have found a more comfortable pew in today's Church, especially the Episcopal branch. Surely the relentless liberalization of the last 75 years has enabled the Church to catch up with Watts?

Surprisingly, the answer is: no, not at all. Or perhaps not surprisingly; for the "liberalizing" in question has mostly in the political sense.

---

[134] Online here: http://biography.yourdictionary.com/alan-watts#GXWzZXEDVzEBmxvv.99.

True, a church that positively welcomes gay and transgendered clergy would find Watts' serial monogamy charmingly old fashioned; or perhaps dangerously cisgendered and triggering?

But more importantly, Watts—as clergyman or congregant—would find the contemporary Church even more boring and pointless than before, for liturgies, both Catholic and Protestant, have been rationalized and "popularized" more than ever, making contemplative prayer all but impossible, and the Social Gospel, the Good News in the Protestant, adolescent form of changing the world in the light of rigid principles of justice (all men are equal here and now, not in the Spirit), has not faded away in the growing light of the Spirit, but instead metastasized and taken over.

However much Watts might agree with those politics—in his autobiography he mentions the tedium of having to kowtow to the conservative businessmen who make up (then) the most important congregants—Watts was interested in the Spiritual, not such surface fripperies. As he insisted in his new Preface, itself now almost 50 years old, all this is a

> [M]ere matter of changing the externals–of having rock bands instead of organs and Kyrie eleison set to jazz, [or] *even of turning churches into social service centers* with the idea that this would be practicing Christianity seven days a week instead of just talking it on Sundays. Indeed, one may well hope that monarchical Christianity will not be practiced, even on Sundays, since the dutiful spirit in which it dispenses charity breeds resentment in the giver and the receiver alike, for when the one gives with reluctance the other receives with guilt.

Speaking of social service centers (today, most likely to be "Mary and Joseph were illegals" – style immigrant service centers), Watts goes on to frame the issue in blunt, Trumpian terms of real estate:

> The practical problem is, what are we going to do on Sunday mornings? How are ministers to continue their work? What is to be the use of church buildings, funds, and administrative machinery? Naturally, institutional Christianity will, in its

present form, continue to supply the demand which remains for a monarchical [civil] religion. But a considerable number of ministers and even congregations—not to mention millions of reasonably intelligent young people—realize that churches must 'put up or shut up,' and that the chief business of religious facilities and assemblies is to provide a social milieu for religious experience. ... Ministers and their congregations must instead consider what need there may be for churches as temples for contemplation and meditation, stripped of the courthouse furniture of stalls, pews, pulpits, lecterns and other equipment for throwing the Book at captive audiences. They must consider also the need for retreat houses and religious communities, and for guidance and instruction in the many forms of spiritual discipline which are conducive to mystical vision [non-dual knowing]." (pp. xx – xi).

Ironic, since the Episcopal Church has indeed taken the path of forcing change down the throats of those conservative vestrymen, and taken over the very buildings themselves—a quirk of the Episcopal Church is that the national body owns the buildings, while the churches control their own endowments and other investments—but hardly to promote contemplation:

> Convention attendees were told that *they had spent $18 million this year suing their own local congregations* —those which have protested the denomination's policies by trying to secede. The New York hierarchy has consistently won in court—asserting that the local members signed over their buildings decades ago. As a result, some of the largest Episcopal congregations in the United States have been forced to vacate their buildings and meet elsewhere. So now, convention delegates were told, *the denomination is the proud owner of scores of empty buildings nationwide – and liable for their upkeep in a depressed real estate market* where empty church buildings are less than prime property. It's the classic "dog in a manger." The denomination has managed to keep the buildings—*for which it has little use*. However, they made their point—refusing to allow the

congregations which built the facilities to have any benefit after generations of sacrifice, donations and volunteerism.

"One former Episcopal priest wrote me, 'The irony is that after all their property suits to get control of empty buildings, they now are losing their main property.'"[135]

One might hope that at least some of these buildings could be turned over to or acquired by some new Peter Gatien, who could turn them into pagan dance clubs, which at least would be more in line with Watts' program.[136]

Ironies abound, of course. Watts makes the interesting point that while he has no doubts at all that Jesus really existed,[137] the refusal to "crack the shell" of scripture to obtain the nut of spirit has led, especially among Protestants, to obsessions with Biblical literalness and inerrancy. Today, of course, the very existence of Jesus is a hot topic,[138] but ironically the last man standing among the candidates for the stripped-down, 100% real Jesus tends to be the wandering Jewish teacher or political zealot; the Spirit seems to have been "found" in the supposed political shell, not even the scriptural shell.

Indeed, the Episcopal Church's new leader has proudly made his motto "We are the Episcopal branch *of the Jesus Movement*," a pretty explicit statement of a proud retreat to the most adolescent stage of the Western Spirit, rather than an advance to the fully mature life of the Holy Spirit.[139]

---

[135] Online here: http://granitegrok.com/blog/2017/07/update-continuing-self-destruction-episcopal-church.

[136] See "From Ultrasuede to Limelight: Halston & Gatien, Aryan Entrepreneurs in the Dark Age" in my collection *Green Nazis in Space! New Essays on Literature, Art, & Culture*; edited by Greg Johnson (San Francisco: Counter-Currents, 2015).

[137] "May I say I have no doubts in my mind as to the reality of the Incarnation and as to the fact that something actually exists which might be called the Body of Christ." Letter to Gertrude Moakly of the New York Public Library, August 22, 1950. *Letters*, p. 270.

[138] See my review of Kenneth Humphreys' *Jesus Never Existed: An Introduction to the Ultimate Heresy*; with an interview by Chip Smith (Charleston, W.V.: Nine-Banded Books, 2014), Counter-Currents, May 20, 2015; and Aedon Cassiel, "Is Jesus a Myth?" on Counter-Currents, July 13, 2017.

[139] The Holy Spirit, saddled with its ridiculous symbol—a pigeon—is apparently still a

Of course, the Episcopal Church has always been mostly the WASP elite at prayer (answering Watts' question, what are we going to do on Sunday mornings?) so it's hardly surprising that it serves mainly as a vehicle for SJW virtue signaling in the Present Year; thus:

> In America last week a church in Virginia took down two plaques of men who had worshipped there, one of George Washington, the other of Robert E. Lee. The plaques distracted our worshippers, said the cowardly rector.[140]

Rather than openness to other religions, it's the phony openness of multiculturalism and unlimited immigration, in the service of global conformity.[141]

Watts seems to have underestimated the ability of the adolescent Protestant conscience to sustain itself in its infinite regress of idealistic guilt. Like a collapsing neutron star, it needs more and more fuel. As we now know, SJW's always double down.

No matter how bohemian his lifestyle, no matter how welcoming to other religions, spiritually Watts was profoundly conservative – or rather, archeofuturistic. Perhaps another of Russell Kirk's "Bohemian Tories"?

---

problem: See *Forgotten God: Reversing Our Tragic Neglect of the Holy Spirit* by Francis Chan (David C. Cook, 2009); for his part, Chan never mentions Watts. For his part, Bishop Curry is the author of *Crazy Christians: A Call to Follow Jesus* (Morehouse, 2013). With a title like that, one might hope for some Wattsian playfulness or even "crazy wisdom" but it turns out to be more of that creepy Christian forced-cheerfulness that Watts deplores as the flip side of the torment of total depravity, with an extra helping of Jesus-centered politics: "What the Church needs, what this world needs, are some Christians who are as crazy as the Lord. Crazy enough to love like Jesus, to give like Jesus, to forgive like Jesus, to do justice, love mercy, walk humbly with God-like Jesus. Crazy enough to dare to change the world." The publisher says it "encourages all of us to let go of conventions and embrace the craziness of believing we can change the world for the better." Hot diddley-doo!

[140] Online here: http://takimag.com/article/sadiq_khans_cesspit/print#ixzz4xUffdYib.

[141] "Why is modern Christianity eerily in sync with the worldview of those nice folks sitting on giant piles of money left over from the glory days of the Standard Oil Company, Ford Motor Company and US Steel? Mainline Protestants have to get out the tweezers now and separate the Christian mustard seeds from the Fabian Society and Rockefeller Foundation mouse droppings." Cagey Beast, commenting at Unz.com.

In any event, Watts was aware of the difference between biblical symbols intended to promote the awareness of the indwelling Holy Spirit, and secular notions of purported social improvement.

Individual morality cannot just be mapped onto social morality or politics. Discussing the Old Testament image of a vengeful God, Watts observes that

> God has no need to punish in the vengeful sense because he has no need to protect himself. He is not weak and vulnerable *like human society*. (p. 211)

> Delivered from the vicious circle of bad self-consciousness, the infinite regression of chasing oneself around and around, it is possible for man to move forward. But in moving forward his principle of action will no more be a moral code; it will be the indwelling Holy Spirit. (p. 211)

> Mature Christian morality … will lose the adolescent's itch to change the world overnight, which has long characterized Western Christianity in its schemes[142] for spiritual and material reforms. (p. 214)

> This will help free our idea of the Christian life from the false heroics of adolescence, that running around in search of great moral deeds to do, which is so often no more than hypocritical interference with the lives of others. (p. 224)

> It is not charitable to the poor to try all at once to abolish poverty, with the exception, indeed of really abject poverty. … Most of the wholesale and impersonal charity we practice today is mere patronization of the poor, motivated by pity and fear of their estate and not by respect and honor. (p. 220)

In short,

> The work of the Church is to share a sense of union with God by all the means at its disposal, symbolic or otherwise. The *Christian*

---
[142] God is not a schemer, as the Joker would say.

morality of love, as distinct from the secular morality of justice, has meaning and value only in relation to this background. Apart from it, it disrupts the *natural* order of society, which based as it is on fear and collective self-interest, is to be preferred to Christian and supernatural virtues running amok in separation form their source. (pp. 221-222; italics in original)

Some people still understand this:

Christian belief contests all politics, its visions of human flourishing and the ethical claims it makes of people being so demanding that *no political leader or political programme can fully satisfy them.*[143]

Again, as the dog returns to his vomit, the Christian returns to his infinite regress.

EXCURSUS: NEVILLE AND WATTS – THE SAME MAN?

"Alan Watts is the Norman Vincent Peale of Zen."[144]

Right about the time Watts was writing *Behold the Spirit* and serving as a "paradox priest," as he titles the relevant chapter in his autobiography, Neville Goddard was in the initial stages of a very successful career as a "metaphysical lecturer," author, and broadcaster.[145]

---

[143] *The Mighty and the Almighty: How Political Leaders Do God*; ed. by Nick Spencer (Biteback Publishing, 2017), p.346.

[144] H. Braun, "The Politics of Zen." *New Politics: A Journal of Socialist Thought*, 1(1), pp.177-89; quoted in *Alan Watts — In the Academy: Essays and Lectures* (SUNY series in Transpersonal and Humanistic Psychology); edited and with an introduction by Peter J. Columbus and Donadrian L. Rice (Albany: State University of New York Press, 2017).

[145] Though, as we will see, a British subject, Neville had been drafted in 1942, but used what we would call "meme magic" to get an honorable discharge within a few weeks. His Army records show he was "discharged from service to accept employment in an essential wartime industry": delivering metaphysical lectures in Greenwich Village. Mitch Horowitz has recently verified Neville's story; see "Neville Goddard: A Cosmic Philosopher," in *At*

These are essentially the roles Watts took on after leaving the priesthood, and I've called attention before to the remarkable resemblances between Watts and Neville (he always went by name alone).[146] Revisiting Watts gives us a chance to review and expand on those similarities.

Both men occupied adjacent slices of the space/time continuum, and although Neville Lancelot Goddard was born in 1905 and Alan Wilson Watts in 1915, both died within months of each other (October 1, 1972, aged 67; 16 November 1973, aged 58, respectively). Both men had long before emigrated to the USA from parts of the British Empire (Neville from Barbados) to seek their fortune, mostly in California. Although Watts fitfully attended good schools he described himself in his autobiography with Shaw's line about being "half-miseducated;"[147] Neville seems to have skipped schools altogether.[148]

On a somewhat more relevant note, both men were tall, handsome, spoke with those authoritative British accents (Neville's with an island lilt to it); charismatic, in short. I call this "more relevant" because this was an essential element to their careers: both men became great successes on the modern lecture circuits, utilizing the cutting-edge technologies of radio, TV, LP recordings, even airplanes (to appear at venues from coast to coast). And, although Neville was fading a bit as Watts was getting into stride,[149] both men have had a remarkable "resurrection" on the internet,[150] where

---

Your Command: The First Classic Work by the Visionary Mystic Neville (Tarcher Cornerstone Editions, 2016).

[146] See my kindle edition of Neville's *Feeling is the Secret* (Amazon, 2016).

[147] "You've gone to the finest school, alright Miss Lonely / But you know you only used to get juiced in it." Nobel Laureate Bob Dylan, "Like a Rolling Stone."

[148] Horowitz describes him as "self-educated."

[149] As Neville shifted his message from what he called The Law (cf. "The Law of Attraction") to The Promise (realizing unity with Christ) "audiences drifted away. Urged by his speaking agent to abandon this theme, "or you'll have no audience at all," a student recalled Neville replying, "Then I'll tell it to the bare walls." Horowitz, *op. cit.*

[150] "His books, audios and videos are as relevant now as they were decades ago, and most of his body of work is still available through the usual sources and the website devoted to his life and work. If he is rediscovered four decades after his passing, it would be a

Neville's books and lectures are freely available,[151] and both men are all over YouTube.

But what did they lecture *on*, surely *that* is the relevant point here? Again, the similarities are remarkable.

Both men had been attached to oddball gurus – Watts first with the "rascal guru" Dimitrije Mitrinovic,[152] then with the iconoclastic Krishnamurti;[153] Neville with a "black, Ethiopian rabbi" named Abdullah[154] – but the ironic lesson they took from both was: ignore gurus and do it yourself![155]

As for the content of their teaching, Watts' concerns here and later in *Beyond Theology* can perhaps be expressed in the title of Neville's 1944 book: *Feeling is the Secret*.

Writing in 1949, Neville summed up what he modestly calls his "simple formula for changing the future:"

---

well-deserved resurrection. He would probably light up a cigar and have a good laugh. "Alan Watts: Reborn in [the movie] *Her*" by Philip Goldberg; online here: http://www.huffingtonpost.com/philip-goldberg/alan-watts-reborn-in-her_b_4848864.html. One could say the same but even more strongly of Neville.

[151] Unlike Watts, Neville never copyrighted any of his books, and encouraged taping and sharing his lectures; a strikingly modern attitude, reminiscent of the Grateful Dead, Mystery Science Theater ("Keep Circulating the Tapes!") and the general Millennial attitude that "information wants to be free."

[152] The editors of *Alan Watts – In the Academy* refer to "the tutorage from 1934 to 1936 of Serbian philosopher Dimitrije Mitrinovic (1887–1953)," whom they identify as "A formative thinker in the pre-World War I Young Bosnia movement and subsequent New Europe Group and New Britain Movement, Mitrinovic integrated mystical metaphysics and transformative political-social philosophy."

[153] See, in addition to *In My Own Way*, the Perry article, *op. cit.*

[154] Here again Mitch Horowitz has done yeoman's service tracking down and verifying Neville's somewhat vague accounts of his teacher, who may have been Arnold Josiah Ford, a Barbados-born leader of the Ethiopian Movement (a precursor to Rastafarianism) in New York City; see "A Cosmic Philosopher," *op. cit.*

[155] They also learned a disdain for ascetism; Watts and Neville, like their gurus, became legendary drinkers and lovers of fine food (although there are no stories of Neville falling down drunk). There is precedent: "The Son of Man came eating and drinking, and they say, 'Look at this glutton and drunkard, a friend of tax collectors and of sinners!' But wisdom is vindicated by her actions." Matthew 11:19-20.

> People have a habit of slighting the importance of simple things; but this simple formula for changing the future was discovered after years of searching and experimenting. The first step in changing the future is *desire*—that is: define your objective—know definitely what you want.
>
> Secondly: construct an event which you believe you would encounter *following* the fulfillment of your desire—an event which implies fulfillment of your desire—something that will have the action of *self* predominant.
>
> Thirdly: immobilize the physical body and induce a condition akin to sleep—lie on a bed or relax in a chair and imagine that you are sleepy; then, with eyelids closed and your attention focused on the action you intend to experience—in imagination—mentally feel yourself right into the proposed action—imagining all the while that you are actually performing the action here and now. You must always participate in the imaginary action, not merely stand back and look on, but you must feel that you are actually performing the action so that the imaginary sensation is real to you.
>
> It is important always to remember that the proposed action must be one which *follows* the fulfillment of your desire; and, also, you must feel yourself into the action until it has all the vividness and distinctness of reality.[156]

We can see two things here: first, the demand for experimental verification, not dogma; the same post-Protestant, post-adolescent demand Watts identifies as still necessary for the new mysticism to be acceptable to modern man.

The second, the importance of desire, or more generally, *feeling*, or aesthetic perception. As I noted above, in Partings I, Watts insists that our feeling is as valuable as our thinking, and that if we think otherwise it is only because we have, in fact, neglected to develop our feelings as we have our intellect. As it is, our outdated and in any

---

[156] *Out of this World: Thinking Fourth-Dimensionally* (1949); Chapter 1, "Thinking Fourth Dimensionally."

event inadequate symbols of God, Christ, etc. make it impossible for modern man—or someone from a traditional culture as aesthetically developed as the Chinese or Hindu—to take the Christian message seriously.[157]

As we've seen this is the nub of Perry's disagreement over Watts' iconoclastic approach to symbols,[158] but *pace* Perry, it is soundly based in Tradition. Neville's method seems definitely related to the discussion of the "dry" and "wet" paths discussed in the journals that Evola edited in the 30s, *UR* and *KRUR*, in which one must first create a mental image, and then bathe it in love and devotion, until it is *realized* on the material plane.[159]

> Another technical detail is in order. *In order for any image to act in the way I am talking about, it must be loved*. It must be assumed in a great, inner calm and then warmed up, almost nourished, with sweetness, without bringing the will or any effort into play, and much less without expectations. The Hermeticists called this agent "sweet fire," "fire that does not burn," and even "fire of the lamp" since it really has an enlightening effect on the images.[160]

As Neville explains the general conception behind the method:

> Sensation precedes manifestation and is the foundation upon which all manifestation rests. There is an unbroken connection between your feelings and your visible world.

---

[157] Schuon mentions the impudent absurdity of expecting a Brahmin, the product of millennia of Traditional culture, to be "converted" on the basis of the half-baked "arguments" of some missionary; see Frithjof Schuon, *The Transcendent Unity of Religion* (London: Faber, 1953); Watts' *The Supreme Identity* would find the same publisher in 1950.

[158] Due, no doubt, to the notorious lack of aesthetic appreciation in the Guénonian wing of Traditionalism; interestingly, Watts was closely associated with Coomaraswamy, who managed to combine both metaphysical and aesthetic interests, as shown by the two volumes of his collected papers.

[159] See the detailed discussion in my Afterword to *Feeling is the Secret* and "Magick for Housewives," *infra*.

[160] "Commentary on the *Opus Magicum*," in Evola, *Introduction to Magic* (Rochester, Vt.: Inner Traditions, 2001), p. 57. The Tooth Fairy comes to mind: an investigator muses over one of his tell-tale *moths*: "Somebody grew this guy. Fed him honey and nightshade, kept him warm. Somebody loved him." *Silence of the Lambs* (Jonathan Demme, 1990).

> All creation occurs in the domain of the subconscious.
>
> The subconscious transcends reason and is independent of induction. It contemplates a feeling as a fact existing within itself and on this assumption proceeds to give expression to it.
>
> Ideas are impressed on the subconscious through the medium of feeling. No idea can be impressed on the subconscious until it is felt, but once felt—be it good, bad or indifferent—it must be expressed. Feeling is the one and only medium through which ideas are conveyed to the subconscious....[161]

As Neville unpacks his "simple method," more parallels to Watts appear. As we've seen, the central insight Watts propounds in his mystical Christianity is that the Incarnation, God becoming Man, is a timeless event, always and already, so that rather than being pursued—which implies it hasn't happened yet, and thus creates a Zeno-like infinite regress—it must simply be assumed as the ground note of our existence.

And so Neville emphasizes:

> To impress the subconscious with the desirable state, *you must assume the feeling that would be yours had you already realized your wish.* In defining your objective, you must be concerned only with the objective itself. The manner of expression or the difficulties involved are not to be considered by you. To think feelingly on any state impresses it on the subconscious. Therefore, *if you dwell on difficulties, barriers or delay, the subconscious, by its very non-selective nature, accepts the feeling of difficulties and obstacles as your request and proceeds to produce them in your outer world.*
>
> You are already that which you want to be, and your refusal to believe this is the only reason you do not see it.[162]

---

[161] *Feeling is the Secret*, Chapter One, "The Law and its Operation."
[162] *Feeling is the Secret*, loc. cit.

Watts says that trying to achieve union presupposes its lack right now, thus stultifying the effort; Neville says that asking/praying for some change of circumstance assumes and therefore concretizes the present situation of lack.[163]

We might also note a subtle implication: ordinary political "action," especially of the SJW type, falls under that same ban.

> The world cannot change until you change your conception of it. "As within, so without".
>
> Nations, as well as people, are only what you believe them to be. No matter what the problem is, no matter where it is, no matter whom it concerns, you have no one to change but yourself, and you have neither opponent nor helper in bringing about the change within yourself. You have nothing to do but convince yourself of the truth of that which you desire to see manifested.[164]

This certainly comports with what we've seen of Watts' disinterest in the Social Gospel aspects of Christianity.

What's interesting here is that while Neville never, like Watts, attempted to take on a formal role in mainstream religion, he also never abandoned Christianity – or rather, the Bible.

> Neville once said that if he was stranded on an island and was allowed one book, he would choose, The Bible, without hesitation. If he could squeeze in more, he would add Charles Fillmore's *Metaphysical Dictionary of Bible names [sic]*[165], William

---

[163] Colin Wilson identified the same methodological problem: "This 'controlling ego' *does not realise it is in control.* It believes itself to be passive and helpless, so it is inclined to lie in bed all day praying for peak experiences. The real solution to the 'Outsider problem' is to induce that basic insight again and again until it finally takes root, and we grasp that we already possess the power. This is why the mystics felt that there is an element of absurdity in the visionary experience, a sudden realization that made them want to kick themselves and shout "Of course!" the solution lies in the recognition that the left-brain is the *gatherer of power*." "A Retrospective Introduction" to the 1984 reprint of *Religion and the Rebel*; reprinted in the Aristeia Press edition, London, 2017.

[164] Loc. cit.

[165] "This Metaphysical Bible Dictionary is offered by the Unity School of Christianity to meet a very definite demand, on the part of Bible students and of metaphysicians generally,

Blake, ("Why stand we here trembling around, Calling on God for help, and not ourselves, in whom God dwells?") and Nicoll's *Commentaries*.[166] These were the books he recommended at his lectures.[167]

How was Neville able to express his teachings entirely within the world of the Bible, while Watts found himself forced to increasingly make use of Eastern teachings? Perhaps because, although Watts, as we've seen, rejected the uniqueness of Christ, he still assumed the Bible, especially the New Testament, to be basically historical, while for Neville, the Bible, like all scriptures, is *a psychological document*, not a historical one: it is man's own psychological drama, taking place within his own skull (Golgotha).

> Today those to whom this great treasure has been entrusted, namely, the priesthoods of the world, have forgotten that the Bibles are psychological dramas representing the consciousness of man. In their blind forgetfulness they now teach their followers to worship its characters as men and women who actually lived in time and space.[168]

This point is closely connected with the previous emphasis on experience, experiment, and testing, rather than dogmatic wrangling:

> [The resurrected Christ] offers his knowledge of Scripture based on his own experience, for that of others based on speculation. Accept his offer. And it will keep you from losing your way

---

for a work setting forth in simple language the inner, esoteric meanings of Scriptural names." For sale here: https://www.truthunity.net/mbd.

[166] "Henry Maurice Dunlop Nicoll (19 July 1884 – 30 August 1953) was a Scottish psychiatrist, author and noted Fourth Way teacher. He is best known for his *Psychological Commentaries on the Teaching of Gurdjieff and Ouspensky*, a multi-volume collection of talks he gave to his study groups." – Wikipedia.

[167] "Neville Goddard (1905-1972) Influential New Thought Teacher," no author, at this Neville website: http://www.nevillegoddard.wwwhubs.com/.

[168] *Your Faith is Your Fortune*, 1941.

among the tangled speculations that pass for religious truth. [169]

And, of course, it puts the kibosh on drawing any political instructions from what is intended to be an entirely psychological document.

Although Watts firmly believed in some kind of historical core to the New Testament,[170] and in *Behold the Spirit* even provides some kind of Chestertonian-Thomist metaphysical argument for historicity (a timeless event must be communicated in time to creatures like us[171]), while Neville just as firmly denied that the whole Bible was anything but an entirely psychological document, Watts surely would have had sympathy with Neville's idea that the more you understand it historically the less you think to apply it to yourself – instead of the story of You, it becomes a story about those people out there and back there. As Watts says about Protestants, they cracked the shell but devoted all their time to studying the fragments and trying to put them back together in improved ways (including, pre-eminently, by the "search for the historical Jesus."), rather than consuming the kernel.[172]

---

[169] *Resurrection*, 1966.

[170] "Of course the whole thing is symbolic, but not merely symbolic… there is more actual evidence for the story of Christ than for a great many other historical events which we believe implicitly, such as the Battle of Thermopylae." Letter to "Mummy & Daddy," October 24, 1943, in *Letters*, pp. 152-53. The "clouds of witness" claim, first made by St. Paul, has been refuted over and over again, for which see almost any "mythicist" work, but especially Richard Carrier's monumental attempt to apply Bayesian analysis to the historicist hypothesis, *On The Historicity of Jesus: Why We Might Have Reason to Doubt* (Sheffield, UK: Phoenix Press, 2014). In the present context, his Chapter One is especially *a propos* to Neville, as he starts with a discussion of the process whereby Haile Selassie, Emperor of Ethiopia, became deified by the Rastafarians.

[171] Cf. Schuon, *op. cit.*: "The Redemption is an eternal act which cannot be situated either in time or space, and the sacrifice of Christ is a particular manifestation or realization of it on the human plane; men were able to benefit from the redemption as well before the coming of Jesus Christ as after it, and outside the visible Church as well as within it. If Christ had been the only manifestation of the word… the effect of his birth would have been the instantaneous reduction of the universe to ashes." (p. 37).

[172] In his lecture "Parabolic Revelation," Neville, talking about David and Saul not being historical personages, but psychological states of ourselves, says that if you regard them as such, you "see Jesus, Abraham, Moses, Jacob, or any of the characters of scripture as men of flesh and blood and *external to yourself* in the pages of history." When describing his method of "feeling it real" he insists that you do not see yourself as outside yourself, as if

Writing in 1947—the same year as *Behold the Spirit!*—Israel Regardie (formerly Aleister Crowley's private secretary), noted that Neville would seem to have some difficulty dealing with the more legalistic portions of the Old Testament.[173] Yet Protestants routinely interpret such passages, or the risqué parts, such as the Song of Songs, in more or less forced analogies to Christ or the Church. And why not? As Neville says,

> [The writers of the Gospels do not] hesitat[e] to interpret the Old Testament according to their own supernatural experiences.[174]

Indeed, many suggest today that the "writers of the Gospels" composed those pseudo-historical narratives entirely from their re-interpretations of the Old Testament.[175] Either from being "self-educated," or from the secret teachings of Abdullah, Neville's psychological interpretation of the Bible is actually consistent with what was the early 20th century scholarly consensus, which is now, like Neville himself, being "resurrected" via the Internet; while Watts' "academic" seminary training has rooted him in the mid-century historicist consensus.[176]

---

looking at a movie screen, but as you would see things from your own perspective (such as climbing a ladder). Regarding the Bible as historical is the same mistake as, and probably leads to, the mistake of seeing yourself as an external being when "feeling it real."

[173] The chapter on Neville, whom Regardie regards as "the most magical" of the proponents of New Thought, from the out of print *Romance of Metaphysics* is reprinted as the Introduction to *The Power of Imagination: A Neville Goddard Treasury* (Tarcher/Penguin, 2015) which reprints ten of Neville's little books.

[174] *Resurrection.* As Watts admits, "It is notorious that scripture can be quoted to prove almost anything." (p. 81).

[175] For the mythicist, a likely source of the New Testament narratives are the typically Judaic homilies known as *midrash*. As mythicist academic (and Lovecraft scholar) Robert Price says, if we want to learn about Jesus, we turn to the New Testament; but what did the folks back then read? The Old Testament, suitably re-interpreted. "The gospel literature emerged at a time of mass illiteracy. A tiny clique of scribes and priests wrote and had access to the texts. By the time the era of fabrication…drew to a close, the texts had become sacred literature, too precious for vulgar eyes. Priests extracted whatever homilies they thought suitable for their flock. Kenneth Humphreys: *Jesus Never Existed: An Introduction to the Ultimate Heresy*, with an interview by Chip Smith (Charleston, W.V.: Nine-Banded Books, 2014), pp. 103-04.

[176] Bart Ehrman, in *Did Jesus Exist?: The Historical Argument for Jesus of Nazareth*

But it must be emphasized that this is not clever hermeneutical sleight of hand or interpretive strait-jacket. In fact, while the laws, battles and genealogies Regardie refers to may indeed require a good deal of re-working, on an everyday basis Neville relies on a handful of familiar passages where he simply takes at face value texts that the usual clergyman strains[177] to "explain":

> "Therefore I say unto you, What things soever ye desire, when ye pray, believe that ye receive them, and ye shall have them." – Mark 11:24

> Now faith is the substance of things hoped for, the evidence of things not seen. – Hebrews 11:1

> He calleth things that were not seen as though they were and things that were not seen become seen. – Romans, 4:17

> Jesus answered them, "Is it not written in your law, I said, Ye are gods?" – John 10:34

> "I and my Father are one, but my Father is greater than I" – John, 10:30

> "Before Abraham was, I am." – John, 8:58

> "The Kingdom of Heaven is within" – Luke 17:21

While giving overall a positive, even enthusiastic account of Neville, Regardie has makes a few negative points, at least one of which is also relevant here. While never questioning Neville's own success, or his sincerity, Regardie doubts that Neville has fully realized the difficulty his audiences would have with his "simple method."

(San Francisco: HarperOne, 2012), claims to have never heard or heard of any scholar—as opposed to internet trolls—doubting the historical existence of Jesus, which is either a remarkable admission of ignorance of the history of his field, or a classic example of paradigm blindness and academic "gatekeeping."

[177] "Blind guides! You strain your water so you won't accidentally swallow a gnat, but you swallow a camel!" Matthew 23;24, New Living Translation.

The method, as we've seen, requires entering a "state akin to sleep," a state of profound relaxation, on the very edge of sleep, but with the imagination still under conscious control; today, we might call this "lucid dreaming." Regardie suggests that Neville underestimates the ability of his audience to achieve this kind of deep relaxation, due to his own previous training—as a professional dancer on Broadway.

> "[T]he fundamental psychological factor in Neville's teaching, [and] the fundamental fact about Neville himself…is a very simple fact: Neville is a dancer."[178]

This has been a frequent criticism of Watts throughout his career: that he counsels an easy, fake, non-practicing kind of practice. As we've seen, Watts takes the Incarnation, the union of God and Man (or Atman and Brahman, in Hindu terms) as a given fact, which cannot be "gotten" by any method (prayer, sacraments, penance, meditation, austerities, whatever); in fact, the use of such methods presupposes and reinforces the presumption of a lack of union, leading to an infinite regress of futility. Such methods are as useless as "painting legs on a snake," and to the extent that they trap us in a hall of mirrors, they are futile, unless, indeed, one suddenly "wakes up" and drops the pretense of needing to re-unite with that which we have never been severed from; the only subsequent use of such methods as prayer or meditation is simply to express or celebrate that union. At times Watts even adopts Neville's talk of sleep and relaxation:

---

[178] Not only is Neville's stage training an important part of his method, I would add that as a dancer Neville is symbolically linked to Krishna, who "from time to time" reincarnates to "re-establish the Dharma." (*Bhagavad Gita*). From Krishna to Alain Danielou, the dancer has always been an archetype of the Realized Man. Watts says that the mystic and saint "are in a special way possessed by this life which is God, somewhat as the heart and mind of a dancer are possessed by the music which he interprets in bodily movement." [p. 12] Clifton Webb was also, like Neville, originally a Broadway dancer, making him the perfect choice to incarnate Krishna in the Mr. Belvedere movies; see my essay "The Babysitting Bachelor as Aryan Avatar: Clifton Webb in *Sitting Pretty*, Part Two," online here: http://www.counter-currents.com/2013/02/the-babysitting-bachelor-as-aryan-avatarclifton-webb-in-sitting-pretty-part-2/. Such dancing, of course, in its calm, hieratic gestures and world-creating power, has nothing to do with the jitterbugging of today.

> Egoism is like trying to swim without relying on the water; your whole body becomes tense, and you sink like a stone. Swimming *requires a certain relaxation*, a certain giving of yourself to the water, and similarly spiritual life demands a relaxation of the soul to god…If it is *hard to relax the superficial tensions of jumpy nerves and insomnia*, it is impossible *to relax by any contrivance of our own* a tension which grips the very core of our being. (p. 70)

Obviously, this can seem like an excuse for inaction, a kind of more or less hypocritical perfectionism, along the lines of "Well, if something is worth doing, it *must* be done well" – although here, and throughout his career, Watts does a pretty good job of relating it to the darker extremes of Protestant self-doubt.[179]

Now, Neville doesn't have this problem because his method is part of what he calls The Law, rather than The Promise; the latter deals with realizing our union with God, which the former is the method given us by God to enable us to realize the good things of life, in preparation for acquiring the freedom to realize union. He takes this union—I and the Father are one—as a given, and asks his audience to simply see if the method works.[180]

When taken to task for this seeming materialism—his reports of student successes do seem rather heavy with wealthy physicians finding just the right summer house—Neville simply noted that

> One day you will be so saturated with wealth, so saturated with power in the world of Caesar, you will turn your back on it all and go in search of the word of God … I do believe that one must

---

[179] Already, in his 1941 essay "The Problem of Faith and Works in Buddhism" (reprinted in *Alan Watts – In the Academy, op. cit.*), Watts had identified a recurrent pattern in all world religions, in which this problem of right work generates a demand for a no-work method of faith or grace. Here, to the charge of "quietism," Watts points out that "human action has also its part, not, however as effort to earn the divine state, but as effort to express it and give thanks for its bestowal." (p. 85) Besides, in a typical Wattsian touch, the "error of quietism" is that "inaction is merely an indirect form of action; it is trying to possess God by doing nothing rather than by doing something." (p. 93)

[180] As noted above, his audiences seemed not really interested in this aspect of his teaching.

completely saturate himself with the things of Caesar before he is hungry for the word of God.[181]

And Watts agrees with this division of labor:

> To the extent that the poor man is a real materialist he is a real Christian, because he reverences matter. (p. 221)

> A Christian gives material benefits to those in need for the reason that, lacking things necessary for the body, they are distracted from their true aim as human person, which is God himself. (p.222)

When we turn to the world of action, based on this supposed union, Watts and Neville agree on the need for mental discipline. Neville says that

> Control of your feeling is all important to a full and happy life.

> The man who does not control his feeling may easily impress the subconscious with undesirable states. Never entertain an undesirable feeling, nor think sympathetically about wrong in any shape or form. Do not dwell on the imperfection of yourself or others. To do so is to impress the subconscious with these limitations. What you do not want done unto you, do not feel that it is done unto you or another. This is the whole law of a full and happy life. Everything else is commentary.[182]

Watts agrees, noting anarchic madness unleashed in the Middle Ages by such misguided cults as The Brethren of the Free Spirit.

> People who…have never dared to receive union with god, naturally have misgivings. They say that those who presume so

---

[181] Mitch Horowitz *(op. cit.)* notes "This passage sounds a note that resonates through various esoteric traditions: One cannot renounce what one has not attained. To move beyond the material world, or its wealth, one must know that wealth. But to Neville—and this became the cornerstone of his philosophy—material attainment was merely a step toward the realization of a much greater and ultimate truth."

[182] *Feeling is the Secret*, loc. cit.

cocksurely that God accepts them and that they are united with him will abandon themselves without qualm to a life of vice.

Yet it must be remembered that [such saints] had been through the impasse of self-consciousness, and had realized thoroughly and profoundly the impossibility of self-improvement. But when a similar attitude was adopted by certain cults of the middle Ages, such as the Brothers of the Free Spirit, the results were sometimes disastrous because of the lack of self-conscious experience.[183] (p. 201-202)

Watts then quotes C. G. Jung:

This attitude would be poison for a person who has already been overwhelmed by things that just happen (in the psyche), but it is of the highest value for one who, *with an exclusively conscious critique, chooses from the things that happen only those appropriate to his consciousness.*[184]

On the other hand, we must not confuse this "conscious critique" with a rigid control (as in Catholic scrupulosity or the Protestant's morose delectation over the total depravity of his will). Neville says that "By control of feeling is not meant restraint or suppression of your feeling, but rather the disciplining of self to imagine and entertain only such feeling as contributes to your happiness,"[185] and here again Watts agrees, bringing up a now-familiar metaphor:

We have confused control with partial or total abstinence. But a controlled dancer is not one who dances rather seldom; he is one who dances often and well. (p. 216)

---

[183] Needless to say, the 60s Situationists thought this was OK; see Raoul Vaneigem: *The Movement of the Free Spirit: General Considerations and Firsthand Testimony Concerning Some Brief Flowerings of Life in the Middle Ages, the Renaissance and, Incidentally, Our Own Time* (French, Editions Ramsay: 1986; New York: Zone Books, 1998).

[184] *Secret of the Golden Flower*, pp. 91-91.

[185] *Loc. cit.*

Dancing is indeed almost the only metaphor for *method* that is consistent with the *goal*; elsewhere Watts brings together those elements Regardie emphasized in understanding Neville:

> When ... you realize that you live in, that indeed you are this moment now, and no other, that apart from this there is no past and no future, *you must relax* and taste to the full, whether it be pleasure or pain. At once it becomes obvious why this universe exists, why conscious beings have been produced, why sensitive organs, why space, time, and change. The whole problem of justifying nature, of trying to make life mean something in terms of its future, disappears utterly. Obviously, it all exists for this moment. *It is a dance, and when you are dancing you are not intent on getting somewhere... The meaning and purpose of dancing is the dance.*[186]

Even later, the fully-New Age Watts makes the same point:

> We could say that meditation doesn't have a reason or doesn't have a purpose. In this respect it's unlike almost all other things we do except perhaps making music and dancing. When we make music we don't do it in order to reach a certain point, such as the end of the composition. If that were the purpose of music then obviously the fastest players would be the best. Also, when we are dancing we are not aiming to arrive at a particular place on the floor as in a journey. When we dance, the journey itself is the point, as when we play music the playing itself is the point. And exactly the same thing is true in meditation. Meditation is the discovery that the point of life is always arrived at in the immediate moment.[187]

So, what "point" have we arrived at here? I've been comparing Watts and Neville—in the spirit of Watts' own hermeneutical or "Chinese box" comparative method, of which more anon—to suggest that

---

[186] *The Wisdom of Insecurity* (New York: Pantheon, 1951), p. 116.

[187] Alan Watts Teaches Meditation (Macmillan Audio; Unabridged edition (November 15, 1992)

while Watts may have grown to find the Church an uncomfortable fit, he could have continued his teachings, however independently, within the Christian tradition.

One suspects the real problem here was that Watts had a low threshold of boredom, and no one tradition or scripture could hold his attention for long. Watts was destined for quite another role: what he called a "philosophical entertainer," or what I've called "the first alt-academic;" a Joker, in short.

EXIT – STAGE LEFT, EVEN

Passing from Neville, we move on to another, more contemporary doppelganger.

The "philosophical entertainer" is Watts' take on the classic American figure, the self-improvement lecturer. As I've noted before, he exists in an uneasy relationship with another American archetype, the con man; both the New Thought lecturer and the diddler trade on the listener's store of that uniquely American virtue, *confidence*.[188]

As such, the entertainer may have one final card up his sleeve – a joker.

To start at the beginning, Watts in *Behold the Spirit* is very definitely of the foundationalist persuasion; for his life to have meaning, man must establish a connection with something "real" and permanent:

> For creativity and sanity man needs to have, or at least to feel, a meaningful relation to and union with life, with reality itself… He knows that men and peoples die, and that beyond them is *a more permanent reality – the reality of the natural universe*, and still beyond that the gods of God. Religion must relate man to

---

[188] See my "Don Draper's Last Diddle," reprinted in *The End of an Era: Mad Men and the Ordeal of Civility* (San Francisco: Counter-Currents, 2015). The *locus classicus*, of course, is Melville's *The Confidence Man*, where modern good-thinkers are apt to be disconcerted to find Emerson and Thoreau among the disguises of the titular scallywag.

the root and ground of reality and life. Without this man cannot feel that his life as any *actual and objective meaning. Without this he feels that reality itself is an inane vacuum, a chaos, in which he creates purely artificial and make-believe meanings out of his own head.* He feels, however dimly, that the emptiness of reality will at last engulf his make-believe, and that therefore to continue with it is mere postponement of ultimate frustration... [T]he sense of futility remains as an undertone of feeling breaking out into consciousness in times of crisis. At such times man knows his need of religion... (p. 4, italics added)

Again, outlining how, as rationalism metastasized, "reason destroyed itself," Watts argues that

Man himself was part of this system, and man too was the product of statistical necessity, together with his reason, his hears, his ideas. ...But if all ideas were equally the result of statistical necessity, the possibility of a true idea vanished. Reason itself disappeared in meaningless mechanism. Vision became a change form of blindness, consciousness a special form of unconsciousness, sense a special form of nonsense. ...But a meaningless whole cannot evolve a meaningful part; a Godless universe cannot provide a sufficient cause for a rational man.[189] (p. 47)

This is not only a common attitude, it is also consistent with—as well as assumed if not always argued for—among Traditionalists. Conversely, Watts' move from Traditionalism to the "hermeneutic" approach of his later writings is, implicitly, an abandonment of foundationalism, with the later given up as either nonexistent, or impossible to obtain.

---

[189] This line of argument is often found among conservative intellectuals, especially Traditionalists – Schuon uses it in *Logic and Transcendence*. This is another motif Watts would continue to use for the rest of his career, developing a unique synthesis of LSD-fueled New Ageism and what would today be called Intelligent Design; in Beyond Theology he writes that "A universe which grows human beings is as much a human, or humaning, universe as a tree which grows apples is an apple tree. ...There is still much to be said for the old theistic argument that the materialist-mechanistic atheist is declaring his own intelligence to be no more than a special form of unintelligence." See my essay "'PC is for Squares, Man:' Alan Watts & the Game of Trump," *infra*.

This move from Guénonian foundationalism to Nietzschean perspectivism is often seen—from the former side—as a move into a pre-suicidal nihilism. The existence of the philosophical entertainer, however, suggests it might be exactly the opposite: a (literally) liberating realization, exactly the kind of "throwing oneself into the current" that Watts recommended as the only viable way to live.[190]

Looking around on the—not very extensive—grounds of serious thought on the so-called "alt Right," one can immediately find a very similar figure in the person of Jason Reza Jorjani, whose *Prometheus and Atlas*, as I've said in my review of the aforementioned *Alan Watts - In the Academy*,

> emphasizes the need for a "mercurial metaphysics" and a literally playful or childlike use of language in order to explore the liminal or "spectral" aspects of our globalized and globalizing Western *Weltanschauung*.[191]

Behold the Spirit allows us to deepen that comparison, as Watts' concern with the existential effects of various kinds of Christian symbolism echo Jorjani's concerns with the divine (or "spectral") archetypes that we inhabit and which thereby shape our perceptions and underlie our worldviews; and Watts' consequent emphasis on the primacy of feeling or aesthetic intuition comports well with Jorjani's privileging of aesthetic Ideas over scientific or philosophical concepts.

That Jorjani has recently published a denunciation of Traditionalism (his objections—the intellectually stultifying consequences of assuming pre-existing "perfect" body of knowledge, which can then only be acquired by attendance on a guru—

---

[190] In Hermann Hesse's early novel, *Beneath the Wheel*, the failed schoolboy, unable to readjust to village life, finally just lets himself fall into a pond and drown. But in Hesse's more mature final novel, *The Glass Bead Game*, the protagonist, having realized the futility of the Game's academic pretensions, allows himself to drown in order to inspire his new pupil -- the death itself is not a negative judgment, but merely a genre convention to bring the immense novel to an end (as is Hans Castorp's death at the end of Mann's *The Magic Mountain*); see my "Two Orders: Evola, Hesse, The Same Man," *infra*.

[191] For Jorjani in general, see my *Aryan Imperium: The Worldview and Geopolitics of the Alt-Right* (Amazon Kindle, 2017).

parallel Watts' own[192]) and both authors are fascinated with the occult, Taoism, Zen and Japan (though perhaps reaching different evaluations of the latter), only adds to what both would likely call the synchronicity. The latter is no mere dilettantism; like Watts, Jorjani sees that the power of the Western or Aryan tradition (or what Watts would call Catholic Christianity) lies precisely in its ability to absorb aspects of other cultures.

> In the great ages of Christian thought theology has always been able to embrace and absorb alien systems much to its own enrichment. In fact, every great advance in Christian theology has involved the absorption of an alien philosophy. (p. 54)

Ironically, Watts reverses the process; where Jorjani discerns the Aryan features of Asian traditions, Watts relies on these traditions to revivify Catholic Christianity. In so doing, he draws on the common core found at their deepest (or, *pace* Perry, highest) levels: Nondualism (the meaning of the Incarnation, in Watts' interpretation), which resembles Jorjani's disparagement of "false binaries."[193]

In general, Watts' project to revive Catholic Christianity as the spiritual center of Western civilization, without further pursuing the futile path of Protestant/scientific rationalism, seems a theological restatement of Jorjani's "search for some ideological basis for the *progress* of Western civilization other than the ahistorical Enlightenment rationalism of the French Revolution."[194]

Speaking of nondualism and "false binaries," one striking dissimilarity is that Watts views mature, Incarnational spirituality as incompatible with not only with vague "pantheism" but also with "such crude dualisms as the Zoroastrian contrast of ultimate light and ultimate darkness, Ormuzd or Ahriman, or the Manichaean dualism of Spirit and Matter;" whereas Zoroastrianism is very much at the heart of Jorjani's project of civilizational reconstruction.[195]

---

[192] Now reprinted in his collection *Lovers of Sophia* (Manticore, 2017)

[193] See *Lovers of Sophia, passim*.

[194] Jorjani, *op. cit.*

[195] See, for example, *World State of Emergency* (London: Arktos, 2017), especially Chapter

But as the example of Watts himself shows, religion *is* whatever it can be interpreted *as*. As I criticized Jorjani for his overly-literal, almost fundamentalist, readings of Islam,[196] there are other kinds of Zoroastrianism:

> But this was not the purely abstract light of the Gnostics and Manicheans. It was not an alien presence imprisoned in the grossness of matter, calling out to the individual to free him out of the stinking body out of this desolate place.[197]
>
> The light did not require the individual to reject matter or retreat into the rarefied world of the intellect. This radiance was an intrinsic property of matter. Man belonged to the earth and the earth belonged to Man. He would never be able to feel himself at home anywhere else but in the material world. The Zarathushtrian conception of this interrelationship of man with nature was very strong. Man was not placed into the universe like an object among other objects in the way that the God of the Old Testament placed Adam into an already-completed garden. Rather he was born out of his environment like an apple from a tree, or ripples from a pond. [198]

Reflecting on Watts' "hermeneutical turn" is also handy for addressing the issue of: is he right? Is there any truth value here, or rather, as William James (another of Jorjani's role models) would say, using what Watts would call a very Protestant turn of phrase, what is the *cash value* of all this? Casting aside any attempt to hold it up for comparison to some unavailable or non-existent "reality," what can we *do* with it?

6, "Aryan Imperium (*Iran-Shahr*)" and 7, "The Indo-European World Order."

[196] See *Aryan Imperium*, Chapters 1 and 2.

[197] Mandaean text in Jonas, Hans: *The Gnostic Religion* (Boston: Beacon Press), p. 88.

[198] "Light in the Philosophy of Zoroaster," by: Ryszard Antolak; October 2004, online here: http://www.iranchamber.com/religions/articles/light_philosophy_zoroaster.php. The idea of man not being "placed" in the world but "growing out of his environment" is a classic Wattsian trope.

Looking at it like one of Watts' Chinese box situations, I can say it is quite illuminating to see Christianity viewed from this angle; puzzles in the history and development of Christianity loosen, and something like a meaning to the process emerges, along with a vision of where we can go with it.

Writing in her Editor's Note to the Aristeia Press reissue of Colin Wilson's *Religion and the Rebel*,[199] Samantha Devin says that "We have forgotten that true religion should be a means of getting in touch with our divine self and that being religious signifies experiencing the mystery that pervades the universe," and that Wilson's book "is not a book about religion in its traditional sense. It is a bold and optimistic … book [that] will appeal to those who have "outgrown" traditional religious systems and ventured on their own into the exploration of their souls…more than fifty years after its first publication, [it] remains ahead of its time." Much the same can be said of *Behold the Spirit*.

But read it for yourself; if you've come this far, I must have succeeded in getting you somewhat interested. Read it and judge for yourself; what other kind of truth is there?

Counter-Currents/*North American New Right*
January 4, 5, 2018

---

[199] London, 2017. For more on this book, see "Neville and the Rebel," *infra*.

PC IS FOR SQUARES, MAN
ALAN WATTS & THE GAME OF TRUMP

"Why...so...serious?" – The Joker[200]

Alan Watts is remembered, if at all, as "that hippie philosopher," meaning perhaps both "a philosopher who was a hippie" (or vice versa), or "a philosopher for or of hippies."[201]

Constant Readers of Counter-Currents know, however, that whatever else, he was above all[202] a "man of the Right."[203]

For example, Greg Johnson points out that

---

[200] *The Dark Knight* (Christopher Nolan, 2012).

[201] See the opening paragraphs of Joyce Carol Oates' novel of madness in Grosse Pointe, *Expensive People*: "I was a child murderer. I don't mean child-murderer, though that's an idea. I mean child murderer, that is, a murderer who happens to be a child, or a child who happens to be a murderer. You can take your choice. When Aristotle notes that man is a rational animal one strains forward, cupping his ear, to hear which of those words is emphasized— rational animal, rational animal? Which am I? Child murderer, child murderer? It took me years to start writing this memoir, but now that I'm started, now that those ugly words are typed out, I could keep on typing forever. A kind of quiet, blubbering hysteria has set in. You would be surprised, normal as you are, to learn how many years, how many months, and how many awful minutes it has taken me just to type that first line, which you read in less than a second: I was a child murderer." (Vanguard Press, 1968; Modern Library, 2006). For more on Vanguard Press, see my "Anti-Mame: Communist Camp Classic Unmasked," Counter-Currents, February 4, 2016.

[202] Or "beneath it all" as he might have preferred; as did my mentor, Dr. Deck, who, in his Canadian way, liked to speak of things *au fond* and of "*approfondising*" some helpless dead philosopher.

[203] See Greg Johnson's "The Spiritual Materialism of Alan Watts: A Review of *Does it Matter?*" in his *Confessions of a Reluctant Hater* (2nd Ed., Revised and Expanded; San Francisco: Counter-Currents, 2016). "Watts was known to be a quiet man of the Right, but it is high time that scholars determine just how far to the Right he was."

Watts tries to reach out to the '60s counter-culture in *Does it Matter?*, but at the same time he makes it clear that he accepts the Traditional idea of historical decline and rejects all cause-mongering and progressivism.

It seems odd to think of Watts as a "rightist" because although

> To most readers, the theory of "Wealth versus Money" seems both amazingly original and astonishingly naïve...that is because Watts is concealing his sources. In fact, the foundation of his proposals is merely a version of C. H. Douglas' Social Credit theory. Of course Watts had good reason not to mention Douglas in the pages of *Playboy* in 1968: Social Credit was the economic system favored by Anglophone fascists like Ezra Pound.[204]

As another example of what might be called "strange not so new respect," a reader of Watts' *Beyond Theology* (Pantheon, 1965) finds that the hip, Zen-meditated, LSD-expanded young intelligentsia of 1965 were applying their psychedelic insights against dreary old Dad by advocating...intelligent design:

> A universe which grows human beings is as much a human, or humaning, universe as a tree which grows apples is an apple tree. ...There is still much to be said for the old theistic argument that the materialist-mechanistic atheist is declaring his own intelligence to be no more than a special form of unintelligence...

> The real theological problem for today is that it is, first of all, utterly implausible to think of this Ground as having the monarchical and paternal character of the Biblical Lord God. But, secondly, *there is the much more serious difficulty of freeing oneself from the insidious plausibility of the mythology of nineteenth century scientism*, from the notion that the universe is *gyrating stupidity* in which the mind of man is nothing but a chemical fantasy doomed to frustration. It is insufficiently

---

[204] Johnson, *loc. cit.* Watts is somewhat more forthcoming about Douglas in his autobiography, but probably thinks—rightly—that it's just a name to his readers. See *In My Own Way: An Autobiography, 1915-1965* (Pantheon, 1972).

recognized that this is a vision of the world inspired by the revolt against the Lord God of those who had formerly held the role of his slaves. This reductionist, nothing-but-ist view of the universe with its muscular claims to realism and facing-factuality is at root *a proletarian and servile resentment against quality*, genius, imagination, poetry, fantasy, inventiveness and gaiety. *Within twenty or thirty years it will seem as superstitious as flat-earthism.*

Well, he seems to have been a little off on that prediction; the argument is still valid, though.[205] Archeo-futurism: who's more "old fashioned" than a "free-thinking" atheist/materialist?[206]

---

[205] I also love how Watts could see, even back then, that the argument was indeed about intelligence, and the phony opposition between Creationist Priests and Materialist Scientists; and what wonderful phrases he comes up with: "insidious plausibility," "gyrating stupidity." I vote we start using these ourselves; what else is the opponent of ID but an advocate of "gyrating stupidity"; any guesses as to how many "factuality-facing" fashionable atheists will have the intellectual courage to grasp the term as indeed articulating their view, or give the reason why not?

[206] Compare Thomas Mann's *Dr. Faustus*, where the combined futurist extremism and atavistic primitivism (as Mann sees it) that led to the rise of Hitler is explored through a series of grotesque figures in "the Kridwiss Circle" who alternatively shock and amuse the "conservative" nobility, such as Daniel zur Hohe (author of a single book, on "hand-made paper"; a "lyrico-rhetorical outburst of voluptuous terrorism"; Stefan George?), and the, in this case at least, rather Wattsian figure of the polymath "private scholar" Dr. Chaim Breisacher, sneering at the very idea of "progress" in a world that has been declining since Solomon built his temple. Miles Mathis writes that "Scientists will say that the current models are superior to Genesis, at any rate, since one who accepts Genesis doesn't continue to ask how the Earth evolved. This much is true. Good scientists continue to study, while religious people and bad scientists do not. But this paper is not about good scientists, it is about bloated atheists and bad scientists, the sort that think they already know how things are. They have barebones models of the early Earth, models less than a century old and ever-changing, and they think they can claim with certainty how things are, who exists and who does not, how things got here and where they are going. They think a theory of how things evolved is equivalent to a theory of how things were created. They think a model of a complex twisting molecule is the same as a blueprint for life or a explanation of self-locomotion or a proof of phylogeny. They think that four-vector fields and non-abelian gauge groups and statistical analysis explain existence, complexity, solidity, and change." The whole article is available online here: http://mileswmathis.com/atheism.html. Seth Macy writes in "Shut Up, Nerd" that "It's really a delight to see people waking up to the lameness of scientists. Nerds belong in labs or basements, not as the subject of memes. Science is extraordinarily useful. Scientists are extraordinarily lame, but they make science, so they have worth to society. The entire "skeptical movement" is filled with the same boring people who love to shit on everything right and lovely. They can't shit on stuff that sucks, because then they'd need to shit all over themselves like some skeptic tubgirl. We

Or their cousins, the political Liberals.

But before we look any further at Watts' suspiciously non-PC attitudes, let's step back and look at their source.

Watts' fundamental insight—equal parts philosophy (Vedanta), psychology (Gestalt) and pharmacology (LSD-25)[207]—was that fundamentally, there are no things. Our experience—and hence any idea we can form of the universe—is of processes or waves.

Now these processes or waves have a kind of duality: they seem to have two parts, or phases, or sides. Up and down, black and white, left and right, front and back, life and death. I say "seem" or "kind of" because we don't want to get into any idea of these phases being like the parts of a transmission, out of which we can build or into which we can disassemble the machine. That's the problem Descartes wound up with, having dissected experience into two utterly different kinds of thing (mind and matter) and then was left wondering how—or if—they interacted.

No, all these processes have aspects that are so closely bound up with each other that one can't even imagine them separated, like front and back.[208] To convey this non-relational relationship Watts suggested we use his neologism "goes-with," as in "Front goes-with Back."

Watts' own expositions of this are so clear, compelling and above all entertaining (and he called himself not a philosopher but a "philosophical entertainer") that one fears sounding like someone

---

need to stop listening to anything they say outside of the confines of laboratory settings. It's like your favorite comedian spewing politics on Twitter. Shut the fuck up." Online here: http://streetcarnage.com/blog/shut-up-nerd/.

[207] See *The Joyous Cosmology* (1965; reprinted 2015 with an introduction by Daniel Pinchbeck). "*The Joyous Cosmology* is Alan Watts's exploration of the insight that the consciousness-changing drugs LSD, mescaline, and psilocybin can facilitate '*when accompanied with sustained philosophical reflection* by a person who is in search, not of kicks, but of understanding'. More than an artifact, it is both a riveting memoir of Watts's personal experiments and a profound meditation on our perennial questions about the nature of existence and the existence of the sacred."

[208] Thus, Jesus says that we should not listen to someone who says of the kingdom of Heaven that lo! It is here or lo! It is there, for the Kingdom is within us. "And indeed We have created man, and We know whatever thoughts his inner self develops, and We are closer to him than (his) jugular vein." (*Quran* 50:16).

over-explaining a joke, or falling into endless quotations. At this point, you might be better off sampling some audio/video remixes an enterprising chap has set up on YouTube.[209]

But it does need a bit of explaining, since for some 2000 years we, in the West at least, have been operating under two very different fundamental understandings.

First, the Jews bequeathed to us the idea of an omnipotent Creator who creates creatures like man from out of the dust, and the dust itself out of nothing at all. Watts calls this the Ceramic Model (with hints of Semite?), after St. Paul's denying the pot the right to question the work of the potter.

There are problems with the model,[210] especially in the underlying, inescapable sense of existential uncertainty it inculcates. But around 500 years ago people began to rethink it, asking in particular why we needed God at all. Deism, which postulated a "watchmaker" god who wound things up and then went on vacation, eventually became outright scientific Atheism. The Ceramic Model was replaced with the Machine Model; more particularly, what I call the Idiot Machine Model. Unfortunately, the existential unease, the damnable contingency and fragility of everything, ultimately ending in the death of ourselves and the universe, remained.

Now this may seem like, indeed, airy-fairy hippie nonsense, but as Watts liked to point out, like all metaphysics, it is "rockily practical." At least, there are practical conclusions.

---

[209] Ironically enough, the company and channel is called Tragedy and Hope, which should again be a "red flag" for conspiracy hounds, as well as connecting Watts to Hillary through Bill's college mentor (and CIA control?) Carroll Quigley. Indeed, "Isaac's videos document his journey from conspiracy theory to spirituality, a path that many of us who have opened the conspiracy can of worms can personally relate to. 'If you look through my channel you will see that it is basically a reflection of my awakening, starting out with conspiracies and politics and then moving into philosophy and spirituality, which I now believe to be the most important truth,' he said."

[210] Such as making sense out of creation *ex nihilo*. See John N. Deck's epochal critique "St. Thomas Aquinas and the Language of Total Dependence;" first published in *Dialogue: A Canadian Philosophical Review*, Vol. 6, 1967, pp. 74-88; anthologized in *Aquinas: A Collection of Critical Essays*, Anthony Kenny, ed., Notre Dame University Press, 1976, pp. 237-254. Deck later generalized his argument as "The Itself: In-Another Pattern and Total Dependence," both of which are on Tony Flood's website devoted to debating the issue: www.anthonyflood.com.

For one, as we've seen, it makes Intelligent Design, well, intelligible. Animals are not bags of meat shoved around by outside forces called Nature; they are processes, and they "go-with" their environment: if there are people, then the universe is a peopling universe; if there is intelligence, it is an intelligent universe. Neo-Darwinism, despite its "neo" prefix, is just the same old Idiot Machine model. Admittedly, they're also right to suspect ID is smuggling in God; it's the Ceramic Model rearing its head again.[211]

To see how all this plays out in the modern political scene, we need to back up a bit first. Both the Ceramic Model and the Idiot Machine Model assume a universe of things, one of which is us. Humans, in particular, are in a forever precarious position *vis a vis* the universe (all the other things). In the Ceramic Model we are the creatures of a supposedly loving but strict and rather unpredictable God; in the Idiot Machine Model we are a random fluke of the universe,[212] subject to the apparently eternal extinction of death at some unknown but inescapable point, followed by the universe itself.

While the Joyous Cosmology of Watts is a *game* between White and Black, the existential unease produced by both of the other models issues in a *fight*, pitting White against Black.

The game of White and Black, where White tries to win, and eventually will,[213] but not without many ups and downs, which lend

---

[211] George Bernard Shaw, a proponent of "vitalism," argued that the public acceptance of Darwinism was not motivated by the supposed evidence—they not being scientists, after all—but rather by weariness at the constant surveillance and intrusions of the Calvinist God, little realizing that the God-less model left them with a literally senseless and meaningless universe. See his Preface to *Back to Methuselah*.

[212] "You are a fluke of the Universe. You have no right to be here. And whether you know it or not, the Universe is laughing behind your back." From *Deteriorata*, the *National Lampoon* parody of the uplifting 70s LP/poster *Desiderata*. *Deteriorata* addresses both the Ceramic Model as well as Watts' Joyous Cosmology: "Therefore, make peace with your god, whatever you perceive him to be: hairy thunderer or cosmic muffin." Oddly enough, Adlai Stevenson was apparently a fan, despite his mean-spirited attack on Norman Vincent Peale (see my "The Secret of Trump's A Peale,"*infra*).

[213] Dr. Deck would correct Watts, or "*approfondise*" him, here; White and Black are a "dialectic couplet," but White is the "senior partner." In this sense, and only in this sense, White *must* win; the necessity is logical, not willful. As Guénon would say, quality and quantity are only logical opposites, not real entities; and while the Whole can be described, as a *façon de paler*, as "Quality," (though really transcending both), "Quantity" (matter,

interest and spice to the game, becomes not a *game* but a *fight* when White feels absolutely positively that he must win. A loss (e.g., one's physical death) would be catastrophic—literally, as Joe Biden would say, apocalyptic.[214]

Life lived according to Watts' Joyous Cosmology is quite different:

It comes, then, to this:

> that to be "viable," livable, or merely practical, *life must be lived as a game*—and the "must" here expresses a condition, not a commandment. It must be lived in the spirit of play rather than work, and the conflicts which it involves must be carried on in the realization that *no species, or party to a game, can survive without its natural antagonists, its beloved enemies, its indispensable opponents*. For to "love your enemies" is to love them as enemies; it is not necessarily a clever device for winning them over to your own side. The lion lies down with the lamb in paradise, but not on earth—"paradise" being the tacit, off-stage level where, behind the scenes, all conflicting parties recognize their interdependence, and, through this recognition, are able to keep their conflicts within bounds.[215] This recognition is *the absolutely essential chivalry which must set the limits within all*

---

darkness, evil, emptiness, etc.) is only a shadow, a point approached asymptotically. Watts does sometimes notice this: "The game doesn't work in reverse, just as the ocean doesn't work with wave-crests down and troughs up."

[214] Dr. Peter Venkman: This city is headed for a disaster of biblical proportions.
Mayor: What do you mean, "biblical"?
Dr Ray Stantz: What he means is Old Testament, Mr. Mayor, real wrath of God type stuff.
Dr. Peter Venkman: Exactly.
Dr Ray Stantz: Fire and brimstone coming down from the skies! Rivers and seas boiling!
Dr. Egon Spengler: Forty years of darkness! Earthquakes, volcanoes...
Winston Zeddemore: The dead rising from the grave!
Dr. Peter Venkman: Human sacrifice, *dogs and cats living together...* mass hysteria!
Mayor: All right, all right! I get the point! (*Ghostbusters*, Ivan Reitman, 1984).

[215] This is the answer to all those Christians who smugly talk about "we are all God's children" as if this required us to throw open the borders, abolish all voting requirements, etc. They have confused (deliberately?) the levels of Heaven and Earth – "immanatized the Eschaton," as Vogelin liked to say.

warfare, with human and non-human enemies alike, for chivalry is the debonair spirit of the knight who "plays with his life" in the knowledge that even mortal combat is a game.[216]

"Chivalry" is the last thing that comes to mind when considering Hillary, and the last thing on her mind as well.

Secretary of State Hillary Clinton shared a laugh with a television news reporter moments after hearing deposed Libyan leader Muammar Qaddafi had been killed. "We came, we saw, he died," she joked when told of news reports of Qaddafi's death by an aide.[217]

In foreign policy, this is the mentality of "The Good War;" which is actually all wars, since America is always in the right.[218] Of course, this is always portrayed as a sin of the Right—first, the obsession with bombing our enemies not into surrender and crude material plundering (which at least would be understandable)[219]—but "back to the Stone Age;"[220] then, turned suicidally on ourselves, smugly professing ourselves to believe it "Better Dead than Red."[221]

---

[216] This all and all the following otherwise unattributed quotes are from *The Book: On the Taboo Against Knowing Who You Are* (Pantheon, 1967).

[217] "We came, we saw, he died." You can, if you want, watch it at https://www.youtube.com/watch?v=Fgcd1ghag5Y.

[218] "And you can believe me...Because I never lie, and I'm always right." Campaign ad for George Leroy Tirebiter's father, running for dog-killer, on the Firesign Theater's *Don't Crush That Dwarf, hand Me The Pliers* (Columbia, 1970). According to Wikipedia, the first late-night movie on the album, *High School Madness*, "is a parody of the Aldrich Family radio show, the *Archie* comic book and of 1950s youth culture in general." See my "Welcome to the Club: The Rise & Fall of the Männerbund in Pre-War American Pop Culture," reprinted in *Green Nazis in Space! New Essays on Literature, Art, & Culture*; edited by Greg Johnson (San Francisco: Counter-Currents, 2015). The second movie, *Parallel Hell* "is a war film set in Korea, where the soldiers (including Tirebiter) debate *the seemingly endless war.*"

[219] Like Chris Rock on OJ, Watts doesn't say traditional war is right, but he *understands* the need and the goals.

[220] Or perhaps at least the Jazz Age. "Leading to a Crowning Moment of Funny as the pilots practice bombing the absolute shit out of the desert while muzak plays: *Crow*: We're gonna bomb 'em back to the Jazz Age!" TV Tropes on Mystery Science Theater 3000, Episode 612, *The Starfighters*.

[221] Christian conservatives like the Buckleyites would often smugly assert that this was a "truly spiritual" view, which is true in the sense that Christianity and other Ceramic Religions seem to lead to it; when it is actually merely the crackpot "spirit vs. matter"

But in reality, it's equally the mindset of the Liberals possessed with the Orwellian-named "Humanitarian Interventionism," from McKinley's "helping" the Philippines and just accidentally acquiring an empire, to Wilson's "War to End All Wars," to Hillary's excellent adventures in North Africa. It's always a war not for plunder or honor, but until the enemy is annihilated: unconditional surrender![222]

And as Watts would point out, since White can't really "win" where "win" means "total annihilation of Black,"[223] it follows that war is endless. Eurasia has always been at war with Eastasia.[224]

For Watts, though, things are entirely different:

> The morality that goes with this understanding is, above all, the frank recognition of *your dependence upon enemies*, underlings, out-groups, and, indeed, upon all other forms of life whatsoever. Involved as you may be in the conflicts and competitive games of practical life, *you will never again be able to indulge in the illusion that the "offensive other" is all in the wrong, and could or should be wiped out*. This will give you the priceless ability of being able to contain conflicts so that they do not get out-of-hand, of being willing to compromise and adapt, of playing, yes, but playing it cool. This is what is called "honor among thieves," for the really dangerous people are those who do not recognize that they are thieves–the unfortunates who play the role of the "good guys" with such blind zeal that they are unconscious of any indebtedness to the "bad guys" who support their status.

As Watts meditates on this, he just keeps digging himself deeper into the role of spokesman for hurtful bullies:

---

spirituality that Watts contrasts with "a really thoroughgoing spiritual materialism."

[222] Sir Fred Hoyle's *October the First is Too Late* imagines that men of present England, dumped into a world where WWI is still raging in France, would immediately try to stop the slaughter. Perhaps, but would they have done the same if it were 1942? See my "Worlds Enough & Times: The Unintentionally Weird Fiction of Fred Hoyle," Counter-Currents, March 4, 2016.

[223] Again, in the phenomenal world. Ultimately, at the end of this *Manvantara*, Black "wins" but the wheel immediately flips, setting up first the sleep of Brahman, then a new Golden Age as the cycle begins again. See "The Basic Myth" in *Does It Matter?*

[224] Needless to say, the global oligarchs are fully onboard this, like all other aspects of the "Liberal" agenda; permanent war means permanent profits.

It is most important that this be understood by those concerned with civil rights, international peace, and the restraint of nuclear weapons. These are most undoubtedly causes to be backed with full vigor, but *never in a spirit which fails to honor the opposition, or which regards it as entirely evil or insane.* It is not without reason that the formal rules of boxing, judo, fencing, and even dueling require that the combatants salute each other before the engagement. *In any foreseeable future there are going to be thousands and thousands of people who detest and abominate Negroes, communists, Russians, Chinese, Jews, Catholics, beatniks, homosexuals, and "dope-fiends." These hatreds are not going to be healed, but only inflamed, by insulting those who feel them, and the abusive labels with which we plaster them—squares, fascists, rightists, know-nothings—may well become the proud badges and symbols around which they will rally and consolidate themselves.* Nor will it do to confront the opposition in public with polite and nonviolent sit-ins and demonstrations, while *boosting their collective ego by insulting them in private.* If we want justice for minorities and cooled wars with our natural enemies, whether human or non-human, we must first come to terms with the minority and the enemy in ourselves and in our own hearts, for the rascal is there as much as anywhere in the "external" world – especially when you realize that the world outside your skin is as much yourself as the world inside. *For want of this awareness, no one can be more belligerent than a pacifist on the rampage, or more militantly nationalistic than an anti-imperialist.*

Watts analyzes the moral crusader in terms straight from the work of Kevin MacDonald:

I would never be able to know that I belong to the in-group of "nice" or "saved" people without the assistance of an out-group of "nasty" or "damned" people. *How can any in-group maintain its collective ego without relishing dinner-table discussions about the ghastly conduct of outsiders?*

Although Watts sees himself, and is, on the side of the Angels here, his refusal to turn this into a Battle in Heaven that the Angels *must* win against damnable devils marks him out, in contemporary terms, as a turncoat or a Fifth Columnist. [225] In the neo-Stalinist language of the SJWs, no matter what ones intentions, if one cuts the "enemy" some slack, or mildly critiques ones own side, one is "objectively" acting for the enemy. For example, when comedian Patton Oswalt retweeted Steve Sailer's remark that Political Correctness is a war on Noticing, he was immediately attacked by people saying that Sailer was "objectively" racist, sexist, homophobic and transphobic. [226]

Watts, like MacDonald, suggests this moral signalling is rooted in Protestantism:

[M]odern Protestantism in particular, *in its liberal and progressive forms*, is the religion most strongly influenced by the mythology of the world of objects, and of man as the separate ego. Man so defined and so experienced is, of course, incapable of pleasure and contentment, let alone creative power. Hoaxed

---

[225] I suppose something like this lies behind the occasional conspiracy theorist who thinks that the drug and hippie movements were "manufactured" by the CIA to derail the burgeoning anti-war movement, turning manly tribunes of the Folk into lethargic burnouts, or else scaring everyone else with tales of the Manson Family. See the various writings of Miles Mathis. Shrine of Eris writes that "He likes to rip the rug from under people I may like quite a bit, such as Rupert Sheldrake, *and Alan Watts*, and Russell Brand, (all three working towards "an agenda of drug use" and pseudo "mysticism" promotion, apparently, and quite plausibly in my opinion), and Terrence McKenna (self-confessed CIA plant). Graham Hancock. Ram Dass. Timothy Leary. Blavatsky, Kerouac, Allen Ginsberg, Hemingway; All the great and cool get a lash of his tongue. Which could be sad.... but I find it refreshing. He sees Red Flags everywhere, this Mathis. Most everyone who has set the foundation for counterculture of any kind, he sees as a plant. We are being lulled into spending lifetimes contemplating unknowable things and being passive—armchair philosophers, who think we can get a handle on consciousness—and this is a deliberate ploy to occupy an intelligentsia that might otherwise be out on the streets actually doing something. I see a lot of truth in this idea. But as he says himself... "the truth is hard to find. It has been made hard to find on purpose, and I am not claiming I know everything or anything.' One would think such an elaborate "cunning plan" (or "Batman Gambit") was hardly necessary; all that was needed was to end the draft and the whole movement faded away. Robin: But suppose something went wrong. Suppose Tut didn't raise his voice, what then? Batman: I prefer not to think about those things, Robin. They depress me. — *Batman* (TV series), "I'll Be a Mummy's Uncle."

[226] For more on Oswalt, see Gregory Hood's review of his film *Big Fan*, here: http://www.counter-currents.com/2011/10/big-fan/.

into the illusion of being an independent, responsible source of actions, he cannot understand why what he does never comes up to what he should do, for a society which has defined him as separate cannot persuade him to behave as if he really belonged. *Thus he feels chronic guilt and makes the most heroic efforts to placate his conscience.*

From these efforts come social services, hospitals, peace movements, foreign-aid programs, free education, and the whole philosophy of the welfare state. Yet we are bedeviled by the fact that *the more these heroic and admirable enterprises succeed, the more they provoke new and increasingly horrendous problems.*[227] For one thing, few of us have ever thought through the problem of what good such enterprises are ultimately supposed to achieve. When we have fed the hungry, clothed the naked, and housed the homeless, what then? Is the object to enable unfortunate people to help those still more unfortunate?[228]

And surely the Ultimate Methodist Scold is none other than Hillary.

To Hillary and all the SJW's who would call this a gospel of passivity or even (ironically) despair, Watts make a simple distinction. He asks, if a pretty girl says she loves you, do you say "Are you serious?" or do you say, "Are you sincere?"[229] To the suicidal Seriousness of the Fighter, Watts contrasts the Sincerity and Good Humor of the Player, the Good Sport.[230]

---

[227] Conservatives call this "unintended consequences," which admittedly is the go-to response to any proposal and a call to do nothing as a policy. For example, we now see the well-intentioned Scandinavian social welfare model upended by the inevitable, almost compulsive impulse to signal yet more moral status by welcoming the unassimilable darkies.

[228] As James Kunstler and others have long noted, the spread of consumer capitalism (what he calls "the world of happy Motoring") would indeed be an apocalyptic catastrophe, in ecological terms.

[229] I feel the need to point out that such "games" have nothing to do with the man-o-sphere's notion of "Game," which is indeed the very epitome of making the game into a fight to be pursued oh so seriously.

[230] Watts might have to admit that those hated English public schools did teach him something valuable.

Be that as it may, Watts' verdict on the morals and politics of the adult world, pursuing scorched Earth in the name of Morality, is dire:

> The political and personal morality of the West, especially in the United States, is utterly schizophrenic. It is *a monstrous combination of uncompromising idealism and unscrupulous gangsterism*, and thus devoid of *the humor and humaneness which enables confessed rascals to sit down together and work out reasonable deals*.

"A monstrous combination of uncompromising idealism and unscrupulous gangsterism" is really the perfect description of the Clintons, who, to be fair, are only the ultimate and most characteristic product of the Liberal Elite.

And as for "the humor and humaneness which enables confessed rascals to sit down together and work out reasonable deals," is this not The Donald himself, the master of The Art of the Deal?[231]

And those same foreign rascals sense this as well:

> Russian President Vladimir Putin had kind words for his "stablemate" Donald Trump during an annual end-of-the-year Q&A session in Moscow.
>
> "[Donald Trump is] a really brilliant and talented person, without any doubt," [Vladimir] Putin told reporters, according to a translation by Interfax. "It's not our job to judge his qualities, that's a job for American voters, but he's the absolute leader in the presidential race."
>
> The GOP front-runner *has been blunt about his plans for defrosting U.S. relations with Russia* should he be elected president.

---

[231] See his *Trump: The Art of the Deal* (1987; Ballantine paperback edition, 2015). The hatred of "deals" is rife on both sides of the political spectrum, but takes its most unctuous form among the Neocons, who find it distasteful to deal with those dubbed "Evil," calling it nothing but "appeasement."

"He says he wants to move on to a new, more substantial relationship, a deeper relationship with Russia, *how can we not welcome that?*" he said. "Of course we welcome that."[232]

For Hillary, though, foreign policy, like everything else, is Serious Business, and rascals like Putin are devils to be threatened with 50s style nuclear annihilation.[233] As Camile Paglia has pointed out with some urgency, Hillary is the New Nixon, the ultimate Brown-shoed Square:

> But Hillary, consumed by her own restless bitterness, has no such tranquility. The wheels must grind! The future must be conquered! Past slights must be avenged! So it's all planning and scheming and piling up loot, the material emblem of existential worth.[234]

What would The Joker say about planning and scheming, and piling up loot?[235] What would Watts say, or even, dare we think it, God Himself?[236] Is Trump the hero we deserve, or the hero we need? Perhaps, as an earlier Joker would say, he's the enema this town needs.[237]

---

[232] http://www.thepoliticalinsider.com/vladimir-putin-just-made-a-massive-donald-trump-announcement/#ixzz47cSUYC8p.

[233] "At a California fundraiser last year, she reportedly compared Russian President Vladimir Putin to Adolf Hitler. …Conservative commentator Paul Craig Roberts, an economist who served as assistant secretary of treasury under President Reagan, warned that Mrs. Clinton will have a difficulty backing down from a confrontation with Mr. Putin after calling him Hitler. "*When you go that far out on a limb, you really kind of have to go the rest of the way,*" he said in an interview at Infowars.com. "I don't think there is any candidate that we can end up with as president that would be more likely to go to war with Russia than Hillary." "Hillary Clinton's hawkish position on Russia troubles both sides of aisle" by S.A. Miller; *The Washington Times*, June 9, 2015.

[234] "It's not about sexism: Camille Paglia on Trump, Hillary's 'restless bitterness' and the end of the elites." Salon, May 5, 2016.

[235] See Trevor Lynch's review of *The Dark Knight* in his *White Nationalist Guide to the Movies* (San Francisco: Counter-Currents, 2012).

[236] "Take no thought for tomorrow.… Lay not up treasure on Earth."?

[237] *Batman* (Tim Burton, 1989).

So, get "with it," kids; save the Earth, and piss off your parents and the all the other squares, too: support Trump!

Counter-Currents/*North American New Right*
May 9, 2016

OF APES, ESSENCE, & THE AFTERLIFE

Ah, Spring! And a young man's fancy turns to…well, that.[238]

I remember reading someone, somewhere that I can't recall—James Hillman?[239] Colin Wilson?—that the kinship of man and monkey was most clearly on display in their reliance on onanism while in captivity.[240]

First, it indicated that they were capable of boredom—which, as Schopenhauer tells us, is one of the two poles of existence.[241] Of course, other animals might get bored, but how could we tell?

That leads to the second point: the recourse to onanism in case of boredom. This, of course, proves the existence of the faculty of

---

[238] Except for Alexander Phipps, the protagonist—or subject—of *A Young Man's Fancy*, the Electrical Institute's short film promoting postwar electrical kitchens. There, the young man "has no time for girls" and prefers to discuss efficient kitchen layouts with his friend's mom. See my "Welcome to the Club: The Rise & Fall of the *Männerbund* in Pre-War American Pop Culture," reprinted in *Green Nazis in Space!*.

[239] For my encounters with "archetypal psychology" see Greg Johnson's "Interview with James J. O'Meara" reprinted in *The Homo and the Negro* (San Francisco: Counter-Currents, 2012; embiggened edition, 2017).

[240] "Unlike other animals, human beings spend a lot of time thinking about what is not going on around them, contemplating events that happened in the past, might happen in the future, or will never happen at all. Indeed, "stimulus-independent thought" or "mind wandering" appears to be the brain's default mode of operation. Although this ability is a remarkable evolutionary achievement that allows people to learn, reason, and plan, it may have an emotional cost. Many philosophical and religious traditions teach that happiness is to be found by living in the moment, and practitioners are trained to resist mind wandering and "to be here now." These traditions suggest that a wandering mind is an unhappy mind. Are they right?" Science says: Yes! "A Wandering Mind Is an Unhappy Mind" by Matthew A. Killingsworth, Daniel T. Gilbert; *Science*, 12 Nov 2010; Vol. 330, Issue 6006, pp. 932.

[241] The other, of course, is pain. Pain either drives us to madness or suicide, or we find relief, which leads to boredom, and madness or suicide. Thus, "Life swings like a pendulum backward and forward between pain and boredom." See "Schopenhauer on Happiness," here: http://www.moodstep.com/schopenhaueronhappiness/

imagination, the ability to conjure up an illusory reality so potent as to lead to physical satisfaction, a result in the empirical world.[242]

Lanz von Liebenfals, the Grand Old Man of Nazi Occultism, brings these themes together:

> The lewdness of apes, especially of the baboon, *exceeds all imagination*. They are Sodomites, pederasts and onanists; they also act in a disgraceful manner toward men and boys. It is universally agreed upon that baboons will attack and mistreat little girls, and that in zoos, women are inconvenienced by their vile forwardness and shamelessness...It is now incumbent upon us to investigate as to why sexual activity with animals is also called Sodomy. The more usual designation is "bestiality."[243]

Despite its bad press,[244] masturbation has a fine pedigree—in fact, a sacred one. Onanaism, as indicated, is connected with both boredom and imagination; and imagination is the power of God in

---

[242] "One is *bored* in a cell; *boredom makes for amorousness*. Genet masturbates; this is an act of defiance, a willful perversion of the sexual act; it is also, quite simply, an idiosyncrasy. The operation condenses the drifting reveries, which now congeal and disintegrate in the release of pleasure. No wonder *Our Lady* horrifies people: it is the epic of masturbation." Jean-Paul Sartre, "Introduction" to Jean Genet: *Our Lady of the Flowers* (London: Panther Books, 1973 [1968]), p. 10.

[243] *Theozoology, or The Science of the Sodomite Apelings and the Divine Electron (An introduction to the most ancient and modern philosophy and a justification of the monarchy and the nobility.)* by Dr. Jorg Lanz von Liebenfels (Europa House 2004); p. 10. The relation of this to Maj. Kong in *Strangelove* is clear. Dr. Lanz also comments on Group Capt. Mandrake's name: "If one looks at the dwarf depicted in Fig. 23, a certain outer similarity to roots (Mandrake roots) cannot be missed. Such Sodom entities were intended by Paul in Hebr. XII.15 when he speaks of "bitter roots," against which Christians have to protect themselves. Fulgentius calls humanity a garden and Christ the gardener. These expressions too stem from Sodomite customs...The Gk. *kepos* means "ape" and "garden" at the same time, as does Heb. '*eden*."

[244] See Andy Nowicki's "Masturbation and Misandry," *Alternative Right*, March 1, 2013. Utah, my go-to model of a Christian no-homo hellhole (despite reports of it being a favored destination of "gay tourists") is now taking aim at that old bugaboo, "pornography" – this time, of course, "for the children's sake."As *CNN* pointed out, a 2009 study by Harvard Business School revealed the state with "the highest per capita purchasers of online adult entertainment" was, you guessed it, Utah.

us; perhaps, simply God in us.

For it is a basic principle of the Hermetic tradition that

> What we think about constantly, what we imagine constantly, we usually end up assuming feeling as being real.[245]

And as Neville constantly reminds us, what we assume, if persisted in, will become reality.

Imagination, then, is the golden chain that links the universe, from ape to man to…God.[246] For what the ape imagines darkly, man can imagine with feeling and persistence, and so bring about.

And God? Well, as Dr. Lektor says, "God's a champ."[247] His imagination is the real, right thing, and what he imagines immediately becomes real.

> And God said, "Let there be light." And there was light.

> In the beginning was the Word, and the Word was God. Through him was made everything, that was made.

So let's look at the other end, as it were: boredom. Are we not made in his image? Does God masturbate, because God, being eternal, all knowing, etc., is eternally, all bored?

I am speaking not even metaphorically but mythologically. And why not? As Watts would insist, if we are bore-able, amorous,

---

[245] Neville Goddard and Tim Grimes: *Mindful Manifestation: A Uniquely Effective Way to practice Mindfulness* (Amazon Kindle, 2015).

[246] See John N. Deck: *Nature, Contemplation, and the One: A Study in the Philosophy of Plotinus* (Toronto: University of Toronto Press, 1967; Reprinted: Burdett. N.Y.: Larson, 1991; Toronto Heritage series, 2017 [Kindle iOS version]), which aims to provide an explanation of Plotinus' claim in *Ennead* III.8 that "Nature contemplates".

[247] Will Graham: Why does it feel good, Dr. Lecktor? Doctor Hannibal Lecktor: "It feels good because God has power. If one does what God does enough times, one will become as God is. God's a champ. He always stays ahead. He got 140 Filipinos in one plane crash last year. Remember that earthquake in Italy last spring?" – *Manhunter* (Michael Mann, 1987). Is this the origin of the taboo on masturbation, hence the supposed sin of "onanism": if one does what God does enough times, one becomes as God is? Of course, Lecktor is just stealing his act from Trump's mentor, Dr. Norman Vincent Peale: "By acting as you wish yourself to be, in due course you will become as you act." *Positive Thinking Every Day: An Inspiration for Each Day of the Year* (New York: Touchstone, 1993), March 18th.

ecstasy-seeking creatures, the God/universe that creates us must in some sense be the same.

> A universe which grows human beings is as much a human, or humaning, universe as a tree which grows apples is an apple tree.... There is still much to be said for the old theistic argument that the materialist-mechanistic atheist is declaring his own intelligence to be no more than a special form of unintelligence...[248]

If it seems odd to consider God becoming bored, think of how bored we would be if we found ourselves faced with immortality. After all, as we've seen, our finite lives are already stuffed to the gills with boredom.

The Christian notion of immortality, at least of the heavenly sort, has always been a bit rum, a bit, well, embarrassing. One the one hand, there is the sense that you only get there by practicing self-denial here and now, and so presumably these same "bad" things will be excluded, *a fortiori*, in the Great Good Place, leading to somewhat uneasy jokes about "there is no beer in Heaven" or wanting to go to The Other Place because that's where all one's friends or all the interesting people will be.

One the other hand, we are given literal promissory notes that Something Else will take the place of earthy pleasures, and will be so satisfying that boredom will be evaded. But What exactly? Ah, there's the rub. The "Beatific Vision" of Dante and the various mystics supposedly does the job, but it's hard for us mortals to be fobbed off with "something so good you literally can't describe it." Right, tell us another.

The "admittedly symbolic" substitutes—endless harping, or sitting on pink clouds, etc.—don't help.

---

[248] See his *Beyond Theology* (Pantheon,1965) and my essay "'PC is for Squares, Man': Alan Watts & the Game of Trump," *supra*. Watts provided a blurb—"A little classic"—for the cover of David Cole Gordon's *Self-Love*, published in Penguins in 1972; his *Overcoming the Fear of Death* appeared the same year in Penguins as well, with no blurb from Watts, who chose 1972 as the year to himself die. Gordon's idea of death as the ultimate form of the desire for self-transcendence – and hence as desirable as auto racing or masturbation (the full title of the hardcover, *Self-Love and a Theory of Unification* shows the connection) – is an obvious influence on the present essay.

It all calls to mind Watts' story of the curate who attended a dinner party where the conversation turned to ideas of Heaven. Growing increasingly agitated, when it came to his turn the cleric finally burst out with "I expect to participate in eternal bliss, but I do wish the conversation could be turned to less unpleasant subjects!"[249]

This conflict goes back at least to Jesus times. In Mark 12.25,

> Our Lord gives his authority to one of the two attitudes current at the time…. Popular opinion sometimes thought of it [afterlife] simply a resumption, with certain modifications, of life as we know it in this world; but some striking rabbinic saying show that at any rate a little later a view similar to that of Jesus was also current. [For example,] the Rab, a third-century Babylonian teacher: "the world to come is not like this world. In the world to come there is no eating or drinking or begetting or bargaining or envy or hate or strife' but the righteous sit with crowns on their head and are satisfied with the glory of God's presence."[250]

Crowns, great. Like getting socks at Christmas. At least they are spared the "eternal cricks in the neck" that Watts predicted would be the fate of those who, in the words of the hymn,

> Prostrate before thy throne to lie
>
> And gaze and gaze on thee.[251]

This explains a curious feature of the Moslem Heaven. We've all heard and laughed at the "79 virgins," but criticism of Moslem Heaven as crudely materialistic and even downright hedonistic goes back to the Crusades. Indeed, it has been pointed out that the Moslem lifestyle, being so enormously burdensome, positively

---

[249] Dr. Ian Paisley, the fiery Irish cleric and politician was reported to have been preaching one Sunday on the End Times–and in particular on the Day of Judgement. As he reached the climax of his address he said that on the Day of Judgement "there would be wailing and gnashing of teeth". At which point an old woman put up her hand and said "Dr. Paisley, I have no teeth" Paisley replied "Madam, teeth will be provided" *Sermon Central*, here: http://www.family-times.net/illustration/Judgment/201583/..

[250] *The Gospel of St Mark* by D. E. Nineham (Pelican Gospel commentaries); Harmondsworth, Eng.: Penguin, 1963, pp. 320-321.

[251] *Beyond Theology: The Art of Godmanship* (New York: Pantheon, 1965).

requires a more robustly imagined Heaven as a reward: the terms need to be spelled out quite plainly. "And I get what, you say?" As a result, deadly sins on Earth become rewards in Heaven!

Thus, while only the most benighted Baptist thinks the Bible forbids all alcoholic drink, rather than only intoxication (creating a cottage industry of booklets "proving" the word translated as "wine" actually means "grape juice," then as now the favorite tipple of thirsty, hardworking fishermen),[252] the Moslem is indeed forbidden all alcoholic beverages, for which the reward in Heaven is rivers of wine, of a vintage far superior to those available down here.[253]

And those 79 virgins? You get to choose them from any gender you please. Imagine a Christian preacher thundering that "God hates the homosexual perversion! And if you restrain yourselves here, He'll give you all the little boys you want, forever and ever, Amen!"

Which is to say, that the harsh discipline of the Moslem way of life, balanced by what to the unbeliever seems an almost comically materialistic Heaven, is from some angles not a bug, but a feature; why else would Islam have appealed to so many, including (hold your ears, conservatives!) many a European, who found it preferable to really-existing Christendom, including the most intelligent and skeptical (e.g., Shelley, or Goethe).[254]

---

[252] Mickey Spillane knows the score. "I don't drink...I'll have a beer once in a while. People say, 'you have a beer, you're a Jehovah's Witness...' but the Bible doesn't proclaim against drinking, it proclaims against drunkenness..." Interview with *Crime Time*, 06 August 2001.

[253] One might compare this to the Wedding Feast at Cana: "When the master of the feast tasted the water now become wine, and did not know where it came from (though the servants who had drawn the water knew), the master of the feast called the bridegroom [10] and said to him, "Everyone serves the good wine first, and when people have drunk freely, then the poor wine. But you have kept the good wine until now." [11] This, the first of his signs, Jesus did at Cana in Galilee, and manifested his glory. And his disciples believed in him." John 2:9-11, ESV. Another case of the Koran borrowing, or "correcting," the Biblical stories? In *The Purple Cloud*, M. P. Shiel writes of "that white wine of Ismidt which the Koran permits," to which the Penguin edition adds this note: "Wine is forbidden by the Qu'ran, but crystal white fountains of wine are forecast in Paradise. Izmit is a wine-producing region of Turkey, within easy reach of Imbros."

[254] "The Moslems, who borrowed the rules of their Religion Game from Jews and Christians alike, did not fail to copy the bad habits of both. Believers were exhorted in the Koran to wage war on the infidel, the slaughter of unbelievers being defined as one sure way of gaining entry into the Moslem heaven (a much lusher paradise than the rather insipid affair offered by their priests to conforming Christians)." *The Master Game: Beyond*

Less salacious though equally crude is the Mormon Heaven, where doughty patriarchs are given their own planets to farm, and multiple wives to bear them sturdy farmhands.[255]

At this point, some New Age goof will smugly point out that "everyone else" believes in reincarnation, but this is hardly a solution. These doctrines seem to imagine some kind of Ur-soul that persists in life after life, which Guénon and Evola both condemned as far from authentically Traditional, and which in any case merely postpones the problem of boredom. Indeed, traditions that seem to incorporate such a notion present it as just more *duhka*, or suffering, from which *nirvana* promises complete extinction – a notion to which we shall return.[256]

Anyhow, it's hard to imagine a form of immortality that wouldn't be, if you will, a deadly bore; a reward, rather than a Sisyphean punishment.[257]

How then do we imagine God makes out? Eternal life, eternal boredom?

Well, we've already touched on that. God's a champ. God, through his imagination, creates this ghastly world, including us. Why, if it's such a bore? Because, otherwise, God himself would be... bored.

Remember those Reader's Digest articles, like "I am Joe's Spleen"? We are God's entertainment.

As usual, Watts puts it best, distilling the august doctrines of the Vedanta into a tale told to a curious child:

---

the Drug Experience by Robert S. de Ropp (1968).

[255] See Rene Guénon, "The Origins of Mormonism," in *Miscellanea* (Ghent, NY: Sophia Perennis, 2003). Guénon of course finds this all typically American and materialistic, though he fails to note the Moslem parallel.

[256] "So we finish the eighteenth and he's gonna stiff me. And I say, "Hey, Lama, hey, how about a little something, you know, for the effort, you know." And he says, "Oh, uh, there won't be any money, but when you die, on your deathbed, you will receive total consciousness." So I got that goin' for me, which is nice." Bill Murray, *Caddyshack* (Ramis, 1980).

[257] *Pace* Camus, whose "We must imagine Sisyphus happy" has never seemed more than desperate hand-waving, to me, at least.

"In the same way, there are times when the world is, and times when it isn't, for if the world went on and on without rest for ever and ever, it would get horribly tired of itself. It comes and it goes. Now you see it; now you don't. So because it doesn't get tired of itself, it always comes back again after it disappears. It's like your breath: it goes in and out, in and out, and if you try to hold it in all the time you feel terrible. It's also like the game of hide-and-seek, because it's always fun to find new ways of hiding, and to seek for someone who doesn't always hide in the same place.

"God also likes to play hide-and-seek, but because there is nothing outside God, he has no one but himself to play with.[258] But he gets over this difficulty by pretending that he is not himself. This is his way of hiding from himself. He pretends that he is you and I and all the people in the world, all the animals, all the plants, all the rocks, and all the stars. In this way he has strange and wonderful adventures, some of which are terrible and frightening. But these are just like bad dreams, for when he wakes up they will disappear.

"Now when God plays hide and pretends that he is you and I, he does it so well[259] that it takes him a long time to remember where and how he hid himself. But that's the whole fun of it—just what he wanted to do. He doesn't want to find himself too quickly, for that would spoil the game. That is why it is so difficult for you and me to find out that we are God in disguise, pretending not to be himself. But when the game has gone on long enough, all of us will wake up, stop pretending, and remember that we are all one single Self—the God who is all that there is and who lives for ever and ever."[260]

If this picture is approximately correct, how do we see our lives?

---

[258] Thus, as we have speculated, God plays with himself.

[259] God's a champ!

[260] *The Book: On The Taboo Against Knowing Who You Are*, by Alan Watts (London, Jonathan Cape Ltd., 1969; Chapter One: "Inside Information."

Little noticed in this sort of picture is that it is, effectively, back at the position of materialistic atheism – "we" do not survive. The "I" that awakens is God's, not mine.

We seem then to have, as Schopenhauer would have predicted, ricocheted back from boredom to fear. This doesn't make sense – why should I want to exit—stage left, even—just to make someone else less bored?[261]

Goddamn it! Might as well just whack your tack.[262]

Wait a minute, that's it!

All this while, we've been bored with ourselves, while, implicitly at least, afraid of death, thought of as a state of nonexistence. We fear hunger, thirst, exposure to the elements, and thus endure the discomfort of striving to prevent or alleviate them (Schopenhauer's pain and fear). And if we succeed, we succumb to boredom. But boredom begets…well, let's say, imagination.

But imagination is what we share with God; in fact, imagination *is* God in us.[263] And the more we do as God does, the more we become as God is.

We have feared and deprecated ourselves becoming nothing, when in fact we are already a Creative Nothing, the no-thing from which all arises as imagination.

God and mankind have concerned themselves for nothing, for nothing but themselves. Let me then likewise concern myself

---

[261] Edina: "I'm sorry if that *sounds selfish, sweetie*, but it's *me! Me! Me! Me!*" *Absolutely Fabulous*, Season 1, "Birthday."

[262] One early morning, having "pulled an all-nighter" in the grad student office, I overheard the tail end of a conversation as a professor of Thomist philosophy arrived at his office: "Well, what else can you do? Just whack your tack."

[263] "I firmly believe, from my own experiences, that this God of whom the Bible speaks is our own wonderful human imagination; that God and the human imagination are one; that all natural effects in the world, though they are created by the Spirit of God, are caused by Spirit. So, 'every natural effect has a spiritual cause, and not a natural. A natural cause only seems; it is a delusion of our'— fading, I would say, "memory." (Blake, from "Milton")" Neville Goddard, "The Spirit Of God," lecture from 5-10-1971, online here: https://freeneville.com/the-spirit-of-god-may-10-1971-free-neville-goddard/.

for *myself*, who am equally with God the nothing of all others, who am my all, who am the only one.[*Der Einzige*]

> If God, if mankind, as you affirm, have substance enough in themselves to be all in all to themselves, then I feel that I shall still less lack that, and that I shall have no complaint to make of my "emptiness." I am not nothing in the sense of emptiness, but I am the creative nothing, the nothing out of which I myself as creator create everything.[264]

As David Gordon says,

> Once insight is gained into the unification experience,[265] it can be seen that what man has depreciated so thoroughly as mere vegetative existence is really the state in which he comes into his own true nature and attains oneness and happiness.[266]

> When one relinquishes his self, he lets go of his thoughts, self-consciousness, and the thought process, and he achieves unification. The unification experience is identical to the loss of self.[267]

We have tried to assuage the fears, or overcome the boredom, by telling ourselves absurd tales of Heavens and Stages of Reincarnation – absurd not so much for being false, as for being no answer anyway.[268] And all the while, the answer was right there, in Death

---

[264] Max Stirner, *The Ego and His Own*. Translated from the German by Steven T. Byington. With an Introduction by J. L. Walker. New York. Benj. R. Tucker, Publisher. 1907.

[265] The pleasurable sense of the loss of self found in activities ranging from sex to sports to stamp collecting; compare my remarks on Steve McQueen and auto racing in "St. Steven of Le Mans: The Man Who Just Didn't Care," here: http://www.counter-currents.com/2016/04/st-steven-of-le-mans/. One might also compare Evola's remarks in *Ride the Tiger* on the elite individual who, lacking access to proper initiatory traditions in the modern world, is driven to put himself various dangerous tests in search of an overcoming of the material ego.

[266] David Cole Gordon, *Overcoming the Fear of Death* (Baltimore, MD: Penguin, 1972). Of Grand Prix racing, Gordon says "Perhaps no other activity in all of sport creates so many and such prolonged states of unification." *Op. cit.*, p 103.

[267] Gordon, *op. cit.*, p. 113.

[268] What we might call the Imaginal view, by contrast, is self-evident, as we see from the ability, already noted, of man's imagination to have effects in the physical world. As usual, the Christian grasped the wrong end of the stick, arguing, as Augustine does,

itself, which deletes our fearful, boring self and reinstates our status as the Dreamer whose dreams are our reality.

> The thing that man fears most is to lose control of himself and his thoughts and to give up his thoughts and the very process of thinking itself. Without his thoughts, he feels he is nothing, but instead of this being the oblivion he fears, it can be his greatest achievement.[269]

Here we find the true meaning of many aspects of Christianity. Resurrection and rebirth, for instance, is not a matter of crude zombie-ism, or an ephemeral heavenly state, but the rediscovery that we are always already God himself; the kingdom of Heaven is within.

> Without the resurrection you would know infinite circuitry, repeating the same states over and over again. But, after moving around the circle unnumbered times, the perfect image is formed, removing you from the circle to enter a spiral and move up as the person who created it all. – Neville

Nor are we able to enjoy our lives, as long as we fear death; he that would have his life must lose it:

> Living with the constant fear of death, rather than just the awareness of death, contaminates life and adversely affects man's capacity to enjoy it.[270]

So Blake was right: "The best thing in life is death but it takes man so long to die that his friends never see him rise from the grave."

---

that erections and natural emission "prove" that man is "possessed" by Original Sin. (*De Civitate Dei*, 14.17). By contrast, "The unification experience is not based on an ineffable or mystical experience. On the contrary, it is based on a natural common experience that occurs frequently and spontaneously throughout our lives and can be verified by all of us independently and empirically." Gordon, *Self Love*, p. 48.

[269] Gordon, *op. cit.*, p. 57

[270] Gordon, *Overcoming the Fear of Death*, p. 20.

Despite our Hamlet-like hesitations, death is indeed a "consummation devoutly to be wished." It is the end of our boredom, and the birth of a divine, infinite Imagination.[271]

Counter-Currents/*North American New Right*
March 29, 2017

---

[271] Shakespeare, *Hamlet*, Act III, Scene I. Rene Guénon: "The end of a world is always the end of an illusion." *The Reign of Quantity, fin.*

CURSES, CUT-UPS, & CONTRAPTIONS:
THE "DISASTROUS SUCCESS"[272] OF WILLIAM BURROUGHS' MAGICK

> My very first question to him, a living, breathing, Beatnik legend in the flesh was... "Tell me about magick?" William was not in the least surprised by my question. "Care for a drink?" he asked. Putting on the TV to watch *The Man from U.N.C.L.E.*, he explained "Reality is not really all it's cracked up to be, you know..." – Genesis P-Orridge

For the longest of times I've repeated the story that I was first exposed to William S. Burroughs through the now-legendary meeting of Burroughs and Bowie brokered by *Rolling Stone*. However, since others have been sufficiently and similarly obsessed enough to document all this on the interwebs,[273] it would appear, assuming as always continuity in the space/time continuum, that this could not be the origin, as I was already sufficiently *au courant* to purchase a copy of *The Wild Boys* in London in the summer of 1972.

Further research on the intertubes would indicate that the source must have been the Robert Palmer interview in May, 1972,[274]

---

[272] Brion Gysin: "Cut-ups: A Project for Disastrous Success," collected in William S. Burroughs and Brion Gysin: *The Third Mind* (New York: Viking, 1978).

[273] "Beat Godfather Meets Glitter Mainman" by Craig Copetas (*Rolling Stone*, February 28, 1974). Jon Savage's account of the past and future of the event, "When Bowie Met Burroughs" is in *The Guardian*, 9 March 2013. When Genesis P-Orridge met Burroughs he asked "Why did you do that stupid interview with David Bowie?" to which Burroughs replied *"Advertising!"* – http://realitystudio.org/biography/nothing-here-now-but-the-recordings/

[274] Robert Palmer, "*Rolling Stone* Interviews William Burroughs." *Rolling Stone*. May 11,

which likely have caught my eye due to the coverage of the Master Musicians of Joujouka, and thus, Brian Jones.[275] I would not be in the presence of the Master—or Uncle Bill, as he liked to be known as—until 1976-77, when I was studying Buddhism at the Naropa Institute and he was in residence at their Jack Kerouac School of Disembodied Poetics.[276]

Now, I take this trip down Memory Lane because the author, Matthew Levi Stevens, author of *The Magical Universe of William S. Burroughs* (Oxford: Mandrake of Oxford, 2014), asserts a more precocious relationship with all things Burroughs:

> I was a 14 year old schoolboy, and already a huge fan of William S. Burroughs, when I first made contact with Industrial Music pioneers Throbbing Gristle. [Later, in] September, 1982, William S. Burroughs is in town for *The Final Academy*. Psychic TV are prime movers, and thanks to Genesis P-Orridge I have a ringside seat. Everybody wants to get their books signed, or have their photo taken with "Uncle Bill" as he is affectionately known. I choose to do neither, deliberately. As well as the PTV connection, I am in touch with J. G. Ballard, Eric Mottram, Jeff Nuttall, and know Bill's old pal Alex Trocchi; I am also a skinny, pale, intense, bookish young boy of nearly 16. I'm sure none of any of these details hurt. Eventually I am in just the right place at just the right time...[277]

Coincidence? Perhaps. But *mere* coincidence?

1972; reprinted in *Burroughs Live: The Collected Interviews of William S. Burroughs, 1960-1997* (ed. Sylvère Lotringer; New York: Zone Books, 2001), pp. 163-91.

[275] See my "Welcome to Club 27: Brian Jones & the Myth of the Rolling Stones" (Counter-Currents, Dec 15, 2014).

276 For an account of the previous, inaugural year of Naropa, see Sam Kasnner's *When I Was Cool: My Life at the Jack Kerouac School* (HarperCollins, 2009).

[277] Peter Christopherson of Throbbing Gristle tops us both: "The discovery of Burroughs' *Naked Lunch* at the back of W. H. Smith's one rainy Saturday afternoon had been a revelation to the 13 year old boy...It changed my life!"

> *In the magical universe there are no coincidences and there are no accidents. Nothing happens unless someone wills it to happen. The dogma of science is that the will cannot possibly affect external forces, and I think that's just ridiculous. It's as bad as the church. My viewpoint is the exact contrary of the scientific viewpoint. I believe that if you run into somebody in the street it is for a reason. Among primitive people they say that if someone was bitten by a snake he was murdered. I believe that.* – William S. Burroughs[278]

Well, surely then this is the man for the job at hand, which is the twofold nature of The Magical Universe of William S. Burroughs:

Firstly, and probably most obvious, is the material that appears in the output of Burroughs the Writer that can be seen as describing or referring to some magical, mystical or occult idea. Invocations of Elder Gods of Abominations, descriptions of Sex-Magick rituals, references to amulets, charms, ghosts, omens and spells, all the thematic set-dressing that we all know and love, from Hammer Horror Movies to *Weird Tales*, from H. P. Lovecraft to Dennis Wheatley and *The X-Files*.

Secondly, and perhaps less obvious, there is the personal interest and involvement of Burroughs the Man with belief systems and practices that come from those strange Other territories that lay outside the bounds of either conventional mainstream religion or scientific materialism… and various other areas that can perhaps be considered Fringe Science (perhaps even pseudoscience), as well as Contested Knowledge of a more Traditional kind: partaking of the Vine-of-the-Soul with Amazonian shamans, attending the Rites of Pan in the Rif Mountains outside Morocco, participating in a Sweat-Lodge with Native American Indian medicine men and as we have seen, latterly an engagement with that most Post-Modern of Occultisms, Chaos Magic.

---

[278] *Literary Outlaw: The Life and Times of William S. Burroughs* (New York: Norton, 2012), p. 252. Burroughs' rejection of both dogmatic science and dogmatic, Abrahamic religion echoes the recent Illuminati Conspiracy; see, for example, Mike Hockney's recent kindle *Richard Dawkins: The Pope of Unreason* (The God Series Book 16), s. l.: Hyperreality, 2014.

Or, as his classic biographer Ted Morgan wrote:

> As the single most important thing about Graham Greene was his viewpoint as a lapsed Catholic, the single most important thing about Burroughs was his belief in the magical universe. The same impulse that led him to put out curses was, as he saw it, the source of his writing...[279]

As Stevens quotes Burroughs Longtime Companion James Grauerholz,

> "He developed a view of the world that was based primarily on Will: nothing happens unless someone wills it to happen. Curses are real, possession is read. This struck him as a better model for human experience and psychology than the neurosis theories of Freud.... He did pursue a lifelong quest for spiritual techniques by which to master his unruly thoughts and feelings, to gain a feeling of safety from oppression and assault from without and from within. The lists of liberational systems that he took up and tried is a long one."

Now, while the first angle has been covered by Burroughs' now numerous biographers and literary scholars,[280] Stevens' unique contribution is using that material, and his own experiences with Burroughs and his acolytes, such as Phil Hine, Peter Carroll, Malcom MacNeill and Genesis P-orridge, to locate in and explain through his life, the magical beliefs and, more importantly, magickal practices therein.

This makes the Matthew Stevens book required reading for anyone interested not just in Burroughs, but in late 20th century literature, music (from the relatively popular Bowie, hip hop, ambient and trance to the unfriendly extremes of punk, Industrial

---

[279] *Op. cit., p632*.

[280] Ranging, as Stevens notes, from the pioneering work of Eric Mottram (*The Algebra of Need*, 1971; see Jed Birmingham's tribute) to *The Secret of Fascination* (1983) by "the most eminent living scholar of William Burroughs and his works," Oliver Harris. For some reason Stevens never mentions one of my favorite ones, Timothy Murphy's *Wising Up the Marks: The Amodern William Burroughs* (University of California, 1998).

and Noise), film (again, from the relatively mainstream David Cronenberg to Anthony Balch) and even painting. [281]

Stevens suggests a genetic component in Burroughs' lifelong involvement with the occult. His mother claimed to be psychic,[282] while his father was a relatively poor relation of the Burroughs office machine creator; perhaps this mixture accounts for Burroughs' fascination not just with the occult but what might be termed the machinery of fringe science: Scientology e-meters, Reich's orgone boxes, Brion Gysin's Dreamachine, and even his famous "cut-up" technique of chance composition and the experiments with altering reality with tape recordings.

Appropriately, then, Stevens begins with Burroughs' childhood, and the curses he learned from family servants,[283] and which he later used both in books and in life.[284]

---

[281] Admittedly, Burroughs "shotgun" paintings haven't been all that influential, but from the other direction, the cut-up techniques are obviously attempts to employ collage and Dada-ist chance procedures to literature, while when Stevens summarizes Burrough's "magical thinking" as an attempt to "exploit the ability of the brain to perceive apparent connections or resemblances between things which, rationally speaking are not linked" he explicitly links it to Dali's "paranoiac-critical method."

[282] "[Kim's] mother's character was enigmatic and complex...[She] was extremely psychic and was interested in magic." – *The Place of Dead Roads*.

[283] I had an old school English professor from Boston who once casually mentioned learning Italian "from the servants." Burroughs has both an Irish nurse, who taught him to "call the toads," as well as a later Welsh nanny, who taught him, *inter alia*, "the blinding worm." I've identified a similarly occult inheritance from my servant-class Welsh mother; see my interview with Greg Johnson in *The Homo and the Negro* (San Francisco: Counter-Currents, 2012; embiggened edition, 2017).

[284] Stevens gives extensive coverage of Burroughs exuberant use of curses in both. Interestingly, Burroughs seems to have had a longstanding feud with Truman Capote. "This late 1960s document, listed in the archive's finding aid as "An Open Letter to Truman Capote," forms a disconcerting counterpart to Burroughs' interest in magic, with Burroughs taking Capote to task for a "betrayal" of literary talent before concluding by effectively casting a curse on Capote's writing abilities. Read with the benefit of hindsight, the text is all the more disturbing given that history bore out the desired effects of Burroughs' sinister wish. ...Regardless of how seriously Burroughs intended his prediction for Capote's future, his words proved eerily prescient. After the publication of *In Cold Blood*, Capote announced work on an epic novel entitled *Answered Prayers*, intended as a Proustian summation of the high society world to which he had enjoyed privileged access over the previous decades.... Capote's betrayal of the confidences of friends (who recognized the identities lurking beneath the veneer of fictionalized characters) resulted in swift exile from the celebrity world which Capote had courted for much of his career...Burroughs [was voted into] the

Burroughs fitfully studied the occult on own and in the context of stays at Harvard and the University of Mexico City, but it was at the Beat Hotel in Paris at the end of the 50s that he met his next, most important occult mentor, Brion Gysin. Among other things, it was Gysin who made the serendipitous discovery that newspapers, cut up while serving as an improvised cutting board, could be rearranged to create new texts. Burroughs soon realized this was not only a literary technique but an occult one as well, making the connection to Dunne's study of precognitive dreams:

> "You will recall *Experiment with Time* by Dunne. Dr Dunne found that when he wrote down his dreams the text contained many clear and precise references to so-called future events. However, he found that when you dream of an air crash, a fire, a tornado, you are not dreaming of the event itself but of *the so-called future time when you will read about it in the newspapers.* You are seeing not the event itself, but a newspaper picture of the event, prerecorded and pre-photographed." (*The Third Mind*)

Leading to this realization:

> "I would say that my most interesting experience with the earlier techniques was the realization that when you make cut-ups you do not get simply random juxtapositions of words, they do mean something, and often that these meanings refer to some future event... Perhaps events are pre-written and pre-recorded and when you cut word lines the future leaks out." (*The Job*)

Stevens adds that

> Burroughs felt that the cut-up was a way to break through the Word Lines of this insidious, all-pervading enemy and get to the Truth...This was an attitude he would extend increasingly to *all* communications, and eventually all relationships.

American Academy and Institute of Arts and Letters in 1983. After a long decline, wrought by the inability to break a harrowing cycle of alcohol and barbiturate abuse, Capote died the following year at the age of 59." – "In Cold Blood: William Burroughs' Curse on Truman Capote" by Thom Robinson, here: http://realitystudio.org/biography/in-cold-blood-william-burroughs-curse-on-truman-capote/.

> "This was a magic practice he was up to, surprising the very springs of creative imagination at their source." (Brion Gysin, *Here to Go*)

After claiming at the famous Edinburgh Conference that he had actually caused a plane to crash, Stephen Spender noted that

> "It seems to me like a rather medieval form of magic rather than modern science."

Some twenty years later, Burroughs made use of another book, Carlos Castaneda's *The Teachings of Don Juan*, to elucidate the occult significance of the cut-ups. Harkening back again to the Edinburgh Conference, when Norman Mailer had famously proclaimed Burroughs to be "possessed by genius," Burroughs, typically, said that he took the idea of "possession" literally: he did not have genius but was possessed by it.

> To me "genius" is the *nagual*: the uncontrollable—unknown and so unpredictable—spontaneous and alive. You could say the magical.
>
> The role of the artist is to make contact with the *nagual* and bring a part of it back into the *tonal* [the everyday, predictable world] in paint or words, sculpture, film, or music. The *nagual* is also the area of so-called psychic phenomena

Burroughs' cut-up technique, while in one sense merely continuing (as he acknowledged) the innovations of writers as outré as Breton and (at that time) established as T. S. Eliot or John Dos Possos, was, in another sense, something very different: by introducing chance the lines of determinism were cut. Cut ups "had the potential to be oracular":

> Whereas the basis of fiction was "once upon a time" – with the cut-ups it was "once in *future time*."

Among Burroughs earliest cut-ups were phrases that meant nothing at the time but which in hindsight took on an eerie prescience.

"In 1964 I made a cut-up and got...'And here is a horrid air conditioner.' In 1974, I moved into a loft with a broke air conditioner which was removed to put in a new unit. And there was three hundred pounds of broken air conditioner on my floor – a horrid disposal problem, heavy and solid, emerged from a cut-up ten years ago."

"Perhaps events are pre-written and pre-recorded and when you cut word lines the future leaks out."

"He had the ability to *write* ahead." – Malcolm McNeil

"This was a magic practice he was up to, surprising the very springs of creative imagination at their source." – Brion Gysin

In Burroughs' hands, what could have been a mere literary technique, perhaps even just a parlour trick, became an instrument of Archeofuturism:[285]

"Not so much a case of 'life imitating art' as art with a magical *intention attempting to initiate events* in everyday life." – Malcolm MacNeill[286]

After moving to London, Burroughs extended the cut-up and fold-in techniques to film and audio tape. Among other projects, bad service at a local coffee bar led to Burroughs declaring occult war; as recently recalled on a blog:

Morgan: There, "on several occasions a snarling counterman had treated him with outrageous and unprovoked discourtesy, and served him poisonous cheesecake that made him sick."

---

[285] Compare my discussion of Ed Wood's supposed "incompetence" as productive of "accidents" that act archeofutristically ("Future events like these will affect our lives, in the future!") See my review of Rob Craig's *Ed Wood, Mad Genius: A Critical Study of the Films*, Counter-Currents, Oct. 9, 2014.

[286] MacNeill took over Burroughs' Franklin Street loft in Tribeca and discovered Burroughs had set up a Blinding Worm curse directed against *New York Times* reviewer Anatole Broyard, which had remained behind and apparently produced visual hallucinations in MacNeill.

Burroughs "decided to retaliate by putting a curse on the place." He chose a means of attack that he'd earlier employed against the Church of Scientology,[287] "turning up...every day," writes [on his blog *The Great Wen*, Peter] Watts, "taking photographs and making sound recordings." Then he would play them back a day or so later on the street outside the Moka. "The idea," writes Morgan, "was to place the Moka Bar out of time. You played back a tape that had taken place two days ago and you superimposed it on what was happening now, which pulled them out of their time position."

The attack on the Moka worked, or at least Burroughs believed it did. "They are seething in there," he wrote, "I have them and they know it." On October 30th, 1972, the establishment closed its doors—perhaps a consequence of those rising rents that so irked the Beat writer—and the location became the Queens Snack Bar.[288]

It's all rather like Alan Watts on "being a genuine fake":

> You cannot will spontaneity but you can introduce the unpredictable spontaneous factor with a pair of scissors.

The cut-up and later fold-in techniques, as well as the Dreamachine ("a kinetic sculpture—basically a light-bulb mounted on a turntable —designed to induce visions by playing flickering light on the closed eyes of the viewer"[289]), emerged during the intense period of the Beat Hotel, when Burroughs and Brion Gysin "lived in and out of each

---

[287] At the time, scientology was quasi-respectable on the occult fringes, and needless to say the E-meters caught Burroughs' interest, although he quickly "cooled on the set-up" and became an implacable enemy. At the appropriate historical point I began to wonder if Stevens would reference fellow Beatdom author David S. Wills' *Scientologist! William S. Burroughs and the "Weird Cult"* (Temple, PA: Beatdom, 2013). But Levin went one better and devotes a few pages to a review of his "good friend's" book. I should try this labor-saving idea on my next book!

[288] "How William S. Burroughs Used the Cut-Up Technique to Shut Down London's First Espresso Bar (1972)" here: http://www.openculture.com/2014/12/how-william-s-burroughs-shut-down-londons-first-espresso-bar-1972.html.

[289] See *Brion Gysin: Dream Machine* by Laura Hoptman (New York: Merrill/New Museum, 2010). You can make you own with Brion Gysin's *Dreamachine Plans* (Seattle: AK Press, 1994).

other's rooms, minds, and lives as much as any married couple." This "commingling" they dubbed "The Third Mind," the phrase itself a kind of cut-up, having been lifted from Napoleon Hill's 1937 self-help classic, *Think and Grow Rich*:

> "No two minds ever come together without thereby creating a third, invisible intangible force, which may be likened to a third mind."

Stevens doesn't make the point, but this is yet again another link to the Midwest tinkering tradition, Hill's book being a late classic of the New Thought or Mind Cure movement, which I have previously called our native Neoplatonism, home-grown Hermeticism, and our two-fisted Traditionalism: the "New Thought" or "Mind Cure" movement.[290]

Although Stevens tries to make Burroughs' magical obsessions seem more respectable than cranky—by, for example, linking him to Aleister Crowley at various points[291]—I was rather more interested in seeing, for the first time, how similar his pursuits were to Baron Evola's. Indeed, the very title of Stevens' book echoes, no doubt inadvertently, Cesare della Riviera's 1605 treatise *The Magical World*

---

[290] While discussed with respect by no less than William James, and even arch-sceptic Mark Twain, "New Thought" is seen as hopeless square and uncool today, suitable to sweaty salesmen and repackaged as "The Secret" for Oprah's minions. Nevertheless, this kind of "self-help" spiritualism is essentially American and quite similar to Burroughs own life-long pursuit of a means of quelling his possession by what he called "The Evil Spirit."

[291] Burroughs himself was rather "ambivalent" about Crowley, as Stevens notes, calling his books "unreadable" and imitating him with a high-pitched shriek: "The Greeeet Beeeeeeeast!" The feeling was apparently shared by Andrew Lyles, who writes of reverently putting on an LP record of Crowley and hearing "a feeble, effete, well-spoken man…My friend Alex… laughed and said, "What a load of shit, he sounds like Larry Grayson." Of course, when the record was removed and another selected, the record player refused to work. See his "Foreword" to *Mighty in Sorrow: A Tribute to David Tibet & Current 93*; edited by Jordan Krall (East Brunswick, NJ: Dynatox Ministries, Intl., 2014). Burroughs always preferred a kind of Jack Donovan style masculinity, for both his self-presentation and choice of friends and lovers (see Jamie Russell's *Queer Burroughs* [New York: Palgrave, 2001]) and consequently a horror of effeminacy (see the note on Crowley). It was up to his acolyte Genesis P-orridge to take the logical step and apply the cut-up technique to gender, with his concept of Pandrogyny. Similarly, Evola's adversion to homosexuality was relativized by his earlier employment of androgyny as the goal of the hermetic quest throughout the Hermetic Tradition, as well his counsel to "acquire the power of the feminine" in "Serpentine Wisdom" (an UR essay reprinted in his *Introduction to Magic*).

of the Heroes (*Il mondo magico de gli heroi*), which Evola republished with his own commentary in 1932,

> [A]sserting that in this hermetic treatise can be found the most open and clear statement of the principles of spiritual alchemy and hermetic art. Rene Guénon notes in his review, however, that the work of della Riviera is far from being as transparent as asserted in Evola's commentary.²⁹²

As Stevens points out, the cut-up method clearly evokes the Dada techniques of Tristan Tzara, who was also a decisive, though early, influence on Evola:

> Dada seemed more than a mere art movement, something along the lines of *a total reconstruction of the world*, [cutting it up to reach the nagual?], the need for which Evola had come to believe in passionately. ²⁹³

In addition to reconstructing the world, Evola and Burroughs shared interests in magic, Buddhism, and painting.²⁹⁴ But I think the most intriguing similarity occurs when

> Burroughs and Gysin in the 1960s…sought to extend their "Third Mind" to others.

Among other things, Burroughs began a series of monthly articles entitled Academy 23 (later reprinted in *The Job*), and in the Bowie interview claims that

---

²⁹² "ORION, or the Heroes' Conspiracy" by Alexander Dugin, here: http://openrevolt.info/2011/10/18/orion-or-the-heroes-conspiracy/.

²⁹³ An excerpt from Gary Lachman's *Revolutionaries of the Soul* (Wheaton, Il: Quest 2014), online here: http://www.dailygrail.com/blogs/Gary-Lachman/2014/9/Excerpt-Revolutionaries-the-Soul.

²⁹⁴ Lachman suggests another as well: "It is also quite possible that in Dada's leader, Tristan Tzara, Evola found a new role model: photographs of Evola displaying his elegant, smooth shave face, immaculate dress and imperious gaze—complete with monocle—are strikingly similar to Tzara." This surely recalls Burroughs' famous "banker drag;" as Stevens say, "With his three-piece suit, glasses, hat and raincoat, Burroughs seemed like the ultimate undercover hipster."

At the moment I'm trying to set up an institute of advanced studies somewhere in Scotland. Its aim will be to extend awareness and alter consciousness in the direction of greater range, flexibility and effectiveness at a time when traditional disciplines have failed to come up with viable solutions. You see, the advent of the space age and the possibility of exploring galaxies and contacting alien life forms poses an urgent necessity for radically new solutions. We will be considering only non-chemical methods with the emphasis placed on combination, synthesis, interaction and rotation of methods now being used in the East and West, together with methods that are not at present being used to extend awareness or increase human potentials.

We know exactly what we intend to do and how to go about doing it. As I said, no drug experiments are planned and no drugs other than alcohol, tobacco and personal medications obtained on prescription will be permitted in the center. Basically, the experiments we propose are inexpensive and easy to carry out. Things such as yoga-style meditation and exercises, communication, sound, light and film experiments, experiments with sensory deprivation chambers, pyramids, psychotronic generators and Reich's orgone accumulators, experiments with infra-sound, experiments with dream and sleep.

Again, very American, but also very much like the occult groups (or "magical chains") created by Baron Evola with the explicit aim of influencing modern society. On the more public front, there were the journals *UR* and *KRUR*, later collected and published as *Introduction to Magic* (Rochester, VT: Inner Traditions, 2001) as well as his contributions to various Fascist periodicals. This semi-public work continued during his futile attempts to interest the New German Reich, as well as his postwar books for youth (*Orientamenti*, 1950[295]) and for "aristocrats of the spirit" (the subtitle of 1961's *Riding the Tiger* [Rochester, VT: Inner Traditions, 2003]).[296]

---

[295] See the translation published by Counter-Currents, online here: http://www.counter-currents.com/2015/01/orientations/.

[296] Given his well-known animadversion to homosexuality, it's amusing to note that his

> One might even use this similarity to justify applying to Evola's efforts Marianne Faithful's verdict on the Dreamachine: "It's like a wonderful idealistic idea, but you know it's never gonna fly…"

Returning to the theme of archeofuturism, Burroughs and Gysin found another occult escape technique in the Master Musicians of Joujouka, Morroco, whose "secret…guarded even from themselves was that they were still performing the Rites of Pan under the ragged cloak of Islam"(Brion Gysin). "Like a message in a bottle for subsequent generations," this music (oldest in the world: "a four-thousand-year-old rock band" as Burroughs dubbed it) cuts lines of pre-recordings.[297]

Over time Burroughs obsessions became less magickal and more Gnostic, emphasizing not just escape from Control but from Time, Space and especially the Body itself. As Stevens notes, Burroughs still evinced the "show me" attitude of his Missouri forbears (or his New Thought ancestors, I'd add), based not in faith but technology validated in personal experience.[298]

> In the goal of non-body freedom from past conditioning in space, he may have thought that he had found both a solution and an escape.

Here too the analogy to Evola continues, as Burroughs' concern with Egyptian doctrines of psychic doubles and astral travel (most especially in his last novel, *The Western Lands*) finds an echo in Evola's controversial (among airy-fairy New Agers) denial of

---

postwar activities actually got him prosecuted by the Italian government for the rather Socratic crime of "corruption of the youth." Burroughs, through his association with Throbbing Gristle, might also be styled a "wrecker of civilization" himself (see Simon Ford's *Wreckers of Civilisation: The Story of COUM Transmissions and Throbbing Gristle* (London: Black Dog, 1999), a sobriquet suggestive of both Evola's *Revolt Against the Modern World* (1932; Rochester, VT: Inner Traditions, 1995) as well as his *Men Among the Ruins: Post-War Reflections of a Radical Traditionalist* (1953; Rochester, VT: Inner Traditions, 2002).

[297] For more on the Master Musicians, see my "Welcome to Club 27 : Brian Jones & the Myth of the Rolling Stones," Counter-Currents, Dec. 15, 2014, and on this and other archaic music as tool of liberation see "Our Wagner, Only Better: Harry Partch, Wild Boy of American Music" in my collection *The Eldritch Evola…& Others (op. cit.)*.

[298] Compare Evola, "The Nature of Initiatic Knowledge," in *Introduction to Magic*.

universal immortality and reincarnation, relying instead on the need to construct a "Body of Light" with which to survive post-mortem dissolution.[299]

> Even towards the end of his life, William S. Burroughs engagement with The Magical Universe (and struggle against The Ugly Spirit) did not wane. The magical, psychic, spiritual and occult appear in his later fiction like never before, from depictions of astral travel and *"sex in the Second State"* to descriptions of actual rituals, referencing everything from Crowley & The Golden Dawn to the Myths of Ancient Egypt and even the *Necronomicon* all interwoven *with increasingly neo-pagan concerns* for the Environment, *the impact on Man & Nature of the Industrial Revolution with its emphasis on quantity, not quality*…His adoption of the Ancient Egyptian model of Seven Souls, continuing development of a very personalized myth of Hassan-i Sabbah and the Assassins of Alamut, and resistance to Christianity (*the worst disaster that ever occurred on a disaster-prone planet virulent spiritual poison*) made him of increasing interest and relevance to the new occultists who were emerging from successive generations of counter-culture that Burroughs had helped to shape through the example of his Life & Work.

> William S. Burroughs engaged with a number of methods & systems down the years, in the search for some method, special knowledge, or technique, which would free him to be whom he wanted to be, to live how he wanted to lives—and, perhaps most important of all, liberate him from the ever-impending threat of possession—by Control, by junk, or by The Ugly Spirit. Ultimately, the most successful of Burroughs' mechanisms against Control was methadone, for which he was prescribed the last XX years of his life, and over which personal stash of which he worries obsessively lest he find himself without the only thing, despite his 'clean' public image, that keeps him off junk.[300]

---

[299] See *op. cit.*, especially "The Problem of Immortality" and "The Doctrine of the 'Immortal Body'".

[300] "How can anyone endure this furtive, precarious life without junk? Shows me the full power that junk has over me, lying hypocrite that I am. "Oh yes, oh yes - I'm off the junk." -

But there was still one technique left. Confronted with Chogyam Trunpa's insistence that he not bring any writing materials to a Buddhist retreat, Burroughs had to admit that writing was his chief method or technique, "his only salvation."

> I am more concerned with writing than I am with any kind of enlightenment, which is often an ever-retreating mirage like the fully analysed or fully liberated person. I use mediation to get material for writing.
>
> The role of the artist is to make contact with the *nagual* and bring a part of it back into the *tonal* in paint or words, sculpture, film, or music. The *nagual* is also the area of so-called psychic phenomena.
>
> According to Trungpa [psychic phenomena] are mere distractions...[They] are all means to an end for the novelist. I even got copy out of scientology.[301]

Perhaps this (along with writer's block) accounts for Burroughs' return to a more conventional narrative style in his last work, the Dead Roads trilogy.

Another concern was a growing sense that magick, especially curses, was not just a means of communication but what I've called "passing the buck;" karma is never destroyed but only passed on to another, the "sucker" or "rube" to use Burroughs' favorite carny lingo.[302] This is one reason why the "enlightened man" may, in fact, seem – or be – quite far from the conventional "good guy." As one of Burroughs' favorite magickal authors, David Conway, is quoted by Stevens:

> Of common concern to [me and Burroughs] was the access magic gives to a wellspring of power which, *in terms of conventional morality, is staggeringly evil* yet ineffably beautiful. In confronting it, the magician becomes less the knightly hero that slays the

---

Last Words: The Final Journals of William S. Burroughs.

[301] "Retreat Diaries" (1976) in *The Burroughs File* (San Francisco: City Lights, 1984).

[302] I've explored this notion in several movie reviews which will be reprinted in a volume entitled *Passing The Buck*.

dragon than *the damsel who succumbs to its depravity*.[303]

On the other hand, Burroughs was also aware that

> "Sometimes a curse can 'bounce back and bounce back double.' Though he didn't say so – cursing amounts to dialogue." (McNeill, quoting Ted Morgan biography)

In *The Hermetic Tradition*, Evola is keen to disabuse the reader of the cliché that the successful Magus is rich, powerful, etc. Partly, this is because one doesn't reach such a level without giving up such childish desires; but it's also because there can be "psychic repercussions" in the everyday world from actions in the psychic realm. [304] In short, what I like to call "Evola's Boomerang." One's very success in the psychic realms has devastating consequences in the terrestrial.

Perhaps this "disastrous success" (as Gysin, prophetically, termed the cut-up technique) explains the rather subdued ends of occult masters like Crowley, Evola himself, and William S. Burroughs. Less than a month before he died in 1997 he wrote in his journal:

Mother, Dad, Mort, Billy[305] – I failed them all.[306]

Counter-Currents/*North American New Right*
Jan 21, 2015

---

[303] Cf. the remarks above on "Serpentine Wisdom." The idea of being the damsel not the dragon recalls the idea in the Northern Tradition of the shameful effeminacy of *Seidr*, despite Odin himself being a practitioner.

[304] *The Hermetic Tradition* (Rochester, VT: Inner Traditions, 1995), especially Chapter 51: "The Invisible Masters."

[305] "I'm now 36 years old, three years older than Billy Burroughs was when the weight of his father's legacy ravaged his liver and landed him in a ditch in Florida, but less than half as old as William Burroughs was when he exited the world addicted, without a family, and adrift alone in the middle of a lake so muddy my wife refuses to set foot in it. I have a daughter now, who will be a year old in just a couple of weeks. Somehow I'm glad she's not a son." "Burroughs & Son: Memoir" by John Proctor" here: http://numerocinqmagazine.com/2010/05/24/burroughs-son/

[306] 19 July 1997, *Last Words*.

THE NAME IS CROWLEY...ALEISTER CROWLEY:
REFLECTIONS ON ENLIGHTENMENT AND ESPIONAGE

"Mania, my dear Mister Bond, is as priceless as genius. Dissipation of energy, fragmentation of vision, loss of momentum, the lack of follow-through—these are the vices of the herd." - Dr. No[307]

A recent book by Richard B. Spence proposes that the (in)famous Aleister Crowley, in addition to his well-known achievements, both acknowledged—mountaineer, chess master – and disputed – England's greatest poet,[308] master of the Qabalah[309]—was also, perhaps *merely*, a British spy.[310]

I suspect that most readers, either of the general public or Crowley enthusiasts, will find this book frustrating. The frustration arises from both the subject and its execution.

---

[307] For a Hegelian analysis of Dr. No's speech, see "The Dialectic of Dr. No" by Ian Dunross: "For what makes the evil scientist so damn readable is that, despite his fantastical dimension, Fleming went out of his way to make the madman's propensity for world domination a credible one and to provide him with sufficient reasons for behaving as he does."

[308] "It has been remarked a strange coincidence that one small county should have given England her two greatest poets—for one must not forget Shakespeare (1550-1610)." *The Confessions of Aleister Crowley*. Even more strange that one small *street* in Alabama should have produced Truman Capote and Harper Lee.

[309] "From the brilliant misunderstandings and misrepresentations of Alphonse Louis Constant, who has won fame under the pseudonym of Eliphas Levi, to the highly coloured humbug of Aleister Crowley and his followers, the most eccentric and fantastic statements have been produced purporting to be legitimate interpretations of Kabbalism. [Author's Note]: No words need be wasted on the subject of Crowley's "Kabbalistic" writings in his books on what he was pleased to term "Magick," and in his journal, *The Equinox*." - Gershom Scholem: *Major Trends in Jewish Mysticism* (New York: Schocken Books, 1961), p. 2; and Note on p. 353.

[310] *Secret Agent 666: Aleister Crowley, British Intelligence and the Occult* by Richard B. Spence (Port Townsend, WA: Feral House, 2008).

To understand the problems with the execution, it's perhaps best to look at the origin of this book.

Author Spence is professor and chair of the University of Idaho's Department of History, and is, I gather, an authority on the history of espionage and counter-espionage, even appearing on the History Channel, no less.[311] Around the turn of the last century he wrote *Trust No One: The Secret World of Sidney Reilly*,[312] a biography of the crypto-Judaic British "Ace of Spies."

In the course of that project, Spence tells us, he began to notice the name of Aleister Crowley cropping up again and again. Intrigued, Spence put together an article on Crowley's possible connections to British intelligence. And there the matter might have rested, except, it now being the age of the Internet, the article provoked responses, and additional information (or claims to information) from Crowleyites, spy fanatics, and conspiracy theorists from far and wide. Spence continued to follow up these leads, and the result is this book.

Unfortunately, most of those leads seem to have petered out or not amounted to much "at the end of the day" (as British historians seem to like to say). In particular, the hitherto classified files of both American and British intelligence, despite being opened up on many recent occasions, seem to remain closed when the topic of Crowley comes up, or else yield little of substance.

It would seem that if Crowley had anything to do with British intelligence, it either amounted to very little beyond some shared information from time to time over several decades,[313] or else was so massive and central that its existence is still being covered up at the highest levels.

Spence, of course, wants you to believe the latter; his Crowley is

---

[311] When I think of Idaho historians, I think of conspiracy researcher Michael A. Hoffman, II (who, according to no less than Robert Anton Wilson, has "the strangest reality tunnel" ever); and when I think of the History Channel, I think of crazy-haired guys talking about what aliens "might" have done; but Spence seems to be rather more conventional.

[313] I am reminded of how Oliver Stone, at the end of *JFK*, proudly announces that after Clay Shaw's death the CIA "admitted he had worked with them" – leaving the viewer to assume this validates Garrison's whole conspiracy plot – when the "work" actually amounted to Shaw, an international businessman, being asked to provide information from time to time.

the original International Man of Mystery - conniving to embroil the USA in what Yockey called the European Civil War (aka "World War I or "the Great War"[314]) through black propaganda and, ultimately, the sinking of the Lusitania; sundry plots to overthrow the Spanish government and derail Irish and Indian independence movements; and even in his drug-addicted dotage, using fake astrology[315] to demoralize Hitler and luring Rudolf Hess to England.

Alas, the lack of hard evidence leaves Spence with little more than a lot of "could have" and "might be," rather like an "ancient astronaut" theorist, augmented by a good deal of "did Crowley have a hand in" and "perhaps this was Crowley's work." Along the way, one does learn a good deal of actual history, especially about the major intelligence services, and these parts of the book are certainly of interest to the layman.

The other dissatisfaction I mentioned has to do with the object of the book itself, whether or not Spence succeeds in establishing it. If Crowley was a British spy, how do we reconcile this with our idea of Crowley as, in some sense, and to some extent, a Mage, a Realized Man? Does this diminish him by its mean little triviality – the Great Beast cut down to size and revealed as Col. Blimp? As quoted by Spence:

> "I still think the English pot as black as the German kettle, and I am still willing to die in defense of that pot. Mine is the loyalty of Bill Sykes' dog ... the fact that he starves me and beats me doesn't alter the fact that I am his dog, and I love him."

Crowley was a pariah and spiritual rebel, but he also longed for the "regular life of an English Gentleman."

Of course, we might wonder how much of a "regular life of an English gentleman" could resemble the life of one of those grubby little men selling secrets in an alley?

Or, alternatively, does it tarnish his reputation—such as it

---

[314] Conspiracy theorists like Hoffman might wonder if this is Revelation of the Method by smirking reference to Crowley, "The Great Beast".

[315] Is there any other kind?

is—with gross immorality? For leaving aside secret-selling, the "espionage" detailed by Spence is really more a history of what we now call "dirty tricks" and even "state-sponsored terror" or "false flag operations" used to stampede the sheeple into various wars for the benefit of the Deep State.[316] Not so much James Bond as G. Gordon Liddy or even, given his supposed role in the sinking of the Lusitania, Dick Cheney.[317]

The first question or perhaps just disquietude—the Mage as Jingoist—is perhaps best addressed by stepping back and asking what The Mage is doing in general. Here, I find the work of Colin Wilson to be useful, both generally, and specifically for Crowley; indeed, though this "confession" may make orthodox Thelemites and Crowley groupies cringe, I find Wilson's account of Crowley to be the best, or at least the most convincing, around.[318]

Magic (or "magick," as Crowley would prefer) is, Wilson points out, concerned with bringing about changes in the environment through the action of the will (or the "Will"). Thus, the Mage is concerned first and above all with the training, or strengthening, of the will.[319]

Why, then, all the fuss about robes and incense, altars, fasting,

---

[316] "False flag attacks occur when government engages in covert operations designed to deceive the public in such a way that the operations seem as if they are being carried out by other entities. False flag terrorism is a favorite political tactic used by governments worldwide. They influence elections, guide national and international policy, and are cynically used to formulate propaganda and shape public opinion as nations go to war." Kurt Nimmo, "A Brief History of False Flag Attacks: Or Why Government Loves State Sponsored Terror," Infowars.com, August 14, 2012; also includes a handy list from the burning of Rome by Nero to Operation Gladio, which designed "to force these people, the Italian public, to turn to the state to ask for greater security. This is the political logic that lies behind *all the massacres and the bombings which remain unpunished*, because the state cannot convict itself or declare itself responsible for what happened."

[317] Perhaps this explains the popular meme of portraying the otherwise utterly banal Cheney as a Sith Lord.

[318] See his classic survey, *The Occult: A History* (New York: Random House, 1971), which has a chapter on Crowley, as well as his *Aleister Crowley: The Nature of the Beast* (Wellingborough, UK: Aquarian Press, 1980).

[319] "What Crowley realised instinctively was that magic is somehow connected with the human will, with man's true will, the deep instinctive will. Man is a passive creature because he lives too much in rational consciousness and the trivial worries of everyday." – Wilson, *The Occult*.

planetary positions, etc.? Why, in short, all this bother about "magic"?

Because training the Will is *hard*,[320] and one needs all the help one can get.[321] He needs, Wilson says, "a whole scaffolding of drama, of conviction, of purpose." Wilson frequently points out how in ordinary life, a sudden crisis can lead one to concentrate the will, summon up necessary reserves, and achieve almost miraculous feats: "In moments of crisis or excitement, man 'completes his partial mind,' and somehow knows in advance that a certain venture will be successful."

But to do this systematically, some kind of framework of belief is needed, to serve as a focus of belief and provide confidence in ones actions.[322]

Crowley, as Wilson points out, is quite clear that the results are not, as Crowley puts it, "apodictically" related to the truth of the framework:

> Magic is to do with a subconscious process, and the actual ceremonies and rituals are not "apodictically related" to it,

> The "results" produced by a religion are not based upon the apodictic truth of its dogmas, but the dogmas are indispensable to the results, and the results are real.[323]

---

[320] "It turns out making a movie is really, really hard." – Joel Hodgson, creator of *Mystery Science Theater 3000*.

[321] "Man has become so complicated that he is unaware of the relation between his willpower and the spinning of the top called consciousness, and minor discouragements tend to get so out of proportion that he forgets to whip it." Wilson, *op. cit.*

[322] "If an ordinary, rational person tried to perform a magical ceremony, he would be thinking all the time: This is absurd; it cannot work. And it wouldn't." Wilson, *op. cit.*

[323] Wilson, *op. cit.* I find it interesting that Crowley's colleague and private secretary, Israel Regardie, called Neville Goddard the "most magical" of the New Thought or Positive Thinkers, and describes Neville's use of the Bible – interpreted accounting to supposed secret teaching delivered to him by a black African rabbi named "Abdullah" – to not just clothe his message but to engage the emotions of a nominally Christian audience in order to provide them with the confidence and will power to actualize their imaginations. The relevant chapter of his 1947 book is reprinted as the "Introduction" to *The Neville Goddard Treasury* (New

The question here is familiar to Traditionalists and perhaps "neo-pagans" as well. Guénon was insistent that one must follow a "regular" tradition—speaking in a way that was perhaps itself a product of his Catholic upbringing—and denounced Crowley as a representative of "counter-traditional action" precisely because of his unorthodox and seemingly improvised teachings.

But what if, as a child of modernity, one does not belong to any particular tradition? On what basis can one "chose" a tradition to belong to, and assuming one can do so in good faith, how does one practice it in good faith while believing, as a Traditionalist, that all the others are equally valid?[324]

Of course, Crowley and modern "Chaos Magicians" have no such problems, and view themselves as practicing a kind of postmodern magic that is based, in fact, on a radical skepticism about the ultimate truth of any given framework, which may be adopted and discarded for another at…will.

Now I bring all this in because I find it interesting that as soon as Wilson introduces the issue of frameworks and belief, his immediate comparison is to patriotism:

> When a patriot talks about his country, he does not mean the view out of the bathroom window, although that is certainly a part of his country. In order to get that patriotic glow, he needs to think of the Union Jack or Old Glory, and accompany it with some definite image of green fields of some battlefield of the past.

York: Tarcher/Penguin, 2015). Also interestingly, Neville asserted that this was in fact the intention of the writers of the Bible, which he insisted was a collection of "psychological teachings" and not in any way, shape or form a "historical" document; thus he was an early proponent of the "Christ Myth" theory, or rather, a bridge to an earlier form of the theory that was temporarily displaced by a resurgence of fundamentalism among so-called Biblical scholars in the mid-century. See my review of Robert H. Price's *The Human Bible* at Counter-Currents, May 26, 2015.

[324] And what if one believes that one's tradition is no longer traditional, such as the "sede vacantists" among Catholics, for instance, who are "more Catholic than the Pope"? And on what basis does one reach such a belief? What if one comes to believe, as Evola did, that Catholicism was never a valid Tradition anyway?

I wonder, then, if Crowley's "patriotism" was not more of the same sort, a framework to help provide support for the Will.

Bur Crowley did more than contemplate his English garden, or even engage in some trivial, pro forma patriotic acts; he supposedly engaged in several decades of dirty tricks, resulting in the deaths of over a thousand on the Lusitania, and is perhaps somewhat responsible for the deaths of millions in the two "World Wars." Even the harshest critics of the Great Beast never blamed all that on him!

So our second question is: can we think of the Mage, the Realized Man, as a Dirty Trickster?

Uncomfortable as it may be, I think the answer may very well be "Yes." The Realized Man has by definition passed beyond the "pairs of opposites" and is no more bound by our notions of moral law than JHVH himself.[325] I've discussed this many times before when discerning the notion of "passing the buck" – passing on one's karmic burden to a sucker and transcending the Wheel of Becoming – in various films.[326]

Spence certainly seems comfortable with the idea; commenting that

> On the contrary, those very qualities (such as his "contempt for the existing order") helped to qualify him for the job. [And what is the job?] Street-level spying anyway, [which] is at best morally suspect.

He then quotes from a CIA agent's memoir to illustrate the mindset:

> "Where else could a red-blooded American boy lie, cheat, steal, rape and pillage with the sanction and *blessing of the all-highest*?"

---

[325] This is the Jehovah God whose "ways are not your ways," and who "rains upon both the good and the bad." Christianity has introduced an apparently inconsistent Father God who seems bound by a moral law outside himself that requires him to punish mankind for its sins, rather than simply issuing a pardon. Evola, Watts and others have pointed out this as showing that this god must therefore be a lower, relativized entity than the Absolute, Brahman, the Godhead, etc. How someone could infer this, metaphysically, and yet remain a practicing Christian, at the level of practice, returns us to the previous difficulty.

[326] These film reviews will be reprinted in a collection, *Passing the Buck: A Traditionalist Looks at the Movies*, forthcoming from Counter-Currents.

But how does this "contempt for the established order" comport with his supposed "my country right or wrong" patriotism? Part of the problem arises from Spence's systematic confusion of "spy" and 'secret agent."

Now, Spence may be the authority on the history of espionage, but when it comes to fictional spies—and Crowley may be no more than that—my authority is Kingsley Amis, specifically his *James Bond Dossier*.[327]

Amis starts right out by clarifying the difference:

> It's inaccurate, of course, to describe James Bond as a spy, in the strict sense of one who steals or buys or smuggles the secrets of foreign powers...Bond's claims to be considered a counter-spy, one who operates against the agents of unfriendly powers, are rather more substantial.[328]

Bond, then, or at least the American version, would be a "secret agent" working to foil the machinations of a "spy" like Crowley.

Amis also emphasizes Bond's simple-hearted patriotism, already somewhat outdated in his mid-50s – 60s prime, which is a genuine version of Crowley's "non-apodictic" sort.

Moreover, Amis emphasizes that Bond is a "believable fantasy" because he is basically like you and me, only a little better, due to training and experience. He's not the best shot in the service, has to read up on card tricks, undergoes various kinds of training, doesn't really drink *that* much, etc.[329] We can easily imagine ourselves doing

---

[327] London: Jonathan Cape, 1965. As I've said before, I regard this as a model for the intense, "deep" study of a pop culture item, although Amis would hardly approve of my own flights of fancy regarding Ed Wood, say. Apart from his literary authority, and a knowledge of James Bond that led him to be asked to write the first post-Fleming thriller, Amis was assisted in the technical details of espionage by his friend, the historian Robert Conquest.

[328] Amis, Kingsley, *The James Bond Dossier* Jonathan Cape, 1965, p. 11

[329] Amis, an epic drinker who, alas, died a painful, lingering, alcohol-related death—no passing the buck for him—minutely investigates this issue; among other things, trying to find out if the famous "Vesper" martini recipe could possibly be drinkable as written (it's not). See also his three books on drinking, collected as *Everyday Drinking* (New York: Bloomsbury, 2008); ignore the introduction by the vile Christopher Hitchens and read the review by Roger Scruton in *The Guardian*: "Wine occasionally gets a look in, but it is clear that Kingsley despised the stuff, as representing an alcohol-to-price ratio far below the

the same, if given the chance. He is, in a comparison *not* made by the Yankee-phobic Amis, Batman, not Superman.

As for the CIA chap, surely this is not a spy, even, but simply a psychopath; which certainly jibes with the CIA's record: not very good at intelligence gathering, but great at creating chaos.[330]

Of course, it's true that the psychopath seems—misleadingly?—rather like the Realized Man after all; the monsters fought by Will Graham and Clarice Starling seem like Mages who have perhaps, like one of the Bluth family, "made an huge mistake." Taking hermetic metaphors literally, with egos too strong or, being too weak, needing inflation all the more, Buffalo Bill, The Tooth Fairy, and even Anthony Hopkins' operatic Hannibal Lecter illustrate the fine line between enlightenment and psychosis.[331]

But this tells us where we should be looking for our analogue for Crowley; not a secret agent, like Bond, nor even a spy, like Bond's quotidian enemies, the secret-stealers and diamond smugglers, but the man Fleming conceived of as the anti-Bond, his opposite number in every way: Ernst Stavro Blofeld.

---

horizon of a real drinker's need."

[330] See *Legacy of Ashes: The History of the CIA* by Tim Weiner (New York: Doubleday, 2007), which lists dozens of world-historic events completely missed by the CIA, which was too busy planning its next coup. The Europeans seem to have a weakness for anarchic comic strip or movie anti-heroes whose antics go far beyond what American audiences would tolerate. Faced with Mario Bava's *Danger: Diabolik* (1968), a kind of Bond/Batman hybrid, in which the titular super-thief merrily machine guns guards and blows up bridges, plunging trains into the sea, Mike and the 'bots could only wonder at a movie in which "Thousands die to satisfy Diabolik's girlfriend's whims." (Episode 1013). The movie does feature *Thunderball*'s Aldo Celli, who, in the dubbed version used on MST3k (though not the revamped DVD release) delivers the immortal line "Is that Stud…coming?"

[331] Jack Crawford: [about the Tooth Fairy] "You feel sorry for him."
Will Graham: "… My heart bleeds for him, as a child. Someone took a kid and manufactured a monster. At the same time, as an adult, he's irredeemable. *He butchers whole families to pursue trivial fantasies.* As an adult, someone should blow the sick fuck out of his socks. Does that sound like a contradiction to you, Jack? Does this kind of thinking make you uncomfortable?" *Manhunter* (Michael Mann, 1986). Once more, a contradiction. Although the remake of *Red Dragon* contains the Blake etching eating that illustrates my point about the misunderstanding of levels and lateralization, as well as Hopkins' Crowley-like take, I continue to prefer Mann's version, including Brian Cox's working class Lecter (named Lektor here, out of Judaic crypsis); among other things, the way Tom Noonan embodies The Tooth Fairy's realization that he has indeed "made a huge mistake."

That Ian Fleming based the first Bond villain—Le Chiffre in *Casino Royale*[332]—and then the ultimate super-villain, Blofeld, on Crowley is fairly well known.[333] The telling of the tale gives a fairly good example of Spence's method of building what he admits is a "circumstantial" case.

When news of the capture of Rudolf Hess began to get about, Crowley dropped a note to Ian Fleming, working in Naval Intelligence, to offer his services in the interrogation; Crowley could locate Fleming, whom he had never met, because Fleming's boss, Maxwell Knight (the model for Bond's "M") had been introduced to Crowley through occult novelist Dennis Wheatley. Higher ups, including Knight, eventually nixed the idea, and Fleming still never met Crowley.

Spence takes this well-established tale, interesting but ultimately going nowhere, and manages to torture the evidence enough to graft on a new head and tail, as well as some depth. Surely Crowley must have been called in to interrogate Hess; after all, the NID interrogation room was located near Crowley in London.[334] Sure, he was an elderly drug addict by this time, but that just shows he could have brought his long experience with psychotropic drugs to bear on Hess. And speaking of bringing things to bear on Hess, perhaps Crowley had been called in even earlier, to psychically manipulate

---

[332] "And so Fleming chose Crowley—based on their wartime meetings [untrue, they never met, but Crowley was sufficiently infamous already]—as the model for the first ever Bond villain. Fleming described Le Chiffre as 'clean shaven, with a complexion very pale or white, fat, slug-like, with sadistic impulses, constantly using a Benzedrine inhaler and with an insatiable appetite for women.' He also had a rather feminine mouth. It is also written that both called people 'dear boy', and both, like the crazed Benito Mussolini [?], 'had the whites of their eyes completely visible around the iris.'" (http://sabotagetimes.com/life/aleister-crowley-is-back#!). Well, I guess all "fascists" must be "crazed," but as for the whites of their eyes business, Amis notes that he only met one such person in his life, a local Welsh bureaucrat, but then he hasn't seen him around for a while...

[333] Although, as Spence notes, the details mysteriously disappeared from the American edition of Pearson's Fleming biography.

[334] Shades of Jim Garrison's "geographic" theory of guilt: Naval Intelligence, Guy Bannister and Lee Harvey Oswald must have been working together, since they all had offices near one another! See my review of Dave McGowan *Weird Scenes Inside the Canyon: Laurel Canyon, Covert Ops & the Dark Heart of the Hippie Dream* at Counter-Currents, September 29, 2014. Crowley, of course, figures on the cover of *Sgt. Pepper's*.

Hess, perhaps planting suggestions in his dreams?[335] And as for Fleming, well, he must have been Crowley's control all along. Can you prove it didn't happen?[336]

Hess was, supposedly, tricked into flying to Scotland. The Crowley/Scotland connection added another element to Blofeld, which also gets us back to Crowley's patriotism. A key plot point in *On Her Majesty's Secret Service* is Blofeld's mad wish to be recognized as a Scottish aristocrat, a wish shared by Crowley, as Spence narrates:

> Soon after the Golden Dawn meltdown, the Beast retreated to Boleskine, his newly acquired house near Loch Ness. There *he played at being a local laird* and performed "magicakal" operations *to perfect his command of the occult arts.*

This certainly put his supposed "patriotism" in perspective. Although I suppose Scotland is regarded as part of Britain (though not by Sean Connery[337]) the idea of "playing at being a local laird" recalls Wilson's notion of framework, and suggests that Crowley's pose as

---

[335] The aforementioned Neville describes methods to control the future behavior of others through the planting of such suggestions, so I suppose Crowley must have had similar, more sinister methods. "My schooling was devoted almost exclusively to the power of imagination. I sat for hours imagining myself to be other than that which my reason and my senses dictated until the imagined states were vivid as reality – so vivid that passers-by became but a part of my imagination and acted as I would have them. By the power of imagination my fantasy led theirs and dictated tot hem their behavior and the discourse they held together while I was identified with my imagined states." *Out of This World*, Chapter 3, "The Power of Imagination" in Goddard, *op. cit.* Spence is correct to point out as well that this is little different than the methods of "remote viewing" and even "remote influencing" studied by the CIA and others.

[336] Criswell's evidence is actually much sounder: "My friend, you have seen this incident, *based on sworn testimony.* Can you prove that it didn't happen?" Plan 9 *From Outer Space* (Edward D. Wood, Jr., 1959).

[337] Although Bond is a real Scotsman, with a French mother, Amis suggests that Sean Connery was not entirely suited to the role; he could play an Edinburgh businessman, *but never a laird.* Ironically, we never got to test this out, since Connery dropped out of the series before *OHMSS* was filmed; there, Bond—impersonating a Scottish herald to get to Blofeld—is played by George Lazenby, an Australian, who is increasingly seen as being the best Bond after all. Even more ironic, the "new Blofeld" will apparently be Christoph Waltz of *Inglourious Basterds*, a movie that would have dumbfounded Amis, who observes, *a propos* Bond's careful application of violence, that "we would shrink from identifying with a mere terrorist who happens to be killing Nazis."

a John Bull-style patriot was, just that, a pose, useful "to perfect his command of the occult arts."

Oddly enough, although Spence mentions Fleming, of course, and the Bond connection, Blofeld never once turns up. A suspicious absence, is it not? Because once we consider Crowley as Blofeld, it becomes clear that he could never have been so respectably middle-class as to be a secret agent,[338] nor as low-level as to be a mere spy.

Whether Spence or anyone else can "prove" Crowley was an agent of the British, he was much more than that: a Realized Man, and so in some sense, already a super-villain. Fleming's instincts were sounder than Spence's: Crowley can only be adequately dealt with through fiction.[339]

Crowleyites need not fear that anything in *Secret Agent 666* about either his patriotism or dirty tricks will tarnish the reputation, such as it is, of their hero. But unless the files haven't been destroyed, and someone someday feels comfortable releasing them, neither Spence nor anyone else will be able to confirm or deny that he was an International Man of Mystery; and I think Crowley would be quite happy about that.

Counter-Currents/*North American New Right*
August 4, 2015

---

[338] Amis suggests "mid-level Civil Servant" as Bond's correct status, if not title.

[339] What would be interesting would be a comparison of Crowley's activities and those of Baron Evola. Evola, of course, was also a practicing Mage, whose UR Group was definitely attempting to influence Mussolini, who, in turn, seemed to be terrified of him (despite having those Blofeld-like eyes). He seems to have been something of an Italian patriot, but more interested in guiding the Fascist movement as such, and thus more than willing to switch to the German side when it seemed more fruitful. See those invaluable publications from Arktos, *Fascism Viewed from the Right* (London, 2012) and *Notes on the Third Reich* (London, 2014) as well as Guido Stucco's discussion of the activities of the UR Group in his Introduction to Evola's *Introduction to Magic: Rituals and Practical Techniques for the Magus* (Rochester, VT: Inner Traditions, 2001); for Evola on Crowley, see his essay. Both Crowley and Evola seem to have wound up as physical wrecks, but Evola already noted in *The Hermetic Tradition: Symbols and Teachings of the Royal Art* (Rochester, VT: Inner Traditions, 1995) that the condition of the Mage in this phenomenal world is often the inverse of his astral state, the triumphs and struggles in the latter resulting in "karmic boomerangs" (as opposed to the "buck passing" I've described above). A true "Struggle of the Magicians"!

TWO ORDERS, SAME MAN:
EVOLA, HESSE

"It is fortunate you are not a historian," Jacobus commented. "You tend to let your own imagination run away with you."[340]

Some readers of Thomas Mann's *Dr. Faustus*[341] have speculated that the character of Chaim Breisacher, a "private scholar" who torments the culturally cuckservative circles of the minor nobility of Munich during the interwar period,[342] is a caricature of a Kabbalah scholar who occasionally collaborated with Evola; others, (such as me), wonder if Evola himself was the target. Making Breisacher an ultra-conservative Jew rather than a pagan enthusiast would have been both excellent cover and an added poke.

Thomas Mann depended heavily on the Jewish metaphysical philosopher Oskar Goldberg. Although Goldberg is little known today, his views on the significance of the Pentateuch caused quite a stir in Berlin between the two wars. Among those enraged by

---

[340] Hermann Hesse: *The Glass Bead Game*, translated from the German *Das Glasperlenspiel* by Richard and Clara Winston, with a Foreword by Theodore Ziolkowski (New York: Bantam, 1970).

[341] *Doctor Faustus: The Life of the German Composer Adrian Leverkuhn As Told by a Friend*, trans. John E. Woods (New York: Knopf, 1999).

[342] As I described it before: "This was a milieu...where the intellectual extremism and atavistic primitivism (as Mann sees it) that led to the rise of Hitler is explored through a series of grotesque figures in "the Kridwiss Circle," such as the painter Baptist Spengler (Spengler having thought painting an impossible art under modern circumstances), Daniel zur Hohe (author of a single book, on "hand-made paper"; a "lyrico-rhetorical outburst of voluptuous terrorism"; Stefan George?), and my own role model, the polymath "private scholar" Dr. Chaim Breisacher (a "corrosively ugly" Jewish Evola, sneering at the very idea of "progress" in a world declining since Solomon built his temple)." See my "Forward – Into the Past! Circling the Cosmos with Herr Prof. Dr. Ludwig Klages," Counter-Currents, July 7, 2015.

Goldberg's "mystical rationalism" was Gershom Scholem who maintained until his death such an antipathy for this man that he included a series of deprecating anecdotes about Goldberg and his "sect" in *From Berlin to Jerusalem* and, more importantly, *Walter Benjamin: The Story of a Friendship*. Let me quote from the latter, which speaks directly of Thomas Mann's reliance on Oskar Goldberg:

> "After 'Die Wirklichkeit der Hebraer' had appeared (1925), I wrote a long, critical letter about the book; (Walter) Benjamin and Leo Strauss disseminated copies of it in Berlin, and it won me no friends among Goldberg's adherents. That others were impressed, indeed entranced, by the imaginative verve of Goldberg's interpretations of the Torah...is evidenced not only by the writings of the paleontologist Edgar Dacque but above all by Thomas Mann; the first novel of the latter's Joseph tetralogy, 'The Tales of Jacob,' is in its metaphysical sections based entirely on Goldberg's book."

Actually we know that Mann studied intensively under Goldberg while preparing the four novels and used more than Goldberg's published words in his own writings. After directing his "pervasive irony" against Oskar Goldberg's philosophy, Thomas Mann turned it on Goldberg, the man. As Scholem tells it, "(In 'Dr. Faustus') Goldberg appears as the scholar Dr. Chaim Breisacher, a kind of metaphysical super-Nazi who presents his magical racial theory largely in Goldberg's own words." According to a disciple of the philosopher, even though the Breisacher portrait was indeed very funny and accurate, Goldberg was not amused:

> If Dan Jacobson, then, has given us "*his own* (my italics) highly individual understanding of the Bible," Thomas Mann most certainly has not. He has, however, provided us with a literary rendition of the philosophy of Oskar Goldberg—not to mention a nasty sketch of the man—whose major works have never been translated and have virtually been forgotten even in the original German. - Judith Friedlander, Purchase, N.Y.[343]

---

[343] *New York Times*, Letter to the Editor, Dec. 19, 1983.

Now that's interesting; and also sounds rather Evolian. On the other hand, for Bruce Rosenstock, who is bringing those then untranslated works to English readers,

> Goldberg's vitalist metaphysics of God as a living power challenges the mechanistic and reductionist scientific paradigm of the period and represents an imaginative approach to a "transcendental politics" that opposes the rising combination of biology and the nation-state in Germany.[344]

A better-known doubling—since Mann himself commented on it in his Preface to the English translation of *Demian*,[345] and Theodore Ziolkowski discusses it at some length in his Foreword to the English translation of *The Glass Bead Game*—is the resemblance between the latter book and Mann's own *Doktor Faustus*, the writing of which was already underway in Los Angeles when Hesse's book was published in Switzerland.

One, meaning myself, might wonder if there is any kind of Evola figure in *Glass Bead Game*, as in *Dr. Faustus*. There is, I think, but only because there is a much more important parallel. The *Game* itself shows Hesse attempting to come to terms with Evola's notions of Order and Tradition.

Given their similar interests, from comparative mythology to "today's youth," it's not surprising that each was aware—and wary—of the other.

In *Ride the Tiger*, Evola quotes twice from Hesse's *Steppenwolf*, each time approvingly, or at least as examples of some trend he approves of; first, the anti-bourgeois attitude that Evola flaunted from his own earliest youth:

> A partly convergent testimony from another direction is that which Hermann Hesse puts into the mouth of one of his characters: "I'd rather feel burned by a diabolic pain than to live in these sanely temperate surroundings. A wild desire flares

---

[344] Announcement of a lecture, "Bioengineering God," at the University of Arizona. See now *Transfinite Life: Oskar Goldberg and the Vitalist Imagination* (Indiana, 2017).

[345] Published by Holt in 1948, later as a Bantam paperback in 1966.

> up in me for intense emotions, sensations, a rage against this whole toneless, flat, normal, sterilized life, and a wish to destroy something—perhaps a warehouse, a cathedral, or myself—and to commit outrageous follies. ...This in fact is what I have always most hated, abhorred, and cursed: this satisfaction, this complacent healthiness, this plump bourgeois optimism, this life of the mediocre, normal, common man."[346]

Indeed, it's not hard to imagine Evola himself writing such a screed.

A few pages later, Evola paraphrases Hesse on the perception of a lack of a stable ego or "soul" in modern man:

> All this has long ceased to exist for modern Western man, and has long been "superseded" along the road of "liberty"; thus the average modern man is changeable, unstable, devoid of any real form. The Pauline and Faustian lament, "two souls, alas, live in my breast," is already an optimistic assumption; all too many have to admit, like a typical character in Hesse, that they have a multitude of souls![347]

However "typical," the "character in Hesse" is being described here from the "Treatise on the Steppenwolf" that in modernistic fashion interrupts the narrative in the novel,[348] bringing in Evola-like wisdom of the East that deserves quotation at some length to show how profoundly Asian mythology has shaped Hesse's thought:

> The division into wolf and man, flesh and spirit, by means of which Harry tries to make his destiny more comprehensible to himself is a very great simplification...Harry consists of a hundred or a thousand selves, not of two. His life oscillates, as everyone's does, not merely between two poles, such as the body and the spirit, the saint and the sinner, but between thousands

---

[346] *Ride the Tiger*, p. 25.

[347] Ibid, p. 45.

[348] In first editions, the text of this Treatise, supposedly handed to Harry Haller by a carnie, yet seeming to him to acutely diagnose his psychological state, was separately printed and bound into the text of the novel itself.

and thousands. The delusion rests simply upon a false analogy. As a body everyone is single, as a soul never. In literature, too, even in its ultimate achievement, we find this customary concern with apparently whole and single personalities…These conceptions are not native to us, but are merely picked up at second hand, and it is in them, with their common source in the visible body, that the origin of the fiction of an ego, an individual, is really to be found. There is no trace of such a notion in the poems of ancient India. The heroes of the epics of India are not individuals, but whole reels of individualities in a series of incarnations… When Faust, in a line immortalized among schoolmasters and greeted with a shudder of astonishment by the Philistine, says: "Two souls, alas, do dwell within my breast!" he has forgotten Mephisto and a whole crowd of other souls that he has in his breast likewise. The Steppenwolf, too, believes that he bears two souls (wolf and man) in his breast and even so finds his breast disagreeably cramped because of them. The breast and the body are indeed one, but the souls that dwell in it are not two, nor five, but countless in number. Man is an onion made up of a hundred integuments, a texture made up of many threads. The ancient Asiatics knew this well enough, and in the Buddhist Yoga an exact technique was devised for unmasking the illusion of the personality. The human merry-go-round sees many changes: the illusion that cost India the efforts of thousands of years to unmask is the same illusion that the West has labored just as hard to maintain and strengthen.

Again, we see a passage Evola could easily have written.

Of course, these are two, somewhat random issues, and when we look at the whole of their work and lives we can see many points of dissimilarity and even hostility. In the same book, Evola disparages "modern" art in these terms:

> When speaking of modern art, the first thing to mention is its "intimate" quality, typical of a feminine spirituality that wants nothing to do with great historic and political forces; out of a morbid sensitivity *it retreats into the world of the artist's private*

subjectivity, valuing only the psychologically and aesthetically "interesting." The works of Joyce, Proust and Gide mark the extreme of this tendency in literature.[349]

Not many today would consider Hesse a "modernist" but Mann, in his Introduction to *Demian*, makes that case, and uses Joyce and Gide as analogues to Hesse's achievement:

> And need it be states that, as an experimental novel, *Steppenwolf* is no less daring than *Ulysses* and *The Counterfeiters*?[350]

It's interesting that Evola refers to "characters" of Hesse, rather than Hesse himself. Ziolkowski says that the "Hesse cult" has revolved around such "painfully humorless works" as *Demian* and *Siddhartha*,

> In which readers have discovered an anticipation of their infatuation with Eastern mysticism, pacifism, the search for personal values, *and revolt against the establishment*.[351]

Again, a pretty good description of the later Evola "cult," but of course we'd have to switch out that bit about pacifism for something like "warlike Aryan values." And of course, that's a big difference. In the aftermath of WWI, Hesse and Evola (who served in the Italian artillery) drew diametrically opposed conclusions; Hesse embraced and promoted pacifism, while Evola consistently denounced what he called "gutless conscientious objectors."[352]

ALL QUIET ON THE WESTERN FRONT VS. STORM OF STEEL

Sticking with the same book, it's not hard to imagine a confrontation of Hesse and Evola resembling that between

---

[349] *Ibid*, p. 153.

[350] *Demian*, p. ix of the Bantam edition.

[351] *The Glass Bead Game*, p. viii of the Bantam edition.

[352] "Despite any antimilitaristic propaganda culminating in the shallow, spineless, and gutless "conscientious objectors," there is a heroic dimension in the Western soul that cannot be totally extirpated. Maybe it is still possible to appeal to this dimension through an adequate view of life." *Men Among the Ruins*, Chapter 9, "Military Style - "Militarism" – War."

Harry and his old friend, a professor of comparative mythology. Again, it's too rich to avoid quoting at some length:

> He too gave me a hearty welcome and the awkward comedy came to a beautiful climax. He was holding a newspaper to which he subscribed, an organ of the militarist and jingoist party, and after shaking hands he pointed to it and commented on a paragraph about a namesake of mine— a publicist called Haller, a bad fellow and a rotten patriot—who had been making fun of the Kaiser and expressing the view that his own country was no less responsible for the outbreak of war than the enemy nations. There was a man for you! The editor had given him his deserts and put him in the pillory. However, when the professor saw that I was not interested, we passed to other topics, and the possibility that this horrid fellow might be sitting in front of them did not even remotely occur to either of them. Yet so it was, I myself was that horrid fellow. Well, why make a fuss and upset people? I laughed to myself, but gave up all hope now of a pleasant evening. I have a clear recollection of the moment when the professor spoke of Haller as a traitor to his country. It was then that the horrid feeling of depression and despair which had been mounting in me and growing stronger and stronger ever since the burial scene condensed to a dreary dejection. It rose to the pitch of a bodily anguish, arousing within me a dread and suffocating foreboding. I had the feeling that something lay in wait for me, that a danger stalked me from behind.

Indeed, Harry the Steppenwolf proceeds to insult the wife of his host over her sentimental ideas of Goethe; accidentally, but all too honestly to withdraw his words.

> "I sincerely beg your wife's pardon and your own. Tell her, please, that I am a schizomaniac [sic]. And now, if you will allow me, I will take my leave." To this he made objections in spite of his perplexity. He even went back to the subject of our former discussions and said once more how interesting and stimulating they had been and how deep an impression my theories about

Mithras and Krishna had made on him at the time. He had hoped that the present occasion would have been an opportunity to renew these discussions. I thanked him for speaking as he did. Unfortunately, my interest in Krishna had vanished and also my pleasure in learned discussions. Further, I had told him several lies that day…it was my duty to inform him that he had grievously insulted me that evening. He had endorsed the attitude taken up by a reactionary paper towards Haller's opinions; a stupid bull-necked paper, fit for an officer on half-pay, not for a man of learning. This bad fellow and rotten patriot, Haller, however, and myself were one and the same person, and it would be better for our country and the world in general, if at least the few people who were capable of thought stood for reason and the love of peace instead of heading wildly with a blind obsession for a new war. And so I would bid him good-bye. With that I got up and took leave of Goethe and of the professor.

Of course, Evola was certainly no philistine academic,[353] or a run of the mill patriot or "jingoist;" and although he would have agreed that party newspapers were "stupid" and "bull-necked…fit for an officer on half-pay, not for a man of learning,"[354] he was in favor of a return of the Prussian style aristocratic ideal of politics; an idea to which we shall return.[355]

What, then, of the Hesse side of the equation? Although I've been an assiduous reader of Hesse, from the latter part of what the *NYT* called the Hesse Phenomenon,[356] to the recently "rediscovered"

---

[353] Again, a bourgeois class Evola always "professed" to despise, declining to take a degree and even giving away his books so as not to accumulate a library.

[354] See his views on Fascism – *Fascism Viewed from the Right*, trans. with Foreword by E. Christian Kopff (London: Arktos Media, 2013) and especially National Socialism – *Notes on the Third Reich*, trans. with Foreword by E. Christian Kopff (London: Arktos Media, 2013). See also H. T. Hansen's "Julius Evola's Political Endeavours," published as the Introduction to the English edition of *Men Among the Ruins, op. cit.*

[355] In contemplating Evola and Hesse on war, I am again reminded of a book I've referred to several times in other contexts, *The Same Man*, which expounds the idea that Orwell and Waugh shared the same view "against the modern world," while differing in the remedy: an atheistic socialist future, or a return to mediaeval Catholicism and feudalism.

[356] Most paperback covers in the 60s – 70s claimed that "The Hesse Phenomenon 'has

novella *In the Old Sun*, and consumed some of the early critical books, I can't say I've ever seen a comment on Evola therein.

In fact, the only reference I've found is provided in the aforementioned "Evola's Political Endeavors," which might be the germ of this essay. There, Dr. Hansen reports on a letter to publisher Peter Suhrkamp, dated April 27, 1935: "This dazzling and interesting, but very dangerous author," a line that Inner Traditions later appropriated as a blurb for *Ride the Tiger*.[357] Hansen adds:

> Hesse then goes on to accuse Evola of dilettantism in esoteric matters, which seems unjustified considering the many competent and distinguished positive voices, such as CG. Jung, Mircea Eliade, Giuseppe Tucci, and Marguerite Yourcenar. His works about Tantrism and Buddhism were even published in India, which is very rare for Western authors.
>
> Amusingly enough, Hesse adds the following remark: "In Italy, almost no one will fall for him, but it will be different in Germany."[358]

---

turned into a vogue, the vogue into a torrent....He has appealed both to....an underground and to an establishment....and to the disenchanted young sharing his contempt for our industrial civilization." —*The New York Times Book Review*

[357] Hermann Hesse on Evola; letter to Peter Suhrkamp, dated April 27, 1935; quoted from the jacket of Julius Evola, *Ride the Tiger: A Survival Manual for the Aristocrats of the Soul* (Rochester, Vt.: Inner Traditions, 2003).

[358] *Men among the Ruins*, op. cit., p. 99. Evola certainly had his greatest political influence in Italy, where he found protection from the bully boys through certain elements in the Party, while Mussolini himself had a superstitious dread of the "magician" Evola; see Renato del Ponte's Preface to the English translation of *Magic*, as well as Hansen's "Political Endeavors," pp. 46-57. On the other hand, Evola was *persona non grata* in the Third Reich. Just as proponents of a Master Race tend to believe they belong to it, and Traditionalists imagine themselves as wise Brahmins, those who advocate an Evola "style" rule by a uniformed "elite" should reflect on how Evola's influence was stymied by Himmler's reliance on the flim-flam man Karl Maria Wiligut, aka Himmler's guru "Weisthor"; see Hansen, pp. 62-69 and Nicholas Goodrick-Clarke, *The Occult Roots of Nazism* (NYU Press, 2004), pp. 189-190. Ironically, it was Weisthor who was instrumental in setting up the whole Ordensburg or Order Castle system that, as we'll see, was of considerable interest to Evola; see Stephen Flowers and Michael Moynihan, *The Secret King: The Myth and Reality of Nazi Occultism* (Feral House, 2007), pp. 49ff.

Lastly, their postwar fates could not be more different. The world couldn't wait to award the Nobel Prize to this "good German," doing so in 1947 for *The Glass Bead Game*, published in Switzerland in 1943 and hastily—and poorly—translated into English in 1948. Although he subsequently published almost nothing and was largely forgotten, by the 1960s the Establishment, in the form of the *NYT* and others, applauded how his books had been taken up by "youth." While I suppose Hesse never really benefited financially from this largely posthumous surge, he lived in quiet seclusion in his adopted Switzerland, no doubt enjoying the role of World Guru.

Evola, however, remained in an apartment in the capital of his native Italy. His publications, aimed at youth, were met with the full force of the state; rather than lauded in the papers, he was put on trial, literally for "misleading youth," *a la* Socrates (and, he was happy to point out in his *Auto-Defensa*,[359] every other significant Western thinker prior to the French Revolution).

However, it would be unfair—to Hesse!—to contrast his success to Evola's relative obscurity, since the former was largely a manufactured phenomenon, based on certain books, and understood in a certain way. As Serrano says,

> It is absolutely absurd to believe that Hermann Hesse "went out of fashion," as if a writer for the youth of forty years ago. In reality, *Hesse was brought artificially "into fashion"* and was used precisely in order *to disorientate the new generations of the fifties and sixties*.[360] I remember very well that Suhrkamp Verlag, Hermann Hesse's German publisher, was under obligation to sell forty thousand copies of Hesse' *oeuvre* every month and, to that end, resorted to all forms of publicity and pressurizing of the young generations of that time. It was thus that in the United States was transformed and falsified Hermann Hesse, making him appear a "hippie," a proponent of drug abuse, *et cetera*.[361]

---

[359] Translated as the Appendix to *Men Among the Ruins, op. cit.*

[360] By contrast, Evola personally attempted to "orient" postwar youth; see his *Orientamenti, undici punti* (Imperium, 1950); see Gornahoor's translation at Counter-Currents, January 7, 2015.

[361] "The Falsification of Hermann Hesse," *loc. cit.*

The Establishment was quite happy to see the anti-war protesters morph into hippies after reading *Siddhartha* (now out of copyright, it easily dominates the reissues), moving off to communes to meditate.[362]

Though no doubt of a different orientation than Serrano himself, orthodox scholar Theodore Ziolkowski concurs on the limited and meretricious nature of the Hesse Boom:

> *The Glass Bead Game*, then, is indispensable for a complete understanding of Hesse's thought. It is possible to read *Siddhartha* as a self-centered pursuit of nirvana, but Joseph Knecht gives up his life out of a sense of commitment to a fellow human being. It is possible to see in *Steppenwolf* a heady glorification of hip or even hippie culture, but Joseph Knecht shows that the only true culture is that which responds to the social requirements of the times. *The Glass Bead Game*, finally, makes it clear that Hesse advocates thoughtful commitment over self-indulgent solipsism, responsible action over mindless revolt. For Joseph Knecht is no impetuous radical thrusting non-negotiable demands upon the institution and demanding amnesty from the consequences of his deeds. He attains through disciplined achievement the highest status in the Order and commits himself to action only after thoughtfully assessing its implications for Castalia and the consequences for himself. Above all—for the novel is not a philosophical tract or a political pamphlet, but a work of art—Hesse suggests that revolt need and violent, that indeed it is more effective when it is rational and ironic.[363]

Hey, what's wrong with being an "impetuous radical thrusting non-negotiable demands upon the institution and demanding amnesty from the consequences of his deeds"? A glance at today's campuses shows what lessons "youth" took from Hesse; although after all, he's just another dead white male, right?[364]

---

[362] An idea, for what it's worth, that continues to be popular among the conspiracy-minded, such as Miles Mathis.

[363] pp. [?] of the Bantam edition.

[364] Apparently, all those folk on those Bantam covers were drawn by an artist in Maine, using his own family as models; including, I guess, the King Ginger on the *GBG* cover;

So *The Glass Bead Game* is necessary as a corrective to the Hippie Hesse image formed from, and for, his 60s boom.

In fact, more essentially in terms of our theme, we can see a clear progression in the sequence of Hesse's writing, from the *Bildungsroman* and its emphasis on the individual, to the *Bundennovellen* which takes its center of gravity from *the idea of an Order*.

One of the important discoveries Ziolkowski makes is that the spiritual progress of the protagonist in each novel continues where he left off in the successive novel (i.e. *Demian* develops into *Siddhartha* into the *Steppenwolf* into both *Narcissus & Goldmund*, into the realm of Castalia in *The Glass Bead Game*).[365]

Hesse's writing lodged itself from the start solidly in the *Bildungsroman* or novel of education tradition, a study of the protagonist's development, mainly cultural. Hence, his novels tended to have titles taken directly from the main character, almost parody-like, such as *Knulp* or *Gertrude*; others more exotic, like the perennial potboiler *Siddhartha* or the teen fave *Demian*.

Steppenwolf already marks a change; there is a framing narrator, and the bulk of the novel, titled "Harry Haller's Records," is only a document within the book, which takes its title—*Steppenwolf*—from the narrator's self-imposed nickname, which we will learn is really more of the name of a role he plays, reluctantly, within bourgeois society; the phantasmagorical last third drives home the message that one or even two selves (Harry and The Steppenwolf) is already a gross simplification of an endless stream of personalities.

---

see http://servitorludi.blogspot.com/2013/01/lost-cover-art-bantams-hesse.html. And that chapter about the scholar who goes "native" and retires to a Taoist-inspired hut and garden – cultural appropriation at its worst!

[365] Nelson reviewing Theodore Ziolkowski's insightful study of Hesse, *The Novels of Hermann Hesse* (Princeton University Press, 1965) on Amazon.com. Actually, Dr. Timothy Leary makes the same point in "Poet of the Interior Journey" (*Psychedelic Review*, No.3, 1966, reprinted in *The Politics of Ecstasy*, 1970); he lists the novels and adds: "different versions of spiritual autobiography, different maps for the interior path. Each new step revises the picture of all the previous steps; each experience opens up new worlds of discovery in a constant effort to communicate the vision."

Narcissus and Goldman is something of a step back[366] but the banal back-and-forth chapter structure takes place within the context of a literal Order, as well as the relatively freer but still highly structured society of mediaeval times.[367] By the time of *The Journey to the East* Hesse has his new theme well in hand, basing himself not on the well-known *Bildungsroman* but the more esoteric *Bundennovellen*, of which Jean Paul's *The Invisible Order* and parts of *Wilhelm Meister* are best known in English; both, of course, seminal influences on Hesse.[368]

> Though very different, *the Journey to the East* picks up where Siddhartha left off and captures *a crucial transitional phase on the way to Castalia*. Here, Hesse has actually defined his "Third Kingdom" (Third Reich - a term hijacked by the Nazis to Hesse's chagrin when he stopped using the term), the realm of the spirit; which can only be reached through magical thinking.[369]

Here is where Hesse meets up with Evola: The two post-World War I writers share a number of themes, though what Evola would have called their "personal equation" gave them decidedly different interpretations. *Demian*, for example, treats of initiation, paganism, esoteric knowledge and construction of elites, in ways comparable to

---

[366] It's easily the most boring of the major works, though the always perverse John Simon maintained it was the best.

[367] Another anomaly among the titles, his second book, *Beneath the Wheel*, also takes place within a seminary-type school.

[368] "The *Bundesroman* is German for the lodge or "league novel", a style popularized in the latter half of the 18th century when secret orders such as the Masons were emerging in response to an un-invigorating status quo. ....The common theme is a secret society with a hierarchy of orders similar to the Rosicrucians. There is a Superior who represents the spiritual ideals of the order whose seat is in some mysterious castle or building with archives and secret chambers." - From Christopher Nelson's review of Hesse's *Journey to the East* on Amazon.com. A lengthier description of this type of novel as it related to *Journey to the East* can be found in Theodore Ziolkowski's study, *op. cit.* See also *Hermann Hesse: life and art* by Joseph Mileck, p221. Recent books in the Dan Brown genre might be considered an example of Marx's "repetition as farce," although it might make me sound like a prickly defender of the *Lord of the Rings* genre, and even Germanists refer to the genre as *Trivialroman*.

[369] Nelson, *op. cit.*

Evola's personal investigations with the UR group;[370] but apart from Hesse's overall Jungian lens, his war-derived pacifism would have disgusted Evola. And his Buddha "is certainly not the one depicted by Hermann Hesse in his novel [*Siddhartha*]."[371]

But in the 30s, both Evola and Hesse began to seriously meditate on the post-war need for an Order. Their "personal equation" determined that Hesse would seek an aesthetic, pacifistic Order, Evola a more militaristic one.

Hesse, as we've seen, had already written his "Lodge Novel" in the early thirties. By 1936, according to Ziolkowski, he was already expanding it by adding the idea of a game of ideas to serve as a unifying principle, both for the Lodge and the narrative:

> What is the "Glass Bead Game"? In the idyllic poem "Hours in the Garden" (1936) which he wrote during the composition of his novel, Hesse speaks of "a game of thoughts called the Glass Bead Game" that he practiced while burning leaves in his garden. As the ashes filter down through the grate, he says, "I hear music and see men of the past and future. I see wise men and poets and scholars and artists harmoniously building the hundred-gated cathedral of Mind." These lines depict as personal experience that intellectual pastime that Hesse, in his novel, was to define as "the *unio mystica* of all separate members of the *Universitas Litterarum*" and that he bodied out symbolically in the form of an elaborate Game performed according to the strictest rules and with supreme virtuosity by the mandarins of his spiritual province. This is really all that we need to know.[372]

Well, maybe we need a little more info. This would be the tedious point of explaining the Game, but fortunately for all of us, the intertubes (a sort of Glass Bead Game itself) brings us a chap calling himself Servitor Ludus who has done the job for us:

---

[370] And as recorded in their journal, later reprinted in three volumes, the first available in English as *Introduction to Magic: Rituals and Practical Techniques for the Magus* (Inner Traditions, 2001). See also my "Battle of the Magicians: Baron Evola Between the Druid & the Dancer," *infra*.

[371] Gianfranco de Turris, Preface to *The Doctrine of Awake*ning, p. xv.

[372] Foreword to *The Glass Bead Game*, p. ix (Bantam edition).

People have had trouble explaining exactly what this Glass Bead Game (GBG) thing is all about since Hesse first wrote about it in the 1940s. His novel won the Nobel Prize for literature, despite it being a scathing critique of the academic Ivory Tower literati. The story itself is about a future utopian society, where the world's intellectuals have walled themselves up in monastic orders to study their chosen arts and sciences. Chief among these pursuits is a strange GAME played by the monks that involves making connections between disparate ideas. My favorite quote from the novel, which many other people have also used to describe the game, is as follows:

The Glass Bead Game is thus a mode of playing with the total contents and values of our culture; it plays with them as, say, in the great age of the arts a painter might have played with the colors on his palette. All the insights, noble thoughts, and works of art that the human race has produced in its creative eras, all that subsequent periods of scholarly study have reduced to concepts and converted into intellectual values the Glass Bead Game player plays like the organist on an organ. And this organ has attained an almost unimaginable perfection; its manuals and pedals range over the entire intellectual cosmos; its stops are almost beyond number. Theoretically this instrument is capable of reproducing in the Game the entire intellectual content of the universe.

Heady stuff! Still, Hesse takes it further. There's a new language that has to be invented in order to compare and contrast all of these ideas on equal footing. Also, in this postulated future age, where religion seems like it's lost its hold on people, the GBG becomes a virtual sacrament that delivers deep meaning to its players.[373]

The Game, then, kind of anticipates structuralism, and perhaps also the internet, or at least the idea of hyperlinked texts. But as Ziolkowski observes, this is really a universal idea that Hesse has merely foregrounded for his purposes here.

---

[373] "More about the Glass Bead Game," http://servitorludi.blogspot.com/2011/01/more-about-glass-bead-game.html.

For the Game is of course *purely a symbol of the human imagination* and emphatically not a patentable "Monopoly" of the mind.[374]

And what is that purpose? Significantly, for a character who bills his blog as "Thoughts on Old School Role-Playing Games and Hermann Hesse's Glass Bead Game," the political dimension is missing.

For the scholars do not merely "wall themselves off" for their own purposes, but to serve as a model of the pursuit of truth—or, I suppose, Truth—untainted by commercial or political considerations—and thus, distortions—so that modern Western or European civilization can recover from the intellectual perversions that drove the Age of Wars (what we know as the 20th century).[375]

In short, metapolitics. But a peculiar, idealistic, aesthetical, defeatist kind of metapolitics. Recognizing the impact of ideas on politics, these scholars no longer seek to influence society directly at all; they choose to contribute to society by *not* contributing, other than contributing the example of their own ascetic devotion to the ideal of Truth as a kind of societal Standard Meter Rod that measures nothing—cannot measure anything—but sets the standard of measurement for society's activities.

Well, I think we can see the problem here. As a commenter at Counter-Currents recently noted,

> Castalia was dead, not rigid. The players didn't preserve the "intellectual integrity of a future" as much as they cataloged

---

[374] Indeed, it bears more than a little resemblance to the drug-induced state of "loose cognition" which Michael Hoffman has identified as the basis of religion experience and ritual. Psychedelic experience *a la Steppenwolf* but with strict rules and meditation. My own modest contributions might also be described as attempts to create a Glass Bead Game effect: "Reading James O'Meara is a psychedelic experience." – Jack Donovan, jacket copy for *The Homo and the Negro* (San Francisco: Counter-Currents, 2012; embiggened edition, 2017).

[375] Such perversions are well described by Evola: "a culture, which even when it comes to that which is most sacred to us, like the ancient Roman world, remains confined to the same patterns of a positivistic ignorance, decked out with academic conceitedness, which really belong to the Enlightenment and the rationalistic world of the previous century." See "The SS, Guard & Order of the Revolution of the Swastika," translated at Counter-Currents, September 13, 2016. The significance of this passage in an article on the SS will become clear in what follows.

an old library in slightly novel ways. *As in a modern university (and almost the entire modern world)* all the arts and all original thought were dead. Source material was used as fodder for the Game, not produced or studied on its own merits. *Like Leftists with their many isms (different styles of playing the Game) players filtered everything of value from the past through an inane system with the goal of gaining the recognition of other sterile players and receiving a prestigious post*...This wasn't a problem of rigidity, but of the leveling impulse of bureaucracy and modernity.[376]

Castalia is not the answer to the modern world, but the ultimate form of it, to the extent that the PC university *lumpenstudenten* are seeking to impose its own form on the whole of society: Castalia, the Pedagogic Province,[377] is the ultimate Safe Space.

But so far, we've been unfair to Hesse. Like those who try to create their own Glass Bead Games, to take Castalia as Hesse's utopia is to miss the whole point of the book. As Ziolkowski notes, the ultimate irony of the book is that the Introduction, "The Glass Bead Game: A General Introduction to Its History for the Layman," and which is likely the only part some people read, is a sort of PC, corporate

---

[376] "AE," commenting on "A Castle of the Order." Could "AE" be Evola, who used the pseudonym EA, reborn?

[377] "But apart from being a mild political manifesto, the novel relies on the German philosopher Oswald Spengler's famous *Decline of the West* (*Das Untergangdes Abendlandes*, 1918-1923) in order to define its main categories. ...In Spengler's terms, Castalia is conceived by its author as an ahistorical, artificial society, built on the logic of the spiritual "province". In *The Decline of the West*, Spengler also stipulated an antithesis between two destinies of culture, defined respectively as the culture of the city and the culture of the province. Both represented in their author's mind a way of spiritual survival within the organic process of turning the organic "culture" into a hyper-organized "civilization", which consists the decadent end of each culture. The culture of the city—Spengler asserted—is based on the social logic of the impulsive and faceless mob, which fixes the destiny of cultural evolution by turning it into distraction and intelligence, as contrary to the culture of the province, which keeps tradition alive, preserving its organic vividness through wisdom and originality. Spengler imagined that in a hyper-socialized, incessantly massifying Europe, the spiritual cloistered enclave can be a solution for culture, by the natural tendency of the "cultural province" to produce a highly qualified and dedicated elite. Spengler's idea has always been very familiar with Hesse, whose other great novels—*Demian, Journey to the East, Steppenwolf* or *Narcissus and Goldmund*—have been built on the logic of the spiritual elite." "Hermann Hesse's 'Glass Bead Game'" by Ştefan Borbély; https://www.quora.com/What-is-Hesses-The-Glass-Bead-Game-novel-about

boilerplate brochure written by a full-on ideological believer, who, as the "biography" of Knecht progresses, comes to agree—somewhat —with Knecht, that Castalia is both doomed, and not really worth preserving anyway.

And why is it doomed? Because it has deliberately neglected politics. The over-bred Castalians have come to consider politics as a vaguely dirty necessity, best ignored, an almost ignoble concession to practical life; like the way liberals view the military, or evangelicals sex.

In the two central chapters, "Two Orders" and "The Mission," Knecht is sent to snoop around a Benedictine monastery that has served, over the centuries, as a sort of Bilderberg where world leaders meet up; there he confronts the imperatives of history in his discussions with Fr. Jacobus, a venerable historian (who counsels, however, "a profound distrust of all philosophies of history"). The Castalians arrogantly assume their Order to be an obvious benefit to society – when forced to think of society at all; indeed, perhaps a timeless feature of nature. Fr. Jacobus, however, sees it, like all human institutions (his Church, of course, is created and maintained by God) as fragile structures, each finite and ultimately doomed; despite his "distrust of all philosophies of history," he is a Spenglerian in effect.

> It is through Father Jacobus that Knecht truly comes to understand that the rarefied study of aesthetics and art, divorced from realpolitik, can only end in terminal decline, while pragmatism is the key to understanding how true harmony must be achieved by the synthesis of the discrete world views offered by Castalia, the monastery, the world and the searchers for self-knowledge. Without Father Jacobus, it is likely that Knecht would have remained a successful *Magister Ludi* for the rest of his days, presiding unknowingly over the decline of the organisation he loved. Instead, he renounces his magistracy and, in so doing, saves both Castalia and himself.[378]

---

[378] Tom Conoboy's blog: http://tomconoboy.blogspot.com/2011/04/glass-bead-game-by-hermann-hesse.html.

Another thing that impresses Knecht is the Benedictine Order itself.[379] Though presumably sustained by God himself, its millennial-long survival cannot help but suggest it may know a thing or two that its Younger Brother (to bring back the Chinese scholar's self-deprecating title) could learn about survival.

One obvious difference is the lack of what Traditionalists would call "the vertical" axis. The *lusores* (or "losers" in the ominous slang of *hoi polloi)* have no particular reason to exist, no purpose or goal, other than playing the Game and educating new players (drawn from the pool of students provided by their secular educational institutions). As you'll recall, the Gamers, to use a contemporary term, have divorced scholarship and intellect from political or social concerns, so as to shield both from the intellectual perversions of ideology. But can an Order, or a society, long exist without a goal or ideal?

One might even compare the conceptual knot here to the inconsistency that stands behind another utopian vision, the world of Star Trek, as outlined by Trevor Lynch:

> *Star Trek* combines two incompatible worldviews, both of which appeal to large numbers of people.
>
> First, there is the Faustian quest for exploration and adventure, the desire to see mankind ascend to space and explore the universe...Second, there is liberalism, multiculturalism, and (literal) universalism, which assume that everybody in the universe (except the bad people who wish to cling to their eccentric identities), no matter how apparently different, is basically the same insofar as they can become part of a United Federation of Planets.

[This corresponds to the "universal" language and institutions of the Game.]

---

[379] Another odd synchronicity: Evola stayed in a Benedictine Monastery—in 1930s, when Hesse was writing *Journey and Glass*—but hated the atmosphere and left ASAP. See *The Path of Cinnabar* (London: Arktos, 2012), p133. Fr. Jacobus calls Knecht "arrogant," as Eliade did Evola.

> Unfortunately, as we have discovered since *Star Trek* first debuted in 1966, Faustianism and multiculturalism are not compatible.[380]

Thus Hesse's (or rather, the Castalians' as he conceives them) vision of politics without metapolitics, as well as metapolitics without politics, is, in the literal sense, a utopian vision: a futile illusion.

What then of Evola? Given his aristocratic background and his Traditionalist worldview, it's clear that Evola, like Heidegger, would be equally repulsed by what the latter called the "great pincers" of both Bolshevism and Americanism.[381]

> As today and in the imminent future, a decisive struggle is being waged against the tide of dark forces tied to the symbols of the various internationals.[382]

Yet for the same reasons, Evola could only take a dim view of what we might call "really existing" Fascism and National Socialism, which he saw as insufferably and irredeemably plebian and indeed modernist movements; so *infra dig*.[383]

As John Morgan writes:

> He also saw Fascism as flawed, especially in its socialist aspects —Evola had no tolerance for any form of socialism, whether nationalist or internationalist—but he nevertheless believed that *it had the potential to become something better, especially if it were to become guided by Traditional principles.*

---

[380] See his review of *Star Trek: Beyond* at Counter-Currents, August 24, 2016.

[381] "This Europe, in its unholy blindness always on the point of cutting its own throat, lies today in the great pincers between Russia on the one side and America on the other. Russia and America, seen metaphysically, are both the same: the same hopeless frenzy of unchained technology and of the rootless organization of the average man." *Introduction to Metaphysics*, 40. See Collin Cleary's "Heidegger: An Introduction for Anti-Modernists, Part 2," Counter-Currents, June 5, 2012. For a comparison of the two anti-modern thinkers, see Greg Johnson's "Notes on Heidegger & Evola," Counter-Currents, February 10, 2016.

[382] "The SS, Guard & Order of the Revolution of the Swastika," *loc. cit.*

[383] See the aforementioned post-war books *Notes on the Third Reich* and *Fascism Viewed from the Right,*

Evola had no illusions that he could convert the entire Fascist movement into a Traditionalist one, but he did hope that he might be able *to help to forge a Traditionalist elite within the Party* by influencing some of its intellectuals and leaders.[384]

And so we see that almost simultaneously, during the chaos of the 30s and 40s, both Evola and Hesse began to grope towards the idea of an intellectual and spiritual Order that would rise from the ashes of "the Century of Wars" (Hesse) or the Kali Yuga (Evola) to preserve the fragments of Tradition and pass them on (*traditio*) to a new age.

The conclusion of the Second World War put paid to that idea,[385] and as we've seen, Evola himself would have been about as welcome as Leon Trotsky in the Greater German Reich. Still, as John Morgan writes:

> Although he remained on friendly terms with political activists, it seems that Evola himself gave up on the idea of a political solution to the problems of our age after 1945. His advice, as he offered in post-war writings such as his book *Men Among the Ruins, was to establish orders of elite individuals who could preserve Traditional principles and pass them down through a chain of initiations until an age would return in which their seeds could again bear fruit.* But Evola had no interest in the democratic party politics of our age.[386]

It would seem, then, that the two men, from very different starting points, both gravitated toward the same solution to the problem of modernity—an intellectual and quasi-spiritual Order—while then pursing widely divergent paths.

---

[384] See "What Would Evola Do?", the text of the talk that Counter-Currents editor John Morgan delivered to The New York Forum, Counter-Currents, May 23, 2017.

[385] Interviewer: "And what in your opinion is the tragic element of our epoch?" Celine: "It's Stalingrad. How's that for catharsis! The fall of Stalingrad was the end of Europe. There's been a cataclysm. Its epicenter was Stalingrad. After that you can say that white civilization was finished, really washed up." "The Art of Fiction No. 33," Louis-Ferdinand Céline interviewed by Jacques Darribehaude and Jean Geunot; *Paris Review*, 1960.

[386] "What Would Evola Do?", *loc. cit.*

Hesse, snug in his little Swiss village, begins by imagining an isolated, apolitical, supposedly "spiritual" Order, but as he develops the plot of his novel he—the narrator—and the reader come to learn, along with his protagonist, that metapolitics must be as much politics as it is "meta."

Evola, by contrast, plunges into what we might call "occult politics" in Rome, attempting to create "magical chains" of initiates to influence Mussolini, then writing *Pagan Imperialism* to persuade him to abandon the Catholic Church; stymied, he re-writes it in German as *Heathen Imperialism*, playing up the Nordic content to interest the National Socialists, only to be checkmated again by Himmler's disinterest. Finally, he gets his chance to work with the SS itself, cataloging confiscated Masonic documents in Vienna, where he receives a crippling injury while deliberately wandering the streets during an Allied air raid, spending the rest of his life in his Rome apartment.

As John Morgan writes: "In later life, Evola advocated for what he terms *apoliteia*, by which he meant disengagement from political affairs." A return to Castalian isolation?

It seems we have come full circle, but not quite. As always, in true or Traditionalist metaphysics, the apparent circle is really a spiral, leading not to repetition but to a new level.[387] To paraphrase a well-known remark at the time, he was our Hesse, only better.[388]

But long before Hesse's 60s guru period, he had already projected such a future for his Magister Ludi:

> On the contrary, all the trappings of office, the strictures of rigid Castalian life, they serve only to obscure from Knecht his true purpose. And that, he realises finally, is to teach, to pass on the harmonious understanding of life and existence *to a*

---

[387] See the application of this to topics as various as Henry James and the folly of Western harmonic theory in the essays in my collection *The Eldritch Evola... & Others: Traditionalist Meditations on Literature, Art, & Culture*; ed. Greg Johnson (San Francisco: Counter-Currents, 2014), as well as my film reviews which will be collected in the upcoming collection *Passing the Buck: A Traditionalist Goes to the Movies*.

[388] According to John Morgan, "The leader of the neo-fascist Italian Social Movement, Giorgio Almirante, famously remarked of Evola that he was "our Marcuse, only better.""

new generation, to boys as yet untouched by formal learning and discipline.[389]

Both men had come to learn, each in his own way—Hesse through imaginative projection in the form of a novel,[390] Evola through bitter experience—that what was needed was not an Order, or a League; not another institution no matter how noble in purpose, but rather, something outside of any institution: the primal *Männerbund*, outside of society and the family but necessary for their survival.[391] As in Brian de Palma's *The Untouchables*:

> Malone: [*to Ness as they assemble their team*] If you're afraid of getting a rotten apple, don't go to the barrel. Get it off the tree.

Indeed, at the end of the novel, as Knecht strips down and dives into the icy lake—a rather pointless and ultimately fatal act of daring,[392] intended to somehow inspire his new pupil—we sense we have transitioned primitive and semi-mythical realm; the Narrator's Castalian intellectual conscience requires him to title this chapter of rumors and suppositions about Knecht's fate "The Legend."

Speaking of stripping down and diving in icy lakes, something like this seems to be on Jack Donovan's mind:

---

[389] Conoboy, *ibid.*

[390] As Ziolkowski explains in his Foreword, Hesse had planned several small novellas, but eventually the one set in the future absorbed his attention. Three other completed novellas, set in various past eras and lands, are printed as "Joseph Knecht's Student Writings," under the pretext that Game students are required during their "Years of Freedom" only to write one such work per year. The pious Narrator is quick to point out that these were exercises in imaginative identification with the past, and no literal belief in reincarnation was involved; however, we'll see evidence that Hesse knew what he was playing with, as his own intense involvement with the East would lead us to believe.

[391] See "A Band Apart: Wulf Grimsson's *Loki's Way*" and "'God, I'm with a heathen': The Rebirth of the *Männerbund* in Brian De Palma's *The Untouchables*," both reprinted in *The Homo and the Negro*. As the future M, Judi Dench, intones at the beginning of *The Chronicles of Riddick*: "In normal times, evil would be fought with good. But in times like these, well, it should be fought by another kind of evil."

[392] We might compare it with Evola's "testing his fate" by walking around Vienna during air raids; see his discussion of this in *The Path of Cinnabar* (London: Arktos, 2012).

> I want to be surrounded with people who share not only my vague common ancestry, but my values and beliefs. Anyone who read *Becoming a Barbarian* knows I don't care about "the politics of the Empire." I want to leave it all behind. I just want to hang out in the woods with my friends and build something beautiful—I want to build a new culture. I want to invest in the people I know personally and my family and the people I am oathed to—my tribe, The Wolves of Vinland.
>
> I'm not a White Nationalist, I'm a Wolves Nationalist.
>
> My aim as a writer isn't to get you to support some major political movement or to join mine.
>
> It's to inspire you to find a group of people you'd be willing to say the same thing about.[393]

Seeing the death of Knecht as part of a myth somewhat redeems Hesse's ending, which looked at more prosaically seems to be simply a rather sudden and crude way to end the novel. In the past, I've dismissed such concerns as being merely "genre conventions;" the story is over, and has to end somehow.[394]

But Knecht's somewhat pointless death is actually intended to, as Donovan would say, inspire his pupil, and presumably, the reader as well. How? To answer that, let's go back to Evola; as John Morgan writes:

> In later life, Evola advocated for what he terms *apoliteia*, by which he meant disengagement from political affairs. But if you really examine what he says on the subject, he never advised

---

[393] Jack Donovan, "Why I Am Not A White Nationalist," JackDonovan.com, May 31, 2017; for a White Nationalist response, see Greg Johnson, "A Reply to Jack Donovan," Counter-Currents, June 1, 2017.

[394] When Lily opens the box in *Kiss Me Deadly* (Aldrich, 1955) and turns into a pillar of fire, this is not the punishment of a femme fatale but rather her triumphant apotheosis; Steven Spielberg's homage to this ending, in *Raiders of the Lost Ark*, is rather a crude melodrama where the good guys "don't look in the box!" and live, while the bad guys are liquified. See "Mike Hammer, Occult Dick: *Kiss Me Deadly* as a Lovecraftian Tale" in *The Eldritch Evola, op. cit.*

that one shouldn't become involved in politics. Rather, what he meant is that *one shouldn't become attached to whatever result might come from such activities.* In this, again, Evola is being consistent with what many of the sacred texts have to say on this. So in other words, sure, get involved with a political party or join the military or vote for Trump or whatever, but *do so because it helps you to attain the goals that you set for yourself rather than because you have staked everything on its success and will be shattered if it fails.* In the Kali Yuga, political restoration may not be possible, but the opportunity still remains for the individual to triumph over modernity in his own way. *Besides which, the fact that we may lose the battle doesn't mean that we are absolved of the responsibility of fighting it and standing for what is true.*

The best illustration of this that I know of comes from the *Bhagavad Gita*. At the opening, a Prince, Arjuna, is preparing to fight a battle against an opposing army. Although he knows his cause is just, he hates war, and knows that there are members of his own family on the other side who he may have to kill in order to win. The god Krishna is acting as his advisor. Just before the battle, Arjuna loses his resolve, and tells Krishna that he will put down his weapons and go into the forest to meditate instead of fighting. Krishna basically says to him, "Stop being such a pussy! You're a *kshatriya* (the Hindu warrior caste)! It's your job to do your duty and fight for justice. Meditating in the forest is for *brahmanas* (priests)." The rest of the *Gita* is Krishna explaining the entire metaphysics of existence, and Arjuna's place in it, and at the end, of course Arjuna does his duty.[395]

Knecht's icy plunge is likely symbolic of bravely entering the dangerous waters of phenomenal existence; that he dies doing so is also a lesson: do what is right, because it is your duty, no matter what the cost, and even if it is futile. So are Evola's "men among the ruins," still standing; or Spengler's Roman soldier buried under the ashes of Pompeii because he was never ordered to leave.

---

[395] "What Would Evola Do?" *op. cit.*

It's a message Keven Costner seems to deliver well:

Jim Garrison: "Let justice be done though the heavens fall." [396]

Ness: [*in court*] Never stop, never stop fighting till the fight is done.
Capone: What'd you say? What're you saying?
Ness: I said, "Never stop fighting till the fight is done."
Capone: What?
Ness: You heard me, Capone. It's over.
Capone: [*sneering*] Get out, you're nothing but a lot of talk and a badge.
Ness: Here endeth the lesson.[397]

Counter-Currents/*North American New Right*
June 6, 2017 & June 7, 2017

---

[396] Oliver Stone, *JFK* (1991). William Murray, 1st Earl of Mansfield: *Fiat justitia, ruat coelum.*

[397] Brian De Palma, T*he Untouchables* (1987); script by David Mamet.

BATTLE OF THE MAGICIANS:
BARON EVOLA BETWEEN THE DANCER & THE DRUID

A Constant Reader has called my attention (keep those cards and letters coming in, folks!) to some critical commentary on the magical writings of Baron Evola[398] by none other than John Michael Greer, who is Past Grand Archdruid of the Ancient Order of Druids in America and current head of the Druidical Order of the Golden Dawn. It's entitled "How Not to Learn Magic: An Introductory Note" and you can find it at his blog, The Well of Galabes: Reflections on Druidry, Magic, and Occult Philosophy.[399]

Now, I am neither a Baron[400] nor an Archdruid; indeed, I am not a practitioner of any kind of magic, chaotic or stage, or even Magick.[401]

But I can say I have almost certainly read more by Evola than the Archdruid;[402] and, obviously, made use of it a lot more. Moreover, that interest in Evola has recently proved a valuable

---

[398] Specifically, *Introduction to Magic: Rituals and Practical Techniques for the Magus* (Rochester, Vt.: Inner Traditions, 2001). This is actually only volume one; the other two volume have not appeared in English to my knowledge.

[399] Here at http://galabes.blogspot.ca/2016/07/how-not-to-learn-magic-introductory-note.html. Perhaps some of you, like myself, are already familiar with his other blog, *The Archdruid's Report,* where he posts infrequently reflections on "a wide range of subjects, including peak oil and the future of industrial society," which are as well worth pondering as they are infrequent.

[400] Even a self-styled one like Baron Corvo; see my "E-Caviar for the Masses! Olde Books for the Downwardly Mobile Elite," Counter-Currents, October 15, 2014.

[401] Or as the Druid puts it with deadly whimsy, "the latest oozing-edge products of post-post-*post*modern (insert one: C, K, X)aos magi(insert one: c, ck, k, que)."

[402] "As I paged through *Introduction to Magic,* trying to decide whether to give it shelf space or sell it to the used book store..."

clue to understanding and appreciating what I call America's home-grown Hermeticism, native-born Neoplatonism and two-fisted Traditionalism, New Thought; in particular, the once widely fashionable and now largely—and unjustly—forgotten writings and lectures of Neville Goddard.[403] So although I don't really have a dog in this fight, it does pique my interest, and I think I have a few things I can contribute to it.

Properly, the Archdruid begins by rehearsing his own credentials; it's pretty impressive and nicely written up, so I think it deserves quoting at length:

> From my first tentative dabblings in magic in the mid1970-s until 1994, when I was initiated into the Order of Bards Ovates and Druids (OBOD), I worked pretty much exclusively with the Golden Dawn tradition of practical occultism, as interpreted by Israel Regardie[404] on the one hand, and Dion Fortune and her students W.E. Butler, William Gray, and Gareth Knight on the other. That was partly a choice of necessity, since the Golden Dawn system was very nearly the only thoroughly developed curriculum of occult study and practice you could get in those days – if, that is, you happened to be a geeky young man with very little money, no connections in the occult scene, and no access to occult literature except via a few not very impressive bookstores and the kind of mail order catalogues that carried Anna Riva's Magic Oils, photocopied talismans out of the Key of Solomon, and what passed, in those rather more innocent times, for manuals of racy sex.
>
> Even after I found my spiritual home in Druidry, I continued my Golden Dawn studies and practices. My completion of the OBOD study course in 2001, though, marked a turning point. By

---

[403] See, for example, "The Secret of Trump's A Peale: Traditionalism Triumphant! Or: He's Our Evola, Only Better?," *infra*. There are plenty of accounts of New Thought online but you might do well to read Mitch Horowitz's skeptical but enthusiastic *One Simple Idea: How Positive Thinking Reshaped Modern Life* (Crown 2014). For more on Goddard, see "Magick for Housewives: The Not-So New and Really Rather Traditional Thought of Neville Goddard," *infra*.

[404] A name that will become significant very soon!

that time it was a good deal easier to get access to a wide range of magical instruction, and I'd also picked up a reading knowledge of Latin and French, which opened doors to a range of traditions most people in the American occult scene have still never heard of. By that time, too, I'd worked my way through the Golden Dawn system in its entirety, and while there was still plenty of work there for me to do—you can easily spend an entire lifetime working through the possibilities of any reasonably complex system of magic, and never run out of things to do—I was ready to explore something else for a while.

Exploring something else, in turn, occupied the next fifteen years. I sought initiation in two other Druid orders, and duly became a Druid Adept in the Ancient Order of Druids in America (AODA) and a Third Order priest in the Reformed Druids of North America (RDNA), but my vagaries weren't limited to Druidry by any means. Among other things, I completed extensive study programs in Renaissance astrological magic and old-fashioned Southern conjure, practiced radionics using a homebuilt Hieronymus machine, devoted some serious time to laboratory alchemy, dove headfirst into sacred geometry, geomancy, and both traditional and modern astrology, got competent at two systems of alternative healing with important ties to occultism, and put ten years into earning instructor's credentials in one of the old temple styles of t'ai chi ch'uan.

Then there were the books. My idea of a good time tolerably often amounts to a quiet room and a good book, so I worked my way through most of the occult literature of the western world, from ancient Greek Neoplatonist theurgic writings (thank Zeus for good translations!) straight through to the latest oozing-edge products of post-post-postmodern (insert one: C, K, X) aos magi(insert one: c, ck, k, que). There were plenty of things I never got around to doing—I've never felt the least attraction to Wicca, for example, so I remain cheerfully ignorant about its inner teachings, and a certain discomfort with the role of clueless white guy has kept me from seeking initiation into any of the Third World magical religions available in America these days—but all in all, I think my wanderings managed to give me a tolerably good glimpse at the landscape of possibilities open to the modern occultist.

As I said, pretty impressive, and I approach this response in the spirit of novice monk who may have a bit to add to the Abbot's lesson to the rest of the brothers.

Turning to the Archdruid's critique, one must start with a few generalities.

First, (what I will hereafter call) *Magic* is described—and dismissed—as a book which

> [S]aw print at the peak of the modern occult boom in 2001... made only the tiniest splash in the English-speaking occult scene on its publication, and pretty much sank without a trace thereafter.

The Archdruid gives no evidence for any of this, but hey, it's just a blog post, and it's his blog. Still, that doesn't seem very accurate. I don't know what "the modern occult boom" is or was, and perhaps he has a definition of it that would make 2001 the "peak". As for its tiny splash (like Trump's small hands?) and subsequent sinking, I don't have any facts and figures, but the book is still in print, fifteen years later, which says something in today's accountant-driven publishing field; and we're still talking about it, now aren't we?

As for its tiny reception, the publisher provides a number of quotes which would seem to indicate a fair amount of interest in the "English speaking occult world":

> "Evola...had a clarity of mind and a gift for explaining tremendously difficult concepts in nonacademic language...His descriptions of subtle states and the practices that lead to them are as lucid as these difficult subjects allow." - *Gnosis*

> "The essays of the UR Group constitute the most complete and the highest magical teaching ever set before the public...The

ultimate goal is the identification of the individual with the Absolute. This is a powerful and disturbing book, and a classic. One can be quite certain that it will still have readers centuries from now." – Joscelyn Godwin, author of *Harmonies of Heaven and Earth* [and much more]

"This collection of essays...cover the practical, the theoretical and the unclassifiable, such as the Mithraic Ritual of the Great Magical Papyrus of Paris, the only ritual from the Ancient Mysteries to have survived intact." – *The Watkins Review*, Winter 2001/02

"Introduction to Magic is a collection of intelligent and erudite essays (many of them admirably concise)." – *Hagal*, May 2001

"...should be standard reading for any serious academic or practical student of occultism. ...Experienced occultists will welcome it as a breath of fresh air and a journey into little discussed territories." – Mark Stavish, The Institute for Hermetic Studies, Mar 2006

And no less than two reviews, in 2001 and then in 2002, in *New Dawn*.

Now, some of these journals and authors are unknown to me, but then again, I'm not an expert. But some are known to me, and pretty impressive, and as whole this sampling would indicate someone was reading and appreciating this book. Moreover, as a book scribbler myself, I think I can tell when a book has disappeared without a trace.

Staying with the publisher's page, another point is that the Archdruid seems to think that *Magic* is intended as some kind of beginner's guide to magical practice.

In recent months, several readers of this blog have raised questions about what constitutes an effective and balanced course of magical training, one that guides the student step by step toward the awakening of the higher potentials of the individual without causing the sort of emotional and psychological imbalances so often seen among failed occultists. As I paged through *Introduction to Magic*, trying to decide whether to give it shelf space or sell it to the used book store mentioned earlier, it occurred to me that one very good way to start that conversation is to take a close look at *a system of magical training that is neither effective nor balanced.*

The fact of the matter is that Evola's UR Group was a wretched flop, and the inadequacy of its system of training is a very large part of the reason why…the practical instructions for training given in *Introduction to Magic* are mediocre at their best moments and seriously problematic at their worst.

All this is true, but the insinuation—that *Magic* contains, or provides, or was intended as, a course of training in magic practice—is a bit misleading.

Although the UR group certainly engaged in magical practices, *Magic* itself is simply a compilation, edited by Evola at several later dates, ultimately almost 50 years later, of the articles appearing in the group's journals, *UR* and later *KRUR*. It is a historical record of their activities, not a manual of instruction. It's mostly, as the Archdruid says,

> Philosophical and symbolic essays included in the UR Group papers, which are generally of a very high quality. Evola himself was profoundly erudite, with an extraordinary if one-sided grasp of mystical philosophy.

True, the title, in English and Italian, seems to promise more, and the publisher says that

> This classic Italian text collects the rites, practices, and esoteric knowledge of the powerful and mysterious UR Group *for the use of aspiring mages.*

But I take the sense of "introduction" to be along the lines of "An Introduction to the Study of Pre-Columbian Archeology" or some such title; it "introduces" the reader to a subject he never heard of, but does not promise that after reading you will qualify for an academic post, or be able to lead an exposition. And "for the use of" means no more than edification, or perhaps "as a warning."

Evola's collection is an "introduction" because it is intended to clarify the subject of magic – hence, his rather cringe-inducing use of the term at all; Crowley, for similar reasons, chose to spell the word with a 'k' to distinguish it from stage foolery. It does so by displaying the activities of an actual magical group, the UR Group. As such, readers, such as the reviewers cited above, are likely to be rather enthused about the whole subject; I know I find it far more enlightening than anything of Crowley's.

Moreover, as the Preface by Renate del Ponte warns,

> Although...the monographs in the *Introduction to Magic* provide invaluable material for those individuals who, even today might combine intention *and capability* in order to repeat the experiences of UR and, if possible, surpass its results on a practical level...[405] we would emphasize that the treatises... are *definitely not designed for the general public* but for a few qualified people *who already grasp the precise sense* of the notion put forth....

In other words, don't try this at home. And it's not likely a careful reader would be inclined to do so, since, as the Archdruid notes,

> [A]ccording to the useful preface contributed to the book by Renato del Ponte, two later groups of occultists who attempted to revive the UR Group's teachings crashed and burned in exactly the same way.

One more small preliminary matter: The Archdruid says that

> Evola, for his part, responded to the parallel failure of the UR Group by *turning from magic* to politics. *His entire involvement*

---

[405] "Dear Avid Fan: Inherit my mantle and surpass my achievements." – Dr. Hannibal Lektor to the Tooth Fairy; *Manhunte*r (Michael Mann, 1986).

with magic began and ended in the three years the UR Group functioned, and these were very early in his life—when the UR Group was founded, he was only twenty-six years old. His decision to turn to political action, and from there to cultural politics, was a sensible one.

Now again, this is true but largely misleading. It ignores that when "only twenty-six years old" Evola had already published his philosophical magnum opus, and embarked with some success on careers as a Futurist painter and a Dadaist poet. He did "turn to political action" (though he did not "spent the last part of the Second World War as an officer in the Waffen-SS"), but also to Pali Buddhism, Taoism, Tantrism, the Hermetic Tradition, the Grail legends, and perhaps above all the Traditionalism first adumbrated by Rene Guénon.[406] In short, his esoteric studies continued, whether technically called "magic" or not, and deepened; he did not go into politics after abandoning magic, like some kind of mystical Richard Nixon: "You won't have the Baron to kick around anymore!"

It's odd that the Archdruid fails to note any of this, since it might even help make his major point that

> Since he was not the sort of person who could submit to another's guidance and instruction, he was never going to get the kind of systematic education in magic he needed to accomplish his goals—and the lack of a systematic education in magic lay at the heart of his failure as a teacher of that art.

Evola, the esoteric dilettante. To others, of course, he might just be multi-talented; as always, your mileage may differ.

Speaking of which, and *a propos* Evola's politics, the ArchDruid gives a rousing defense for reading Evola at all:

> It's common these days for biographical data like these to lead people to insist that books by any such author should never be read, discussed, or even mentioned. I consider that attitude to be

---

[406] For Evola's own account, see *The Path of Cinnabar* (London: Arktos, 2009).

somewhere on the notional spectrum between self-defeating and just plain silly. For the serious student of occult philosophy, in particular, an encounter with Evola's ideas and personality—the two are very much of a piece—is essential. This isn't because I agree with the man; I don't. Neither, though, do I agree with a good many of the attitudes and ideas he chose to attack. Evola is among many other things a near-perfect case study in one of the rules of magical philosophy I've discussed here and elsewhere: the principle that, far more often than not, the opposite of one bad idea is another bad idea.

All that said, let's turn to what's wrong with *Magic* when construed as a training manual:

> Turn the pages of *Introduction to Magic* and...setting aside the philosophical and symbolic essays—which again are generally of high quality—and the turgid rhetoric that seems to have been *de rigueur* for occult authors in that era, what you get, in terms of practical work, consists of: (a) standard advice on developing consciousness and will in everyday life, mostly cribbed from Eliphas Lévi; (b) an assortment of exercises in meditation and visualization, not well integrated with one another; (c) a few exercises with a magical mirror, for one or two persons; and (d) a simple ritual centering on Pietro d'Abano's invocation of the archangel of the Sun, *without any of the preliminary training needed* to make rituals work. *As a set of basic practices*, that has serious problems: it leaves out a number of things essential to the novice in operative magic, and it's imbalanced in ways that will produce (and in fact did produce) predictable problems.

Well, as we've said, it's the archives of a magical group, not really intended to be an instruction guide; so yeah, it's not entirely "original" (not that Evola would care about that), it leaves things out, and isn't well integrated.

Be all that as it may, the Archdruid does make a very valuable—indeed, devastating—point:

The fact of the matter is that Evola's UR Group was a wretched flop, and the inadequacy of its system of training is a very large part of the reason why.

It's a failure that stalks everyone who tries to come up with an original system of magical training without first mastering some existing system from top to bottom, and finding out what systems of magical training are supposed to accomplish. *One of the goals of magical training, to turn to technical language for a moment, is the equilibration of the lower self: in less opaque terms, the balancing out of the habitual imbalances of the personality, so that the aspiring mage can use his or her habits of thought and feeling rather than being used by them.* Magical systems cooked up by people who haven't had such a training inevitably miss this; *having projected the habitual imbalances of their personalities onto the cosmos—and we all do this, until appropriate disciplines teach us how to stop—they end up reinforcing their imbalances rather than equilibrating them.*

Evola's choice of *a basic magical ritual* is a good example of this....From a metaphysical and symbolic perspective, it's entirely appropriate to treat the Sun as a symbol of the Absolute, and so Evola *pulled a solar invocation out of its original context in a carefully designed set of Renaissance-era invocations of the planetary archangels, on the assumption that his students could use a ritual based on that invocation to attain the Absolute.*

The difficulty here is that novice mages don't operate on the plane of the Absolute. They operate on the planes of form, and if you invoke the Sun on the planes of form, you won't get the Absolute; you'll get the kind of solar influence that astrologers, for example, know well; and if you invoke the Sun only, without equilibrating it with the other planetary forces, you can pretty much count on pushing your personality in the direction of too much solar influence, which will make you behave like an arrogant blowhard—the astrologically literate may imagine a really out-of-control Leo here. If your personality already tends toward arrogance and self-glorifying egocentricity, furthermore, this fate is going to be all but impossible to avoid, because the energies of the ritual and the dysfunctions of the self form a feedback loop that drowns out the signals that something's gone wrong.

Now, this really caught my eye, because the sun ritual is where Evola and Neville (he always went by Neville, like Madonna or Cher) link up. First, let's look at Evola's sun ritual:

> [B]efore falling asleep, in a calm state, not being tired, having cleansed the mind of all worries, imagine through meditation to be at the foot of a mountain in the early hours of the morning, ready to begin the ascent. Slowly, let the ascent begin, while darkness fades away and the first light, then the sun, appears. You must continue to ascend, imagining the simultaneous rising of the sun in the sky, its growing, triumphant, expanding light shining over all things. Right at the moment you feel you have reached the peak of the mountain, become aware that the sun has reached its zenith in the clear, bright sky. Contemplation needs to be stopped at this point, as you recognize all this as the sense of that which will effectively happen within, beyond the threshold of sleep, until the middle of the night. Naturally, your ascent of the mountain and the rise of the sun from dawn to noon must be felt in strict correlation. Everything must be experienced from an inner perspective as a progression of awakening. This process, once the top of the mountain is reached, must give rise to a sense of identification with the noon light—radiant, silent, pure in the boundless ether.
>
> In the morning, upon waking up, clear the mind from any residue of sleepiness and return through contemplation to the peak of the mountain, which is where you had remained; slowly head back to the valley below. In the meantime, the sun descends, sets, and every light will disappear by the time you reach the plain. This must be imagined and remembered as the meaning of the period between the middle of the night and the

morning. In the darkness of the day, in which you find yourself when you awake, let the echo of the Light from above or the echo of the Midnight Sun linger in the sensation that I am the bearer of this Light that is now in your center, namely in the heart. Then you will notice the new, animated sense, according to which the light of the physical sun will appear when these disciplines are realized and lived. Also, you should notice and pay much attention to any other new meaning that flashes in the midst of common perceptions. Besides mere imagining, try to really recall some of the impressions of that time in which, aside from dreams, consciousness is interrupted by sleep.[407]

Let's compare this to Neville's basic technique, his "simple method for changing the future." Neville *bases his method on sleep* – a kind of "dream yoga." (For him, prayer is only a waking mode of sleep). Here is Neville detailing his method of invoking not the Sun but anything devotedly wished for:

> Preparing to sleep, you feel yourself into the state of the answered wish, and then relax into unconsciousness. Your realized wish is he whom you seek. By night on your bed you seek the feeling of the wish fulfilled that you may take it with you into the chamber of her that conceived you, into sleep or the subconscious which gave you form, that this wish also may be given expression. This is the way to discover and conduct your wishes into the subconscious. Feel yourself in the state of the realized wish and quietly drop off to sleep.
>
> Night after night you should assume the feeling of being, having and witnessing that which you seek to be, possess and see manifested. Never go to sleep feeling discouraged or dissatisfied. Never sleep in the consciousness of failure. Your subconscious, whose natural state is sleep, sees you as you believe yourself to be, and whether it be good, bad, or indifferent, the subconscious will faithfully embody your belief. As you feel so do you impress her; and she, the perfect lover, gives form to these impressions

---

[407] *Magic*, pp. 55-56.

and out-pictures them as the children of her beloved. "Thou art all fair, my love; there is no spot in thee," is the attitude of mind to adopt before dropping off to sleep. Disregard appearances and feel that things are as you wish them to be, for "He calleth things that are not seen as though they were, and the unseen becomes seen." To assume the feeling of satisfaction is to call conditions into being which will mirror satisfaction. "Signs follow, they do not precede." Proof that you are will follow the consciousness that you are; it will not precede it.[408]

It should be no surprise then, that Neville's method has been called "the most magical" of all the systems of New Thought. But being the Ur-American New Thought, it's a very stripped down, to the point, no bullshit kind of magick. You may find that attractive; I certainly do.

But what might be a surprise is that the man who said that was: Israel Regardie, the Archdruid's mentor.[409]

So when the Archdruid says that Evola's "system" "leaves out a number of things essential to the novice in operative magic, *and it's imbalanced in ways that will produce (and in fact did produce) predictable problems*," it's interesting that Israel Regardie brings exactly the same criticism—mildly—to Neville.[410]

First, the lack of preliminary training. He attributes Neville's own success with his "simple method for changing the future" to his training—as well as his presumed natural talent—as a professional dancer.[411]

---

[408] *Feeling is the Secret, op. cit.*

[409] See Mitch Horowitz, ed.: *The Power of Imagination: The Neville Goddard Treasury* (New York: Tarcher/Penguin, 2015). This not only collects 10 of Neville's short books, but reprints the relevant chapter from Israel Regardie's *The Romance of Metaphysics* (1946).

[410] *Romance of Metaphysics*, cited from Horowitz (ed.), *The Power of Imagination: The Neville Goddard Treasury*.

[411] "[T]he fundamental psychological factor in Neville's teaching, [and] the fundamental fact about Neville himself… is a very simple fact: Neville is a dancer" (Regardie, *op. cit.*). Not only is Neville's stage training an important part of his method, I would add that as a dancer Neville is symbolically linked to Krishna, who "from time to time" reincarnates to "re-establish the Dharma" as the Bhagavad Gita says. From Krishna to Alain Danielou,

This is what enabled Neville to achieve, without appreciable effort, states of tremendously profound relaxation, without actually dropping off into sleep and unconsciousness.[412] And this is exactly why Neville never provides, and seems never to have seen a need for, elaborate instructions and training methods so as to bring his listeners up to his level. One can only assume that the ones with natural ability—like those who supposedly make "good" subjects for hypnosis—found the method worked, while the rest gave up after a few failures.

More generally, there's the criticism of imbalance; psychic imbalance. Regardie criticized Neville's neglect of the unconscious; it is the unconscious that is the source of our desires, which are "outpictured" as the world around us. One the one hand, it is futile to try to impose our conscious desires, using Neville's method, when the far more powerful unconscious has other ideas; on the other, it may be wrong to try to override those unconscious desires, since *they may be trying to tell us something*. Before trying to "become a success" perhaps you should find out just why you *really* want to be a failure.

This, I think, clearly syncs up with the point made by Regardies' student, the ArchDruid: the need, before embarking on a magical career, of getting the lower self in order.

So, what do we have here? Two systems of magic, neither of which really works unless you've already gotten yourself psychically straighten up. Pretty useless, then, eh?

Well, maybe not. I think there's a kind of trap door, or a trick, in both systems, and in Crowley's system as well. Hey, they call it magic, right?

Take the latter; Crowley's magick, inducing changes in the world through will, only works if you have achieved the Knowledge and Conversation of the Holy Guardian Angel. Having identified your

---

the dancer has always been an archetype of the Realized Man. Clifton Webb was also originally a Broadway dancer, making him the perfect choice to incarnate Krishna in the Mr. Belvedere movies. See my essay "The Babysitting Bachelor as Aryan Avatar: Clifton Webb in *Sitting Pretty*, Part Two," Counter-Currents, February 5, 2013.

[412] Neville occasionally tells stories—like Jesus, his favorite method—where he seems to be able to drop into such states at will, at the drop of a hat, if you will, and then snap out of them after only a few moments, but having accomplished all his set tasks.

will with that entity, it is that entity's will that magick instantiates. "Not my will, but Thine, be done." As Augustine, not Crowley, said, "Love and do what thou wilt." As Crowley would say, not only "Do What thou wilt" but "Love is the Law, Love under Will."

As Alan Watts said, the Westerner thinks that if you say, I am God, then you should be able to "prove it" by doing random, meaningless things like make lightning strike. But if you are God, what you want to do is exactly what's happening now all around yourself and within yourself; you've simply chosen to get out of your own way.

Now, getting back to Evola and Neville, both systems require the practitioner to invest an enormous emotional commitment to object of desire. Evola:

> Another technical detail is in order. *In order for any image to act in the way I am talking about, it must be loved.* It must be assumed in a great, inner calm and then warmed up, almost nourished, with sweetness, without bringing the will or any effort into play, and much less without expectations. The Hermeticists called this agent "sweet fire," "fire that does not burn," and even "fire of the lamp" since it really has an enlightening effect on the images.[413]

And Neville? Neville no doubt enjoyed fluttering the dovecots of his ladies-who-lunch listeners with his risqué reading of the *Song of Songs*. Many have wondered what on Earth it has to do with the "wise" Solomon to whom it is attributed; Neville reveals that it is, in fact, the key to the Bible itself, and his method:

> What more beautiful description of this romance of the conscious and subconscious is there than that told in the "Song of Solomon": "By night on my bed I sought him whom my soul loveth [3:1]...I found him whom my soul loveth; I held him and I would not let him go, until I had brought him into my mother's

---

[413] "Commentary on the *Opus Magicum*," *op. cit.*, p. 57. "The fire of the lamp" recalls Neville's "You must be like the moth in search of his idol, the flame." Again, Dr. Lechter comes to mind: an investigator muses over one of Buffalo Bill's tell-tale *moths*: "Somebody grew this guy. Fed him honey and nightshade, kept him warm. Somebody loved him." *Silence of the Lambs* (Jonathan Demme, 1990).

house, and into the chamber of her that conceived me" [3:4].

Preparing to sleep, you feel yourself into the state of the answered wish, and then relax into unconsciousness. Your realized wish is he whom you seek. By night, on your bed, you seek the feeling of the wish fulfilled that you may take it with you into the chamber of her that conceived you, into sleep or the subconscious which gave you form, that this wish also may be given expression.

This is *the way to discover and conduct your wishes into the subconscious*. Feel yourself in the state of the realized wish and quietly drop off to sleep.

Night after night, you should assume the feeling of being, having and witnessing that which you seek to be, possess and see manifested. Never go to sleep feeling discouraged or dissatisfied. Never sleep in the consciousness of failure.

Your subconscious, whose natural state is sleep, sees you as you believe yourself to be, and whether it be good, bad or indifferent, the subconscious will faithfully embody your belief.

As you feel so do you impress her; and she, the perfect lover, gives form to these impressions and out-pictures them as the children of her beloved.

"Thou art all fair, my love; there is no spot in thee" [Song of Solomon 4:7] is the attitude of mind to adopt before dropping off to sleep.[414]

Note: the way *to discover* as well as to conduct your wishes into the subconscious. Again, not some random, "show off your magic powers" wish, but literally our heart's inmost desire. And once it is discovered, we know it is God's will for us, since it is He who placed it there. We can "make changes in accord with our will" because our True Will is, in fact, God's will for us; we only need to discover it, and then get out of the way.

---

[414] *Feeling is the Secret*, op. cit.

So if you must find a "system" of magic expounded in Evola's book, I suggest it can be defended from the charge of ignoring, as Regardie would say, the importance of getting in touch with the unconscious as an essential preliminary; at least, the materials are there, if read against the much clearer presentation given by Neville, the "most magical" of the New Thought teachers.

And this is why I regard New Thought, for all its trailer park hucksterism, to be superior to all the "magickal" systems; no robes and chants and waiving wands around; just a continuous attitude of gratitude (Wallace Wattles) and positive thought (Norman Vincent Peale, Trump's guru) directed toward what we confidently expect God to provide.[415]

Not surprisingly, Neville seems to have had the most successful life of the three (especially in the very American terms of the New Thought). Marriage and family, living in swanky hotels and apartments, lecturing in New York and San Francisco to sell-out crowds, even a TV show! He also tells stories of successes ranging from getting tickets to a sold-out performance at the Met to getting out of the Army.[416] The rather dismal later lives of Evola, and especially Crowley, are well known.

But is this a fair, or relevant, issue? Evola points out in *The Hermetic Tradition* (one of those many works the Archdruid fails to mention) that we cannot judge the mage's accomplishments by his life on this plane; he may be hiding, or he may suffer from "boomerang" effects in this world from his activities in another. Above all, he has risen above all concern for material shows and

---

[415] "Faith is the underlying reality of things hoped for, the proof of things unseen." Hebrews 11.1; "He need only petition God, the one who gives to everyone unstintingly and without asking embarrassing questions, and it will be given him. Only let him be sure to ask in faith, without ambivalence, for the doubter wavers like the tossing of the sea, driven and tossed by the wind." James, 1. 6-7 (From Robert M. Price's *The Human Bible*; see "Lovecraft's Bible: Robert M. Price & the [Un]-Making of the New Testament," Counter-Currents, May 26, 2015).

[416] Horwitz has verified a number of these, including the story of how he dreamed his way out of the Army. Official records show he was honorably discharged in 1942, *and* awarded American citizenship, in order to, as the discharge paper say, "conduct important wartime activities in civilian life" – giving lectures in New York.

material gain; just the psychic "adjustment" ("so that the aspiring mage *can use his or her habits of thought and feeling rather than being used by them*") demanded by the Archdruid.[417]

After all, it is Neville, after a lifetime of success, who is largely forgotten today; except for a few rarified souls, which happy band now includes…you.

Counter-Currents/North American New Right
July 29, 2016

---

[417] *The Hermetic Tradition* (Inner Traditions, 1995), "The Invisible Masters."

EVERYTHING YOU KNOW IS WRONG![418]
EMERICUS DURDEN'S PHILOSOPHICAL FIGHT CLUB

"I don't want to be a product of my environment. I want my environment to be a product of me." – Frank Costello, *The Departed*

Who is Emericus Durden? At first, literally the first few minutes at most, I automatically assumed it must be a pseudonym, referencing *Fight Club*'s Tyler Durden. This was reinforced by the photo purporting to be the "author," whose style (surely deliberately, as he purports to be a photographer as well) rather resembles the avatar used by "Tyler Durden," the moderator of the financial blog ZeroHedge.

Being a natural born cheapskate, the best part of the kindle revolution is the plethora of books cheaper than hard copies would be, even if available at all, and liable to sudden, unexplained drops to $0.99 or even less; a plethora so multitudinous that I subscribe to an email alert service to notify me of sudden price reductions.

So when a kindle entitled *Aiming Higher Than Mere Civilization: How Skeptical Nihilism Will Remind Humanity Of Its Long Forgotten Purpose*, by one bearing the name Emericus Durden, and costing zero, zip, nada, appeared on my update, I could not stand to live another minute before downloading and examining it.[419]

---

[418] "Dogs flew spaceships! The Aztecs invented the vacation! Men and women are the same sex! Our forefathers took drugs! Your brain is not the boss! Yes, that's right – *everything you know is wrong!*" Firesign Theatre. *Everything You Know Is Wrong*. Columbia Records, LP - KC-33141 (1974).

[419] *Aiming Higher Than Mere Civilization: How Skeptical Nihilism Will Remind Humanity Of Its Long Forgotten Purpose* (Emericus Durden Philosophy Series Book 1) by Emericus

According to his Amazon page,

> Mr. Durden strives to create works that are intellectually challenging, perhaps even disturbing, though always exciting, suspenseful, and entertaining. In his writings, Mr. Durden has focused on a wide variety of topics, ranging from the sublime—philosophy and spirituality (e.g., "Aiming Higher Than Civilization") to the much more hellish—murder and brainwashing (e.g., "Two Heads Equal Two Hands" and "Great & Mighty Things").

Since a lot of this Alt-Right literature I've been looking at recently indeed seems to gravitate around the hellish, I was glad to take a break from all the nerds and losers and attend to something more sublime.

The book certainly tries to rise above the usual hipster nihilism of today:

> The book represents an attempt by Emericus Durden to sum up, codify, and present in clear language a practical method of allowing each and every human being to rise above their own humanity, surpass the norms of civilization, and become a higher being.

Specifically,

> The goal of this book is to wake people up – to awaken them from the sleep of their most cherished beliefs and allow them to become the sole authorities over their own lives.

Waking someone requires disturbing them, and of course *"no one likes to be disturbed, and therefore everyone resists being awakened;"* especially when they *believe they, and only they, are right about themselves.* [Durden's italics].

Perhaps as an enticement, Durden adds that not only will grasping this point benefit the reader "far more than you can imagine," but if that reader continues on, completing not only

---

Durden; Radical Academic Press, 2014.

the book but practicing the exercises provided, the reader will be transformed into "something else beyond humanity."[420]

You might think that sort of thing would be attractive, but you would be wrong. To become something beyond humanity is terrifying to almost everyone, since it contradicts everything we have been taught, seemingly "destroy[ing] all human knowledge and truth."

First, awakening implies that there exists a higher realm, independent of human beings or indeed of any biological organism, immaterial, beyond the reach of scientific research, instruments, or devices. But the rejection, or more precisely, the relativization, of the god Science is anathema (think of the squawking of Dawkins, Hawking, and other intellectual scolds).

Secondly, there is the implication that you can gain access to that immaterial realm, become a higher being yourself, and that of course runs afoul of our so-called "Judeo-Christian heritage."

And finally, transforming yourself into this Higher Thing implies that

> *You can create whatever world or reality you exist in*, based on your inner vision, imaginations, and the focused intentions underlying beliefs you *choose*.

And that, as the reader may have already exclaimed, contradicts plain old common sense.

So far, we are on solidly Traditionalist ground: the refusal to restrict knowledge to that which is revealed by the scientist's gauges, the corresponding appeal to a kind of higher empiricism that rejects religious "faith" in favor of "work on self" with the aim of attaining higher states of being, and the world-creating powers of that higher being, the Realized Man or *Chakravartin* at the Center of the Garden or the axis of the World Tree, are well documented in the works of Guénon and Evola.[421]

---

[420] "If you were never a special person, you are a special person now." – Firesign Theatre, *op. cit.*

[421] Evola, in particular, given his focus on practical methods of realization; see his *Introduction to Magic: Rituals and Practical Techniques for the Magus* (Inner Traditions, 2001) and *The Hermetic Tradition: Symbols and Teachings of the Royal Art* (Inner Traditions,

Speaking of Evola, Durden also deals with the pesky accusation of elitism in an especially Evolian tone of voice:

> Democracy and democratic ideals are second only to scientific progress as my favorite "punching bag" of skeptical nihilism.
>
> Once awakened however, we become part of a "higher" order. So let's be honest here – the awakened ones form a kind of aristocracy in the sense they have a superior ("higher," "transcendent") perspective on humanity compared with the sleepers.

Indeed, Evola's defense of the Traditional notion of an Elite is based almost entirely on it comprising the members of a spiritual Order whose Authority is legitimized by their access to transcendental realms, vouchsafed to them by their ascetic practices;[422] while, conversely, the justification of a Traditional society is its ability to produce and sustain such Orders (rather than, say, the good of the greatest number, progress, *la gloire*, *Lebensraum*, and other paltry materialistic aims).

Indeed, Durden then goes full Kali Yuga on us:

> A fourth implication of the idea is that centuries of so-called "progress" have, in fact, been quite the opposite, a steady retrogression and reduction in our creative abilities. Rather than a belief we are the active creators of the world we exist in, we have, in the name of progress, chosen a belief ... *that we are reactive participants in a universe govern by impersonal, random physical forces.* [Durden's italics]

Durden wants us, the sleepers, to wake up, by realizing that, contrary to what we've been told our lives long, our much vaunted "knowledge base" is actually "a field of persuasion and disposable beliefs, leaving us without a foundation of truth."

1995). From the former:"Those who are called "scientists" today have hatched a real conspiracy; they have made science their monopoly, and absolutely do not want anyone to know *more* than they do or in a *different* manner than they do." (p. 4)

[422] Danielou remarks somewhere that far from the invidious picture of the Brahmin lording it over the lower castes, the Sudra laughs at the Brahmin, who cannot enjoy a nice juicy steak and must spend all day reciting boring scriptures.

JAMES J. O'MEARA

Although he immediately brings up Nietzsche, I find his language here extremely reminiscent of the Grand Old Man of that boring old school of analytic philosophy, Willard Van Orman Quine, who famously dismissed the whole idea of our knowledge having "foundations" composed of empirical "data" uncontaminated by the theories to be proved by them, or of "logically true" propositions that no one could doubt; instead, there was a "web of belief" in which any proposition, however "central," could be rejected if one were willing to make drastic enough adjustments elsewhere.[423]

Quine, I understand from those unfortunate enough to have been his teaching assistants, was not one to suffer fools gladly, and I can only imagine the disdain with which he would greeted any darwinomaniac, student or the Oxford "Professor of the Public Understanding of Science", who suggested that the acceptance of a mere biological theory like natural selection was the criterion of rationality, to say nothing of the stern warning that an increase of .000128 ppm in atmospheric CO_2 will bring about global disaster.

To get back to the "method of skeptical nihilism," it basically consists in itemizing all our beliefs, (especially the "core" beliefs such as "there is no higher realm of being" or "only science produces knowledge," etc.), then locating their origins in "a particular place and time, unavoidably limited by history and locale," and then concluding that they are "necessarily lacking in any universal qualities." And then reminding oneself that such half-assed beliefs are "not any more deserving of your respect and admiration than any other." Repeat as necessary until you recognize "your total detachment from beliefs and habits" as manifested in "a state of awareness devoid of fear, hope, and desire."

This sort of "genetic" skepticism is often associated with Nietzsche,[424] but although Durden mentions Plato and Descartes as forerunners of his method, it really seems to originate with the

---

[423] Quine, W.V.O., "Two Dogmas of Empiricism," *The Philosophical Review* 60: 20–43. Reprinted in *From a Logical Point of View* (Harvard, 1953). This "paper [is] sometimes regarded as the most important in all of twentieth-century philosophy" – Peter Godfrey-Smith, *Theory and Reality (University of Chicago,* 2003), pp. 30-33.

[424] e.g., his *Genealogy of Morals* (1887).

Greek Skeptics, such as Sextus Empiricus.[425] Hence, therefore, "*skeptical* nihilism."

Rather than getting into this millennia-long discussion, readers are encouraged to try what Durden rather grandiosely calls his "exercises" for themselves; their mileage may vary from his or mine. What's more interesting is his next move.

Durden immediately sets himself apart from "all those brilliant thinkers…from Descartes through Hume to Nietzsche, Wittgenstein and the postmodern philosophers" by pointing out that nihilism is "very useful if you know what to do with it and how to act on it."

Here again, we find Durden sounding like Evola, who lauded Nietzsche for his very useful destruction of bourgeois complacency, while mourning his lack of access to the transcendental dimension that would have given his whole project a telos in the beyond, and prevented his tragic destiny.[426] Thus "nihilism" is not really the right word for this, although it does still have a sexy ring in some quarters. We might call this "completed nihilism" or "integral nihilism," as per Evola.

"Cologero" makes a similar point in this context:

Nietzsche needs to be adapted to Tradition, not the reverse. This is what Evola tries to do. …. In the Traditional view, the world, too, is absurd, since it is the result of an illusion or a fall. *The task, therefore, is self-transcendence, to overcome the world. Yet, Nietzsche's naturalism does not recognize any such transcendence; hence, the world can only be overcome by more power. Unfortunately, that is a Sisyphean task and can only lead to insanity…*

Evola rejects the "revolution of nothing" and claims that Nietzsche is merely using rhetorical techniques to appear

---

[425] My view of the Sceptics, especially Sextus Empricus, derives from a reading of *Scepticism* by Arne Naess (Universitetsforlaget, 1968), rather than the rather duller works of classical scholars such as Michael Frede or Myles Burnyeat. See *David Hume and Contemporary Philosophy*, edited by Ilya Kasavin (Cambridge Scholars Publishing, 2013), p58, Notes 1-2 for a discussion of Naess vs. Burnyeat

[426] See *Ride the Tiger: A Survival Manual for the Aristocrats of the Soul* (Inner Traditions, 2003) especially Part 2: In the World Where God Is Dead.

shocking or sensational. His real target, in Evola's view, is really "petty morality" and "herd morality", *in order to make room for the higher morality of the superman*. It should not be necessary to point out, however, that many Nietzscheans today *simply stop at the point of idol smashing and immoralism*, i.e., those who cannot *recognize any higher principle within themselves*. I suppose this is the "danger" that Evola refers to.[427]

Durden is clearly on Evola's side here, proposing that "*what we will do with nihilism here…is use it as a tool to transform ourselves.*" [Durden's italics] When all our beliefs—*all*—are firmly out of play, we will become aware of ourselves as being really, always already, an immaterial, timeless center of pure awareness.

And just as nihilism is incomplete without that transformation, so the transformed being, as Plato recognized, is incomplete without his return to the social realm, which can now be reconstructed in an optimal manner, based on a new set of "core beliefs" free of the restrictions of scientism, faith, and "common sense."[428]

It's useful, I think, to dwell a bit on some aspects of his portrait—apparently from personal experience—of the Higher Being and its lifestyle.

One odd point is his going to the trouble of pointing out that there are

> [N]o indications that [his] awakening caused the human organism to vanish or become modified in some unpredictable way…it does not affect the general appearance or functioning of the human organism.

---

[427] "Evola and Nietzsche, 40 Years Later," by "Cologero;" Gornahoor.net, December 31, 2012.

[428] Evola's interest in Guénon's Tradition was sparked by the idea that his previously arrived at notion of the Absolute Self could be grounded in historical reality by being identified with the primordial lawgivers of Tradition; see *The Path of Cinnabar* (London: Arktos, 2009). See also the discussion of how the Realized Man reconstructs his own new, immortal Diamond Body (Tantric Buddhism; cf. St. Paul's resurrection body) in *The Hermetic Tradition*.

"Functioning" might address the rather mundane concern about physical well-being, rather like those New Age books that have a preface about not being a substitute for medical advice, etc.[429]

Otherwise, it seems to be directed at Guénon's idea that the Realized Man, having transcended the conditions of space and time, would essentially resolve into a point and then just disappear, like a three-dimensional creature in *Flatland*.[430] If Guénon is right, it would appear that Durden has not achieved the ultimate level of transcendence.

What he purports to have achieved, however, seems consistent with the best accounts of so-called "mystical" experience:

> Because awakening from the *dream* of your beliefs puts you into contact with a "higher" inner reality, *your attention or awareness is now "split," as it were, between two realities*, the higher reality you "discover" using this book's exercises and the lower, human reality you have experienced since birth. The way you access the higher reality is through internal processes like imagination, feeling, *contemplation* and meditation.

This picture of the Realized Man's conscious awareness taking place on two, simultaneous levels, one recognized as relatively "dreamy" and the other, higher level accessed through a process of contemplation, is easily recognized as a recapitulation of Plotinus.[431]

As is the next point, the more you give attention to the higher, or inner, reality, the more you realize that, contra Dawkins, *"it is the inner reality that gives rise to the outer reality."*[432]

---

[429] In Salinger's *Franny and Zooey*, Franny's doltish boyfriend, Lane, listening to her narrate her spiritual crisis, observes that "you could do some real damage to your heart" by synchronizing it, as suggested by *The Way of the Pilgrim*, to recitation of the Jesus Prayer.

[430] I think this is towards the end of his *Introduction to the Study of the Hindu Doctrines* (Ghent, NY: Sophia Perennis, 2001).

[431] See *Plotinus' Psychology: His Doctrines of the Embodied Soul* by H.J. Blumenthal (The Hague: Martinus Nijhoff, 1971) and *Nature, Contemplation and the One: A Study in the Philosophy of Plotinus* (University of Toronto Press, 1967; Paul Brunton Philosophical Foundation, 1991), by John N. Deck (who taught a popular "gut" philosophy course entitled "Dream Worlds and Real Worlds"); see especially "Is Nature "Real" For Plotinus?"

[432] See Deck, *op. cit*, especially "Making and Efficient Causality." It's important to note

While the Traditionalist will agree with Durden's validation of higher realities, one place Durden goes off the rails in that perennial (if you will) bugaboo, reincarnation.

> Our identity, then, is located *forever* in the higher reality, not in the lower reality where human organism exists. And if we do choose a human experience, we will *unavoidably* be at the mercy, so to speak, of core beliefs 1 through 4 (and only those beliefs, not one more, not one less). [Italics Durden]

> The nonphysical point of awareness may enter, exit and reenter human experience as many times as it chooses. This process we might call "reincarnation." *The tendency to choose the same human experience over and over again*...we might call "karma." The opposite tendency of choosing a series of *widely different human experiences* we might call "consciousness expansion." Indeed, the intentional exploration of *a wide variety [of] human experiences* could itself comprise a science of sorts, though one quite different in its structure and assumptions form physical science. [Italics mine]

Indeed, there is such a science, and it is very different from physical science. It's called "metaphysics," at least as defined and practiced by Guénon. In that light, he is correct to emphasize that the nature of the experience chosen depends on what he calls "core beliefs," which here correspond to what Guénon would call the "conditions of three-dimensional existence" (space, time, and extension). Unfortunately, Durden, as he repeats almost obsessively, seems to be completely hung up on "human" experience, to which the reincarnating spirit is assumed to return, varying only in the *type* of human experience chosen; however "widely" it may vary, it is still recognizably *human*.[433]

---

that this does not involve a cliché "dreamy" or "otherworldliness;" historians record how Plotinus was sought after for practical advice and even toke over the guardianship of several orphans; Durden notes that the "mundane daily decisions of an awakened one" are "no longer based n selfish desires and needs" but on higher laws; this is what makes ordinary consciousness, by contrast, the true 'dream world.'"

[433] At least Durden resists the especially New Age fantasy of reappearing as an animal or plant. In *The Big Chill*, an admirer of the group's dead pseudo guru Alex reminisces that

Here we see, as so often before, the spiral replaced by the circle; rather than exhausting the possibilities of a human existence, and then circling back—*at one higher degree of pitch to the screw*—into an entirely different type of existence, with utterly unimaginable conditions of experience, Durden, and so many "new agers" like him, imagines that any such "return" would be a circling around back to the same place.[434]

Understandably, Durden swings between Nietzschean nihilism, for maximum academic hipster cred, and occasional hints that all this can be found in the mysterious East,[435] to appeal to the hippie types. His method, examining and discarding all beliefs as "relative," recalls Nietzsche in its appeal to history and psychology, but the basic method can be found in the epistemological disputes of the Greek Sceptics. The latter, however, seemed to think that once all opinion was silenced, a state of *ataraxia* would ensue, whose blissfulness was in itself a goal.[436] Durden, fitting his pseudonym, has a different goal: to change oneself, and then to change the world.

Actually, as I've pointed out before, all this can be found already in our native Neoplatonism, our home-grown Hermeticism, our two-fisted Traditionalism, the New Thought or Mind Cure movement (aka "The Secret") from the turn of the previous century.

"He believed in reincarnation. He never ate meat. He said he was afraid he would come back someday as a steak." See my essay on *The Big Chill* as a initiatory drama, "Of Costner, Corpses, & Conception: Mother's Day Meditations on *The Untouchables* & *The Big Chill*," reprinted in *The Homo and the Negro* (San Francisco: Counter-Currents, 2012; embiggened edition, 2017).

[434] "And the same shit starting all over again" – Karl Marx. See the letter explaining, and gently critiquing, Guénon's position by Marco Pallis in *Studies in Comparative Religion*, Vol. 1, No.1..

[435] Referencing among others Nagarjuna (see T. R. V. Murti's *The Central Philosophy of Buddhism* (1955; Routledge, 2008), whom Alan Watts liked to pair up with St. Dionysius as masters of the negative way seeks to "remove obstacle to the direct experiencing of reality;" see his translation of the latter in *Alan Watts–Here and Now: Contributions to Psychology, Philosophy, and Religion* by Peter J. Columbus and Donadrian L. Rice (SUNY, 2012), p. 69; and see my review, "There & Then: Personal & Memorial Reflections on Alan Watts (1915-1973)," *supra*.

[436] Why bliss, rather than sheer terror, was the result of skepticism is a mystery, to me at least.

Like these more academically respectable systems of thought, New Thought relied on the notion of a creative Spirit or Consciousness behind the material world, and accessible by each of us by withdrawing within ourselves. Each of the New Thinkers, in line with their penchant for self-reliance, had their own method to establishing this connection, which provide interesting parallels to Durden's methods.

Christian Larson, for example, favored a transcendental approach rather the more contemporary nihilism; our ability to control our thoughts now and then proves that we have a point of view superior to them, which can be accessed at any time and therefore at all times.

For example, in *Mastery of Self: How To Develop Your Inner Forces And Powers* (1909), Larson urges his readers to abandon the "position of influence" in which our mind, and thus our reality, is shaped by external influences (Durden's "core beliefs") and instead assume the "position of self-mastery":

> Your supreme idea should be that you are above it all, superior to it all, and have control of it all. You simply must *take this higher ground* in all action, thought and consciousness before you can control yourself and direct, for practical purposes, the forces you possess...And though this phase of the subject may appear to be somewhat abstract, we shall find no difficulty in understanding it more fully as we apply the ideas evolved. In fact, when we learn to realize that *we, by nature, occupy a position that is above mind and body*, this part of the subject will be found more interesting than anything else, and its application more profitable. (Chapter 2)

In the first chapter of *Mastery of Fate* (1910) Larson writes that

> When man thinks what he desires to think, he will become what he desires to become. But to think what he desires to think, he must consciously govern the process through which impressions are formed upon mind.
>
> To govern this process is to have the power to exclude any impression from without that is not desired, and to completely

impress upon mind every original thought that may be formed; thus giving mind the power to think only what it consciously chooses to think.[437]

Before man can govern this process, he must understand the difference between the two leading attitudes of mind – the attitude of self-submission, and the attitude of self-supremacy; and must learn how to completely eliminate the former, and how to establish all life, all thought, and all action absolutely upon the latter.[438]

When this is done, no impression can form upon mind without man's conscious permission; and complete control of the creative power of thought is permanently secured.

To master the creative power of thought is to master the personal self; and to master the personal self is to master fate.

This "State of Self-Supremacy" corresponds to Durden's Highest Being. In both cases, the road to true freedom is to realize that we are free already, only at the moment we have allowed ourselves to be bemused by the ideas forced on us by society (Stirner's "spooks"[439]).

There is such a thing as being influenced by conditions that exist in our surroundings; but when we transcend that influence we are in it no more; therefore, to say that we are in it when we are out of it, is to contradict ourselves. And we equally contradict ourselves when we state that we are controlled by environment after we are convinced that we are inherently masters of everything in the personal life.

---

[437] Training the mind to slow down awareness until impressions can be felt, and judged, before allowing them to enter our consciousness, is a basic initiatic practice; see Evola, *Introduction to Magic*, op. cit.

[438] "I have founded by affair on nothing" – Goethe, and the epigraph to Stirner's *The Ego and His Own*.

[439] See my review, "The Sad, Sour Spook: Max Stirner & His Proper Ties;" Counter-Currents, August 8, 2017.

> While you are conscious of the principle of self-supremacy, you are unconscious of the influence of environment; therefore, to speak the truth, you must declare that you are complete master in your own domain.[440]

More recently (post-WWII), Neville Goddard (d/b/a "Neville"), the Alan Watts of New Thought (with a bit of Criswell thrown in), also sounds the Durden note in a more positive, less "nihilistic" way:

> If I can *deny the limitations of my birth, my environment, and the belief that I am but an extension of my family tree,* [abandon all "core beliefs"] and feel within myself that I am Christ [the "Higher Being"], and sustain this assumption until it takes a central place and forms the habitual center of my energy [as we'll see, Durden emphasized the need to enliven that center by concentrating our feelings on it], I will do the works attributed to Jesus [rebuild the world in accordance with new, or at least newly chosen, ideas]. *Without thought or effort I will mold a world in harmony with that perfection which I have assumed and feel springing within me.*
>
> Any enlargement of our concept of Self involves a somewhat painful parting with strongly rooted hereditary conceptions. The ligaments are strong that old us in the womb of conventional limitations. All that you formerly believed, you no longer believe. You know now that there is no power outside of your own consciousness.
>
> A transformation of consciousness will result in a change of environment and behavior. However, our ordinary alterations of consciousness, as we pass from one state to another, are not transformations, because each of them is so rapidly succeeded by another in the reverse direction; but whenever one state grows so stable as to definitely expel its rivals, then that central habitual state defines the character and is a true transformation.

---

[440] Not that there's anything wrong with that.

Neville simplifies the initial process, from skeptical argumentation to simply choosing to believe what you want to be:

> Assume you are already that which you seek and your assumption, though false, if sustained, will harden into fact.[441]

But Neville and Durden both emphasize that the process requires far more than the relatively simple first step (the college freshman's "It's all relative, man" or Oprah's "Just believe it"). Durden says that

> Finding that state of identity with a higher reality, *feeling it, then sustaining it over time* takes a tremendous amount of concerted effort, and it's very subtle work. [My italics]

In Neville's case, the suggestion is not only to simply assume what you want to be, but to hold it in your mind, adore it, feed it, keep it warm, until it becomes a reality in the physical world.

> Concentrated observation of one thing shuts out other things and causes them to disappear. *The great secret of success is to focus the attention on the feeling of the wish fulfilled without permitting any distraction.* All progress depends upon an increase of attention. The ideas which impel you to action are those which dominate the consciousness, those which possess the attention.
>
> To the unenlightened man this will seem to be all fantasy, yet *all progress comes from those who do not take the accepted view, nor accept the world as it is.* As was stated heretofore, if you can imagine what you please, and if the forms of your thought are as vivid as the forms of nature, you are by virtue of the power of your imagination master of your fate.
>
> Your imagination is you yourself, and the world as your imagination sees it is the real world.[442]

---

[441] Neville Goddard, *Five Lessons and Q & A*, Chapter Two.
[442] *The Power of Awareness*, Chapter Six

All of which recalls the "Three Ways" discussed in an essay by "Abraxas" (Ercole Quadrelli) collected by Baron Evola in the first volume of his *Introduction to Magic*.

> You must generate—first by imagining and then by realizing it—a superior principle confronting everything you usually are (e.g., an instinctive life, thoughts, feelings). This principle must be able to control, contemplate, and measure what you are, in a clear knowledge, moment by moment. There will be two of you: yourself standing before "the other."

Then, in contrast to the mystical, or Christian, path, where the Principle remains Other, and the Self remains in the feminine position of need and desire,

> In the magical, dry, or solar way, you will create a duality in your being not in an unconscious and passive manner (as the mystic does), but consciously and willingly; you will shift directly on the higher part and *identify yourself with that superior and subsistent principle*, whereas the mystic tends to identify with his lower part, in a relationship of need and of abandonment.

> Slowly but gradually, you will strengthen *this "other" (which is yourself)* and create for it a *supremacy*, until it knows how to dominate all the powers of the natural part and master them totally. [Then,] the entire being, ready and compliant, reaffirms itself, digests and lets itself be digested, leaving nothing behind.[443]

All of which is to suggest that Durden is incorrect to claim that

> This is the first time, so far as I know, anyone has used this sort of reasoning as a means to a higher end rather than as a logical parlor trick ending in exclamations like "Well, there you

---

[443] Julius Evola, *Introduction to Magic* (Rochester, Vt.: Inner Traditions, 2001), pp. 88-91. The process of "cultivating" the Other as part of the process of initiation is referenced in *The Silence of the Lambs*, where Buffalo Bill cultivates a rare species of moth: "Somebody grew this guy, fed him honey and nightshade, kept him warm. Somebody loved him."

have it—everything is relatively true – there are no absolutes—anything goes."[444]

Or, to put it more positively, he's in the mainstream of esoteric thought.

Speaking of "mainstream," Europeans like to mock Americans' "self-help" obsessions, but it's a perfectly European trait, or rather, a Roman one. Despite all the guff about "democracy" on the one hand (Athens) and the "shining city on a hill" (Jerusalem) on other, Americans have always turned to Rome for serious matters, from our capitols and Senators to the fasces decorating the wall behind the Speaker of the House.

The Greeks of course knew about philosophy as a way of life,[445] but it was the Romans who demanded practicality in all things; under Roman domination, even the Greeks looked more to solace than theory.[446]

Speaking of Stoics and Epicureans, Durden makes an interesting contrast with Lovecraft. The weird author regarded all religious or philosophical ideas of meaning and purpose to be

> Very largely the accidental results of traditions rather than basic antidotes, as we may see by comparing the mods of different types and individuals – older and younger, unsophisticated and sophisticated.

Sounding very like Durden, Lovecraft insists that to have "any chance of holding any genuine opinion of value regarding the universe" requires a "slow and painful process of courageous disillusionment."

---

[444] A knock against Paul Feyerabend's "anarchist theory of knowledge," which he summarized as "The only rule of science is 'anything goes'"?

[445] You could read Foucault on this, but you'd be better off reading Pierre Hadot, such as his *Philosophy as a Way of Life: Spiritual Exercises from Socrates to Foucault* (Wiley-Blackwell, 1995).

[446] The classic work on how much life sucked under the later Empire is, of course, E. R. Dodds, *Pagan and Christian in an Age of Anxiety: Some Aspects of Religious Experience from Marcus Aurelius to Constantine;* (Cambridge, 1991 [1965]). In general, see *The Cambridge History of Latin, Greek and Early Mediaeval Philosophy*; edited by A. H. Armstrong (Cambridge University Press, 1967).

Lovecraft, however, derived his ideas less from the Skeptics or Stoics than from the Atomists, like Lucretius, from whom he learned a materialistic, scientific "skepticism" that confined itself to questioning religious dogmas rather than itself.

> What most persons can rationally expect is a kind of working adjustment or resignation in which active pain is cut down to a minimum...the highest consistent and practicable goal of mankind is simply an absence of acute and unendurable le suffering – a sensible compromise with an indifferent cosmos which was never built for mankind, and in which mankind is only a microscopic, negligible, and temporary accident. This is the most which the average person will ever get out of life, and he might as well trim his sails accordingly.[447]

Lovecraft never examined his own prejudices,[448] which are also a part of Durden's relativized "core beliefs."

Thus, for Lovecraft, the superior man is someone who is honest and brave enough to face oblivion without religious comforts ("I desire only oblivion"). To Evola or Durden, thus would be admirable enough but incomplete, since scientism and "common sense" (Lovecraft's "local traditions") are left in place; thus, like Nietzsche, we can call this "incomplete" nihilism, needing to supplemented by something like Evola's hermetic tradition or Durden's Absolute Being.[449]

Ironically, Lovecraft, for all his Anglo-Saxonism, would not

---

[447] *Lord of a Visible World: An Autobiography in Letters* by H.P. Lovecraft, S.T. Joshi (Ed.), David E. Schultz (Ed.), (Ohio University Press, 2000), pp. 302-04.

[448] Starling to Lechter: "You see a lot, Doctor. But are you strong enough to point that high-powered perception at yourself? What about it? Why don't you. ...Why don't you look at yourself and write down what you see? Maybe you're afraid to." Dr. Lechter recommends Marcus Aurelius to Starling when giving here the clue to Buffalo Bill's identity. Joshi notes that the Skeptics DID question themselves.

[449] The suggestion that Lovecraft's "indescribable horror" is actually what a later generation of less uptight seekers would call "the ultimate high, man" has been developed by Erik Davis (see my review of his *Nomad Wandering infra*) and used by myself to contrast Lovecraft and Evola in the title essay of *The Eldritch Evola...& Others*. For a more completely skeptical approach to Science, though also without any necessary connection to transcendence, see Paul K. Feyerabend's "epistemological anarchism",

be considered by Evola as having a truly Aryan attitude in this. In the chapter on "Discernment of the Vocations" in his *Doctrine of Awakening*, Evola notes that the Aryan does not, as the American Buddhist/hippie cliché has it, react to the perception of the relativity (as Durden would say) of our beliefs about the world with "pain" or "suffering" and seeking an escape, but with sovereign contempt for mere Becoming and a thirst for true Being (as Durden would say). Lovecraft's comfy Epicureanism is a relatively degenerate attitude.[450]

So it really comes down to whatever works for you. Durden writes well; no fancy touches, just good solid philosophical prose, meaning that anyone with a college degree, let's say, should be able handle this. You might think the New Thinkers are too earnest and old-fashioned, but I rather find them comforting.[451]

On the other hand, you may prefer Durden's more up to date version of what the kids might call "hacking your brain,"[452] finding ways to avoid the prison of existing programing (Durden's "core ideas" such as "only what empirical science can prove is real"); or, as the anarchist collective Crimethinc say,

> Putting yourself in new situations constantly is the only way to ensure that you make your decisions unencumbered by the nature of habit, law, custom or prejudice – and it's up to you to create the situations.

Counter-Currents/North American New Right
May 8, 2015

---

[450] Evola, in *Doctrine of Awakening*, is keen to promote what scholars call Early or Pali or Hinayana or "primitive" Buddhism as authentically Aryan, regarding the later Mahayana schools as popularized and degenerate; thus he confines his attention to the earliest presentations of the doctrines. Durden, however, as noted above, finds the Mahayana school of Nagarjuna to be *simpatico* with his project.

[451] They kinda remind me of Prof. E. C. Buehler, who appears in many educational shorts of the 50s, such as "Speech: Using Your Voice" (Centron, 1950). (And don't miss Centron regular Herk Harvey; in about ten years, he'll be filming *Carnival of Souls*!) I like reading them out loud as if they were being delivered in his earnest, Dale Carnegie voice. "One, you must be heard. Two, you must be understood. Three, you must be pleasing." Hey, it makes as much sense as Durden's insistence on using a comfy chair.

[452] A phrase I owe to the blog Practical Application of Neville Goddard Principles Today (http://nevillegoddardnow.blogspot.com/).

LORDS OF THE VISIBLE WORLD:
A MODERN RECONSTRUCTION OF AN ANCIENT HERESY

> As with many ancient teachers of whom we only know about through their accusers, we must read between the lines in examining his system. – Luis Varady[453]

> Conjecture about things not meant to be known, "to explain what ancient authors deliberately concealed," is risky at best. – Robert Conner[454]

Despite a superficial gloss of rebellion and "History" Channel romanticism, the Gnostics themselves are a tough sell. Expositions tend to be either dry as dust academic pinhead-dancing, or else New Age hokum hoping to ride on the coattails of the aforementioned glamour—"Now it can be revealed—by me!"

Partly it's due to the Gnostics, being the losers in the great theological wars of the early AD's, having had their writings torched, in typical Christian fashion, and consequently being known to us only through quotations in the "refutations" of their enemies.[455]

---

[453] *A Life Beyond Change – the Gnostic System of Carpocrates* by Luis Varady (Amazon Kindle, 2015).

[454] *Secret Gospel of Mark: Morton Smith, Clement of Alexandria and Four Decades of Academic Burlesque* [sic] by Richard Conner (Amazon, 2014).

[455] Cioran says somewhere—perhaps *The New Gods?*—that after reading one of the orthodox denunciations of some heretic or pagan, its level of cultural and spiritual foulness would make any reader immediately go over to the Gnostic side.

Over the last hundred or so years, more and more "gnostic" texts[456] have become available—even leading to a "Gnostic Bible"[457]—but even with issuing the texts themselves the same shoals of academic embalming and New Age exploitation rear themselves again.

The discovery and study of the new Gnostic materials was largely an affair of German scholarship, and consequently they had a high profile in NS Germany: Alfred Rosenberg relied heavily on the doctrines of the Gnostics, and especially the example of their alternative canon of scriptures, both in *The Myth of the XXth Century* as well as his attempts to concoct a "Pagan Christ" suitable for his "German Church."[458]

They also rode with others in "Lucifer's Retinue," the "good spirits" of Europe's past that Himmler sought to disinter with the help of Otto Rahn, his personal Indiana Jones.[459]

An essential problem is that these Gnostic chaps, at least the ones literally bedeviling the Christians, though un-orthodox, never the less were still working in the same medium. That is to say, these are an alternate set of gospels, epistles and apocalypses, and just as turgid and borderline-sane as the "official ones."[460]

---

[456] The word itself is, typically, subject to enormous academic huffing and wheezing, leading some scholars to call for it to be forcibly retired from the field. As will become clear, I'm talking about "Christian Gnostics" or "Gnostic Christians," not Persian dualists, Manicheans, Ranters, Levellers, etc.

[457] *The Gnostic Bible: Revised and Expanded Edition* by Willis Barnstone (Boulder, CO: Shambala, 2009).

[458] See "Gnostic Origins of Alfred Rosenberg's Thought" by James B. Whisker, *The Journal of Historical Review*, Fall 1983 (Vol. 4, No. 3), pages 335-355; as well as his *The Social, Political and Religious Thought of Alfred Rosenberg* (Bethesda, MD: University Press of America, 1982).

[459] See Rahn's *Luzifers Hofgesind, eine Reise zu den guten Geistern Europas* (1937), *Lucifer's Court: A Heretic's Journey in Search of the Light Bringers*, translated by Christopher Jones (Rochester, VT: Inner Traditions,2008) and *Otto Rahn and the Quest for the Grail: The Amazing Life of the Real "Indiana Jones"* by Nigel Graddon (Adventures Unlimited Press,2008). "Rahn also equates heretics such as himself (a baptized Catholic) and the Cathars, for example, with the Luciferian tradition, the "Light Bearers." The SS saw themselves in this role and their insignia represented two lightning bolts of Thor. In terms of the Occult, the Luciferian tradition represents the middle path between Satanism and Yahweh – in other words, Lucifer is seen as a sort of Pagan-Christ." - Review by JE Farrow at gnostics.com.

[460] It's always wryly amusing when some standard Christian, scholar or journalist, pooh-poohs some rediscovered text, like the *Gospel of Judas*, as "fittingly excluded from the canon

This is somewhat connected with the notion of the Gnostics teaching a "secret doctrine" of some sort. Partly, of course, due to their eventual suppression by the orthodox as soon as they attained secular power, it's also, I think, another specific trait.

Hebrew has a script so primitive that it lacks both vowels and numerals; the rabbis have made a virtue of this, and have arrogated to themselves the power to "interpret" the "real" meaning of any given word—and hence passage—by supplying a different set of vowels, based on some "oral tradition" supposedly handed down from Moses;[461] or, taking advantage of the use of consonants for numerals, "summing up" the letters of words as if they were equations, then substituting "equivalent" words (*gematria*). [462]

Carpocrates of Alexandria himself made use of a supposed *Secret Gospel of Mark*, which is attested to by Clement, also of Alexandria, though the surviving texts of the latter don't contain actual quotes. Morton Smith, a professor of ancient history at Columbia, claimed to have rediscovered the portion Clement quotes in 1958, spending the next 15 years studying and translating it. Despite—or because of—being endorsed by both academic poohbah Jacob Neusner *and* up and coming guru Bubba Free John (aka Adi Da among other sobriquets), the jury is still out on whether Smith was one of the great Biblical archeologists, a Borgesian trickster, or a disgruntled homosexual trying to forge a scriptural backing for his lifestyle.[463]

---

because of its crazy ideas." Unlike, I suppose, the New Testament? Richard Conner gives an excellent summary of the chaotic welter of texts generated by the turbulent Christians in "Faking Jesus," online here: https://www.scribd.com/doc/125993290/Faking-Jesus#scribd.

[461]   For example, the tribal god's name, YHVH, was never to be pronounced (except by the High Priest, in the Holy of holies, on Yom Kippur), so the phrase "my Lord" (Adonai) was always used in reading; to make this clear, the vowels of the latter were added to the former wherever it appeared in printed texts, thus leading later Christians to think the name was (the impossible form) "Jehovah"!

[462]   This sort of double-talk is the root of Christ's rejection of the Pharisees: "For laying aside the commandment of God, you hold the tradition of men – the washing of pitchers and cups, and many other such things you do." (Mark 7:8, KJV).

[463]   In terms of our previous distinction of dusty academics and New Age hokum, *Clement of Alexandria and a Secret Gospel of Mark* (1973) falls into the first group; *The Secret Gospel* (1973) the second. For the subsequent brouhaha, see *The Secret Gospel of Mark: Morton Smith, Clement of Alexandria and Four Decades of Academic Burlesque* by Robert Conner (2014). Conner comments that "Although the question of authenticity remains unresolved,

So, between lost texts, invidious commentary by enemies, secret doctrines, and Semitic double-talking, the Gnostics are a tough sell.

Comes now this Varady chap, unknown to me and with no apparent internet presence (other than his half dozen or so short little kindles), and offers us a clear, interesting interpretation of the teachings of Carpocrates of Alexandria (founder of an early Gnostic sect from the first half of the 2nd century).

A search of my (admittedly unrepresentative) kindle discloses about 7 titles with references to Carpocrates, and they illustrate the Rashomon Effect in action.

Not surprisingly, the most references are in *The Essence of the Gnostics,* one of those illustrated little gift books for History Channel fans; for example:

> Carpocrates believed in magic and taught that fornication was in order.

> Carpocrates claimed that we are all imprisoned in a cycle of reincarnations by wicked angels, but we will eventually be saved. In order to leave this world, the soul has to pas through every possible condition of earthly life, or it cannot free itself from the material powers. This view is very similar to that of Buddhism.

> Carpocrates is a favorite of Lawrence Durrell, referencing him in both the *Alexandria Quartet* and the (thematically Gnostic) *Avignon Quintet.*

> [Alexandria] has always thrown up one religious libertine— Carpocrates, Anthony—who was prepared to founder in the senses as deeply and truly as any desert father of the mind.

> ...working over those huge parchment tomes, lost in the non-world of Carpocrates – the negative of the printed world we had

---

the controversy has opened a window on the intellectually corrupt nature of apologetic New Testament studies, a subject of greater importance than the authenticity of early Christian texts" since "The case against Smith has advanced over the past four decades on the basis of homophobia, conspiracy theory, amateur forensic demonstrations and repeated misstatements of fact."

thought we knew well, but which now seemed a delusion, and all the more dangerous because it was so enticing.[464]

The Illuminati, no strangers to rumor themselves, state bluntly:

> Carpocrates believed that the route to heaven was to commit every conceivable sin.[465]

And speaking of the Illuminati, the Gnostics in general are always a bugbear, from quasi-reputable scholars like Vogelin ("Immanentize the eschaton!") to conspiracy hounds like Nesta Webster:

> Another Gnostic sect, the Carpocratians, followers of Carpocrates of Alexandria and his son Epiphanus—who died from his debaucheries and was venerated as a god—likewise regarded all written laws, Christian or Mosaic, with contempt and recognized only the γνῶσις or knowledge given to the great men of every nation—Plato and Pythagoras, Moses and Christ—which «frees one from all that the vulgar call religion» and «makes man equal to God.» [466]
>
> So in the Carpocratians of the second century we find already the tendency towards that *deification of humanity* which forms the supreme doctrine of the secret societies and of the visionary Socialists of our day. The war now begins between the two contending principles: the Christian conception of man reaching up to God and the secret society conception of man as God, needing no revelation from on high and no guidance but the law

---

[464] From *Monsieur*; Durrell also blurbs the City Lights edition of Jacques Lacarrière's quasi-scholarly *The Gnostics*.

[465] *Nietzsche: The God of Groundhog Day (The Divine Series Book 3)* by Michael Foust (Kindle, 2014).

[466] Thus, Guénon and the other Traditionalists are often slighted as "Gnostics" with Tradition being the gnosis common to all religions and which makes man a god. Guénon himself seems to have used Gnostic memes only in such very early essays as "The Demiurge" (reprinted in *Miscellane*a [Ghent, NY: Sophia Perennis, 2003]) and for most of his career seems to have shared the usual orthodox aversion to "gnostics." Unlike his epigones (e.g., Huston Smith), Guénon did not consider the exoteric/esoteric to be operant in every Tradition, but mainly in the Semitic ones, for the reasons we've alluded to above.

of his own nature. And since that nature is in itself divine, all that springs from it is praiseworthy, and those acts usually regarded as sins are not to be condemned. By this line of reasoning the Carpocratians arrived at much the same conclusions as modern Communists with regard to the ideal social system.[467]

Well, you see the PR problem.

By contrast, Varady presents, according to the Amazon page,

> A detailed but concise description of the long lost Gnostic system of the Christian Gnostic Carpocrates, giving his teachings on God, reincarnation, magic, salvation, the nature of Christ and how one may realize the ultimate truth.

Early on, Varady gives us a handy summary of the system, such as we can recover it, of Carpocrates:

> The one source of all being, the unbegotten Father, emanates lesser beings distinct from himself. Over time, as these lesser beings become ore and more distant from the unbegotten Father's original purity, they take on malevolent forms and a group of them—Abolus and his angels—take it upon themselves to create the cosmos and bind other emanated beings therein, in hopes that they endlessly reincarnate.[468] The task of salvation, therefore, is to undo this deed and return to the world of the unbegotten Father. And after all experiences have been transcended, one can return to the primordial state. The role of Jesus was to teach this same path.[469]

Varady is not the first to notice there are some problems with this. Why does the perfect produce the imperfect? Why does Good

---

[467] *Secret Societies and Subversive Movements* by Nesta H. Webster; innumerable editions.

[468] "*What scared you all into time?* Into body? Into shit? I will tell you: *"the word."* Alien Word *"the."* *"The"* word of Alien Enemy imprisons *"thee"* in Time. In Body. In Shit. Prisoner, come out." – William S. Burroughs, *Nova Express: The Restored Text* (New York: Grove, 2014), p. 4.

[469] In Alan Watts' terms, the Gnostics teach the religion of Jesus, not, like the orthodox, the religion *about* Jesus, the unique Son of God (and thus, as Watts' points out, a freak).

produce Evil? Why do the devils persecute us, and why does the Father permit it? And so forth.

Since we are here to understand, rather than anathematize, Varady tries to find a coherent picture by presenting what might be called a psychological interpretation of Carpocrates – but that would be misleading, suggesting some kind of Jungian reductionist angle.[470] "Experiential" might be better, especially if we keep Evola in mind.[471]

Reflecting on our experience, we see that it is also quite irrational. That is, in experience, there is nothing prior to it, which can offer a reason or rationale or *raison d'etre*. Since we can experience nothing prior to experience, experience is, indeed, unbegotten. Like the Unbegotten Father, it is the prior potential of all subsequent experience; and since it is *us* at our own deepest level, we and the Father are one.[472]

And, in the same way, we can see that though our experience starts out pure and blissful as consciousness itself, as it expands in space and time it become increasingly ensnared in the fears and delusions that emanate from the mind itself; this is delusion.

This leads to a psychological, or experiential, understanding of karma and reincarnation; each thought leads to and conditions another thought, spiraling—or rather, circling, an important distinction as we'll see—endlessly.

Yet there always remains a way out; there is always The Seer himself, the deepest and most necessary level of our consciousness, which observes but is not these experiences. How then, can we rise

---

[470] "Jung interprets Gnosticism the way he interprets alchemy: as a hoary counterpart to his analytical psychology. As interpreted by Jung, Gnostic myths describe a seemingly outward, if also inward, process which is in fact an entirely inward, psychological one." Richard Segal, "Jung and Gnosticism," in *Religion* Volume 17, Issue 4, October 1987, pages 301–336.

[471] See the discussion of the role of experience in science and mysticism, as opposed to Semitic "faith," in "The Nature of Initiatic Knowledge," reprinted in *Introduction to Magic: Rituals and Practical Techniques for the Magus* (Rochester, VT: Inner Traditions, 2001)

[472] "Who is Number One?" "You are...Number Six." "I am not a number, I am a free man!" (Hysterical laughter in response). "Six of one, half dozen of the other." "I I I I! I I I I!" – various quotes from *The Prisoner*. See Collin Cleary's meditations on the TV show in his *Summoning The Gods* (San Francisco: Counter-Currents, 2012).

(or sink) to the level of the Seer, and become free of the pain and evil of entrapment in experiences?

Here's where Carpocrates' bad reputation arises. But before getting there, where is Jesus in all this?

> Jesus was sent by the unbegotten Father to be born into a conducive environment by natural means yet with full knowledge of what occurred in the upper regions prior to time.[473]

But for Carpocrates, Jesus was not some God-Man sent to redeem us by faith; he also taught the real story (the secret gnosis) to his disciples:

> He taught the real science of salvation, and how to overthrow the authorities of the cosmos.

Rather than believing *in* Jesus,

> The life of Jesus could be looked upon as a symbolic form of what must occur in the life of each individual.

> What must occur is remembrance (*anamnesis*), remembering who we really are.

> Knowing this and using such knowledge (gnosis) as a means of liberation, one completes the same cycle that Jesus completed, and becomes free.

An interesting wrinkle here is that in addition to suggesting that Jesus had a secret or at least more profound teaching, the Carpocratians also believed there was deeper aspect of the "miracles." Rather than just material trickery like changing water into wine, or even healing the sick,[474] there was also "psychological and spiritual miracle working…Jesus had the power to take the passions of human beings and eradicate them."

---

[473] As Number Six, the Prisoner, is repeatedly sent into the Village, each time with more and more knowledge of how it works and how it can be defeated.

[474] Shaw, following Ibsen, pointed out that the miracles, far from "guaranteeing" the message, were actually the biggest stumbling block; no real teacher would resort to such mountebankery.

This aligns Jesus far more with the Eastern *guru*, or the Hermetic Magus, and uncovers a new level to the Gnostic distaste for the Jewish scriptures:

> If one reads the Old and New Testaments, salvation is always portrayed as something exterior—a place one goes after death—and revelation, also, is the unveiling of spiritual truth to a person by an external agent. Yet it is not the spiritual truth of oneself, but rather of events which will come to pass, or the nature of heaven and hell. We never see an angel or God showing a person what the true nature of the soul is, or eradicating their deluded inclinations directly. Everything is outside and pertains to time and space.[475]

In all this, we can see how Carpocrates' system aligns itself not with Judeo-Christian "faith" but with the heroic striving of the Northern or Hermetic Traditions, as well as the Tantric schools of the Hindu and Chinese Traditions.

We can also see how to overcome the biggest puzzle of the Carpocratians. As we've seen, according to the orthodox heresy-hunters, the Carpocratians believed that one had to undergo all possible experiences, in order to transcend them all and thus achieve liberation from the prison of the material world. In particular, they were accused of engaging in every kind of horrifying and revolting practice.

As Varady notes, this is absurd; a moment's thought reveals that no mortal creature could acquire every possible experience, good or bad.

Things become clear, however, when we recall that the Gnostics, unlike their orthodox brethren, are part of the Western tradition of Hermetic Magic.

By using incantations, images, dream control and other methods,

---

[475] We'll see, *infra*, that Neville Goddard also disparaged the idea of the Bible as literal history, as a distraction from it actually being a psychological biography of the reader himself.

> the Carpocratians sought to overpower the forces of the created universe and demonstrate their freedom from the cosmic prison.
>
> Magic is the opposite of prayer...Magic is active and serves to confound the forces of nature, compelling them to align with the magician's wishes.
>
> We could imagine that the Carpocratians were practicing a form of dream magic where they called up in their minds certain specific dream scenarios for the purposes of transcending them.

Indeed, Varady suggests that here lies the origin of the seemingly tiresome phantasmagoria of the Gnostic cosmologies:

> Spiritual traditions rooted in dreaming would likely look very similar to old Gnosticism, incorporating rich mythologies and dramas, mystical pantheons and fragmentary cosmologies.

The use of images is especially interesting, as it ties back to the notion of a Gnosticism as an active, Western tradition versus the passive, Semitic nature of orthodox Christianity. Evola in fact explains the differences between the "dry" and "wet" paths by considering the use of images. The pupil first constructs an image of his ideal Self, concentrating all his thoughts and will on it. In the wet path, the duality remains, the Self is worshipped from afar; while in the dry path, one attempts to gradually achieve unity, to become the Self.

> You must generate—first by imagining and then by realizing it—a superior principle confronting everything you usually are (e.g., an instinctive life, thoughts, feelings) [This is the bondage of experiences]. This principle must be able to control, contemplate, and measure what you are, in a clear knowledge, moment by moment. There will be two of you: yourself standing before "the other."

All in all, the work consists of a "reversal": you have to turn the "other" into "me" and the "me" into the "other."

Then, in contrast to the mystical, or Christian, path, where the Other remains Other, and the Self remains in the feminine position of need and desire…

In the magical, dry, or solar way, you will create a duality in your being not in an unconscious and passive manner (as the mystic does), but consciously and willingly; you will shift directly on the higher part and identify yourself with that superior and subsistent principle, whereas the mystic tends to identify with his lower part, in a relationship of need and of abandonment.

Slowly but gradually, you will strengthen this "other" (which is yourself) and create for it a supremacy, until it knows how to dominate all the powers of the natural part and master them totally. Then, the entire being, ready and compliant, reaffirms itself, digests and lets itself be digested, leaving nothing behind.[476]

And thus, as we have seen, in the orthodox sects Jesus is the unique Self, worshipped by the unworthy believer, so as to obtain the boon of salvation—like a waiter hoping for a tip—while for Carpocrates and the other Gnostics Jesus is the one who brings a technique which each of us can use for ourselves, so as to become one with him and thus with the Unbegotten Father.

Thus, through magic, the Gnostic magus becomes "able to control, contemplate, and measure what you are, in a clear knowledge, moment by moment;" in short, mastery, and thus transcendence, of all experiences in space and time. And this is equivalent to Liberation:

> By demonstrating magical power, the gnostic also demonstrates that they are no longer in bondage to the cosmic authorities,

[476] Julius Evola, *Introduction to Magic* (Rochester, Vt.: Inner Traditions, 2001), pp. 88-91. Actually, this essay, "The Three Ways," is attributed to an author with a very appropriately Gnostic pseudonym: "Abraxas." The process of lovingly "cultivating" the Other as part of the process of initiation is referenced in *The Silence of the Lambs*, where Buffalo Bill cultivates a rare species of moth: "Somebody grew this guy, fed him honey and nightshade, kept him warm. Somebody loved him." I consider this process of imaginal magic in the context of two Hollywood films in my essay "Of Costner, Corpses, & Conception: Mother's Day Meditations on *The Untouchables* & *The Big Chill*," reprinted in my collection *The Homo and the Negro* (San Francisco: Counter-Currents, 2012; embiggened edition, 2017).

and if Gnostics should possess within themselves the power to control events on the material plane, they may also possess the power to transcend matter entirely. In fact, [the two powers] both derive from the same mystic source.

According to the Christian heresiologists, the gnostic adepts claimed to be "lords over even the wicked angels that made the cosmos," the Royal Priesthood that Evola—contra the contemplative Guénon—considered to be the truly primordial condition of Man.

I find this aspect of Carpocrates' teaching—or Varady's version of it—especially interesting, as it seems to offer an historical parallel to some notions I've been finding—or applying to—various movies: endless repetition of experiences—the circle of Samsara—until an escape can be found upward—the circle becomes a spiral[477]—and the related notion, that as this Liberation is beyond the polarity of good and evil, so is the means: any method, such as magic or murder, is fair game, including one I've called "passing the buck," in which ones karma is unloaded on a willing or unwilling sucker.[478]

Varady is not free of the New Age hokum impulse, of course. He's eager to inform us right away that

> As with other Gnostics, the Carpocratian system was also egalitarian, seeing men and women as spiritual and ethical equals – a belief which clearly disturbed the more patriarchal Christens of the time.

The supposedly "feminist" and "egalitarian" tone of the Gnostics has long been a selling point among PC academics, going back at least to

---

[477] See, for example, "Phil & Will: Awakening Through Repetition in Groundhog Day, Point of Terror, & Manhunter, Part 2", Counter-Currents, December 31, 2013 (Phil is an example of Gnostic self-liberation as he gradually improves himself; "The Tooth Fairy" endlessly repeats his crimes until Will Graham crashes through his window with the saving gnosis).

[478] Griffin, the murderous ex-con and bum played by Coleman Francis himself in his masterwork, *Red Zone Cuba*, is an example of a Carpocratian figure who, through the sheer repetition of his crime and brutality, achieves Liberation. See my *Coffee? I Like Coffee! The Metaphysical Cinema of Coleman Francis* (Amazon Kindle, 2017). "The Kingdom of Heaven suffereth violence."

Elaine Pagels.⁴⁷⁹ As academics as well as Traditionalists have pointed out, the idea that women can, if they try real hard, "achieve the male mind" as one Gnostic says, is hardly going to satisfy today's feminists ("Phallocentric rationality!"), and the practices of small, elite religious groups are hardly a model for society as a whole to implement.

On the other hand, Traditionalists, unlike New Agers, will reject the idea of reincarnation, although as we've said, Carpocrates (or Varady's Carpocrates) seems more in tune with Guénon's preferred notion of exhausting all possible states of being on one particular level and then moving to another, entirely different one (rather than repeatedly reappearing as a human or even animal).⁴⁸⁰ The way out for the soul is a spiral, not a circle, as we've frequently said.⁴⁸¹

Especially hurtful to Traditionalist ears will be the combination of reincarnation with the idea of "evolution" of the soul, in the modern sense of the word. For Guénon, the combination of reincarnation and progressivist evolution is always the hallmark of a modern pseudo-tradition.

But Guénon being dead, perhaps everything is now permitted. In any event, Varady presents us with a clear and interesting model which could prove quite useful for those interested in the sort of self-guided pursuit of Liberation through exploration of consciousness that remains for us, now that Tradition has withdrawn in the Kali Yuga. ⁴⁸²

---

⁴⁷⁹   Elaine Pagels, *The Gnostic Gospels* New York, Random House, 1979.

⁴⁸⁰   "He seeks to dismantle all aspects of spiritism, including the theory of reincarnation, whose foundations are false because, he said, involving 'a limitation of the universal possibility.'" - Wikipedia, quoting *The Spiritist Fallacy* (Hillsdale, NY: Sophia Perennis, 2003). For Evola, see the essays on posthumous survival in *Introduction to Magic, op. cit.*

⁴⁸¹   For example, "Our Wagner, Only Better; Harry Partch, Wild Boy of American Music" in *The Eldritch Evola…& Others* (San Francisco: Counter-Currents, 2014), quoting Alain Danielou: "The fifths form a spiral whose sounds, coiled around themselves, can never meet. For us, *this limitless spiral can be the joint in the center of the world, the narrow gate that will allow us to escape from the appearance of a closed universe*, to travel in other worlds and explore their secrets. (*Music and the Power of Sound: The Influence of Tuning and Interval on Consciousness*, Rochester, VT: Inner Traditions, 1995, p. 8)."

⁴⁸²   Cf. of course Evola's *Ride the Tiger: A Survival Manual for the Aristocrats of the Soul*; Rochester, VT: Inner Traditions, 2003.

Though Gnosticism may have been erased as a discernible set of institutions, its undercurrents and values never did disappear from either Europe or the Middle East, and I think that an open-minded reading of their beliefs shows that their systems still have relevance to the modern world.

Those "undercurrents and values" have an archeo-futuristic character. Like paganism, Tradition, or fascism, Gnosticism can never die.[483]

Counter-Currents/*North American New Right*
February 10, 2015

---

[483] "Fascism is a human political system that is deeply rooted in primeval, pervasive biological impulses and patterns that lead to the emergence of distinct communities. Understood in this way, Eco's characterization of ur-fascism as "eternal fascism" is transparent: while fascism always manifests in certain places and times, it can always come back again in unexpected guises and different forms; it can never truly, entirely be eradicated." "Ur-Fascism" by Organon tou Ontos, Counter-Currents, October 30, 2014. See also: "How thousands of Icelanders suddenly started worshiping the Norse gods again" by Terrence McCoy; *Washington Post*, February 3, 2014. The Grail Legend, according to Evola, is a pagan survival, no part of Christianity; like Carpocrates' followers, any method is made use of by the knights, and the hermit Titurel observes with wonder: "The Grail never was won by violence [until Parzifal came along]."

EVER SACRED, EVER VEXED:
ERIK DAVIS, LORD OF THE CODES

"I find the internet-driven pressure to make pieces short, data-dense, and crisply opinionated—as opposed to thoughtful, multi-perspectival, and lyrical—rather oppressive, leading to a certain kind of superficial smugness as well as general submission to the forces of reference over reflection." – Erik Davis.[484]

Nomad Codes[485] collects about twenty years of Erik Davis' essays and journalism. Some has appeared in rather obscure 'zines and websites, but much of it comes from mainstream outlets like the *Village Voice, Wired, Salon,* and *Slate.* That, along with titles like "The Technofreak Legacy of Golden Goa," "UFO Epistemology," and "My Date with a Burmese Transvestite Spirit Medium," might lead you to pass it by, but that would be a mistake.[486]

What's distinctive about Erik Davis's journalism is a unique combination of immersive reportage from the most eccentric subcultures—think Tom Wolfe among the Pranksters or Hunter Thompson riding with the Hell's Angels—with the kind of profound insights derived from a lifetime (at least since the release of *Led*

---

[484] "Erik Davis – *Technoccult* Interview" by Klint Finley; November 23, 2010.

[485] *Nomad Codes: Adventures in Modern Esoterica* by Erik Davis; illustrations by Susan Wilmarth (Portland, OR: Yeti Publishing, 2010).

[486] In the interests of full disclosure, our paths first intersected through mutual interests in lectures given at the New York Open Center when Erik was writing for the *Village Voice;* in the Wild West days of the Internets I passed for something of an expert, believe it or not, and lent research assistance to a piece, post-Oklahoma City, on neo-Right websites; later, as guest editor of an issue of *FringeWare Review,* he solicited an article on my involvement with the Da Free John sect.

Zeppelin IV[487]) of practical study of the mythological and esoteric realms that Wolfe or Thompson could only dream of.

A Klingon Con, for example, is revealed to be rather more than a sad collection of acned-scarred basement-dwellers – an awful lot seem to be drawn from law enforcement or the army, which Davis notes is a hotbed of Neopaganism as well; he quotes one Klingon saying that "The Klingons are very similar to the Norse" and then draws back to offer some commentary:

> But as good myth-weavers know, the potency of myth lies in the magic of ambiguity.... No matter how much you allegorize Klingons, as Russkies or black nationalists or creatures from the id, they are compelling because they retain a certain nomadic volatility – what the 'zine Katra calls "outliness"

Further along, after observing a Klingon ritual and noting that everyone is aware that it's "not real," he neither scoffs like a *Huffington Post* secular bigot nor sniffs about "inauthentic pagan reconstructions" but makes the same point we have been arguing from in our own reviews of pop culture:

> Both fans and witches share a very concrete sense of the power of imagination, seen not as an elite realm restricted to "artists" (or TV producers) but as *a vital phantasmic faculty that links the realms of fantasy with the here and now...*

By performing their spiritual sensibilities in the trappings of a TV show, Karizans also revived the oldest derivation of the word "fan:" *fanaticus*, a devotee of the ancient mystery cults.[488]

---

[487] See his *Led Zeppelin IV*, #17 in the "33 and 1/3" series (Bloomsbury Academic, 2005).

[488] See Greg Johnson's "Interview with James J. O'Meara," in *The Homo and the Negro* (San Francisco: Counter-Currents, 2012; embiggened edition, 2017), where I discuss Jeremy Reed's appropriation of the pop culture "fan" as a model for the intense awareness of the "mundane" that characterizes the poet, and the relationship of this notion to Archetypal psychology (Moore, Hillman) and Sufi mysticism (Peter Lamborn Wilson, to be mentioned later); see also Michael Hoffman's egodeath.com for research on, among much else dear to the hearts of

The term Davis likes to use for this kind of intersection of the sacred and profane is "occulture":

> [The] place where popular culture meets the underground and very real currents of magic, mysticism, and the esoteric – a stream that has always been with us, but which was rediscovered and reaffirmed, in not always healthy ways, in the 60s. "Occulture" is also a way to claim the occult or the religious fringe as a kind of cultural identity or playground, rather than an overly serious and hidden realm.
>
> I try to look at the mysteries from both ends – I think its important to look at, say, the contemporary ayahuasca scene as a scene, *with dress codes and slang and rock stars*, not as a sacred separate realm.[489] (Even though sacred things can and do go down there.) At the same time I think it is important (or at least more rewarding) *to look at our often junky*[490]*world of late capitalist culture as a place where the seeds of insight and vision might be found, if only you look at the landscape in just the right way...*[491]

Davis unpacks this idea right from the start by opening this collection with what he (or his editors) dubs a "Prolegomenon" in the form of an autobiographical account: "Teenage Head: Confessions of a High School Stoner."

> [P]ot also gave me something that has stuck with me far longer than the urge to bake the brain: *a love of slippage, founded in*

Davis and myself, psychedelic rock music as modern mystery rituals.

[489] Compare my discussion of the role of dress codes and themes as constitutive of anti-modern zones in "Fashion Tips for the Far From Fashionable Right" in *The Homo and the Negro*.

[490] He means of course 'filled with junk' (in "The Technofreak Legacy of Golden Goa" he refers to "junky speakers") but the link to Burroughs' *Junky*, his one piece of hardboiled realism, is interesting.

[491] "Follow your Weird: A Conversation with Erik Davis," by Antonio Lopez; *Reality Sandwich*.

the realization that altering perception alters the claims reality makes on you. The various social agendas of parents, teachers, and the ghost of God could be sidestepped not only by sullen monosyllables and the worship of unwholesome heavy metal guitarists but by tinkering with consciousness itself. What greater rebellion than rewiring one's experience of the world?

Davis then adds this intriguing note:

It's no accident that many kids start taking drugs at about the same age when children in traditional societies are tossed into a terrifying rite of passage, often involving some freaked-out combination of blood, darkness, self-sufficiency, and secrets. For better or worse, acid, 'shrooms, and massive bongloads now perform this rite, leaving marks that are both scars and the deep patterns of change.

That's where subculture steps in, collective identities which can shore up the threat of dissolution and excess.

Teenage cults of drugs and music (psychedelic, heavy metal, trance, as opposed to the squeaky-clean world of pop and the thug culture of [c]rap) are the modern equivalents of the traditional adolescent rites of passage, where drugs, music (and sex) are used to break the bonds of childhood and forge new ties with the adult world, or perhaps a "subculture" such as the *Männerbund*, the military, or the priesthood.

[T]hat aimless and reckless quest for the silliest of grails (a party, pot, a parent-free abode)

The particular role of drugs (to an extent shared with music and sex) is to produce a state Michael Hoffman has called "loose cognition," where the tight bonds of what passes for common sense (Kuhn's "normal science") are loosen or broken, allowing new combinations to arise (Kuhn's "new paradigm").[492]

---

[492] For drugs, sex and the *Männerbund*, see the work of Wulf Grimsson, generally, and my review of his *Loki's Way* reprinted in *The Homo and the Negro*; for drugs, music and loose cognition, see the work of Michael Hoffman collected

> Phasing between the reveries of a bookish childhood and the hormone-fueled angst of teendom, *my mind liquified, running through the cracks and creases of a suddenly unfolded world.*

For some, the shamanistic, shall we say, a lasting taste for such adventures in perception is retained, ideally combined with some ability to maintain an ability to function in normal society. The point is not to gain some new dogma, but to retain the ability *to see.*

> Acid *doesn't give you truths; it builds machines that push the envelope of perception.* Whatever revelations came to me then have dissolved like skywriting. All I really know is that those few years saddled me with a *faith in the redemptive potential of the imagination.*

> It produces a bubbling, crackling *connection-machine* which quickly sinks into the mire.

> Trivial objects, words, and glances stitch together webs of deep and intense meaning that uncomfortably thicken—once a Greek salad in New Haven set off a rumination on the flows of Western history which overwhelmed my puny mind like a tidal wave.

> But I take great satisfaction in the fact that many people acquainted with either my writing or my person assume I'm a total stoner.[493]

But Deleuze and Guattari are fairly down on drugs themselves. To quote them quoting Henry Miller, the point is to get drunk on a glass of water.

Or, to quote William Burroughs, the self-styled "master drug addict" himself, "Learn to make it without chemical corn."

This is somewhat like what Peter Lamborn Wilson, subject of another fascinating piece—"The Wandering Sufi"—calls "sacred

---

at his egodeath.com.

[493] I too have had this ambiguous pleasure: "Reading James O'Meara is a psychedelic experience." – Jack Donovan, jacket copy for *The Homo and the Negro.*

drift," which Davis calls "a magical mode of writing: recombinant, luminous, fragmentary." Even so, as Davis notes, "for an anarchist, he has a remarkably traditional respect for rigor and cautious argument, as well as a real love of the dusty bibliographies and arcane disputes of classic scholarship." (He was, after all, part of Seyyed Nasr's Iranian Academy of Philosophy, and remembers their patroness, "Mrs. Shah," with great fondness).[494]

Unlike the kids, not everyone likes the Drift; for example, H. P. Lovecraft, who even though he was dead in his forties, had long since taken to referring to himself as "Old Gandpa." In "Calling Cthulhu,"[495] Davis describes the then-nascent cult of pop-Cthulhu, and noted that Lovecraft's "dread" and "horror" seemed to belong to a 19th century materialist confronting vast new vistas opened up by science, not unlike those opened by the 60s drug culture; as he describes it in a later article on Cthulhu porn:

> In this tangy bon-bon of nihilistic materialism, Lovecraft anticipates a peculiarly modern experience of dread, one conjured not by irrational fears of the dark but rather by the speculative realism of reason itself, staring into the cosmic void. ...This terror before the empty and ultimately unknowable universe of scientific materialism is what gives the cosmic edge to the cosmic horror that Lovecraft, more than any other writer, injected into the modern imagination (though props must be given up as well to Arthur Machen, William Hope Hodgson, and, in the closing chapters of *The Time Machine* at least, H. G. Wells). While many secular people proclaim an almost childlike wonder at the mind-melting prospect of the incomprehensibly vast universe sketched out by astrophysics and bodied forth by doctored Hubble shots, Lovecraft would say that we have not really swallowed the implication of this inhuman immensity—that we have not, in other words, correlated our contents.[496]

---

[494] Wilson is another seminal influence on my own writing and research.

[495] "Calling Cthulhu: H. P. Lovecraft's Magical Realism" in *op. cit.*

[496] Erik Davis, "Cthulhu is not cute!"

Or, as Davis says in "Teenage Head":

> Whether or not the sense that everything fits together is perceived as a holistic liberation or a dire trap depends a lot on *how tightly you are clutching to your frame of mind.*

"Calling Cthulhu" also explores the "curiously literal dimension" of Lovecraft's cult, "made all the more intriguing by the fact that Lovecraft himself was…philosophically opposed to spirituality and magic of any kind." Yet in his work, thanks to the "tension between fact and fable" called magic, "ancient and amoral forces violently puncture the realistic surface of his tales," drawing the reader "into the chaos that lies 'between the worlds' of magic and reality." Davis calls this "Lovecraft's magical realism" but we have elsewhere suggested that it also resembles what has been called "archeofuturism," the continued accessibility of the past in the future, now.[497]

> The resurgence of weed as cultural icon may not be a matter of returning to nature but recovering its flow in the urban milieu: how to slip through the cracks in the concrete,[498] how to grow wilderness in the most degraded or rigidly stratified of circumstances. That's not a spoon or a needle or a bottle on all those caps around town. It's a leaf.

Speaking of Cthulhu, and theurgy (acting on the gods) in general, Lovecraft, in "The Call" and elsewhere liked to bring in voodoo cults and other darkie woo-woo to suggest parallels, or equivalents, to his

---

[497] Thus Ed Wood's Grade-Z films, an equivalent genre to Lovecraft's pulp fictions, paradoxically produced real effects in the present day ("Future events like these will affect your lives in the future, as Criswell predicts) due to the principle that ""any endeavor pursued with sufficient vigor [e.g., magick, even performed by a non-believer] will achieve results, those results potentially surpassing the endeavor's original intentions." Lovecraft might be compared to the bogus psychic is Wood's *Night of the Ghouls* (a rather Lovecraftian title) whose fake séances actually raise the dead and bring about his doom. See my "Getting Wood: Closely Watching the Cinematic Alchemy of Ed Wood Jr.," Counter-Currents, October 9, 2014.

[498] Cf. the Situationist slogan from '68: "Beneath the pavement, the beach!"

fictional cults of the Elder Gods; Lovecraft the Village Atheist no doubt also liked to imply this was the real nature of more respectable religions like Puritan Christianity.[499]

Here again, once you make the connection, you can't really control where it will take you ("sacred drift"); perhaps there's more to those "primitive" cults, perhaps as much as the White man's fancy theology? "Trickster at the Crossroads" explores African cults that may make the White "neopagan" uncomfortable, but may have something to teach us moderns.

Perhaps that discomfort arises not (only) from "a lingering afterimage of colonialism" but from an uncomfortable similarity:

> As one Neopagan I know put it, "why be interested in these grotesque and parasitic deities?" You could answer that these deities are not so much grotesque as rich with character, not so much parasitic as *deeply and reciprocally bound up with the daily lives of their devotees."*
>
> Though they possess godlike powers, the orisha are not transcendent beings; rather, they are idiosyncratic personalities thoroughly bound up with ritual, practice, and the sort of exchanges that define human community.

In short, rather more pagan than the alien Christianity imposed on us.[500] Traditionalists like Guénon and Coomaraswamy scorned the whole notion of "primitive" peoples, either as vertigoes of a past left behind by religious or scientific "progress" or as role models to be emulated, considering them rather as degenerate traces of lost primordial civilizations; but the degenerate culture, by definition,

---

[499] e.g., "The Dunwich Horror" as a blasphemous reworking of the Incarnation and Crucifixion. On gods as malevolent parasites, see Jason Reza Jorjani, *Prometheus and Atlas* (London: Arktos, 2017).

[500] See the essays of Collin Cleary, collected in *Summoning the Gods* (San Francisco: Counter Currents, 2010) and most recently "What is Odinism" in *TYR* 4 (Ultra, 2014); also, Greg Johnson's "The Philosophy of Collin Cleary," the Introduction to Cleary's *What is a Rune? & Other Essays*; edited by Greg Johnson (San Francisco: Counter-Currents, 2015).

bear some connection to the healthy, unlike the deviationism of Judeo-Christianity and Modernity. [501]

In fact, in the spirit of archeofuturism, the *orisha* suggest not merely the past but the present future:

> In our wired world, Eshu can also be seen as the spirit of the network, nomadic lord of the codes and protocols that tie movement and trade, images and perspective, data and sex. Of all the *orisha*, he perhaps speaks most forcefully to us today because he is about the very process that we engage in order to understand and recognize him: the tangled process of communication itself, ever sacred, ever vexed.

Now, I know what many of you are thinking: this Davis cat is just another aging neo-hippie, and no doubt some kinda eco-friendly anti-Westerner, peddling more new-age pap. Admittedly, there are times when Davis does seem to lean perilously close to becoming some kind of Burning Man trendster (see "Beyond Belief: The Cults of Burning Man") or just another fruity California nut (see the section on "Kalifornika" as well as his historical/spiritual/psycho-geographical travelogue, *The Visionary State: A Journey through California's Spiritual Landscape*[502]).

But at his best, which is most of the time, Davis is made of sterner stuff. Take "Snakes and Ladders," an important Gnostic manifesto that echoes, not only in the title, James Hillman's "Peaks and Vales." Here the "tension" we've seen is abstracted into

> [Two] contrasting modes of spiritual movement, two pervasive "styles" or religious impulses. One the one hand, the desire to establish an intense, deeply wedded connection with the imaginative matrix of the natural world; on the other hand, a desire to overcome desire, to ascend towards virtual light, to

---

[501] See "Shamanism and Sorcery," chapter 26 of *The Reign of Quantity* (Ghent, NY: Sophia Perennis, 2001), especially the cautions expressed on p. 181. In the same way, the stoner culture Davis emerged from is a degenerate modern version of the ancient rites of passage, and so more valuable than mere bourgeois normality.

[502] Chronicle Books, 2006.

escape the demands of matter and wake up to a new order of knowledge and being.

This wariness of what Ken Wilber might call "premature unity" leads him to suggest that

> the impulse to transcend—the Neo-Platonist's ascent through the spheres, the Gnostic's sudden awakening, the desert monk's rejection of the élan vital—is not simply a philosophical error or the mark of patriarchy, but is fired by an intensely lucid yearning for the highest of goals: liberation.

Davis avows that he distrusts

> [A]ny easy attempt to shove them under one roof. It's too simple to paper over their real differences be appealing to the supposed unity of mystical experience or the clichéd notion that various religious languages describe the same truth from different perspectives. *What if the truth itself is multiple?*

Like Hillman, Davis sees that polytheism is not—or should not be—just another dogma like monotheism:

> The polytheistic alternative does not set up conflicting opposites between beast and Bethlehem, between chaos and unity; it permits *the coexistence of the psychic fragments* and gives them *patterns in the imagination...*[503]

On the other hand, Davis is admittedly given to the usual knee-jerking; he can't help but interrupt an account of his first encounter with the OnStar system—when he sets it off accidentally in a rental car—to wonder not just what the cops in Skokie would do if they had arrived and he was black. (The answer, of course, is "Nothing as bad as the brothers would do if they found you in Compton.")

But even so. Readers will find his positive take on "The Matrix Way of Knowledge"—"the Wachowski brothers realize that the

---

[503] Davis quoting James Hillman, *A Blue Fire* (New York: HarperCollins, 1989), p. 44.

cybernetic problem of control reboots the hoary old struggle between freedom and fate"—to be an interesting contrast to Trevor Lynch's disgust,"[504] and Davis' musings:

> What, then, is the proper rejoinder to determinism? The Oracle tells Neo that "You are here to understand why you made the choice, not to make the choice." I take this to mean that, to an awakened one, events and decisions have always already occurred, but that understanding and compassion can still dissolve their karmic hold.

Intersect nicely with our own obsession with finding the rather more amoral "passing the buck" motif—escape from karma through a scapegoat or "sucker"—in genre flicks.[505]

"Intersection" is really what it—and Erik Davis' writing—is all about. Knowledge may be fragmentary, but Wisdom arise from the intersection—ever repeated—of the fragments. This collection will expose the intrepid spiritual adventurer to many of those "Shards of the Diamond Matrix," from jazzbo Islamic heresies, to the hash-addled surf epiphanies of California teenagers, to "Scratch" Perry churning out dub from Switzerland. Like another one of its own topics—how appropriately fractal—it is truly "a mighty bizarre volume known as *The Secret Museum of Mankind*."

Yeti has done a great service to esoteric adventurers by bringing out this collection. It has a great personal introduction by Marcus Boon, but one does miss—in the spirit of Peter L. Wilson, and Davis's "bookish" boyhood, if not Melville's Sub-Sub Librarian[506]—a list of first appearances rather than just dates; moreover this sort of writing calls out for an index to guide the reader who is sure Davis

---

[504] "About twenty minutes into *The Matrix Reloaded* I was feeling sick to my stomach — literally." See his review in *Trevor Lynch's White Nationalist Guide to the Movies* (San Francisco: Counter Currents, 2013).

[505] See the discussion in "Getting Wood," *op. cit.*

[506] Melville, of course, was a pioneer of the esoteric methods of linguistic warp and woof; see Harold Beaver's 300-page, line by line commentary attached to the Penguin English Library edition of *Moby Dick* ((New York: Penguin, 1972), itself almost a parody of literary paranoia.

mentioned something about something somewhere.

But perhaps they hope the reader with enter into the spirit of the thing, and just dive in and wait for the sacred drift to take them... somewhere.

Counter-Currents/*North American New Right*
November 17, 2014

MAGICK FOR HOUSEWIVES:
THE NOT-SO-NEW, AND RATHER TRADITIONAL, THOUGHT OF NEVILLE GODDARD

"Assume you are what you want to be. Walk in that assumption and it will harden into fact." – Neville Goddard's "Law of Assumption"

"The fool who persists in his folly will become wise." – William Blake

I. WHO WAS NEVILLE?

Why on Earth have I not heard about Neville before?

My constant readers will recall that I've been wading around in the murky waters of what I call our home-grown Hermeticism, our native Neoplatonism, our two-fisted Traditionalism, the so-called "New Thought" movement.[507]

In Neville, New Thought found its Alan Watts: a self-taught mystic whose tall, handsome, charismatic, British-accented presence thrived on the then-cutting-edge audio-visual lecture circuit; unlike Watts, I imagine his target audience was not proto-hippies or beats, but that distinctively American phenomenon, the society lady in search of occult thrills. In fact, you might say, borrowing the well-known aphorism comparing Marcuse and Evola, that Neville (he

---

[507] Steve Sailer, late to the party as usual, discovers the influence of New Thought on Donald Trump: "Donald Trump, Norman Vincent Peale, and Ned Flanders," VDare.com, August 26, 2015.

went by his first name, like Cher or Madonna) was our Alan Watts, only better.

Writing only about ten rather short books—booklets, mostly—over a longer career than Watts (though both died in 1972), Neville not only lectured every week at the Wilshire Theatre in Los Angeles to overflow crowds, he even had his own TV show (rather like Criswell, another suggestive *Doppelganger*).

His popularity waned in his last decade, for reasons we'll get to later, and in the decades after his death he seems to have been mostly forgotten. Even Penguin/Tarcher, the big hitter in the repackaging of public domain New Thought books, seems to have largely ignored him, until now.[508]

In fact, with the 21st century, and the arrival of the Intertubes and the Googles, along with the expiration of copyrights, Neville is everywhere, if you know where and how to look for him.[509] His books are not only republished cheaply by others, but electronic copies and Kindles proliferate like magic mushrooms on Amazon, many "featuring" clip art or hand-made inspirational-poster style covers and editorial addenda from guys no doubt making big bucks running laptop "life coaching" businesses "inspired" by Neville's teachings.

And you can too! Not only are all his books available online for the plucking, but so are hundreds of audio recordings and

---

[508] *The Power of Imagination: The Neville Goddard Treasury* New York: Tarcher/Penguin, 2015. This collection includes *Your Faith Is Your Fortune* (1941); *Freedom for All: A Practical Application of the Bible* (1942); *Feeling is the Secret* (1944); *Prayer: The Art of Believing* (1945); *The Search* (1946); *Out of this World: Thinking Fourth-Dimensionally* (1949); *The Power of Awareness* (1952); *Awakened Imagination* (1954); *Seedtime and Harvest: A Mystical View of the Scriptures* (1956); *The Law and the Promise* (1961). This volume features "Neville: A Portrait" from a long out of print 1947 book on New Thought leaders by Israel Regardie, journalist, philosopher, and private secretary to the Beast himself, Aleister Crowley. However, if you find yourself jonesing for Neville, as I hope you do, I suggest trolling the internets for the collection *Resurrection*, which reprints most of all that, plus the rare title booklet, in a nicely designed paperback (though without the French flaps and deckle-edges of the Penguin) you can get for about $0.01 plus postage, and makes a handy book to read while sipping a Gimlet on a Sunday afternoon.

[509] *Navigating the Aether* (http://www.navigatingtheaether.com/) seems to be the most complete and best organized collection of books and audio lectures online, and I'll be drawing on it here. AudioEnlightenment seems to have the most audio tapes – 475!

transcriptions.[510] Watch him (or a picture of him, as no video footage seems to exist) lecture on YouTube! Follow him on Facebook!

Like Criswell, Neville could truly say, "Future events such as these will affect us in the future."[511]

And of course I have plenty of my usual paranoid-critical reasons to be interested in Neville. He was born same year as my father (and died in the same year as my early mentor, Alan Watts). But Neville was born in the West Indies, like my mother.[512] And, as we shall see, he seems to have developed a technique for consciousness development via "the state akin to sleep" that rather resembles my mother's self-induced astral projections she called "visiting."[513]

II. WHAT WAS NEVILLE'S METHOD?

Born into a large merchant's family, Neville came to New York in his and the century's twenties and took to the stage as a dancer. Though somewhat successful, he spent his money as fast as he made it ("I'd work for a year and spend it in a month"), and then ran into the Depression. He acquired an interest in the occult, and then met, in the usual mysterious manner, his equally mysterious guru: a black Ethiopian Jew named Abdullah. Abdullah taught him Hebrew, the

---

[510] To continue the comparison, Watts' estate, in the form of his son, Mark, has not only zealously guarded his copyrighted books, and carefully doled out his audiotapes, there also have been rumors of plans to let the original books go out of print in favor of new, Mark Watts-approved anthologies. Arguably, much of Watts' later production was undertaken to support his three wives and eleven or so children and grandchildren, the pace of production contributing, biographers have speculated, to his alcoholism and early death.

[511] *Plan 9 From Outer Space* (Ed Wood, Jr., 1959). See my reflections on the archeofutristic depths of this popular saying of Neville's *doppelganger*, Criswell, and of Ed Wood's work in general, in my review of Rob Craig's *Ed Wood, Mad Genius: A Critical Study of the Films*, "Getting Wood: Closely Watching the Cinematic Alchemy of Edward D. Wood, Jr.," Counter-Currents, October 9, 2014.

[512] Although, to my ears, his accent sure sounds Australian. In fact, rather like Lord Athol Layton, an Australian wrestler who performed on, but most notably hosted, the "Big Time Wrestling" TV show in Windsor/Detroit during my youth.

[513] Discussed in Greg Johnson's "Interview with James J. O'Meara," reprinted in *The Homo and the Negro* (San Francisco: Counter-Currents, 2012; embiggened edition, 2017). What was going on in the West Indies?

Qabalah, and, most importantly, a method of interpreting the Bible as a psychological document.[514] From all this evolved a method that Neville called "The Law."

The story of what, and how, Abdullah taught Neville is frequently retold, especially by Neville himself. I think it might be best to give it in his own words, transcribed from one of his last lectures, as it has considerable merit, and gives you an idea of his speaking style.

> I can tell it best by telling you a story. The year was 1933. Roosevelt was elected. I had been in this country for eleven years. I never really wanted to go back to Barbados. My parents came up in that year, and they pleaded with me to come to Barbados and join the family – become a member of the family; and I declined. I said, "No." I saw them off at the boat; and strangely enough, as they sailed—and they were on the deck and I waved "goodbye" to them—a peculiar feeling came over me, and I had a desire that I had never had in eleven years to go to Barbados. I had just said "goodbye" to them, and said "No" to their request. They would have paid all expenses and brought me back, and everything would have been perfect.
>
> Then from the boat, I went to my old friend Abdullah. He was born, so I am told, in Ethiopia. He was a black man, raised in the Jewish faith, but really understood Christianity as few men that I ever met understood it. He understood the Law, not the Promise. He understood the Law.[515] So, I went to him and I told him the feeling that came over me: that I wanted to go to Barbados. I had just waved at my parents, and a peculiar feeling possessed me; and he said to me, "You are in Barbados."
>
> Well, that did not make sense to me. I am standing in his place on 72nd Street, off Central Park West; that's where he lived. He lived at 30 West 72nd Street. And here I am in his place, and

---

[514] Even to the last sentence of his last book: "There is no secular history in the Bible. The Bible is the history of salvation and is wholly supernatural." *Resurrection* (1961).

[515] This is the later development I mentioned that led to a decline in Neville's drawing power.

he's telling me that I am in Barbados! He didn't explain what he meant. So, as the days went by, I said to him, "Ab, I am no nearer to Barbados than I was when I spoke to you."

And he said to me, "If you are in Barbados, you cannot discuss the means of getting to Barbados.[516] You must actually live in Barbados in your imagination as though you were there—just as if—and view the world from Barbados. If you sleep in Barbados and view the world from Barbados, the means will appear, and you will go to Barbados. But as far as I am concerned, you are already in Barbados, because you desired it with intensity. All you had to do was simply to enter it; and you enter it now in New York City even though it is two thousand miles across water – and you aren't going to walk across water; but you enter Barbados and view the world from it. If you see the world from Barbados, then you have to be in Barbados."

He did not explain to me then, but I learned later that *man, being all imagination, is wherever he is in imagination;*[517] *and imagination is the God-in-man.* That is the Eternal Body of the Lord Jesus Christ, and "all things are possible to Him," and "by Him all things were made, and without Him was not anything made that was made" – that what is now proven was once only imagined. These things I did not know then. He simply talked in the over-all picture.

But I did my best, and I slept mentally in Barbados in my mother's home. I looked at the world, and saw it from Barbados. I looked at the world, and saw it from Barbados. I saw New York City two thousand miles to the north of me – northwest, for we

---

[516] A key point. You do not imagine the means, which are innumerable; that is for the world to decide. You imagine the end, the goal, *as if it were already accomplished*, and let the means take care of themselves. As Jesus says, "I AM the Alpha and the Omega;" our feeling imagination is the link.

[517] Pete: "I'm not imagining!" Bert: "The Japanese have a saying: a man is, whatever room he is in. And right now, Donald Draper is in this room." *Mad Men*, Season 1, Episode 10, "Nixon versus Kennedy. For more on this episode and *Mad Men* in general, see my collection *The End of an Era*: Mad Men *and the Ordeal of Civility* (San Francisco: Counter-Currents, 2015).

are at a certain Latitude 13 North; New York is 42 North. We are the 59th Longitude; New York is the 74th; so I saw it northwest, as I could imagine it.

I heard the tropical noises. We call this land tropical. It really isn't tropical in the really true sense of the word. When you go into the tropics, it's something entirely different, and I was born in the tropics – almost on the Equator. It's an entirely different odor. Sunsets go like this: you look at the sun, and the sun disappears suddenly. A ball of red light becomes green. You are looking at the sun, and suddenly, in the matter of a split second, you are seeing a green sun. You are seeing the complement of red. So, we have no twilights in Barbados. The sun goes down rapidly from a red ball to a green ball, and you see the green ball.

So, the whole atmosphere differs. Well, I put myself into that, and felt that my mother and father were in their room, and that my brothers—those who were not yet married—were in the house. It's a huge, big, old home of ours. And there I "slept."

This was, now, late October. When it came to the end of November, I said to Ab, I said, "Ab, I am no nearer Barbados." He said, "You are in Barbados." Then he turned his back on me, walked towards his bedroom, and slammed the door, which was not an invitation to follow him, if you understood Ab. He was teaching me a lesson, the lesson of faith.

If I am actually sleeping in Barbados, no power in the world could interfere with my journey to Barbados. This is, now, late November. The last ship out of New York City sailing for Barbados was the 6th of December. I wanted to get there by Christmas, and so I could not raise the question any more. But on the morning of the 4th or the 3rd of December I got a letter from my brother Victor. I did not ask him or any member of my family to bring me to Barbados.

He wrote a letter and justified the contents in this manner: He said, "We are, you know, a large family" – nine brothers and a sister. "We have never been united around our Christmas table at Christmas since we were a family" – for there was an interval between my sister Daphne and the last two boys of eight years.

By that time, my oldest brother had left for Demerara in British Guiana; and by then, when he came back, my brother Lawrence went off the McGill to study medicine, and we were always moving around. But this time, every one was present but Yours Truly. And he said, "I am enclosing a small, little draft" – $50.

But in 1933 when there were seventeen and a half million unemployed, and we didn't have two hundred and four million citizens, we only had a hundred and twenty-odd million – it was an enormous thing. If you were old enough to know it, may I tell you? It was really a horror! Well, I was numbered among the unemployed; so he knew that I could come if the terms were there, that I had my passage paid; so he enclosed a $50 draft to buy a suit. Well, you could buy a suit in those days for $12, $10. You could buy a pair of shoes, McCann shoes, for $3.00.

So, I went down to the steamship company because in the letter he said, "I've notified the Company to issue you a ticket; then with the $50 you buy what you need for the trip, and then sign the chips; and when the ship comes in, I will meet the ship and pay all the things that you have incurred, all the debts."

So, when I went down to the ship company, they said to me, "I am sorry, Mr. Goddard, but I do not have a first-class passage for you. We can accommodate you third class. You have the first-class accommodation for meals, and you can have all the other areas of first class; but for sleeping, you have to move into the third class." I said, "That's perfectly all right with me. I'll take it."

I went back to Abdullah and I told him. Do you know what he did when I said, "I am going third class to Barbados, but I have the accommodations of the first for the daylight hours?"

He said, "Who told you you're going third class? You are already

> in Barbados, and you went first class." Again, he closed the door on me.
>
> I went down to the ship the morning it sailed, on the 6th of December; and the ticket agent said to me, "Mr. Goddard, I have good news for you. We have a cancellation, and now you can go first class, but you will share it with two others. There are three in the cabin." "That is perfectly all right with me." So, I went down first class.[518]

Neville later found the same method worked to get him honorably discharged after he tired of being in the Army. It also works, according to another frequently told story, if you want to buy tickets to a sold-out production of *Aida* at the Met.

After years of practice and lecturing, Neville eventually boiled the whole technique down into a remarkably "simple method for changing the future": Desire, physical immobility bordering on sleep, and imaginary action. No more wandering around Manhattan for days at a time, imagining being surrounded by palm trees.

> People have a habit of slighting the importance of simple things; but this simple formula for changing the future was discovered after years of searching and experimenting. The first step in changing the future is *desire*—that is: define your objective—know definitely what you want.
>
> Secondly: construct an event which you believe you would encounter *following* the fulfillment of your desire—an event which implies fulfillment of your desire—something that will have the action of *self* predominant.
>
> Thirdly: immobilize the physical body and induce a condition akin to sleep—lie on a bed or relax in a chair and imagine that you are sleepy; then, with eyelids closed and your attention focused on the action you intend to experience – in imagination –

---

[518] "I am all Imagination," June 3, 1971. You can hear it in the aforementioned YouTube video, "How Abdullah Taught Neville the Law."

mentally feel yourself right into the proposed action—imagining all the while that you are actually performing the action here and now. You must always participate in the imaginary action, not merely stand back and look on, but you must feel that you are actually performing the action so that the imaginary sensation is real to you.

It is important always to remember that the proposed action must be one which *follows* the fulfillment of your desire; and, also, you must feel yourself into the action until it has all the vividness and distinctness of reality.[519]

How on Earth is that supposed to happen? Well, speaking of "Earth," the book just quoted, *Out of this World*—Neville's most metaphysical book, in the academic sense—posits (or proves; we'll get to that "proof" question in a bit) a four-dimensional universe.[520] The fourth dimension of course is time, and through the faculty of imagination—by a kind of controlled dreaming[521]—one can both see the already determined future, and, by concentrated thought, enter it, and alter it.

And how can that be possible? Neville, though barely referring to anyone but Blake and the Bible, links up with the New Thought tradition and its roots in Emerson, Hegel, Plotinus, and the Idealist and Hermetic Traditions in general, by asking the reader or listener to seriously consider that before he can say "I am this or that," he must acknowledge himself to be "I AM" - he is, *au fond*, God;

---

[519] *Out of this World: Thinking Fourth-Dimensionally* (1949); Chapter 1, "Thinking Fourth Dimensionally."

[520] This, we'll see, is the "block-universe" of Michael Hoffman, who posits that the ancient Mystery Religions used psychoactive or "entheogenic" drugs to induce a vision of this state of total determinism and loss of agency, then proposed a liberating Savior, such as Mithras or Christ; see, generally, the research collected at egodeath.com. As we'll see immediately, Neville finds freedom rather than determinism here. If Neville were more than fitfully in a philosophical mood, he might admit that our preferred futures are "determined" as well, but insist that the only meaningful notion of "freedom" is "free to do what we in fact want, unhindered" rather than "free to choose what we want." As he says in *Feeling is the Secret*: "Free will is only freedom of choice."

[521] *Out of this World*.

"imagination is the God-in-man."[522]

The method works, because it is, in fact, "the mechanism used in the production of the visible world."[523]

Wallace Wattles, the Grand Old Man of New Thought, presents the basic notion, known as Idealism in philosophy or Hermeticism in mysticism, thus:

> THERE is a thinking stuff from which all things are made, and which, in its original state, permeates, penetrates, and fills the interspaces of the universe.
>
> A thought in this substance produces the thing that is imaged by the thought.
>
> Man [also] can form things in his thought, and by impressing his

---

[522] Cf. Evola: "In the *Heliand* [the Saxon version of the Gospel], Christ is the source of the *Wurd* (Destiny, Fate) and this force finds in him its Master, thus becoming 'the wondrous power of God.'" *Revolt against the Modern World* (1937; Rochester, Vt.: Inner Traditions, 1995); Chapter 31, "Syncope of the Western Tradition," p. 294, note 8. The glory to be revealed, spoken of in Romans 8:18, "is nothing less than the unveiling of God the Father in us, as us" (*Resurrection*). Regardie, *op. cit.*, thinks Neville's readers would be shocked if he admitted he is, in fact, "an atheist," but I think that's being a bit too Crowley-like; there's plenty of American precedent for such a pantheistic and self-deifying version of the Biblical God, from Emerson and Joseph Smith to, well, Oprah. The writers of the Gospels do not "hesitat[e] to interpret the Old Testament according to their own supernatural experiences." (*Op. cit.*).

[523] *Feeling is the Secret* (1944). Feeling is "the secret" (the phrase appropriated by Oprah) because "you must feel yourself into the action until it has all the vividness and distinctness of reality." As Dr. Wayne Dyer puts it: "This is how God works. Your imagination, when aligned with the highest principles of your highest self, is God at work. You can make your imagination a place where you absolutely 'call things' [Romans 8:13] as you insist that they are, even though they may not have appeared in the third dimension as reported by your five senses." Dyer, *op. cit.*, p85. Or, as Dr. Hannibal Lecter opines, (*Manhunter* (Michael Mann, 1986), "And if one does what God does enough times, one becomes what God is." Tall, handsome, well-spoken, Neville is the charismatic figure the Tooth Fairy wishes to be. ("You owe me awe!"). Neville is the master communicator in print, audio and person; the Tooth Fairy writes notes on toilet paper and kidnaps a reporter to force him to read a message into a tape recorder. Both Neville and The Tooth Fairy are assiduous readers of Blake, but only Neville has really assimilated him; The Tooth Fairy tattoos "The Red Dragon" on his back, and tries to *eat* a Blake etching. The Tooth Fairy, a cold psychopath, is unable to truly *feel* his obsessions ("Someone made a child a monster" – Will Graham) until he meets the blind girl, Reba, but only after it's too late to save himself. Repetition is the key, at least to build up emotional charge ("Once more with feeling!" as they say).

thought upon formless substance can cause the thing he thinks about to be created.[524]

As Neville says:

> Consciousness is the one and only reality, not figuratively but actually. This reality may for the sake of clarity be likened unto a stream which is divided into two parts, the conscious and the subconscious. In order to intelligently operate the law of consciousness, it is necessary to understand the relationship between the conscious and the subconscious.
>
> The conscious is personal and selective; the subconscious is impersonal and non-selective. The conscious is the realm of effect; the subconscious is the realm of cause. These two aspects are the male and female divisions of consciousness. The conscious is male; the subconscious is female.
>
> The conscious generates ideas and impresses these ideas on the subconscious; the subconscious receives ideas and gives form and expression to them.
>
> By this law—first conceiving an idea and then impressing the idea conceived on the subconscious—all things evolve out of consciousness; and without this sequence, there is not anything made that is made.[525]

---

[524] *The Science of Getting Rich* by Wallace D. Wattles; Chapter 17: "Conclusion: Summary of the Science of Getting Rich;" published in 1910, with innumerable editions since, and online. For the idea that physical and material causality are actually lower, relatively weak forms of the divine act of intellectual contemplation (*Nous*), which is shared by man at his highest level, see *Nature, Contemplation and the One: A Study in the Philosophy of Plotinus* by John N. Deck (Toronto: University of Toronto Press, 1967; Burdett, NY: Larson Publications, 1991; Toronto Heritage series, 2017 [Kindle iOS version]) and my review (*Alexandria*, Vol. 2, 1993, pp. 400-01). "The whole drama [of enlightenment] belongs to a world far more real and vital than that which the [everyday human] intellect inhabits for the historical imagination to understand it." (Neville, *Resurrection*). For the interaction of Idealism and Hermeticism, see Glenn A. Magee: *Hegel and the Hermetic Tradition* (Cornell University Press, 2001).

[525] *Feeling Is the Secret*, Chapter 1: "Law and Its Operation."

Now, I know that long before now, many of you, not only Manly Men of the alt-Right Man-o-sphere, have been muttering "What a steaming pile of hockey pucks!"

Mitch Horowitz has tried to track down and confirm this "Abdullah" story; whatever its basis in our common reality, it conforms not just to a known pop culture meme—the "Magic Negro"—but it encapsulates a higher kind of truth.[526]

Evola, contrary to Guénon and Schuon, held that the regular, Traditional initiatory current was not lost by or hidden within Christianity, but that Christianity was a pseudo-Tradition from the start; primordial or hermetic tradition came back into Christian Europe via the Jews (who stole the so-called Qabalah from the Greek Neoplatonists).[527]

> Thus, in comparison with historical Judaism, primitive Christianity may be credited with a mystical character along the same lines of prophetism, but *not with an initiatory character*, contrary to what F. Schuon claimed (*The Transcendent Unity of Religions* [Paris, 1937]) on the basis of sporadic elements found mostly in Eastern Orthodoxy. We should never forget though that if Christianity developed from the ancient Jewish tradition, *Orthodox Judaism developed in an independent fashion through the Talmud and the Kabbalah, which represents an initiatory tradition that was always missing in Christianity*. This is how, later on, *true esotericism developed in the West, that is, outside*

---

[526] See his "Neville Goddard: A Cosmic Philosopher" in *At Your Command: The First Classic Work by the Visionary Mystic Neville* (Tarcher Cornerstone Editions, 2016; also my review, Lord Kek Commands! A Look at the Origins of Meme Magic," *infra*. Interestingly, Neville casually notes in one of his lectures that Abdullah lived (rent-free?) in a basement apartment in a building owned by the father of Henry Morgenthau, FDR's Treasury Secretary and the architect of the genocidal Morgnethau Plan to exterminate the German race. See "How Abdullah Taught Neville the Law", YouTube.

[527] Ironically, Evola concurs with Michael Hoffman, for whom the Eucharist is merely a placebo for the original, effective entheogenic plant, though Evola would no doubt agree with Eliade and insist that the plant, rather, is substitute for a spiritual force.

Christianity and with the help of non-Christian currents such as the Kabbalah, Hermeticism, or movements of a remote Nordic origin.[528]

Thus, Neville's encounter with Abdullah, and subsequent training in esoteric Biblical interpretation, is in fact wholly regular and Traditional.[529]

In fact, I would go further: Neville's teaching, simple and "popularized" as it may be, is wholly Traditional, a veritable restatement of Tradition for our time, the Kali Yuga.[530]

Keeping with Evola as our source for Tradition, Neville's method seems definitely related to the methodology discussed in the journals that Evola edited in the 30s, *UR* and *KRUR*.[531]

---

[528] *Revolt against the Modern World* (1937; Rochester, Vt.: Inner Traditions, 1995); Chapter 31, "Syncope of the Western Tradition," p. 281, note 1 Cf.: "[Guido von] List claimed that [the Renaissance humanists'] revival of neo-Platonism and hermetic-cabbalistic ideas marked an efflorescence of the ancient national gnosis following the weakening of the Catholic stranglehold in medieval Europe." In particular, "List claimed that the original [Teutonic] priest-kings had entrusted their gnosis verbally to the rabbis of Cologne during the eighth century, *in order to safeguard its survival during a wave of Christian persecution.* The rabbis had then set these secrets down in cabbalistic books which were erroneously thought to represent a Jewish mystical tradition." Nicholas Goodrick-Clarke: *The Occult Roots of Nazisim* (New York: New York University Press, 1985; 2004 ed.), pp. 62-63.

[529] This would not come as a surprise to Crowley, or most esoteric figures; see Marco Passi's *Aleister Crowley and the Temptation of Politics* (New York: Routledge, 2014) for a thorough discussion of how esoteric currents, especially the Qabalah, have attracted those seeking to abandon a played-out or otherwise repugnant Christianity since the turn of the last century.

[530] "[T]he fundamental psychological factor in Neville's teaching, [and] the fundamental fact about Neville himself...is a very simple fact: Neville is a dancer" (Regardie, *op. cit.*). Not only is Neville's stage training an important part of his method, I would add that as a dancer Neville is symbolically linked to Krishna, who "from time to time" reincarnates to "re-establish the Dharma." (Bhagavad Gita) From Krishna to Alain Danielou, the dancer has always been an archetype of the Realized Man. Clifton Webb was also originally a Broadway dancer, making him the perfect choice to incarnate Krishna in the Mr. Belvedere movies. See my essay "The Babysitting Bachelor as Aryan Avatar: Clifton Webb in *Sitting Pretty,* Part Two," Counter-Currents, February 5, 2013.

[531] Not republished until 1971 (and not translated into English until 2001) and presumably unavailable to Neville at the time. Abdullah, however, was an Ethiopian; did he have some connection to or in Italy? A simpler explanation, of course, is simply that Abdullah was one – *one who knows?*

First, *the importance of acquiring control over our sense impressions*. Neville says:

> The habit of seeing only that which our senses permit, renders us totally blind to what we otherwise could see. To cultivate the faculty of seeing the invisible, we should often *deliberately disentangle our minds from the evidence of the senses* and focus our attention on an invisible state, mentally feeling it and sensing it until it has all the distinctness of reality.[532]
>
> The perfectly disciplined man is always in tune with the wish as an accomplished fact. He knows that consciousness is the one and only reality, that ideas and feelings are facts of consciousness and are as real as objects in space; therefore *he never entertains a feeling which does not contribute to his happiness* for feelings are the causes of the actions and circumstances of his life.
>
> On the other hand, the undisciplined man finds it difficult to believe that which is denied by the senses and usually *accepts or rejects solely on appearances of the senses*. Because of this tendency to rely on the evidence of the senses, *it is necessary to shut them out before starting to pray, before attempting to feel that which they deny*. Whenever you are in the state of mind, "I should like to but I cannot," the harder you try the less you are able to yield to the wish. You never attract that which you want but always attract that which you are conscious of being.[533]

Bringing sense impressions under voluntary control is a basic, initial step in the Hermetic path, discussed throughout the essays published by Evola in *UR* and *KRUR*:

> These people [the initiated] can bind and freeze the Waters. Having been conquered by them, the Waters are now a magical force that obeys them. The Sun rises over the Waters and controls them with its reflection. Desire, the unleashed centerless lunar force...finds here a center.[534]

---

[532] *Out of this World*, loc. cit.

[533] *Feeling is the Secret*.

[534] Knowledge of the Waters" by "Leo"; reprinted in Evola, *Introduction to Magic*

> The struggle for immortality is a battle for the control over the sounds and ghosts that dwell in us; the waiting for our "Self "to become King is the waiting for the Messiah.
>
> Frightening or splendid apparitions will confront you, making you believe they are beings from another world. In truth, they are only thoughts in visible form over which you do not yet have full control![535]
>
> At the center of yourself, *like a spider that keeps under control all the strings of its web and their vibrations*, let there be a calm self-control and a scrutinizing lucidity, purified and fearless, open to every voice.[536]
>
> I will not discuss here at length the methods I employed. It will suffice to say that I spent a few years *alternating study with a slow and tenacious attempt to gain a greater control of my thought*, and be purified from the "being of desire." I also practiced focusing, meditation, and concentration exercises, combining them, as I saw fit, with breathing exercises.[537]
>
> On getting accustomed in that (practice), passions will not arise; or should they do so, they are controlled by the mind.[538]

And in this next passage we see the skill—controlling thoughts before they can control us—in the context of facilitating the practice of extracting "the 'subtle' from the 'dense,' to use Hermetic terms, or of the 'real' from the 'unreal,' to use Hindu terms":

> I would like to say beforehand that since the "external" world is, as we are, *an expression of occult spiritual powers*,[539] we can engage in a relationship with external things that *transcends the*

(Rochester, Vt.: Inner Traditions, 2001), p. 17.

[535] "The Path of Awakening According to Gustave Meyrink." p. 37, 39.

[536] "The Hermetic Caduceus and the Mirror., p. 74

[537] "First Experiences," p. 142.

[538] "Tibetan Initiatic Teachings," p. 234.

[539] Neville: What we *impress* on the imagination is *expressed* in the world.

ordinary relationship of the senses, and one in which our inner being is forced to reveal itself.

We must try to perceive, parallel to every sensible impression, an impression that always accompanies each one yet is of a totally different kind (i.e., an echo in us of the intimate, supersensible nature of things) and *which seeps silently into us*...

We can do the same with our thoughts, always through the exercise of distancing ourselves...; then *we will become increasingly capable of seizing our thought and using it, even before it begins to be articulated in its cerebral formulation.*

An analogous practice may take as object either the emotional contents of our consciousness or the various impulses. I do not want to dwell on this. The meaning is the same: *it is a rapid and subtle attentiveness at the threshold of the Self, which catches and stops perceptions in midair, thus realizing a knowledge of the elements that replaces ordinary, provisory, gross, and sensual consciousness.*[540]

As Evola adds himself:

One of the instruments of operative magic is the ability to fix a feeling, to realize it as an objective something, not connected by the reference to my physical body; as a state that I can posit outside of myself, in space, so to speak, without it ceasing to be a conscious event. *Nothing can be done in operative magic without the capability to evoke, nourish, and then free oneself (by inducing or projecting) from a feeling or a thought.* This skill is somewhat connected to the descent to the center of the earth, and thus to the seat of the heart.[541]

"Fixing a feeling" brings us to the next, the key element: feeling or emotion. This is indeed Neville's "secret," the key to his method.

---

[540] "First Steps Toward the Experience of the 'Subtle Body'" by "Leo"; reprinted in Evola, *Introduction to Magic* (Rochester, Vt.: Inner Traditions, 2001), p. 61.

[541] "Commentary on the *Opus Magicum*," *op. cit.*, p. 57

You must not—merely—dream or contemplate or wish; you must *feel* the state desired, as intensely as possible; *you must love it.* Only thus can it be *impressed* on the Higher Self, which will then—out of necessity—express it as a reality.

> You must make your future dream a present fact. *You do this by assuming the feeling of the wish fulfilled.* By desiring to be other than what you are, you can create an ideal of the person you want to be, and assume that you are already that person. If this assumption is *persisted in until it becomes you dominant feeling,* the attainment of your ideal is inevitable. The ideal you hope to achieve is always ready for an incarnation, but unless you yourself *offer it human parentage* it is incapable of birth. …You must be the thing itself and not merely talk about it or look at it. You must be like the moth in search of his idol, the flame.[542]

Neville no doubt enjoyed fluttering the dovecots of his ladies-who-lunch listeners with his risqué reading of the *Song of Songs*.[543] Many have wondered what on Earth it has to do with the "wise" Solomon to whom it is attributed; Neville reveals that it is, in fact, the key to the Bible itself, and his method:

> What more beautiful description of this romance of the conscious and subconscious is there than that told in the "Song of Solomon": "By night on my bed I sought him whom my soul loveth [3:1]… I found him whom my soul loveth; I held him and

---

[542] *The Power of Awareness* (1952). Neville goes on to say that "This is what wholeness means, this is what integrity means." Integrity, that is, one-ness, is both a mystical and typically American ideal; see, for instance, my discussion of Integrity as the leitmotif of Harry Partch's career, in "Harry Partch, Wild Boy of American Music," reprinted in *The Eldritch Evola* (San Francisco: Counter-Currents, 2014). In *The Right Stuff*, Tom Wolfe talks about the American rocket scientists and their obsession with the leader of their Russian counterparts, always one step ahead of them and known only as The Integral.

[543] Elsewhere, Neville must have enjoyed telling his audience, in response to a question about how to know when you've imagined "enough" to bring something about, that it's just like the act of love: when you're accomplished your goal, you become impotent. Neville works with the traditional—and Traditional—idea of the male consciousness implanting its seed in the female unconscious, which then brings it forth. In Chapter One of *Feeling is the Secret*, he corrects St. Paul: man may be the "head" of the woman, but in our day, women prefer to be persuaded rather than commanded, treated as lovers, not servants.

I not let him go, until I had brought him into my mother's house, and into the chamber of her that conceived me" [3:4].

Preparing to sleep, you feel yourself into the state of the answered wish, and then relax into unconsciousness. Your realized wish is he whom you seek. By night, on your bed, you seek the feeling of the wish fulfilled that you may take it with you into the chamber of her that conceived you, into sleep or the subconscious which gave you form, that this wish also may be given expression.

This is the way to discover and conduct your wishes into the subconscious. Feel yourself in the state of the realized wish and quietly drop off to sleep.

Night after night, you should assume the feeling of being, having and witnessing that which you seek to be, possess and see manifested. Never go to sleep feeling discouraged or dissatisfied. Never sleep in the consciousness of failure.

Your subconscious, whose natural state is sleep, sees you as you believe yourself to be, and whether it be good, bad or indifferent, the subconscious will faithfully embody your belief.

As you feel so do you impress her; and she, the perfect lover, gives form to these impressions and out-pictures them as the children of her beloved.

"Thou art all fair, my love; there is no spot in thee" [Song of Solomon 4:7] is the attitude of mind to adopt before dropping off to sleep.[544]

Again, the Hermetic or Magickal Tradition contains parallel formulations, especially here where "Abraxas" delineates the Two Paths: the Wet and the Dry, Love and Knowledge, Christianity and Gnosis:

It is a method that *essentially acts through the soul and feelings.*

---

[544] *Feeling is the Secret*, Chapter Three, "Sleep."

In order to understand how it must be realized, be aware that *the secret* of its inception consists in creating in yourself a dual being. You must generate—first by imagining and then by realizing it—a superior principle confronting everything you usually are (e.g., an instinctive life, thoughts, feelings). This principle must be able to control, contemplate, and measure what you are, in a clear knowledge, moment by moment. There will be two of you: yourself standing before "the other." Then you will know the meaning of "inner dialogues,"[545] the inward commanding and obeying, the inward asking for and obtaining of advice, as in the case of many Christian and Muslim mystics, and similarly reflected in many Hindu texts that were compiled in dialogue form; *the characters depicted in them are not real persons, but are seen by a skilled disciple as two parts of his own soul.*

All in all, the work consists of a "reversal": you have to turn the "other" into "me" and the "me" into the "other." Depending upon which of the two principles the person focuses on, you will have the Dry Way or the Humid Way, the magical method or the mystical method.

In the mystical method, the mind creates an "other" that still remains "other" (the Master, "Christ" to be imitated, and even the image of the Deity itself). The Self is not transformed; it remains in the feminine part, which consists of desire and need. As soul, the feminine "other" reaches out to Him in an élan of renunciation, love, adoration, and complete devotion. *Sui iuris non esse* (not to be one's own law), letting one's will die completely, to give oneself to God with inner poverty and humility, consecrating to Him every act with pure faith, wishing nothing for oneself, experiencing an untold suffering and love;

---

[545] Neville: "The seemingly harmless habit of "talking to yourself" is the most fruitful form of prayer. A mental argument with the subjective image of another is the surest way to pray for an argument. ...Unfortunately, man forgets his subjective arguments, his daily mental conversations with others, and so is at a loss for an explanation of the conflicts and misfortunes of his life. As mental arguments produce conflicts, so happy mental conversations produce corresponding visible states of good tidings. Man creates himself out of his own imagination." Prayer, Chapter 6: "Good Tidings."

this is what the *mortificatio* requires from those who follow the Humid Way, since they do not possess the strength of an active detachment, but rather yearn for the Eternal, their center being located in the "Waters," in the "soul," or, in other words, precisely in what needs to be depotentized.

However, this way has many imperfections. First among them is the difficulty of transcending *the dualism proper to love* (in the union proper to love, the loved one and the lover communicate with each other but also remain distinct) and of achieving the identity that is the law of every initiatic realization. Thus even at the peaks of Christian mystical theology (which follows exactly this path) we still find a dualism that rarely generates the true substantial transformation into the "other," in which duality, together with the corresponding divine personifications, marks the appearance of a given phase of the process.

A relationship saturated by desire and love is, moreover, negative and dependent; it has the character of need. To turn it into the purely affirmative, central, and self-sufficient solar nature requires a qualitative leap and a daring that is very difficult for a mystic to achieve, considering the contrary nature of the previous mortification.

In addition, through the disposition from which one begins (which is not an active attraction and determination, but a waiting and a desiring), it so happens that the transcendent states appear as a revelation: you are not integrated in them, but remain passive and rootless under their strikingly miraculous power. Ruysbroeck said: "Amidst a feeling of astonishment, something is born: it is an act of grace. Lord, I am not worthy of it!" Moreover, in a text called Light On the Path, it is written: "*You will enter the Light, but you will never touch the Flame.*"

Thus, if you follow the mystical path, make sure to realize the "unitive state." It will transport you and absorb you; flowing into the universal Light, you will suddenly become this very same

Light. With the extinction and fulfillment of your yearning for God, your center will "drown," and this drowning will appear to you as the Ultimate Good and as the highest goal. Our way sees "ecstasy" only as a test to be passed and as a "solvent," but never as the ultimate goal. We do not seek "to go outside" ourselves (ecstasy-displacement), but rather to return and to take possession of the "seat of the Center." The mystical Light represents for us the "Higher Waters," in which your individuality must not diminish, but rather reawaken.

The positive side of this path consists in the room left to individual initiative. Be aware, though, that the mystic, both by believing in the objective, personal, and distinct reality of the ideal of his superior principle (Jesus Christ, as an example to be imitated, or God himself) and by referring to himself the regenerating action ("the action of grace"), unconsciously actualizes some general laws of transcendent praxis. According to these laws, an image "acts" precisely when it is not thought, but presented figuratively and contemplatively fixed in the imagination, and loved as if it were a true reality, distinct from the contemplator. According to these laws, the yearning for growth needs to be killed and your inner being needs to rise in silence *due to an impersonal, calm,* and occult force and *not under the desire to grow.*[546] This desire, in fact, would paralyze growth itself and harden you, due to an unavoidable strengthening of the bond of the Self. These are purely technical details that have nothing moral, religious, or sentimental about them, even though the mystic experiences them under this illusory and mythological guise. For instance, in the "imitation of Christ," we find a series of images that act by arousing subtle forces *that would first produce a "death" and then a "resurrection," even if Christ had never existed.*

In the magical, dry, or solar way, you will create a duality in your being not in an unconscious and passive manner (as the

---

[546] As Neville says elsewhere: "Keep in mind though, that *wanting* to remember pushes memories away. What needs to be done is to *attract* memory, invoking it without desire, *loving it.*"

mystic does), but *consciously and willingly*; you will shift directly on the higher part and identify yourself with that superior and subsistent principle, whereas the mystic tends to identify with his lower part, in a relationship of need and of abandonment. Slowly but gradually, you will strengthen this "other" (which is yourself) and create for it a supremacy, until it knows how to dominate all the powers of the natural part and master them totally. What is required of you is a discipline of firmness and sobriety until an equilibrium is created, namely the quality of a life that owns itself and is free with regard to itself, cleansed from instincts and from the obscure appetite of the natural being, in both flesh and mind. Only then will you be able to employ, usefully and in an auxiliary fashion, some "corrosive water" (an alchemical expression denoting violent methods such as toxic substances, the use of wine and sex, suspension of breath, and so forth). By attacking the natural connections, these give the fixed and pre-established nucleus the possibility of expanding and bursting forth more energetically. However, if this nucleus were not already established, the "corrosive waters," by dissolution, would lead you not above but below the condition from which you first started. The affirmative discipline is enhanced by transformations provoked by some direct method, upon which the entire being, ready and compliant, reaffirms itself, digests and lets itself be digested, leaving nothing behind.

These leaps are faster rhythms in which you must be able to transform the slow tempo of your incarnated being, in the same way that a surfer rides a wave; wherever the wave goes, so does the surfer, thus rejoining himself, remaining affirmative, firm, and centered.

Then the solar and golden nature in you will be able to break the equilibrium and be the stronger one: the other nature (your Self, your senses, and your mind) will be under your control. At that point you can even suspend them, make them inert, neutralized, fixed. This is Silence, the "extinction of mania," the dissolving of the fog. Then, in your clarified eye, the cyclical, integral vision will shine forth; you will see your transcendent essence, the destiny of beings and of all things, and the kingdom of "Those Who Are." You will grasp the mode of action in a pure state, and you will grasp the mode of immaterial motion that operates outside every space or body in a timeless, creative rapidity. The center in you will amalgamate with universal, non-becoming nature, and will derive from it a divine strength that expresses itself through miraculous powers. You will be able to focus on the knowledge of the Names and on the wedding with the Letters. You will be initiated.

The "knowledge of the Waters" and the sense of awakening need to be integrated with the awareness of these various methodical possibilities, in order to obtain a power of awareness and discrimination, before the elements of magical practice are revealed to you.[547]

And again, Evola himself:

Another technical detail is in order. *In order for any image to act in the way I am talking about, it must be loved.* It must be assumed in a great, inner calm and then warmed up, almost nourished, with sweetness, without bringing the will or any effort into play, and much less without expectations. The Hermeticists called this agent "sweet fire," "fire that does not burn," and even "fire of the lamp" since it really has an enlightening effect on the images.[548]

Both paths, the Wet and Dry, or the Mystical and Magickal, require that our imagination create an ideal to serve as a focal point of concentration, meditation, love. The Wet path, however, is defective, in that it preserves and rests content in the duality of love, while the Dry path will not "cease from mental strife" (Blake) until unity is achieved.

---

[547] "Three Ways," pp. 49-51; all italics mine.

[548] "Commentary on the *Opus Magicum*," op. cit., p. 57. "The fire of the lamp" recalls Neville's "You must be like the moth in search of his idol, the flame." Again, the Tooth Fairy comes to mind: an investigator muses over one of his tell-tale *moths*: "Somebody grew this guy. Fed him honey and nightshade, kept him warm. Somebody loved him." *Silence of the Lambs* (Demme, 1990).

Similarly, Neville, like the Gnostics, distinguishes worshiping some purportedly historical Christ in some religious context, and becoming Christ as a psychological act here and now. *What we entertain in imagination we become.* And as was pointed out in the quote just now, this also implies that the Bible, like all scriptures, is a psychological document, not a historical one: a point to which we shall return:

> Today those to whom this great treasure has been entrusted, namely, the priesthoods of the world, have forgotten that the Bibles are psychological dramas representing the consciousness of man. In their blind forgetfulness they now teach their followers to worship its characters as men and women who actually lived in time and space.
>
> Man has so long worshipped the images of his own making that at first he finds this revelation blasphemous, but the day man discovers and accepts this principle as the basis of his life, that day man slays his belief in a God apart from himself.[549]

Thus Neville's method is based not on faith, but experience: a "Confession of faith *in terms of experience*."

> [The resurrected Christ] offers his knowledge of Scripture based on his own experience, for that of others based on speculation. Accept his offer. And it will keep you from losing your way among the tangled speculations that pass for religious truth.
>
> [The writers of the Gospels do not] hesitat[e] to interpret the Old Testament according to their own supernatural experiences.[550]

In the same way, Evola distinguishes "initiatic knowledge" from both science and faith, as a path in which "the criterion of direct experience is [is applied to higher realms but] never abandoned."[551]

As we've seen, Neville *bases his method on sleep* – a kind of

---

[549] *Your Faith is Your Fortune* (1941).

[550] *Resurrection*.

[551] Ea [a pseudonym of Evola], "The Nature of Initiatic Knowledge," *op. cit.*, p. 27.

"dream yoga." For him, prayer is only a waking mode of sleep. Here is Neville detailing his method:

> Preparing to sleep, you feel yourself into the state of the answered wish, and then relax into unconsciousness. Your realized wish is he whom you seek. By night on your bed you seek the feeling of the wish fulfilled that you may take it with you into the chamber of her that conceived you, into sleep or the subconscious which gave you form, that this wish also may be given expression. This is the way to discover and conduct your wishes into the subconscious. Feel yourself in the state of the realized wish and quietly drop off to sleep.
>
> Night after night you should assume the feeling of being, having and witnessing that which you seek to be, possess and see manifested. Never go to sleep feeling discouraged or dissatisfied. Never sleep in the consciousness of failure. Your subconscious, whose natural state is sleep, sees you as you believe yourself to be, and whether it be good, bad, or indifferent, the subconscious will faithfully embody your belief. As you feel so do you impress her; and she, the perfect lover, gives form to these impressions and out-pictures them as the children of her beloved. "Thou art all fair, my love; there is no spot in thee," is the attitude of mind to adopt before dropping off to sleep. Disregard appearances and feel that things are as you wish them to be, for "He calleth things that are not seen as though they were, and the unseen becomes seen." To assume the feeling of satisfaction is to call conditions into being which will mirror satisfaction. "Signs follow, they do not precede." Proof that you are will follow the consciousness that you are; it will not precede it.
>
> You are an eternal dreamer dreaming non-eternal dreams.[552]

In "Commentaries on the *Opus Magicum*," Evola sketches a remarkably similar discipline:

---

[552] *Feeling is the Secret* (1947).

To these matters, I want to add a practice with which it is possible to go further in this direction, and thanks to which many other disciplines will be greatly enhanced and vivified. This practice breaks down into two phases, namely the moment that precedes falling asleep and the moment that follows waking up in the morning.

[B]efore falling asleep, in a calm state, not being tired, having cleansed the mind of all worries, imagine through meditation to be at the foot of a mountain in the early hours of the morning, ready to begin the ascent. Slowly, let the ascent begin, while darkness fades away and the first light, then the sun, appears. You must continue to ascend, imagining the simultaneous rising of the sun in the sky, its growing, triumphant, expanding light shining over all things. Right at the moment you feel you have reached the peak of the mountain, become aware that the sun has reached its zenith in the clear, bright sky. Contemplation needs to be stopped at this point, as you recognize all this as the sense of that which will effectively happen within, beyond the threshold of sleep, until the middle of the night. Naturally, your ascent of the mountain and the rise of the sun from dawn to noon must be felt in strict correlation. Everything must be experienced from an inner perspective as a progression of awakening. This process, once the top of the mountain is reached, must give rise to a sense of identification with the noon light—radiant, silent, pure in the boundless ether.

In the morning, upon waking up, clear the mind from any residue of sleepiness and return through contemplation to the peak of the mountain, which is where you had remained; slowly head back to the valley below. In the meantime, the sun descends, sets, and every light will disappear by the time you reach the plain. This must be imagined and remembered as the meaning of the period between the middle of the night and the morning. In the darkness of the day, in which you find yourself when you awake, let the echo of the Light from above or the echo of the Midnight Sun linger in the sensation that I am the bearer of this Light that is now in your center, namely in the heart. Then you will notice the new, animated sense, according to which the light of the physical sun will appear when these disciplines are realized and lived. Also, you should notice and pay much attention to any other new meaning that flashes in the midst of common perceptions. Besides mere imagining, try to really recall some of the impressions of that time in which, aside from dreams, consciousness is interrupted by sleep.[553]

You can see why Israel Regardie says that "Of all the metaphysical systems with which I am acquainted, Neville's is the most magical."[554] But being New Thought, it's a very stripped down, to the point, no bullshit kind of magick.[555] You may find that attractive; I certainly do.

But you may also find it unsatisfying, even unworkable, due to this very simplicity, or barrenness. Where are the robes, the chants, the magical instruments? Even the disillusioned postmodern acolytes of Chaos magick grant the importance of such frippery to create the right support for the training of the Will, what Colin Wilson calls "frameworks."[556]

---

[553] Op. cit., pp. 55-56. Evola adds the helpful detail: "The memory is also facilitated by a slight scent of musk, rose, or Florentine iris." Not coincidentally, mountains were Evola's passion, his framework; see the essays and article collected in *Meditations on the Peaks* (Rochester, Vt.: Inner Traditions, 1998).

[554] Speaking of magick, there is, as with so many mystics, a sexual undercurrent in Neville's teaching. The tall, handsome man with the pleasing voice and vaguely British accent must have stirred some hearts among the housewives seeking something more spiritual than Liberace; and unlike Liberace, he's teaching you how to do it yourself! (Liberace himself was, like Phyllis Diller, an outspoken devotee of Claude M. Bristol's *The Magic of Believing* [1948]). In explaining the role of sleep in transferring our conscious desires into concrete reality, he asks us to conceive of the unconscious as a willing and adept lover, accessed during sleep, and likes to dwell on passages from the *Song of Songs*, especially one where the beloved is invited "into the chamber of her that conceived me." And in answer to a question about when to know that the desired end has been fully realized in imagination, Neville blithely says it's like sex; when the man reaches his goal, his desire fades, and he becomes impotent. "Oh, Captain Spaulding!" Pretty racy stuff for 40s and 50s America!

[555] New Thought is the typically American presentation of the Hermetic Tradition, right down to marketing its Traditional wisdom as "New," which continues to mislead scholars and critics.

[556] See my review of Richard B. Spence's *Secret Agent 666*, supra.

These "frameworks" are part of what provides the emotional saturation we spoke of earlier. Regardie suggests that Neville, a professional entertainer, obviously had a richly developed talent for imagination, or rehearsal, and vastly underestimated his audience's ability to simply "see the world from Barbados."

But Regardie also notices that Neville does have a framework to produce emotional intensity: The Bible.

It may be hard to imagine (if you will) today, in our postmodern, multicultural and above all illiterate world, but as recently as the 60s one could count on an audience, for better or worse, to be pretty familiar with the Bible, and pretty willing to take it as an authority of some kind. [557]

But Neville is actually more modern than his audience. For he is insistent, right up front and over and over again—a sign of how trusting his audience's faith is—that the Bible is not history, but psychology.[558]

> Tonight I will use scripture, but my premise will not be along any orthodox concept of Christ, for scripture is…God's secret, which cannot be read with complete understanding, but must be experienced.[559]

> When you read in the Book of Revelation, "Jesus Christ, the faithful witness, the first born from the dead," you may think—as the world does—of a unique being who came into the world two thousand years ago.

---

[557] Although, as already noted, Neville was a successful platform lecturer and broadcaster, today the language, both Biblical and sophisticated, is perhaps no longer comprehensible to the average American. Dr. Wayne Dyer has also apparently discovered Neville only recently, despite about 40 years in the Oprah-sphere. His recent book, *Wishes Fulfilled: Mastering the Art of* Manifesting (New York: Hay House, 2012), was written when he discovered, after sharing Neville's *The Power of Awareness* with his children, that each of them complained about having to "read each paragraph over and over and stop to think about what he's saying," and expressing the need to "have it explained more." (p. 32).

[558] See "Tales of the Christos Mythos," my review of Kenneth Humphreys' *Jesus Never Existed: An Introduction to the Ultimate Heresy* (Charleston, W.V.: Nine-Banded Books, 2014), Counter-Currents, May 20, 2015.

[559] Again, the Hermetic/Evolian emphasis on experience (perhaps mystical) over faith.

> The Bible is sacred history, not secular history, and the events recorded there go on forever and ever.
>
> After making hundreds of millions of dollars out of the poor people by selling little medallions and statues of these saints, the church now proclaims they never existed. They were all one grand myth, started by the church for monetary purposes. Millions of these little medallions were sold as intermediaries between man and God, when the human imagination is God, whose name is I AM![560]
>
> While reading scripture, always bear in mind that it is a story of salvation and not secular history, that the characters—from Adam to Jesus—are states of consciousness.

Even his last book, *Resurrection*, which we've described as little more than a scriptural pastiche, ends with a quote from Blake—"Moses and Abraham, are not here meant, but Stories Signified by those Names," etc.)—and the blunt statement:

> There is no secular history in the Bible. The Bible is the history of salvation and is wholly supernatural.

Now this is fascinating, for while the Bible as Myth was well established in scholarly circles around the turn of the last century, an Evangelical counter-attack has driven it from the field, only to be revived more recently, partly due, once more, to the Internet. Neville, thus, represents both a retrograde and a progressive trend, a kind of missing link existing between the great skeptical periods.[561]

---

[560] "Spiritual Sensation," 05-16-1969. In the last paragraph, Neville seems to be referencing the post-Vatican II Church's admission that many if not most of the "saints" of the liturgical calendar were fictional; no refunds, however, were offered. Although not essential to the Christ Myth theory, most advocates seem to delight in such quotes as "This fable has served us well" (Pope Leo X).

[561] "A State Called Moses," 4-29-1968. The earlier New Thought writers frequently presented their teachings as Gospel-based, or as a new revelation completing or supplementing the Gospels, but I don't believe any of them rejected the "historicity" of the Bible as such. "Neville once said that if he was stranded on an island and was allowed one book, he would choose The Bible, without hesitation. If he could squeeze in more,

III. THE TURN

At the end of the 50s, Neville's message changed. I like to give it the Heideggerian name of The Turning: from what he called The Law (as in Oprah's "Law of Attraction") to The Promise. It was as a result of an experience in San Francisco, on July 20, 1959, and like Abdullah teaching Neville the Law, it deserves to be told in his own inimitable way:

> One night I went to sleep quite normally in the city of San Francisco and in the wee hours of the morning a most intense vibration was taking place in my head and I begin to awake. Instead of awakening on the bed in my hotel room, I am awakening in my skull to find my skull not a room – my skull is a sepulcher, a tomb, and I am fully awake in my skull – alone. For the first time in eternity I really was awake. There was one moment of panic, and after that moment of panic I began to feel around, and I felt the base of my skull and I pushed and something gave, and out I came, head first, just like a child being born, and down I came, inch by inch by inch. I pulled myself out of my skull and there I lay on the floor for a few seconds. Then I arose, and looked back at the bed and there was my body on the bed. It was ghastly pale, tossing my head from side to side. Then I heard this wind—a fantastic wind, as described in the book of Acts—and here came a sudden wind from heaven. I looked over to the corner of the room because it came from that direction,

---

he would add Charles Fillmore's *Metaphysical Dictionary of Bible Names*, William Blake, and [Maurice] Nicoll's *Commentaries*. These were the books he recommended at his lectures." Online at http://www.nevillegoddard.wwwhubs.com/). Neville was glad to share this opinion with his greatest precursor, Blake: "In Blake's "Visions of the Last Judgment," he said: "It ought to be understood that the Persons Moses and Abraham are not here meant, but states signified by those names as they were revealed to mortal man in a series of divine revelations, as they are written in the Bible." Having seen the entire play, Blake added: "When you see them from afar they appear as one man, but as you approach they appear as multitudes of nations, as the One Man becomes the many." See also his booklet *Blake on Imagination*. Fillmore was one of those Christianizing New Thinkers; Maurice Nicoll's *The Mark* and *The New Man* offered an equally psychological approach to the Bible after the War, outwardly Jungian but actually covertly Gurdjieffian (as in his six-volume *Psychological Commentaries on the Teaching of Gurdjieff and Ouspensky*); once more, we see Neville as a missing link, this time from Fillmore to Nicoll.

and then I looked back to the bed where the body was and the body was gone; they removed the body, a body that was so real only a few seconds before. But here sat three witnesses, three men; they didn't see me and I am more real than I have ever been in eternity. I suddenly became aware of the reality of my own invisibility. I am more real than anything in eternity, and yet no one sees me. I can see them, I not only see them, I can discern their thoughts. Their thoughts are to me [as] objective as you are. They are all curious about the wind, but one is the most curious and he got off the bed and started toward the same direction that I thought the wind originated. As he started over he looked at the floor and he said: "Why it's Neville's baby!" And they together asked in the most incredulous manner: "How could Neville have a baby?" He doesn't argue the point; he lifts an infant wrapped in swaddling clothes and places that infant on the bed. Then I took that infant in my hands, looked into its smiling face—it does that—and I asked it: "How is my sweetheart?" And this heavenly smile broke upon its face – and then the whole thing dissolved, and I am on my bed in the hotel in San Francisco. That is the beginning of the unfolding of God's promise: "I will give you a son."[562]

---

[562] "God's Promise to Man – Feb 2, 1963." I don't believe anyone has tried to compare this with the awakening of the Kundalini and the breaking through of the Crown chakra during the ultimate stages of the process of enlightenment, described by many mystics; for example, Franklin Jones (aka Da Free John, Adi Da and numerous other titles); see his autobiography, *The Knee Of Listening: The Divine Ordeal of The Avataric Incarnation of Conscious Light. Book Four of the Seventeen Companions of the True Dawn Horse* (1st ed. 1972 subtitled "The Early Life and Radical Spiritual Teachings of Franklin Jones", 2nd ed. 1973, 3rd ed. 1978, 4th ed. 1984, standard ed. 1992, new ed. 1995 subtitled "The Early-Life Ordeal and the Radical Spiritual Realization of the Divine World-Teacher, Adi Da (The Da Avatar)", standard ed. 2004); this was first published in San Francisco in 1972, the year Neville left this third dimensional world. Da's Vedantic teaching method of "self inquiry" ("Who AM I") might be usefully compared to Neville's Judeo-Christian "Before Abraham, I AM." (Neville, like most everyone, relies on a translation that some recent scholars question; see my review of Robert M. Price's *The Human Bible* at Counter-Currents, May 26, 2015; although in general Price is one of the leading scholars of the modern Christ Myth school). Fortunately, the similarities stop there: "Showing promise of becoming a great spiritual adept and brilliant teacher of self-inquiry and Self-realization (with a strong emphasis on grounding this realization in heartfelt relationship and "enlightenment of the whole body"), very quickly, within less than two years of public work, all evidence indicates that Franklin Jones/Da Free John fell deeply and dangerously into monstrous ego-inflation,

As one follower recalls:

> From that moment on Neville's lectures changed. Having awakened from the dream of life, Neville's outlook on the world changed. He knew, as the visions came upon him from that point on, that the garment he wore, and answered to its name, was simply a covering, hiding his true, immortal being who was God the Father. And he tried to tell all those who would listen that they were not the little mask they wore, but a being far greater than they could ever conceive themselves to be.
>
> And from that day forward, until his departure on October 1, 1972 Neville, like Paul, expounded from morning till night, testifying to the kingdom of God and trying to convince all about Jesus, both from the Law of Moses and the prophets. And some believed, while others disbelieved.[563]

Although not, as we have seen, strictly inconsistent with his previous message, it was not a good marketing move. According to Mitch Horowitz:

> His audiences, however, seemed to prefer the earlier message of self-affirmation. They began to drift away. Urged by a speaking agent to abandon this theme, "or you'll have no audience at all," a student recalls Neville replying, "Then I'll tell it to the bare walls." His popularity would partly rebound as he settled into teaching a mixture of both the mystical and creative-mind aspects of his

---

abusively toxic relationships towards his disciples and wife/wives, and heavy addictions to personal power, sexual debauchery, drugs, and extravagant material possessions. We have here the sad story of a gifted and highly educated young man endeavoring for spiritual mastery who became, instead, an unknowing egocentric slave to aspects of a very needy, sick, 'shadow' part of the psyche. He then exploited his trusting disciples and turned them into his own serfs in a slavish cult—often descending into a nightmare—that pretended to create a heavenly scene around the 'Incarnate God,' Adi Da." See "Adi Da and His Voracious, Abusive Personality Cult" by Timothy Conway, http://www.enlightened-spirituality.org/Da_and_his_cult.html.

[563] "Who Was Neville Goddard?" by Margaret Ruth Broome, from *The Miracle of Imagination;* online at https://freeneville.com/margaret-ruth-broome-on-neville-goddard/

philosophy.[564]

Indeed, his last book, *Resurrection* (1971), though hailed by some as his summa, is a short work, really a booklet, seemingly stitched together from a hatful of Biblical quotes, with very little of the distinctively Neville hermetic interpretation.

Neville left this dimension in 1972, the same year as Alan Watts, leaving, for some reason, no obituary.

IV. SO WHAT?

We've said that Tradition and magick rely on experience, not faith, and Neville was by no means uninterested in proving his ideas. In one of his very first books, *Freedom for All: A Practical Application of the Bible* (1942), right in the very first paragraph, he writes

> Public opinion will not long endure a theory which does not work in practice. Today, probably more than ever before, man demands proof of the truth of even his highest ideal.

In fact, one of his last books, *The Law and the Promise* (1961), consists mostly of "case studies" of the usual "a reader/listener writes that…" variety.

> The purpose of the first portion of this book is to show, through actual true stories, how imagining creates reality. Science progresses by way of hypotheses tentatively tested and afterwards accepted or rejected according to the facts of experience. The claim that imagining creates reality needs no more consideration than is allowed by science. It proves itself in performance.

Actually, what passes for "science" has for some time now been

---

[564] "Searching for Neville Goddard." Originally published in the March 2005 issue of *Science of Mind*, it also appears as the introduction to *The Neville Reader: A Collection of Spiritual Writings and Thoughts on Your Inner Power to Create an Abundant Life* (DeVorss, 2005).

the province of smug hypocrites ignorantly[565]—or perhaps disingenuously—defending an arbitrary personal metaphysical preference for dead-level materialism as if it were an essential component of scientific method, or indeed of rationality itself, it's not likely they or their blind followers will be very impressed, even if they should deign to pick up the book.[566]

But Neville is admittedly not really interested in "scientific" proof; right after that sentence above about what the public demands, he goes on to specify that:

> For ultimate satisfaction man must find a principle which is for him a way of life, a principle *which he can experience as true*.[567]

Already by 1944, Neville was becoming less sanguine about proof, in *Feeling is the Secret*:

> Were it possible to carry conviction to another by means of reasoned arguments and detailed instances, this book would be many times its size. It is seldom possible, however, to do so by means of written statements or arguments since to the suspended judgment it always seems plausible to say that the author was dishonest or deluded, and, therefore, his evidence was tainted. Consequently, I have purposely omitted all arguments and testimonials, and simply *challenge the open-minded reader to practice the law of consciousness as revealed in this book*. Personal

---

[565] Having proclaimed that philosophy is nonsense, and therefore not worth reading, Steven Hawking—a genius in his own field—decides nevertheless to do it himself; badly, of course, as he would have predicted had a child proposed to re-invent quantum mechanics out of his own head.

[566] As Alan Watts pointed out, it is metaphysics that is "rockily practical," and the hard-headed man of facts is in fact beholden to an unexamined—and long since refuted—metaphysical system. For an antidote to the Mad Hatter of Oxford and his ilk, try *Richard Dawkins: The Pope of Unreason* by the Illuminati's Mike Hockney (Hyperreality Books, 2014).

[567] Similarly, Rene Guénon disdained the demand that he "prove" his metaphysical Tradition, before embarking on the path to transformation: "It is one of the worst characteristics of modern Western man to substitute the philosophy of knowledge for knowledge itself." Or as Zen would say, mistaking the finger pointing to the moon for the moon itself.

success will prove far more convincing than all the books that could be written on the subject.

As a wisdom older than Francis Bacon would have it, *the proof is in the pudding*.[568] And this is very much in tune with Neville's whole *Weltanschauung*: as he says, an assumption, however wrong, if persisted in, will *become* true. Like William James' Will to Believe, by adopting the hypothesis we create the evidence, in the future.[569]

As John N. Deck says of Plotinus: he is not so much interested in proving his ideas as he is in circling around them over and over, thereby "accustoming the reader to their truth."[570]

As should be clear, I am less interested in Neville's magick as a testable hypothesis than as a entailment, or a pragmatic application, of a general metaphysical standpoint, found throughout East and West, which someone like Evola might identify with the Hermetic Tradition, or if not perhaps with what Guénon would apply the honorific term Tradition *tout court*.[571]

And so, Dear Reader, I recently put Neville's method into practice myself. After staying over two years as a "temp" employee, I decided to try to visualize my way into a "permanent" position, or if not, at least a substantial wage increase as a reward for long and apparently acceptable service. Here is another chap describing how he—and I—utilized Neville's method:

> All the while I persisted in seeing and feeling myself shaking hands with the owner congratulating me and my friend who works at the company giving me a congratulatory hug. I experienced myself walking through the office with my new supervisor who introduced me to the other employees and

---

[568] "Don't dream it, just be it." – *The Rocky Horror Picture Show* (Jim Sharman, 1975).

[569] "Future events such as these will affect you in the future."

[570] John N. Deck, *Nature, Contemplation, and the One: A Study in the Philosophy of Plotinus* (University of Toronto Press, 1969; Toronto Heritage series, 2017 [Kindle iOS version]); Preface.

[571] In much the same diffident way Alan Watts once said that astrology was "obviously" true, since it is simply an application or consequence of the general view that "Everything is Connected" if not One; however, *how* it's true, and more importantly, *how* it works, seems to be still unknown.

showed me my workspace. I saw and felt this all in "first person," not from a detached "third-person" state.[572]

And sure enough, one day, I was called into the boss's office, and notified that the position would not be made permanent, and in fact was being eliminated. So, not only did I not get a permanent position, or a raise, but I was now fully unemployed for the first time in almost three years. Pretty spectacular failure, eh? *Peenemunde* class.[573]

Fortunately, Neville has a whole chapter on "Failure," for

> This book would not be complete without some discussion of *failure* in the attempted use of the law of assumption.[574]

Already in his very first book, *At Your Command,* Neville addresses the problem of what he calls "conditioning" a desire – asking for a specific result, as if that were the only way to accomplish one's goal.

> The reason men condition their desires is because they constantly judge after the appearance of being and see the things as real – forgetting that the only reality is the consciousness back of them. To see things as real is to deny that all things are possible to God. The man who is imprisoned and sees his four walls as real is automatically denying the urge or promise of God within him of freedom.
>
> A question often asked when this statement is made is; If one's desire is a gift of God how can you say that if one desires to kill a man that such a desire is good and therefore God sent? In answer to this let me say that no man desires to kill another. What he does desire is to be freed from such a one. But because he does not believe that the desire to be free from such a one contains

---

[572] A reader's "Thrilling Success Story," at FreeNeville.com.

[573] "Well, that escalated quickly." Ron Burgundy, *Anchorman: The Legend of Ron Burgundy* (Adam McKay, 2004). Again, as in Wolfe's *The Right Stuff,* the German-Americans watch one rocket after another crash and burn, while The Integral moves from launch triumph to launch triumph.

[574] *The Power of Awareness* (1952), Chapter 24, "Failure," italics Neville's.

within itself the powers of freedom, he conditions that desire and sees the only way to express such freedom is to destroy the man – forgetting that the life wrapped within the desire has ways that he, as man, knows not of. Its ways are past finding out. Thus man distorts the gifts of God through his lack of faith.[575]

Again, Wallace Wattles gives a similar response to the question of failure:

> Go on in the certain way, and if you do not receive that thing, you will receive something so much better that you will see that the seeming failure was really a great success.
>
> A student of this science had set his mind on making a certain business combination which seemed to him at the time to be very desirable, and he worked for some weeks to bring it about. When the crucial time came, the thing failed in a perfectly inexplicable way; it was as if some unseen influence had been working secretly against him. He was not disappointed; on the contrary, he thanked God that his desire had been overruled, and went steadily on with a grateful mind. In a few weeks an opportunity so much better came his way that he would not have made the first deal on any account; and he saw that a Mind which knew more than he knew had prevented him from losing the greater good by entangling himself with the lesser.
>
> That is the way every seeming failure will work out for you, if you keep your faith, hold to your purpose, have gratitude, and do, every day, all that can be done that day, doing each separate act in a successful manner.
>
> *When you make a failure, it is because you have not asked for enough; keep on, and a larger thing then you were seeking will certainly come to you. Remember this.*[576]

---

[575] *At Your Command* (1937).

[576] *The Science of Getting Rich* by Wallace D. Wattles; Chapter 16: "Some Cautions, and Concluding Observations." Published in 1910, with innumerable editions since.

Thus, my real goal was financial freedom; my idea of keeping this job is a condition laid upon that goal by my implicit belief that this is the only path to that goal.[577] One must, Neville says, will the end, not the means; live in the assumption of the goal *being* here now, not concerned with *how* to get it; the latter is impious, as it implies one isn't it *now* already. Don't imagine becoming a writer; imagine the circumstances that imply you *are* one, now.[578]

Which is another way of saying that you can only employ The Method when what you desire is what you are now; what is your very nature. Not some random act chosen to "test" the Method, or "prove" you're God making it rain, or something logically impossible. These true desires Neville calls "basic desires":

> God speaks to man only through the medium of his basic desires.
> Your desires are determined by your conception of yourself.
> Your desires are *the natural and automatic result* of your present conception of yourself.[579]

---

[577] Dyer, *op. cit*,. speaks about the need to not conceive of what he calls "the Highest Self" in egoic terms, as if one were claiming to be a big guy in the sky, just as you are, but all-powerful. Similarly, Watts used to point out that if asked "If you're God, then why don't you make it rain" the proper response is "Well, it happens without my conscious knowledge or decision; I don't know how to breathe or beat my heart, either." Both Dyer and Neville are allowing their Gnostic conceptions to show, by denying that "God" could be an egotistic monster. As many, from Marcion to Jung have noted, the Hebrew JHVH shows all the signs of not being not just all-too human but an outright murderous psychotic—Marcionites called him "the Exterminator," identified him will an evil, false god, and edited out the Hebrew scriptures from their canon. Gnostic or not, Neville is quite orthodox in re-interpreting or else ignoring anything in the so-called Old Testament that conflicts with his New Thought, if not New Testament, Jesus.

[578] You can't become a writer, you can only be one, now; see my DIY essay "How I Write, and You Can Too!" at Counter-Currents, Sep 21, 2015.

[579] *Freedom for All,* Chapter 7: "Desire: The Word of God." As Neville interprets Christ's "I AM the Alpha and the Omega," our basic desires (what I want to be) are what we are, already. To try and visual or figure out the means is not only futile, as the Universe has many means available to bring it about; but it is even more deeply impious, implying these are separate and need to be brought together. In the chapter just quoted from, Neville inveighs against "individuals and nations alike [who] are constantly violating this law of their basic desire by plotting and planning the realization of their ambitions;" this suggests *The Dark Knight*'s Joker and his jihad against "planners" and "plotters." The modern world has so cut itself off from Tradition that, as Trevor Lynch has suggested, Traditional ideas are only allowed in our popular culture if assigned to master criminals and madmen.

So, looking at it another way, to imagine what you are, now, is to imagine your own true nature. So Neville says in his chapter on Failure:

> The fact that it does not feel *natural* to you to be what you imagine yourself to be is *the secret of your failure*. Regardless of your desire, regardless of how faithfully and intelligently you follow the law if you do not feel *natural* about what you want to be *you will not be it*. If it does not feel natural to you to get a better job you will not get a better job.[580]

In truth, I didn't belong at that job anyway. I hated the people—smug New York jerks—and the operation, I gradually realized, was an academic con game, designed to sell hapless low-IQ students into lifetimes of debt slavery, while funding the faculty's 60s era feel-good Liberal "activism."

Moreover, as Wattles suggested, I did not go unrewarded. They felt so guilty over the obvious outrage that they tried—successfully—to buy me off with two weeks severance (as opposed to the unseal no-weeks given to temps). Then, that same weekend, an old friend came into some money, recalled an old debt, and presented me with the cash equivalent of another week's salary. I now had almost a month paid for, enabling me to do some writing—this essay, for example—while engaging in an unstressed job search. And after the weekend passed, I got an unsolicited call from another nonprofit doing real work, and since then I've been employed pretty consistently and at far more enjoyable locations.

To revert to another American Transcendentalist, Henry David Thoreau: in the "Conclusion" of *Walden*, Thoreau says,

> I learned this, at least, by my experiment; that *if one advances confidently in the direction of his dreams, and endeavors to live the life which he has imagined, he will meet with a success unexpected in common hours*. He will put some things behind, will pass an invisible boundary; new, universal, and more liberal laws will begin to establish themselves around and within him; or

---

[580] *The Power of Awareness*, loc. cit., italics Neville's.

the old laws will be expanded, and interpreted in his favor in a more liberal sense, and he will live with the license of a higher order of beings. *In proportion as he simplifies his life*, the laws of the universe will appear less complex, and solitude will not be solitude, *nor poverty poverty*, nor weakness weakness.

Remember, Neville's instructions to pare down one's fantasy to *a simple statement* or action that presumes the fulfillment of the thing wished for? And the all-purpose one he suggests is *a simple "Thank you."*

Just as Neville has a chapter on "Failure," Wattles has one on "Gratitude."

> The whole process of mental adjustment and atonement[581] can be summed up in one word, gratitude.
>
> Many people who order their lives rightly in all other ways are kept in poverty by their lack of gratitude. Having received one gift form God, they *cut the wire which connects them with him* by failing to make acknowledgment.
>
> It is easy to understand that the nearer we live to the source of wealth, the more wealth we shall receive; and it is easy also to understand that *the soul that is always grateful lives in closer touch with God* than the one which never looks to Him in thankful acknowledgment.
>
> The more gratefully we fix our minds on the Supreme when good things come to us, the more good things we will receive, and the more rapidly they will come;[582] and the reason simply is that *the mental attitude of gratitude draws the mind into closer touch with the source from which the blessings come.*[583]

---

[581] Not creepy Protestant "total depravity" but as Watts suggests, "at-one-ment." Man is imagination, imagination is God, "I and the Father are One," the world is just my projected imagination; I don't "control" it, I AM it.

[582] Hence, the puzzling saying of Jesus: "To those who have, more shall be given." Neville explicitly relates that saying to his Law of Assumption: act as if you already have now what you desire and you will have it.

[583] *The Science of Getting Rich*, Chapter 7, "Gratitude."

Yet more profoundly, Neville, and Tradition, tell us that we need not even try to draw the mind closer, as it is so close as not to be even "near"– implying as that word does some spatial distinction, however small. As Christ says, "I and the Father are One." Man is Imagination, and Imagination is God. That is why Christ "always does the Father's will;" if he and the Father are one, their wills are one. What God wills, I will; and thus "Thy will be done."[584]

As with Crowley's "knowledge and conversation with the Holy Guardian Angel," the secret of magick is to so identify oneself with (or realize one's existing identify with) God that God's will, what "happens," is one's own will anyway.[585]

It seems that, despite starting off with all that exciting talk about getting "whatever" you desire, one ultimately winds up with a simple instruction to face the universe with confidence and gratitude— Colin Wilson's self-fulfilling self-confidence, Chesterton's "absurd good news"—what else can you do, what with our being God and all. No goals are really necessary, since whatever happens is God's will, which is our will, and is for the best.

Aristokratia IV (2017)

---

[584] I, like Neville, pass over will sovereign contempt the centuries of bloody Christian wrangling over the "nature" of Christ's will: human, divine, or both?

[585] Again, as when Watts was challenged to "prove" his was God by performing some act like making it rain or thunder: Well, look around you; I'm already doing all this! And don't ask me how; I don't even know how I beat my heart!

NEVILLE AND THE REBEL:
REFLECTIONS ON COLIN WILSON AND NEVILLE GODDARD

"What was needed was not some new religious cult but some simple way of accessing religious or mystical experience, of the sort that must have been known to the monks and cathedral-builders of the Middle Ages." – Colin Wilson[586]

"The serpent said that every dream could be willed into creation by those strong enough to believe in it." – Eve to Adam, in Shaw's *Back to Methuselah*

Colin Wilson spent his life and his career—for him, as an existential philosopher, the two are one—pursuing a method, first in philosophy and literature, then in the occult, that would "crystallize into a philosophy of life that will bring order out of chaos and unity out of discord."[587] Can we say that another occult figure taught such a method before Wilson was even born? Most decidedly, we can![588]

One of the most irritating tropes of our age—at least among the dominant SJW journalistic class—is when the journo starts off by

---

[586] *The Angry Years: The Rise and Fall of the Angry Young Men* (London: Robson Books, 2007; Kindle, 2014), p66.

[587] Chap calling himself Zeteticus who conducted an online reading of *Religion and the Rebel* at the Soul Spelunker website; this is from Part Four, here: http://soulspelunker.com/2017/07/religion-rebel-part-4.html.

[588] Neville, *At Your Command* (New York: Snellgrove Publications, 1939); see *At Your Command: The First Classic Work by the Visionary Mystic Neville* (Tarcher Cornerstone Editions, 2016), which includes Mitch Horowitz's essay on Neville's life and work, "Neville Goddard: A Cosmic Philosopher;" and see also my review, Lord Kek Commands! A Look at the Origins of Meme Magic," *infra*.

narrating some incident that just happened to them, or something they just happened to overhear, which constitutes a total validation of some supposed problem or assumption on their part, thus kicking off the essay or article exploring this continuing abuse crying out for immediate attention. For example, after The Coming of Trump, tormented snowflakes tweeted and youtubed endless stories like this one:

> So, I was in line to vote, and these two guys behind me, real frat boy-looking, starting talking real loudly about how they were gonna get some ropes and take care of the immigrants. And I'm like, dudes, don't you see I'm Hispanic, and everyone around you is too? And they just laughed and said "it's Trump time, bitch!" I was never so scared in my life, but I voted anyway!

And for my part, I'm like, Bullshit! Two "frat boys" not only living in an overwhelmingly Hispanic voting district, but they're taking the opportunity, while standing in line, no doubt next to some cops and voting overseers, to rant about lynching immigrants. Yeah, that happens.

Although this is obviously rampant in the current tsunami of rape accusations and hate hoaxes, it occurs on smaller scales throughout our sorry culture. And I was reminded of it when Phil Baker, attempting to convey the deep loathing of the British literary establishment (yes, there still is such a thing, or at least something that thinks it is) for the late Colin Wilson, produced this supposed anecdote:

> Meanwhile Iain Sinclair, master of the ambulant put-down, has been less restrained. Walking round a book market in his semi-autobiographical novel White Chappell Scarlet Tracings, he notices a haggler "beating down some tattered Colin Wilsons from 20p to 5p: unsuccessfully. Overpriced at nothing."[589]

---

[589] Phil Baker (*TLS*, Feb. 15, 2017) "Overpriced at Nothing: The Life and Work of Colin Wilson"; reviewing Gary Lachman, *Beyond the Robot: The life and work of Colin Wilson* (New York: TarcherPerigee, 2017) and Colin Wilson, *The Outsider* (New York: TarcherPerigee, 2017; first published 1956).

Yeah, I know, it's a novel, but it's "his semi-autobiographical novel," meaning it has a claim to a footing in reality; he's not leaping over a tall building, or plotting 9/11. The anecdote is supposed to be actual, or at least leave the reader with the impression, like a Russian novelist, that "the like of this happens nowadays." Or as Trollope would say, "The Way We Live Now."[590]

It's the purest expression of PC dogma, offered, perversely, as evidence therefor.

And indeed, Baker's "review" is just another opportunity for an establishment Insider (which is even to use Wilson's own terms) to put the boot in to the man who, ironically enough, seems to have replaced Aleister Crowley as "The Most Evil Man in Britain."[591]

Towards the end of his non-stop smirk-sneer-and-smug-fest, Baker lets drop a very significant insult (it's not relevant enough to call a 'point'): Lachman's publisher blurbs that they "also publish Napoleon Hill's *Think and Grow Rich*." My God, the jumped up little pseudes! And proud enough of it to put it on the cover, too![592]

This, a more specific version of his querulous complaints about Wilson being popular among those American colonials, establishes a tenuous connection between Wilson and New Thought. And this accusation leaves my withers—whatever they are—unwrung. For as Constant Readers know, I've long been thumping the drum for what I call our native-born Neoplatonism, our home-grown Hermeticism, our two-fisted Traditionalism.

And although it would be too much to expect that Baker has any more respect for those traditions—he strikes me as the kind of pretentious parlor pinko who mocks parapsychology but adheres

---

[590] For his part, Wilson himself says that "Second hand shops told me that certain people were obsessive collectors of my books, and would pay fairly high prices for them." "*The Outsider*, Twenty Years On," printed as the Introduction to *The Outsider* (New York: Diversion Books, 2014).

[591] "Former home of 'most evil man in Britain' burns down," *The Telegraph*, 23 December 2015. Crowley is usually called "the Most Evil Man in the World;" is it not enough that his house should burn down, they have to put the boot in by demoting him? Or did Osama Bin Laden retire the title?

[592] At least they don't publish Savitri Devi...

to some kind of "science"-based progressivism—they are definitely European.[593]

On the other hand, it may not matter much, whether we insist on Neville and New Thought in general being colonial outbreaks of the Western (European) Tradition – in Spengler's terms, a "second religiosity" characteristic of senescent cultures; or as the birth of the spirituality of a new cultural cycle in the New World.[594] Surely what matters is: it works!

Or is that oh so American an attitude? Fine; we'll leave our epicene cousins to their thrilling games of U and Non-U and other One-upmanship,[595] and get on with the task of living. And that, of course, was Colin Wilson's greatest sin: taking life seriously.

It's a synecdoche of Wilson's problematic, shall we say, reputation that while *The Outsider* has been more or less in print since 1956, his second book, *Religion and the Rebel*, has been out of print for 27 years. However, the end of 2017 brings news that Aristeia Press of London are bringing out a new edition (with an "Historical Introduction" by ubiquitous Wilsonian Gary Lachman).

As famous and as oft-told as the story of Wilson's overnight fame after *The Outsider* is, just as famous and oft-told is the second act, the universal hatred, contempt and loathing that greeted its follow-up, *Religion and the Rebel*. Without rehearsing all that, it's clear, to me at least, that Wilson's own account[596] (despite what must be some

---

[593] See my "Magick for Housewives," *supra*, as well as Mitch Horowitz' *One Simple Idea: How Positive Thinking Reshaped Modern Life* (Crown: 2014).

[594] Watts takes Spengler to task for not perceiving that great spiritual wisdom—such as Neoplatonism, Stoicism, and Christianity—not just New Age quackery, is found during these periods; and also speculates that the USA may not be part of the European old age but the birth of a new cycle.

[595] "A battery of old grey men in club chairs, frozen in stony disapproval of this vulgar drunken American. When will the club steward arrive to eject the bounder so a gentleman can read his *Times*? ...Old Sarge screams after them...'You Fabian Socialist vegetable peoples go back to your garden in Hampstead and release a hot-air balloon in defiance of a local ordinance. We got all your pansy pictures at Eton. You wanta jack off in front of the queen with a candle up you ass?'" William S. Burroughs, *The Wild Boys* (London: Calder, 1972). Wilson famously camped out on Hampstead Heath in his pre-fame youth.

[596] Both in his "Retrospective Introduction" here and in his more recent *The Angry Years*.

amount of bias and self-interest) is fundamentally correct. While one might expect his sophomore effort (an all-to appropriate word in his critics' opinion) to fall below the standard of the first, or to fail in its perhaps overambitious goals, the wholesale revision of Wilson's reputation from genius to fraud, from earnest if not angry young man to charlatan, often announced by the very same critics, is impossible to justify.

Religion and the Rebel is clearly the sequel, or continuation, of *The Outsider*, advancing its concerns and maintaining the same high level. The vociferous negative response, and Wilson's subsequent banishment from "serious" discourse, can only be explained as one of those all too typical changes in critical fashion, where a book, say, is picked up and relentlessly promoted by Those Who Know, and then the author's next book is the occasion for an equally relentless thrashing, after which the author is forgotten and a new one selected to repeat the process. [597]

Thought criminals on the Right are well acquainted with the Cathedral and the Megaphone,[598] and if not already fans of Wilson can be assumed ready to give him a fair shot – the enemy of one's enemy, after all.

I assume a certain basic familiarity with Wilson and especially his first and most famous book, *The Outsider*, on the part of any reader; who could be more of an Outsider than the reader of a book called *Magick for Housewives*? If not, I can refer you to John Morgan's excellent survey, "A Heroic Vision for Our Time: The Life

---

[597] Kingsley Amis, no friend of Wilson's – he once proposed throwing him off a roof, as Wilson notes with some bemusement in *The Angry Years* – wrote much later that "Toynbee...after finding Colin Wilson's *The Outsider* worthy of the highest praise... shiftily backtracked and condemned....*Religion and the Rebel*, as a 'vulgarizing rubbish bin' unaware that it was actually *part two of the same book...*." *Memoirs* (London: Hutchinson, 1991), p182; quoted in Colin Stanley: *Colin Wilson's Outsider Cycle: a guide for students* (Colin Wilson Studies #15); Nottingham (UK): Pauper's Press, 2009.

[598] It's really very simple: "The media, at all levels, is a racket financed by monied interests in order to promote the policies and programs that are good for rich people." Z-Man's Blog, "The Rackets," December 14, 2017. Outsiders—real ones, not the safe opposition promoted by the media—need not apply.

& Ideas of Colin Wilson,"[599] as well as a contemporary review by Sir Oswald Mosley.[600]

Tom X. Hart provides a nice summary of the arc of Wilson's thought, which oddly enough seems easier to see by moving backwards, and has the advantage of tying in many of the strands, especially the political:

Wilson's philosophy can be divided as follows:

I. Human beings have a hidden potential, Faculty X, which once fully realised will allow humans to greatly augment their powers, and possibly transcend death itself;

II. An aspect of Faculty X is manifested in the 'peak experience', a term Wilson borrowed from the psychologist Abraham Maslow. The peak experience is, in essence, the ego destruction that is associated with meditation, sex, and near-death experiences. A person can obtain a peak experience through intense concentration on an object or thought. When the person shifts their attention from concentration an ecstatic moment follows as the person returns from a state where their ego is temporarily suspended;

III. There have been people through history who have attained or understood Faculty X. These include extraordinary figures such as TE Lawrence and Van Gogh – as well as more marginal figures, such George Gurdjieff and Rasputin;

IV. Faculty X and its associated properties may be involved in many 'unexplained', occult, or mysterious events through history. These include UFO sightings, Jack the Ripper, and other elements connected to the supernatural. Phenomenon that are discarded as pseudo-science, such as telepathy and synchronicity, are manifestations of hidden human potential;[601]

---

[599] Counter-Currents, December 12, 2013, now reprinted in *North American New Right*, Volume 2; edited by Greg Johnson (San Francisco: Counter-Currents, 2017

[600] *The European*, February 1957; reprinted online at Counter-Currents, November 16, 2017. This is still one of the best analyses of the book; it was also reprinted in the anthology *Colin Wilson, A Celebration: Essays and Recollections* (London: Woolf, 1988), edited by Colin's bibliographer, Colin Stanley, who will soon reappear here.

[601] Hart will later note the tie between this and the alt-right, especially Jason Reza Jorjani.

> V. The existentialists and atheistic philosophers are depressing, and lack optimism in their materialist conception of man without God. There are grounds for optimism, and there is a possibility for human improvement – if only we have the will to find it. In this respect, Wilson echoes 19th Century optimism rather than 20th Century despair. The world can—will—get better. This salvation will be partly scientific. In this he resembles the 19th Century psychical researchers who thought that a scientific method would uncover evidence for the existence of an afterlife, and that communication with that afterlife would be possible.
>
> What this philosophy represents is a hierarchical, optimistic, and occult approach to life that contains an implicit authoritarian politics.
>
> His optimism tips the implicitly rightist ideas in his work towards fascism. Far-right ideas are not simply conservative in nature, but revolutionary conservative ideas. This not a glum defence of the old order. And revolutionaries must be optimistic about the world to come, if not their chances of achieving that world. [602]

Quite an intellectual achievement for one man's life! For our purposes, I want to concentrate on the earliest part of his thinking, as developed in the newly republished *Religion and the Rebel*, and draw out some comparisons with our favorite New Thinker, Neville Goddard.

Neville likes to present his teaching in the mode of commentaries on the famous "I Am" (or as he prefers to put it, "I AM") sayings of the Bible – "I AM the Way," "Before Abraham was I AM," etc. One might well put together a similar set of Wilson's pronouncements on the nature of The Outsider:

> "The Outsider is a symptom of civilization's decline; Outsiders appear like pimples on a dying civilization."
>
> "The Outsider's final problem is to become a visionary."
>
> "The Outsider must raise the banner of a new existentialism."

---

[602] "Outsider: Fascism and Colin Wilson," online at Medium, July 8, 2017.

"The Outsider is the man who has faced chaos. The Insider is the man who blinds himself to it."

"The Outsider must find a direction and commit himself to it, not lie moping about the meaninglessness of the world."

"The Outsider cannot help feeling that men do not learn from experience – not the really important things."

Interesting, but what does all this mean? Wilson considers *Rebel* to be an extension of the ideas discussed in *The Outsider*, and it is, but in two directions; reading it is rather like watching *The Godfather Part II*, in that it takes up the story both before and—in this case, speculatively—after the first book.[603]

Schematically, it looks like this:

Rise of civilizations—Decline of civilizations and appearance of the Outsider[604]—Renewal(?)

The middle part is largely covered by *The Outsider*, while *Rebel* takes up the before and after. I say *largely*, because the nature of Wilson's method, what he calls the existential method, is to develop his ideas by examining—sometimes at great length – the way ideas have come to be worked out in the lives of great men – the Outsiders —and in his own life.[605]

Colin Stanley says Wilson feels

---

[603] "*The Outsider* was an incomplete book" (p. 1). Like Coppola, Wilson says there were other ideas he wanted to deal with in *Religion and the Rebel* that he did not have the space for in *The Outsider*. He intends to "probe deeper into the Outsider himself, while at the same time moving towards the historical problem of the decline of civilizations" (p. 2).

[604] "The Outsider is a symptom of a civilization's decline; Outsiders appear like pimples on a dying civilization. An individual tends to be what his environment makes him. If a civilization is spiritually sick, the individual suffers from the same sickness. If he is healthy enough to put up a fight, he becomes an Outsider." (pp. 1-2).

[605] The essence of *Existenzphilosophie*, according to Wilson, is "systematising one's knowledge of how to live *by the most rigorous standards* – by the Outsider's standards. Very few men can serve as examples of this kind of development." Neville agrees: "For ultimate satisfaction man must find a principle which is for him a way of life, a principle which he can experience as true." *Freedom for All* (1942), Preface.

The need to demonstrate that his philosophy is not just words on paper but ideas that can and should be proved by living. Personal anecdote becomes an integral part of his message, making it accessible to his audience.[606]

And so there is some overlap as *Rebel* continues this method; for example, the discussion of possible civilizational renewal takes place largely in terms of another long (overlong, for this reader) discussion of Shaw's career; adding as well three Wilson-centric introductions, an "Autobiographical" one, a "Retrospective" one from a later printing, and a "Historical" one by Gary Lachman for this edition.[607]

Already we can see a parallel with Neville, who presents his teachings almost exclusively through personal anecdote and, especially as his audiences grew, the stories told or written to him by his (successful, of course) listeners.[608] Like Wilson, as we'll see, he had no interest in religious dogma or philosophical theory, insisting that everything he said had been proven in his own experience, and simply asking his listeners to go and do likewise.

> Public opinion will not long endure a theory which does not work in practice. Today, probably more than ever before, man demands proof of the truth of even his highest ideal. For ultimate satisfaction man must find a principle which is for him a way of life, a principle which he can experience as true...

> Having laid the foundation that a change of consciousness is essential to bring about any change of expression, this book explains to the reader a dozen different ways to bring about such a change of consciousness.

---

[606] Colin Stanley, *loc. cit.*

[607] Wilson himself later admitted "there is simply too much in the book, and it is like an overstuffed pillow." See "Afterword: Colin Wilson on *The Outsider Cycle*," in Stanley, *op. cit.*

[608] For example, *The Law and the Promise* (1961): "The purpose of the first portion of this book is to show, through actual true stories, how imagining creates reality... I want to express my sincere appreciation to the hundreds of men and women who have written me, telling me of their use of imagination to create a greater good for others as well as for themselves; that we may be mutually encouraged by each other's faith. A faith which was loyal to the unseen reality of their imaginal acts. The limitation of space does not allow the publication of all the stories in this one volume."

> This is a realistic and constructive principle that works. The revelation it contains, if applied, will set you free.[609]

At times, the aim to be practical even supersedes the testimonial method:

> Were it possible to carry conviction to another by means of reasoned arguments and detailed instances, this book would be many times its size. It is seldom possible, however, to do so by means of written statements or arguments since to the suspended judgment it always seems plausible to say that the author was dishonest or deluded, and, therefore, his evidence was tainted. Consequently, I have purposely omitted all arguments and testimonials, and simply challenge the open-minded reader to practice the law of consciousness as revealed in this book. Personal success will prove far more convincing than all the books that could be written on the subject.[610]

For our purposes, I am going to follow the latter method, and try to pull out what Wilson says on various—related—topics in order to compare them with Neville, especially his "simple method for changing the future."

And in the spirit of Wilson's existentialism, perhaps I could begin with some biographical comparisons.

First, Wilson was a product of the pre-War British working class – no doubt the basic root of the animosity directed at him by his "betters" among the chattering classes.

Neville, while born into a large, not particularly wealthy family in the British colony of Barbados (he likes to tell a story about the correct way to feel ducks for dinner, as he did as a child, and how it relates to our "mental diets"), they did eventually become— due, Neville insists, on father and brothers making use of his own imaginal methods—the proprietors of a chain of grocery stores

---

[609] *Freedom for All* (1942), Preface.

[610] *Feeling is the Secret* (1944), Foreword.

which ultimately became, under the name Goddard Enterprises, the largest conglomerate based in the Caribbean.[611]

Nevertheless, Neville, like Wilson, never received much job-related training and struck out early for the big city—New York, in his case—and lived hand to mouth at menial jobs until achieving some success as a dancer, ultimately starring in several Broadway shows.

Despite his success, he later said that the income of any one year was wiped out in a few months the next, and then the Depression put everyone out of work. However, as Israel Regardie pointed out, Neville's natural aptitude and professional training as a dancer formed a crucial part in the method he taught; a point to which we shall return.[612]

In addition, Neville was tall, handsome, and spoke with the sort of exotic accent Americans just love;[613] he was made for the lecture stage. Wilson, though a fashionable enough Angry Young Man in his turtleneck jumper and RAF-issued hornrims,[614] was never particularly charismatic on stage, at least in my experience.[615]

Wilson the existentialist would agree, I think, that all this has an impact on their ideas; at least, it made it inevitable that Neville flourished on the lecture circuit, Wilson in books. And here again, things conspired against Wilson. Productivity in books is looked down on, again, by the Establishment.[616]

---

[611] "Goddard Enterprises Ltd has been operating since 1921 and the elements of its success include Vision, Creativity, Expertise, Tenacity and Location" according to their website.

[612] See Mitch Horowitz, ed., *The Power of Imagination: The Neville Goddard Treasury* (New York: Tarcher/Penguin, 2015), which not only collects ten of Neville's short books, but reprints, as an introduction, the relevant chapter from Israel Regardie's *The Romance of Metaphysics* (1946).

[613] "Americans always assume a British accent means intelligence, so Sargon's fans are being told they are right about the world, by a smart British guy, who sounds confident and reasonable. It's why his clash with Spencer was a disaster for him. He was revealed to be a petulant, argumentative airhead." Z-Man's Blog, "A Pointless Ramble About YouTube Stars," January 10, 2018.

[614] Lachman ("Historical Introduction") says he "looked the part of the 'young genius.'"

[615] Though admittedly confined to a lecture at the Open Center in New York about twenty years ago, where Wilson put the audience of New Agers on edge by calling one of his Establishment foes "a right cunt."

[616] Consider Stephen King. In the MST3k episode "The Dead Talk Back," a detective

Although Neville lectured constantly, he wrote only a handful of small books (booklets, really)—which he never copyrighted; the contents of which, along with recordings of the lectures (again freely made)—fill the internet. And again, Wilson could hardly afford to eschew copyright, as much of his productivity was necessary to support his family.[617]

And the topics! Parapsychology, sure, but Atlantis,[618] pyramids, alien abductions...for Christ's sake, Bigfoot? Not that there's anything wrong with all that—for Feyerabend reasons,[619] I think fringe areas are the *most* worthy of investigation—but it's hardly likely to help your reputation.[620]

After this dip into biography, let's shift our focus back to ideas. The upshot of Wilson's exploration of his selected Outsiders, against the theoretical background provided in *Religion and the Rebel* by Spengler and Toynbee, could be put this way:

> Religion is the glue that holds society together; more importantly, from the Outsider's perspective, it provides a refuge for the world at large, and a method or discipline to provide for the meaning of life missing from the secular world.[621] It does so by providing a

---

(who rather resembles Neville) contemplates a wall of book shelves, and one of the crew overdubs: "And on the shelf behind you every book Joyce Carol Oates released last month." Oates is or at least was a fan of Wilson and provided an Introduction to a reprint of *The Philosopher's Stone*, which was my own introduction to his work. I don't recall who the publisher was, but a later reprint of Oates' version is from Tarcher – the publisher slagged above for printing Napoleon Hill. Pulling it off the shelf to check the date, I see that I had it autographed by Colin Wilson in 1995, presumably at that Open Center lecture.

[617] Alan Watts had a similar motive, although he seemed able to achieve a better balance of lectures to books; on the other hand, it drove him to drink and possible his early death at 57; Neville lasted to 67, Wilson to 82, in line with his speculations in *The Philosopher's Stone* on the relation between genius and longevity.

[618] This is where Hart draws in the work of Jason Reza Jorjani; see *Prometheus and Atlas* (London: Arktos, 2016).

[619] Well laid out by Jorjani in *Prometheus and Atlas*, Chapter Two.

[620] Weirdly, it was *The Occult* (1971) that led Philip Toynbee to perform a second 180 turn and proclaim Wilson once more a genius; one might suspect these "respected critics" were simply desperately trying to one-up each other.

[621] "What was needed was not some new religious cult but some simple way of accessing religious or mystical experience, of the sort that must have been known to the monks

means, a method, of disciplining the will and the imagination so that the Outsider can fulfill his destiny and become a visionary.[622]

As Wilson proceeds through the "Outsider Cycle" of books, the topic becomes more and more clearly a search for a method, as Sartre might say. While Sartre moved from existentialism to Maoism, Wilson wants to move from Sartre's pessimistic existentialism to his own, optimistic version, "the New Existentialism." Wilson's optimism arises from the Shavian insight that The Outsider represents an evolutionary advance of consciousness; or rather, it would, if only a method could be found.

Method for what? In *Religion and the Rebel*, Wilson says that the inspiration for *The Outsider* was William James' *Varieties of Religious Experience*, and goes on to combine James with Whitehead's concept of "prehension," a primal form of consciousness (or, in Husserl's language, 'intentionality') that permeates organic life:

> [James'] argument amounts to this: Man is at his most complete *when his imagination is at its most intense*. Imagination is the power of prehension; without it, man would be an imbecile, without memory, without forethought, without power of interpreting what he sees and feels. The higher the form of life, the greater its power of prehension; and in man, *prehension becomes a conscious faculty, which can be labelled imagination*. If life is to advance yet a stage higher, beyond the ape, beyond man the toiler or even man the artist, it will be through a further development of the power of prehension. This craving for *greater intensity of imagination* is the religious appetite. (Loc. 6636-38)

The "conscious faculty" which satisfies the "craving for greater intensity of imagination" and thus solves the Outsider's problem, is

---

and cathedral-builders of the Middle Ages." *The Angry Years, loc. cit.* Essentially the same as Watts' tripartite historical scheme (see my review of *Behold the Spirit, supra*), with the Outsiders gradually becoming dominant in the Third Age of the Holy Spirit and demanding a suitable religion for their expanded consciousness; not surprising, since both rely on Spengler.

[622] "The Outsider's final problem is to become a visionary."

what Wilson will explore, as "Faculty X," in his subsequent "Occult Cycle."[623]

Having brought in the notions of conscious control, imagination, and the occult, we can usefully circle back to compare these ideas to the teachings of Neville. Let's start with a rather long quote from his very first book, *At Your Command*;[624] patience will be rewarded.

> Now let me instruct you in the art of fishing. It is recorded that the disciples fished all night and caught nothing. Then Jesus came upon the scene and told them to cast their nets in once more, into the same waters that only a moment before were barren – and this time their nets were bursting with the catch.[625]
>
> This story is taking place in the world today right within you, the reader. For you have within you all the elements necessary to go fishing. But until you find that Jesus Christ, (your awareness) is Lord, you will fish, as did these disciples, in the night of human darkness.[626] That is, you will fish for THINGS thinking things to be real and will fish with the human bait—which is a struggle and an effort—trying to make contact with this one and that one: trying to coerce this being or the other being; and all such effort will be in vain. But when you discover your awareness of being to be Christ Jesus you will let him direct your fishing. And you will fish in consciousness for the things that you desire. For your desire – will be the fish that you will catch, because your consciousness is the only living reality you will fish in the deep waters of consciousness.

---

[623] See Colin Stanley, *Colin Wilson's 'Occult Trilogy': a guide for students* (Alresford [UK]: Axis Mundi Books, 2013).

[624] *At Your Command*, op. cit.

[625] As we'll later point out, Neville typically presents his teaching in the form of esoteric interpretations of Biblical stories; here, Luke 5:5.

[626] Again, as will be noted, Neville disdains the literal interpretation of the text, and consequently the organized religions built upon it, insisting instead that it is an entirely psychological document meant to be applied to and by ourselves.

If you would catch that which is beyond your present capacity you must launch out into deeper waters, for, within your present consciousness such fish or desires cannot swim. To launch out into deeper waters, you leave behind you all that is now your present problem, or limitation, by taking your ATTENTION AWAY from it. Turn your back completely upon every problem and limitation that you now possess.

Dwell upon just being by saying, "I AM," "I AM," "I AM," to yourself. Continue to declare to yourself that you just are. Do not condition this declaration, just continue to FEEL yourself to be and without warning you will find yourself slipping the anchor that tied you to the shallow of your problems and moving out into the deep.

This is usually accompanied with the feeling of expansion. You will FEEL yourself expand as though you were actually growing. Don't be afraid, for courage is necessary. You are not going to die to anything by your former limitations, but they are going to die as you move away from them, for they live only in your consciousness. In this deep or expanded consciousness you will find yourself to be a power that you had never dreamt of before.

The things desired before you shoved off from the shores of limitation are the fish you are going to catch in this deep. Because you have lost all consciousness of your problems and barriers, it is now the easiest thing in the world to FEEL yourself to be one with the things desired.

Because I AM (your consciousness) is the resurrection and the life, you must attach this resurrecting power that you are to the thing desired if you would make it appear and live in your world. Now you begin to assume the nature of the thing desired by feeling, "I AM wealthy"; "I AM free"; "I AM strong." When these 'FEELS' are fixed within yourself, your formless being will take upon itself the forms of the things felt. You become 'crucified' upon the feelings of wealth, freedom, and strength. – Remain buried in the stillness of these convictions. Then, as a thief in the night and when you least expect it, theses qualities will be resurrected in your world as living realities.[627]

I think it's good to get the flavor of Neville thinking; but more succinctly, his "mechanism of creation" can be outlined thus:

1. Formulate a definite desire, an obsession, and then imagine a dramatic scene that would be consequent of your desire being fulfilled, clearly articulated in every detail.

2. Induce a state of total relaxation, a "state akin to sleep."

3. In this state, rise in consciousness until you are aware of yourself only as pure existence—"I AM"—without and before any definite determination, such as "I AM this or that."

4. Turn your attention to the preconceived drama, and hold it in your imagination until you *intensely feel the emotion* consequent to having attained your desire.

Reading this, one is immediately reminded of the central chapter of *The Outsider*, where Wilson, having concluded that "the Outsider problem is essentially a living problem [and] beyond a certain point, the Outsider's problems will not submit to mere thought, *they must be lived*,"[628] proceeds to examine the lives of three types of Outsider: the intellectual (T. E. Lawrence), the emotional (Van Gogh) and the physical (Nijinsky).[629]

And, at the conclusion of *Religion and the Rebel*, Wilson reiterates the Outsider's problem as:

Our civilization…is suffering from…*too much intellect, and the consequent starvation of the emotional and physical factors.* Existentialism is a protest on behalf of completeness, of balance

---

[627] *At Your Command, op. cit.*

[628] *The Outsider*, p. 70; Wilson's italics.

[629] This chapter, "The Attempt to Gain Control," is the one Wilson showed to Victor Gollancz, resulting in Gollancz offering to publish the completed manuscript.

[and] clearly plays the same role in the twentieth century that Christianity played in the roman Empire in the first century… The solution…is for the individual Outsider to continue to bring new consciousness to birth.[630]

Neville's method is uniquely qualified to do so, as it addresses each of these factors. Schematically:

1. Decide on a desired state, in great detail, ideally as a mini drama: intellectual

2. Induce a state of relaxation akin to sleep: physical

3. Feel the emotion consequent on the realization of this desired state: emotional

No wonder Neville lived a more successful life than Lawrence, Van Gogh or Nijinsky, at least in existential terms. Neville is the ultimate existentialist, as Wilson understands the term. He has discovered and refined a method for rising in consciousness to the I AM (existence) that precedes any determinate form (essence), from which position I can chose any future state I desire.[631] Remember all those "I AM" statements?

> Unconditioned consciousness is God, the one and only reality. By unconditioned consciousness is meant a sense of awareness; a sense of knowing that I AM apart from knowing who I AM; the consciousness of being, divorced from that which I am conscious of being.

> I AM aware of being man, but I need not be man to be aware of being. Before I became aware of being someone, I, unconditioned awareness, was aware of being, and this awareness does not depend upon being someone. I AM self-existent, unconditioned

---

[630] *Op. cit.*, p 321.

[631] Wilson points out how Sartre had pointlessly sabotaged his philosophy by denying the reality of any such "transcendental ego." Wilson, Sartre and Neville all agree, though, that there is no "unconscious" that determines or controls my life.

consciousness; I became aware of being someone; and I shall become aware of being someone other than this that I am now aware of being; but I AM eternally aware of being whether I am unconditioned formlessness or I am conditioned form.

As the conditioned state, I (man), might forget who I am, or where I am, but I cannot forget that I AM.

This knowing that I AM, this awareness of being, is the only reality.

This unconditioned consciousness, the I AM, is that knowing reality in whom all conditioned states—conceptions of myself—begin and end, but which ever remains the unknown knowing being when all the known ceases to be.

All that I have ever believed myself to be, all that I now believe myself to be, and all that I shall ever believe myself to be, are but attempts to know myself – the unknown, undefined reality.

This unknown knowing one, or unconditioned consciousness, is my true being, the one and only reality. I AM the unconditioned reality conditioned as that which I believe myself to be. I AM the believer limited by my beliefs, the knower defined by the known.

The world is my conditioned consciousness objectified. That which I feel and believe to be true of myself is now projected in space as my world. The world—my mirrored self—ever bears witness of the state of consciousness in which I live.

There is no chance or accident responsible for the things that happen to me or the environment in which I find myself. Nor is predestined fate the author of my fortunes or misfortunes.[632]

This rising in consciousness and return also parallels Wilson's discussion, via Toynbee, of the social role of religion and the Outsider, showing the connection between the social and personal aspects of the problem of the Outsider, which we will develop below.

---

[632] *Freedom for All*, Chapter One.

Earlier, I noted Wilson's second thoughts, 45 years later, about *Religion and the Rebel* as an "overstuffed pillow;" he specifically felt that the early biographical material on Rilke was "unnecessary." But actually, it supplies us with a remarkable parallel to Neville's method, as well as a hint of Wilson's future development.

Wilson says if Rilke had died at age twenty-five, no one would have remembered him. Instead, he *willed himself to be a poet*. "It is the fact *that he so thoroughly dramatised himself in the role of poet*. The life of Rilke is an astounding case of *self-creation*" (p. 50).

> Rilke might almost be said to *have made himself a poet by an act of will*. As I have already mentioned, his early poetry shows very little talent; unlike a Rimbaud, a Hugo von Hofmannsthal, he did not create a great poetry at sixteen. *He envisaged his ideal of the poet, and then quite deliberately acted the poet until he became one*. (p. 56)

And if all this sounds too airy-fairy, remember that between that second book and those second thoughts twenty years later, Wilson had already turned to the parapsychological investigations of his "Occult Cycle;" his subsequent theory of synchronicity supplies a link to this earlier thought.

> Now I would argue that *our natural power of intentionality can create visible effects*. For example, I believe it is responsible for what Jung calls 'synchronicity'. I note that when I begin to focus on the idea of synchronicity, odd synchronicities begin to happen…

> This…suggests that there is some mutual interaction between the mind and the universe, and that the key to 'retrieving information' is to be in the right state of mind: a state of deep interest or excitement: Albertus Magnus' "excess of passion."

(Or, I would suggest, Neville's "feeling is the secret")

It is my experience that coincidences like this seem to happen when I am in 'good form' – when I am feeling alert, cheerful and optimistic, and not when I am feeling tired, bored or gloomy. ...*We are all at our best when the imagination is awake*, and we can sense the presence of that 'other self', the intuitive part of us.[633]

And this in turn clearly links him to Neville's simple method.

With this linkage established, we can begin to notice and call attention to a great many similar features and concerns in both thinkers.

As we've seen, Wilson agrees with Spengler that our society—Western Man—is in decay; he connects this to his own thought by adding that the Outsider is the symptom. Why is this? Because in a healthy society, religion (such as the Catholicism of the Middle Ages) holds society together, providing a sense of purpose and optimism. For the sub-par majority, this takes the form of myths and rituals, but for a minority (Wilson infamously suggested 5%, leading to cries of "Fascism!") it provides more or less esoteric techniques for satisfying the evolutionary impulse to develop greater and higher levels of consciousness. In the absence of such a religion, society decays, and the 5% become the Outsiders who rebel.[634]

What is needed is not a return to some Mediaeval ideal, but to go forward; we need now a method, "a spearhead of conscious intellectual effort."[635]

If man can "change himself," he must establish certain means to do so; he must work out a discipline.[636]

Neville agrees; since imagination is what produces real effects in the "outside" (or what Neville would call the "out-pictured" or "ex-pressed") world, we must acquire a disciplined imagination: Prayer is an art and requires practice. The first requirement is a

---

[633] "Afterword: Colin Wilson on *The Outsider Cycle*," in Stanley, *op. cit.*

[634] Mildred: Hey Johnny, what are you rebelling against? Johnny: Whadda you got? Marlon Brando, *The Wild One* (1953).

[635] *Religion and the Rebel*, "The Outsider and History" loc. 2825.

[636] *Religion and the Rebel*, "The Making of a Religion," loc. 3214.

controlled imagination.[637]

Man is warned to be selective in that which he hears and accepts as true. Everything that man accepts as true leaves an impression on his consciousness and must in time be defined as proof or disproof…A man must discipline himself to hear only that which he wants to hear, regardless of rumors or the evidence of his senses to the contrary.

As he conditions his perceptive hearing, he will react only to those impressions which he has decided upon. This law never fails.[638]

The disciplined man transforms his world by imagining and feeling only what is lovely and of good report.[639]

Perhaps surprisingly, the key to this discipline is…*relaxation*; or rather, the ability to relax and strengthen the will as needed, as one would exercise any other muscle.[640] Wilson says:

For sensitivity—essential to maturing—means relaxing the will, making the personality transparent, becoming completely receptive; and analysis means essentially reacting, using the will, strengthening the personality.

The ideally great existentialist, then, would have the ability to use his will power in analysis, and yet at a moment's notice to become completely negative, transparent and receptive.[641]

Here, as we've seen,[642] Regardie lodges his main criticism of Neville:

---

[637] *Prayer* (1945), Chapter One.

[638] Your Faith is Your Fortune (1941), Chapter 10

[639] *Prayer*, Chapter Three.

[640] "Freedom and imagination are also muscles that we never exercise; we rely upon external stimuli to make us aware of their possibilities." "Postscript," *loc. cit.*

[641] *Religion and the Rebel*, "Bernard Shaw," loc. 5031.

[642] "Magick for Housewives,"*supra.*

it is unreasonable for Neville to expect his audience to have the same level of control over inducing states of relaxation as he himself, a talented and trained dancer, possessed.

Wilson, for his part, would disagree; he thought the method was eminently teachable:

> The next day, I taught them a basic 'trick' for inducing deeper intentionality, the 'pen trick.' This demonstrates the basic principle: that if the senses can contract violently, and then relax and expand, the result is a sense of relief, and a perception of the objective value of being alive…One simple method is to take a pen or pencil, and hold it up against a blank wall or ceiling. Now concentrate on the pen as if it is the most important thing in the world. Then allow your senses to relax, so you see the pen against the background of the wall. Concentrate again. Relax again. Keep on doing this until you become aware of the ability to focus the attention at will. You will find that this unaccustomed activity of the will is tiring; it produces a sense of strain behind the eyes. My own experience is that if you persist, in spite of the strain, the result is acute discomfort, followed by a sudden immense relief – the 'peak experience'. The result is less spectacular—because less dangerous—than Greene's Russian roulette, but it is, in some ways, more interesting, for we become aware that we can alter our perceptions with an act of will. They are not just something that 'happens to us'.[643]

This last point about will recalls Regardie's other criticism, that Neville neglects the role of the unconscious.[644] Wilson, as we've seen, rejects the idea of an unconscious that is beyond our control:

> The 'controlling principle' in man…lies in the ordinary conscious mind, and not (as D. H. Lawrence thought) in the solar plexus or

---

[643] *Access to Inner Worlds* (Rider & Co., 1983), p36; see also his "Postscript to *The Outsider*,", loc. cit.

[644] Of course, at the time Regardie was in the process of evolving from Crowley's secretary to a psychotherapist, so he *would* say that, wouldn't he?

[as Freud thought] in the instincts.[645]

And so does Neville; he urges us to reject the wisdom of the world —seeing is believing—and instead asserts that "believing is seeing":

> To accomplish this seemingly impossible feat, you take your attention away from your problem and place it upon just being.[646]
>
> To dissolve a problem that now seems so real to you *all that you do is remove your attention from it.* In spite of its seeming reality, turn from it in consciousness. Become indifferent and begin to feel yourself to be that which would be the solution of the problem.[647]

Now, let's circle back to Neville's method of *rising* and *returning* in consciousness.

> To accomplish this seemingly impossible feat, you take your attention away from your problem and place it upon just being. You say silently but feelingly, "I AM". Do not condition this awareness but continue declaring quietly, "I AM – I AM". Simply feel that you are faceless and formless and continue doing so until you feel yourself floating. …In this state of complete detachment, a definite singleness of purposeful thought can be indelibly engraved upon your unmodified consciousness.[648]

Typically, Neville presents this as a Biblical doctrine, if we could but see it:

> When it is recorded that Jesus left the world and went to His

---

[645] "A Retrospective Introduction" to the 1984 reprint of *Religion and the Rebel*; reprinted in the Aristeia Press edition, *op. cit.*

[646] *Your Faith is Your Fortune* (1941), Chapter Three.

[647] *At Your Command*, Chapter One.

[648] *Your Faith is Your Fortune*, Chapter Three.

Father ["He was received up into heaven", Mark 16:19, Luke 24:51], it is simply stating that He turned His attention from the world of the senses and rose in consciousness to that level which He desired to express.

There He remained until He became one with the consciousness to which He ascended. When He returned to the world of man, He could act with the positive assurance of that which He was conscious of being, a state of consciousness no one but Himself felt or knew that He possessed.

To rise in consciousness to the level of the thing desired and to remain there until such level becomes your nature is the way of all seeming miracles. "And I, if I be lifted up, I shall draw all men unto Me" ["And I, if I be lifted up from the earth, will draw all men unto Me", John 12:32]. If I be lifted up in consciousness to the naturalness of the thing desired, I shall draw the manifestation of that desire to me. "No man comes unto Me save the Father within Me draws him" [John 6:44], and "I and My Father are one" [John 10:30].

My consciousness is the Father who draws the manifestation of life to me. The nature of the manifestation is determined by the state of consciousness in which I dwell. I am always drawing into my world that which I am conscious of being.

If you are dissatisfied with your present expression of life, then you must be born again [John 3:7]. Rebirth is the dropping of that level with which you are dissatisfied and rising to that level of consciousness which you desire to express and possess.[649]

This individual, subjective process has an objective, societal parallel which Wilson derives from his meditations on Toynbee. The Outsider has been forced, by social decay, to go his own way; but once he has obtained his end, he must return and revitalize his society.[650]

---

[649] *Your Faith is Your Fortune* (1941), Chapter Three.

[650] We discussed this dialectic in "Two Orders, Same Man: Hesse And Evola," *supra*.

Zeteticus gives us a nice outline here:

> How do the visionaries, the Outsiders, gain this supreme knowledge, and how do they convince the masses their ideas will heal their cultures? And Wilson asks, "How does the man of genius persuade the uncreative majority to follow him"...
>
> Toynbee offers an idea called *"withdrawal and return"*...The course followed by the creative minority, the mystics and supermen, who lead civilizations into new glories, "pass first out of action into ecstasy and then out of ecstasy into action on a new and higher plane." Just as Moses ascended Sinai to commune with Yahweh in solitude for forty days and nights, to be illuminated, and then to return to his people with a new way of living, so the creative individuals withdraw into solitude to solve the hard problems facing their people.
>
> Toynbee writes, "The withdrawal makes it possible for the personality to realize powers within himself which might have remained dormant if he had not been released for the time being from his social toils and trammels."
>
> The creative ones must escape to be alone for a time to receive insight and enlightenment. And "when they emerge, it is with the power to stimulate the rest of society to overcome the challenges" (Wilson 113). These creative individuals are Outsiders, the rebels of society who have a vision for the future.
>
> The task that lies ahead for the Outsider is nothing less than formulating solutions that will transform our world.[651]

For Wilson, this is the "crucial question":

> "Society held together by discipline...but what discipline? ...Is the Outsider strong enough to create his own tradition, his own way of thought, and to make a whole civilization think the same way?"[652]

---

[651] Zeteticus, "Religion and the Rebel, Part Six," *loc. cit.*

[652] *Religion and the Rebel*, "The Making of a Religion," loc. 3203; Wilson's italics.

Frankly, though Wilson has done much hard, valuable work, it's not likely his pencil method would capture the attention of the masses like Mormonism or Islam. Indeed, it's hard to imagine how one would, in the modern world, establish a religion.

Here, however, Neville again has the advantage over Wilson. While sharing a barely concealed contempt for organized religion, Neville never the less retains the Bible, Old and New Testaments, as the foundation of his teaching. He does this through a rejection of not only organized religion but the literal understanding of the Bible that grounds it, [653] substituting the understanding that God is our own Imagination, and that the Bible is consequently an inner, psychological drama.

> The Bible has no reference at all to any persons that ever existed, or to any events that ever occurred upon earth.
>
> The authors of the Bible were not writing history, they were writing a great drama of the mind which they dressed up in the garb of history, and then adapted it to the limited capacity of the uncritical, unthinking masses.
>
> You know that every story in the Bible is your story, that when the writers introduce dozens of characters in the same story they are trying to present you with different attributes of the mind that you may employ. You saw it as I took perhaps a dozen or more stories and interpreted them for you.[654]

---

[653] "There is a little statement in the book of Exodus which bears this out. Millions of people who have read it, or have had it mentioned to them throughout the centuries have completely misunderstood it. It is said, "Steep not a kid in its mother's milk." (King James version, "Thou shalt not seethe a kid in his mother's milk." Exodus 23:19). Unnumbered millions of people, misunderstanding this statement, to this very day in the enlightened age of 1948, will not eat any dairy products with a meat dish. It just is not done. They think the Bible is history, and when it says, "Steep not a kid in its mother's milk," milk and the products of milk, butter and cheese, they will not take at the same time they take the kid or any kind of meat. In fact they even have separate dishes with which to cook their meat." *Neville Goddard Lessons 5*: "Remain Faithful To Your Idea." Or again: "The formula for the cure of leprosy as revealed in the fourteenth chapter of Leviticus is most illuminating when viewed through the eyes of a mystic. A literal application of this story would be stupid and fruitless, while on the other hand a psychological application of the formula is wise and fruitful." *Freedom for All*, Chapter Six.

[654] *Lesson 5, loc. cit.*

Regardie, *op. cit.*, thinks Neville's readers would be shocked if he "admitted he is, in fact, an atheist." But he is not a materialist, either. Like the writers, mystics and scientists whose lives Wilson studies, Neville is threading his way between an ossified religious tradition and an all too lively dogmatic materialism.[655] He has proven to himself, and offers to prove to others, that the only real God *is* the human imagination. "I and my Father are one, but he is greater than Me;" and His Kingdom is within us.[656]

> You are God conditioned as man. All that you believe God to be you are; but you will never know this to be true until you stop claiming it of another, and recognize this seeming other to be yourself. God and man, spirit and matter, the formless and the formed, the creator and the creation, the cause and the effect, your Father and you are one. This one, in whom all conditioned states live and move and have their being, is your I AM, your unconditioned consciousness.[657]

Rather than the Herculean task of creating a new religion, and getting everyone to sign on, Neville simply avails himself of the same method of "reinterpretation" practiced by Christians themselves lo these many centuries.[658]

Like a true existentialist, Neville interprets scripture in the light

---

[655] Perhaps he resembles the 45% of self-identified UK Christians who say they do not believe in God, either; see the Times Survey results here: https://d25d2506sfb94s.cloudfront.net/cumulus_uploads/document/6v34wr1cpg/TimesResults_150209_atheism_Website.pdf.

[656] Neville says that the reason people think prayer doesn't produce results, is that "you are praying to a God that doesn't exist;" i.e., an external God elsewhere.

[657] *Freedom for All* (1942), Chapter One.

[658] In fact, many scholars today think that the Gospels are not historical or biographical but simply narrative reinterpretations of the Hebrew scriptures by the earliest Christians, a method the rabbis call *midrash*. Remember, the Christian faith *predates* the New Testament. As Robert Price says, if we want to read about Jesus we go to the Gospels, but where did the early Christians go? Neville, as usual, is *au courant* with the latest scholarship of our time: "It is said that, beginning with Moses and all the prophets and the psalms. Paul interpreted to them in all the scriptures the things that concerned him. Remember: in Paul's day there was no New Testament. It was written to record the passages of the Old Testament which were fulfilled. So when you read the New Testament, pay strict attention to any passage that is quoted by the Risen Lord and taken from the Old Testament." Neville, "The Mystery of Inspiration," January 27, 1969.

of his own experience, seeing how it helps to make sense of his life, and asks us to do the same.

> Now, not everything in the Bible is inspired. Paul's passages about marriage are not. Paul confesses he is not married and wishes that everyone were as he is...This was his opinion, not his inspiration. In his letter to the Romans, Paul states his opinion about the homosexual – only because he forgot that in the Old Testament God made everything and pronounced it good and very good. If God made everything, then God made the homosexual, did he not? So not every word of scripture is inspired; but you will know the passages that are, for when you awake, scripture unfolds in you.
>
> If you are meant to experience scripture consciously, you will be sent, and tell your experiences to those who will be drawn to you, to show them the parallel between what happened to you and what the word of God said through His inspired prophets...
>
> We are in the act of awakening as God, and when the visions come they cannot be stopped. Coming suddenly and unexpectedly, their power possesses you as though something is wearing you. Then you begin to see and hear that which kings and prophets long to see, and cannot because the time has not fully come for them.
>
> As passage after passage of scripture unfolds within you, you will recognize the inspired ones as they take place; but not everything written in scripture was inspired. They wrote certain dietary laws based upon what they called the need of the time, but these are not inspired.
>
> There are passages in both the Old and the New Testament that were not inspired, but man-made traditions which have enslaved the minds of men. We are asked [by Jesus]: "Why do you deny the word of God for the traditions of your fathers?" If you are going to accept the man-made traditions, you will never know

the inspired word of God.[659]

In this way, Neville can leverage the existing knowledge and prestige of the Bible to give his teaching maximum impact among his listeners.[660] It sure beats the pencil trick.[661]

At this point one might pull in the oars, sit back and ask: if Neville and Wilson seem to be on the same track, how explain this remarkable converge of two thinkers who never met nor, as far as we know, even knew of one another's existence?

Of course, one answer is simply that Neville and Wilson *are right*; each has found the truth and therefore their answers are obviously convergent. As John Deck wisely said:

> [If] it is good to keep our eyes open to spot "sources," it is even better to bear in mind that a philosopher is one who *sees things*, and to be ready to appreciate it when sources are handled uniquely and, in fact, transmuted.[662]

Indeed. But still, this is not graduate student source-mongering, but as plain as, to use Deck's own subject, the "influence" of Plato or Aristotle on Plotinus (however "transmuted" or, as we would say, "spun"). For not only did Wilson devote a whole chapter to Blake in *The Outsider*, and refer to him often, Neville also devoted a fairly scholarly and widely read lecture to Blake,[663] and moreover,

> Neville once said that if he was stranded on an island and was allowed one book, he would choose, The Bible, without hesitation. If he could squeeze in more, he would add [three others, including] William Blake, ("...Why stand we here

---

[659] "The Mystery of Inspiration," *loc. cit.*

[660] Or was able; it may be questionable not only how much reverence is given the Bible today, but even how much of it is still read and remembered.

[661] Though the Joker's trick is still pretty cool.

[662] John N. Deck, *Nature, Contemplation, and the One: A Study in the Philosophy of Plotinus* (University of Toronto Press, 1969; Toronto Heritage series, 2017 [Kindle iOS version]); Preface.

[663] "Blake on Religion," 1963; many editions and available all over the internet.

trembling around, Calling on God for help, and not ourselves, in whom God dwells?")...[664]

Blake, Neville, Wilson; for all three, God dwells within us, and our task to realize it – to become a visionary.[665]

Wilson seeks a method to produce visionary or peak experiences "as needed." Neville's method does so: it is a clear, easy to use technique; and as for Wilson's demand for a "new existentialism" that would dispense with the pessimism of Sartre and Heidegger, what could be more inspiring than the ability to take control of oneself and even one's destiny and change the future to fit our desires? To have found the savior, and found him *in oneself*?

Surely this is Chesterton's "absurd good news," the phrase Wilson uses frequently to describe the peak experience.

In *Feeling is the Secret*, Neville quotes the Song of Solomon:

> What more beautiful description of this romance of the conscious and subconscious is there than that told in the "Song of Solomon": "By night on my bed I sought him whom my soul loveth [3:1]...I found him whom my soul loveth; I held him and I not let him go, until I had brought him into my mother's house, and into the chamber of her that conceived me" [3:4].[666]

And adds:

> Our understanding of and delight in what sleep has to bestow will cause us, night after night, to set out for it as though we were keeping an appointment with a lover.[667]

---

[664] "Neville Goddard (1905-1972) Influential New Thought Teacher," no author, at this Neville website: http://www.nevillegoddard.wwwhubs.com/.

[665] "How can an individual hope to escape the general destiny of futility? Blake's solution was: Go and develop the visionary faculty. Good. But how?" *The Outsider*, "The Outsider and the Visionary."

[666] i.e., The imagined Beloved state of affairs is brought into the womb of imagination.

[667] Chapter Two, "Sleep." Neville plays his audiences like a fiddle; he delights in slyly making sexual allusions and metaphors, no doubt causing a flutter among the suburban housewives. Asked by one how to know when one's imagining has done the job, he says

The following passage might be said to tie all these threads together:

> [The] Bible is a message of the soul and must be interpreted psychologically if man is to discover its true symbology. Man must see this story as a psychological drama rather than a statement of physical fact. In so doing, he will discover the Bible to be based on a law which, if self-applied, will result in a manifested expression transcending his wildest dreams of accomplishment. To apply this law of self-expression, man must be schooled in the belief and disciplined to stand upon the platform that "all things are possible to God."[668]

In *Beyond the Outsider*, the penultimate book in the Outsider Cycle, Wilson says that "The first man to learn the secret of control of consciousness will be the first true man..." Perhaps he has already been here among us, and we knew him not.

Counter-Currents/North American New Right
February 12 & 13, 2018

"Well, it's like making love. How do you know when you're done? You just can't go on."

[668] *Your Faith is Your Fortune*, Chapter Eight ("Christmas"); cf. Matthew 19:26; Mark 9:23; 10:27; 14:36; Luke 18:27; Acts 8:37.

THE SECRET OF TRUMP'S A PEALE:
TRADITIONALISM TRIUMPHANT!
OR: HE'S OUR EVOLA, ONLY BETTER?

"Personally, I find the Apostle Paul appealing and the Apostle Peale appalling." – Adlai Stevenson on hearing Norman Vincent Peale was supporting Eisenhower.

"I know that with God's help I can sell vacuum cleaners." – Rev. Norman Vincent Peale

In all the hoopla about Donald Trump, candidate, President, redeemer, God-emperor, not really all that much attention has been paid to what would seem like an important issue in American politics – his religion.

I mean his real religion, not his occasional attempts, strained and painful, to acknowledge the American obsession by pretending an interest in some kind of Christianity.[669]

The Republican presidential front-runner said in an interview with CNN's Don Lemon Wednesday that Perkins, the president of the Family Research Council, had given him notes on what to say when he visited the evangelical university in Lynchburg, Virginia.

"Tony Perkins wrote that out for me – he actually wrote out 2, he wrote out the number 2 Corinthians," Trump said. "I took exactly what Tony said, and I said, 'Well Tony has to know better

---

[669] "Our government makes no sense unless it is founded on a deeply held religious belief – and I don't care what it is." – Dwight Eisenhower.

than anybody."[670]

One does recall an earlier bumptious businessman, Rex Mottram in Evelyn Waugh's *Brideshead Revisited*, who, perfectly happy to convert to Catholicism to get access to Julia Flyte and the family monies, is played the fool by Julia's younger sister, Cordelia, who fills his head with a lot of Catholic truthiness:

> "For instance," says Rex, "that you have to sleep with your feet pointing East, because that's the direction of Heaven, and if you die at night you can walk there… And what about the Pope who made one of his horses a cardinal? And what about the box you keep in the church porch, and if you put in a pound note with someone's name on it, they go to Hell. I'm not saying that there mayn't be a good reason for all this, but you ought to tell me about it and not let me find out for myself."

When Father Mowbray and Lady Marchmain puzzle "who could Rex have been talking to?" the mischievous young Cordelia laughingly bursts, "What a chump!…who would have dreamed he'd swallow it all. I told him such a lot besides…About sacred monkeys in the Vatican…"[671]

Anyway, looking around for something or other, I recently found this intriguing clue provided by Steve Sailer:[672]

> As a child, Donald Trump attended Norman Vincent Peale's church in Manhattan, which was part of the Reformed Church of America, which is, I think, kind of like Presbyterian but a little more liberal.

---

[670] "Trump blames Tony Perkins for '2 Corinthians'" by Eric Bradner, CNN, Thu January 21, 2016. Alas, the headline led me to anticipate an interesting discussion of the influence of *Psycho* on Trump's religious views.

[671] "Cordelia's Sacred Monkeys," The Evelyn Waugh Society, posted on December 28, 2015 by Jeffrey Manley.

[672] "Donald Trump, Norman Vincent Peale, and Ned Flanders," by Steve Sailer; Unz.com., August 25, 2015.

JAMES J. O'MEARA

Peale (1898-1993) was associated with Protestant business leaders such as Thomas Watson of IBM and Branch Rickey of the Brooklyn Dodgers. He was the author of the huge self-help bestseller *The Power of Positive Thinking.*

Sailer notes that an anonymous commentator at his source adds:

Peale's positive thinking is definitely evident in Trump's attitude and speaking style and presentation. Trump is relentless in applying positive thinking. Everything he says about himself and his projects and goals is unequivocally positive.

The positive thinking "philosophy" was very much a part of bourgeois, pro-business, Protestant American mainstream culture, but now largely persists among some evangelicals e.g. Rick Warren's "Purpose Driven Life" and in a non-Christian, New Age context. The self-help tropes about having a positive attitude, thinking positive, waking up in the morning and staring at the mirror while repeating positive mantras about yourself to yourself every day, etc., derive from positive thinking. Mainline Protestants today find it declasse and are sort of embarrassed by it.

Now *this* is interesting. I've never read a word of Norman Vincent Peale, although I do have a Cultural Literacy type understanding of the reference. What I do know is that this puts Trump in the lineage of what Constant Readers will recall as one of my current obsessions, what I have call America's home-made Hermeticism, our native-born Neoplatonism, our own two-fisted Traditionalism, the movement generally known as New Thought.[673]

With this clue, I began googling around and scored this gossipy article in the *Washington Post* from just last January: "How Trump got religion – and why his legendary minister's son now rejects him."[674]

---

[673] The lineage is basically Neoplatonism, Hermeticism, Transcendentalism, Mind Cure, New Thought, Positive Thinking, and The Law of Attraction (The Secret).

[674] "How Trump got religion – and why his legendary minister's son now rejects him," by

The article is about what you'd expect: one third contempt for people who take religion seriously (except as a cudgel to shame conservatives), one third contempt for people who would take this hokey cult in particular seriously, and one third contempt for Trump as a hypocrite anyway.[675]

The link between New Thought and Tradition is clearest in my own personal favorite of the bunch, Neville Goddard. As Israel Regardie said back in 1946, "Of all the New Thought systems, Neville's is the most magickal."[676] And for "magickal" I suggest you read "Traditional."

Who was Neville Goddard, and what was this system? Let's say that Neville (he always went by his first name, like Cher or Madonna) was the Alan Watts of the mid-century; tall, handsome, and delivering his metaphysical lectures to vast crowds in New York, Los Angeles and San Francisco in an irresistible British accent.

Born in Barbados, he approached metaphysics with a typically swashbuckling New World attitude. After finding his guru, a black Ethiopian rabbi named "Abdullah,"[677] he stripped down the message

---

Paul Schwartzman; January 21, 2016.

[675] The nadir comes when one Jack Peale turns up, the hitherto unknown son, described as a 79-year-old retired philosophy professor (whereabouts unrevealed) who bitches about Trump distorting his father's real Christian message and emphasizing the self-hypnosis aspects. Ordinary readers, like myself, will be surprised to hear that there *was* any Christian message from Peale. The nadir of the nadir comes when he dredges up some story about Trump gifting his father a painting on his 90th birthday: "'he made some remarks that were particularly inane...He repeatedly said, "This is a very great painting," as if he didn't know anything else to say about the painting,' John Peale recalled, adding that from then on the moment became a recurring source of humor within his own family." I guess joking behind people's backs and gleefully retailing gossip to the national media is John's idea of Christian behavior.

[676] Regardie should know, having been personal secretary to no less than Aleister Crowley. The comment occurs in his book of 1946, *The Romance of Metaphysics*, a study of New Thought; the chapter on Neville is reprinted in *The Power of Imagination: A Neville Goddard Treasury*, edited by Mitch Horowitz (New York: Tarcher/Penguin, 2015); both Tarcher and Horowitz will reappear here soon.

[677] Although Abdullah regarded him as being sent; he greeted Neville by exclaiming "Neville, you are late!"

of the Vedanta—and, according to him and his guru, Judeo-Christianity as well—to its basic and most literal form. You are, *au fond* at least, God; and therefore, you are, au fond at least, the Creator of your world.[678]

And this was no armchair notion. Neville provided as well what he modestly called "the simple method for changing the world:" Desire, physical immobility bordering on sleep, and imaginary action.

> People have a habit of slighting the importance of simple things; but this simple formula for changing the future was discovered after years of searching and experimenting. The first step in changing the future is *desire*—that is: define your objective—know definitely what you want.
>
> Secondly: construct an event which you believe you would encounter *following* the fulfillment of your desire—an event which implies fulfillment of your desire—something that will have the action of *self* predominant.
>
> Thirdly: immobilize the physical body and induce a condition akin to sleep—lie on a bed or relax in a chair and imagine that you are sleepy; then, with eyelids closed and your attention focused on the action you intend to experience – in imagination – mentally feel yourself right into the proposed action—imagining all the while that you are actually performing the action here and now. You must always participate in the imaginary action, not merely stand back and look on, but you must feel that you are actually performing the action so that the imaginary sensation is real to you.[679]
>
> It is important always to remember that the proposed action must be one which *follows* the fulfillment of your desire; and, also, you must feel yourself into the action until it has all the vividness and distinctness of reality.[680]

---

[678] *Tat Twam Asi*; I AM that I AM; I and the Father are one.

[679] "I like daydreaming. You know that state before you get to sleep? Except in my life my daydreams came true." Steve McQueen, interview given while he was dying from lung cancer in 1980. *Steve McQueen: The Man and Le Mans* (Clarke, 2015).

[680] *Out of this World: Thinking Fourth-Dimensionally* (1949); Chapter 1, "Thinking Fourth

And how can that be possible? Neville, though seldom referring to anyone but Blake and the Bible, leaps over the New Thought tradition to its roots in Emerson, Hegel, Plotinus, and the Idealist and Hermetic Traditions in general, by asking the reader or listener to seriously consider that before he can say "I am this or that," he must acknowledge himself to be "I AM" – he is, *au fond*, God (I AM that I AM); "*imagination is the God-in-man.*"[681]

The method works, because it is, in fact, "the mechanism used in the production of the visible world."[682]

One way to impress those desired states on the mind so that they will then be ex-pressed is through self-talk, and here we meet up again with Rev. Peale. Alan Watts used to talk about "silencing the chatter in the skull" so as to experience the pure NOW state of consciousness. This is because our "inner conversations" serve to

---

Dimensionally."

[681] Cf. Evola: "In the *Heliand* [the Saxon version of the Gospel], Christ is the source of the *Wurd* (Destiny, Fate) and this force finds in him its Master, *thus becoming 'the wondrous power of God.'*" *Revolt against the Modern World* (1937; Rochester, Vt.: Inner Traditions, 1995); Chapter 31, "Syncope of the Western Tradition," p. 294, note 8. The glory to be revealed, spoken of in Romans 8.18, "is nothing less than the unveiling of God the Father in us, as us" (Neville, *Resurrection*). Regardie, *op. cit.*, thinks Neville's readers would be shocked if he admitted he is, in fact, "an atheist," but I think that's being a bit too Crowley-like; there's plenty of American precedent for such a pantheistic and self-deifying version of the Biblical God, from Emerson and Joseph Smith to, well, Oprah. The writers of the Gospels do not "hesitat[e] to interpret the Old Testament according to their own supernatural experiences." (*Op. cit.*).

[682] *Feeling is the Secret* (1944). Feeling is "the secret" (the phrase appropriated by Oprah) because "you must feel yourself into the action until it has all the vividness and distinctness of reality." As Dr. Wayne Dyer puts it: "This is how God works. Your imagination, when aligned with the highest principles of your highest self, is God at work." *Wishes Fulfilled: Mastering the Art of Manifesting (Hay House,* 2013), p. 85. Or, as Dr. Hannibal Lecter opines in *Manhunter* (Michael Mann, 1986), "And if one does what God does enough times, one becomes what God is." Tall, handsome, well-spoken, Neville is the charismatic figure the Tooth Fairy wishes to be. ("You owe me awe!"). Neville is the master communicator in print and person; the Tooth Fairy writes notes on toilet paper and kidnaps a reporter to force him to read a message into a tape recorder. Both Neville and The Tooth Fairy are assiduous readers of Blake, but only Neville has really assimilated him; The Tooth Fairy tattoos "The Red Dragon" on his back, and tries to *eat* a Blake etching. The Tooth Fairy, a cold psychopath, is unable to truly *feel* his obsessions ("Someone made a child a monster" – Will Graham) until he meets the blind girl, Reba, but only after it's too late to save himself. Repetition is the key, at least to build up emotional charge ("Once more with feeling!" as they say).

impose various identities on the pure state of I AM (the "original face before you were born" of Zen).

Neville, in line with the activist stance of the Hermetic tradition, emphasizes learning to take control of such "inner conversations" so as to actively create your future.[683] Rather than the vague "affirmations" of Peale—"I'm great! Everything's going my way!"[684]—Neville asks us to construct *a scene which would follow on* the achievement of our goal, and someone congratulating us on our achievement, for which we, of course, thank him. This scene, impressed on our subconscious by our fervent imagining, will compel outside circumstances to create that exact scene in the future.[685]

How? Because, as I AM, Atman, etc., I (again, *au fond*) am a four-dimensional being, not bound by the "facts" of the three dimensions, but able to access and manipulate the four dimensional continuum that includes time. Imagination accesses that causal continuum and if sufficiently strong the imagined scene will alter the continuum and supersede the previously fated outcome.

"An assumption, however false, if held firmly, will become reality" – Neville.

Is Trump empowering his improbable, against all odds success with such techniques? Possibly so. Discussing this at a recent Counter-Currents meet-up in New York City (just a few blocks from Peale's Marble Collegiate Church) someone brought up a recent snafu where Bibi Netanyahu [686] rejected a meeting with the Don, and Trump, instead of "lashing out" as the MSM would suggest he does

---

[683] See the recent collection of taped lectures form the 50s, *Your Inner Conversations are Shaping Your World*.

[684] Not actual Pealisms, but you get the idea. For more such, see Peter DeVries, *Comfort Me With Apples* (1958), where the main character is a man trapped in a job writing such inspirational thoughts for the local newspaper.

[685] Neville was the original Criswell, both in popular lecturing and in theme: "Future events such as these will affect us all, in the future!" – *Plan Nine From Outer Space*.

[686] Who, some have suggested, rather resembles Trump himself; see "President Trump's America? Think: Netanyahu's Israel on Bad Steroids" by Bradley Burston; *Haaretz*, Jan 05, 2016.

habitually, calmly commented that "When I'm President, I'll go and see him." *When I'm President, I'll do that.*

I haven't really found anything else reported that strikes the same note, but I did find this, which is interesting because it's someone with a blog devoted to ruminations on Neville and other New Thinkers, who in a moment of existential doubt takes heart from… Trump:

> I was thinking about Donald Trump, for example. It is impossible for Donald Trump to believe, claim and feel himself to be poor. Poverty and lack are completely alien to him. *These states never even enter his mind, or if they do, they leave as quickly as they came. He is only aware of being wealthy.* Even if he loses his money due to a bad deal or debt, he will make it right back up again. Donald Trump's perception of himself, his conception of himself, is that of a successful and wealthy businessman, soon to be a successful and wealthy president. *I guarantee you that he already sees himself living in the white house, writing laws and changing policies he wants to change…*
>
> I have wandered off-topic…Realizing that Trump could no more see himself as poor than I could see myself as wealthy I think I finally came to understand what is needed, what is required, for the desired changes in my own life. Somehow I have to stop seeing myself as poor, soon-to-be homeless, suffering, alone, lonely, single, undesirable, unwanted, not fitting in, etc.
>
> Enough is enough! If I want to be successful and wealthy, somehow, I am not sure how, I must see myself as these things. I must claim these desired states for myself. Part of what I can do to that end is make a public declaration that I am successful and wealthy. *Another part is feeling it,* [remember, "feeling is the secret" to Neville's method] but I don't know how I am supposed to feel something I have never felt, *The best I could do is imagine how it must be to wake up as an immediate member of Donald Trump's family.* Probably a California King-size bed and silk sheets, next to a beautiful woman, in some ornate room with a

balcony overlooking the city. I guess I have to figure out what success and wealth mean for me, and imagine how that feels.[687]

Since you are Imagination, *wherever you imagine yourself to be, you are* (or, from our 3 dimensional point of view, *will be*); a point to which we will return.

Assuming you're still reading this and haven't turned away in disgust at "more hippie nonsense," you may still find the idea of tying this "New Age" sort of stuff to Tradition, and tying either to Republican politics, odd or absurd; and you have reason. It's what I call the "New Age Bookstore" effect.

Go into any such establishment, and look for books by Evola: not one in sight, despite mounds of History Channel pseudo-hermetic rubbish from his English language publisher, Inner Traditions. You used to find some René Guénon, back in the day, mostly because there was a proto-ancient astronauts strain in him; see *The King of the World* or, better, *The Kingdom of Agarttha: A Journey into the Hollow* (Inner Traditions, 2008) by Marquis Alexandre Saint-Yves d'Alveydre, the hoaxer who took in Guénon and others, with an introduction from Joscelyn Godwin.

Godwin himself is fairly typical. In his *Arktos: The Polar Myth in Science, Symbolism and Nazi Survival* (First Last, 2015; originally Phanes, 1993), he gingerly broaches the possibility of what he calls "Nazi spirituality," a kind of ascetic death cult typified by Himmler and his *Gita*-quoting SS elites, and carried on by oddballs like Miguel Serrano and Savitri Devi. Earlier, in an article on Guénon's *The Reign of Quantity* for *Gnosis* magazine, he prefaced his account of Guénon's anti-progressive eschatology with the words "Get ready for the Dark Side."[688]

'Twas not always thus. My actual introduction to the Traditionalists came from a sparkly orange-spined paperback,

---

[687] https://blisswriter.wordpress.com/tag/neville-goddard/.

[688] As usual, the problem with this is that evil is attractive (and absolute evil absolutely); perhaps this is his way of sneaking these names out to a larger audience? I know it worked for me: see my meditation on Evola's Lovecraftian worldview in the title essay of *The Eldritch Evola ...& Others* (San Francisco: Counter-Currents, 2012).

The Sword of Gnosis, published around 1972 by Penguin in their "Metaphysical Library" series, both book and series edited by Jacob Needleman;[689] and found, in this case, in the mass market paperback rack (remember those?) at a college bookstore. I recognized the names from Alan Watts, so I bought it – best $1.65 I ever spent!

Penguin later reprinted it in the 80s—in a larger, so-called "trade" edition—in a later "Arkana" series, but it and the others are long out of print now, and it's hard to imagine Penguin finding any profit in such a series today. [690]

Even that anthology contains no mention even of Evola or Danieleou;[691] I first heard of the former when Titus Burckhardt's wary review[692] of *Ride the Tiger* turned up in his collection *Mirror of Intellect* (SUNY, 1987), but otherwise the surviving Traditionalists seemed to think it better to not let the name slip their lips.[693]

Needless to say, when I did get around to finding some Evola in English, it was quite the revelation – i.e., apocalyptic. Metaphysics that grappled with the material world of the Kali Yuga, rather than hiding out in Cairo like Guénon. And without hippies![694]

---

[689] The other books in the series included some more Traditionalists, but mostly Gurdjieffian or pseudo-Gurdjieffian works; only later would I realized Needleman was a Gurdjieffian, and the series was no doubt intended to get the very un-Traditional Gurdjieff out to a wider audience.

[690] However, through a series of corporate reshufflings, they now have the venerable New Age psychology publisher Jeremy Tarcher as an imprint, which they are using for a series of bright and shiny reprints of New Thought warhorses as Tarcher Success Classics, which includes *The Power of Imagination: The Neville Goddard Treasury*, edited by Mitch Horowitz, who will soon reappear further along.

[691] Admittedly, it confines itself to pieces published in the journal *Studies in Comparative Religions* in the 60s, but either author might have at least been cited or even critiqued.

[692] The editor of Evola's *Path of Cinnabar* in English (Arktos, 2009) calls it "highly complementary" (p. 231, note 30) but my memory of it is quite different, although I don't have access to it at this time.

[693] Some might say the situation is little changed; see "Our Conclusion on Evola and Radical Traditionalism" by Jason Thompkins, KRYST-AL AL-KRYST, THULEAN ARIOSOPHY, March 14, 2016.

[694] Despite his reputation, Watts had always been a Man of the Right, and became suspicious and eventually downright contemptuous of the hippie culture he seemed to have created; see the essay on Watts *supra*.

No, today the "New Age" seems firmly the province of the Left – the loony Left, at that. So when New Thoughters are called upon to reflect on politics, the results are typically like this, from a blog supposedly devoted to a "hardheaded" contemporary examination of New Thought notions:

> Can New Thought principles help us make tough choices in this contentious presidential election year? Rev. Sara Nichols argues for embracing Bernie Sanders big vision and New Thought adherent and political consultant Rob Foreman makes a case for Hillary Clinton. I write that while both Clinton and Sanders have their virtues our actions as citizens may be more important to social and political transformation than which candidate receives the Democratic party nomination. – *Harv Bishop*

It's as bad as you'd imagine, or almost as bad. Right off the bat, there's no mention of Trump. In fact, there's no mention of any Republican, just two references to shadowy forces known as "Republicans" but who might just as well be called The Nazgul. So yes, the idea from the start is that "the choice" is "which Democrat."[695]

Mr. Foreman's piece does indeed read like a "political consultant," specifically one paid handsomely to spew a squid ink cloud of nonsense in support of his boss.[696] Baffle 'em with bullshit! Take this gut-churning opening:

> Here are two spiritual principles that come to mind when I think about why I support Hillary Clinton for president.
>
> *1) But none of these things moves me (Acts 20:24).*
>
> This woman has had so many falsehoods hurled at her over the years and not only is she still standing, but she is continually moving forward. She's been accused of having some part in the death of her best friend, of ripping off people in a shady real

---

[695] That old comedy LP *The First Family* had a bit where the ubiquity of the Kennedy brothers was satirized with a supposed public service ad asking that you "Get out and vote! Vote for the Kennedy of your choice, but vote!"

[696] I do not say he has been hired by Clinton to write this; only that it read as if he were.

estate deal, and allowing a U.S. Ambassador to be killed on her watch. In politics, it almost never matters if none of these things are true. In fact, political careers have been derailed for far less.

But Hillary Clinton faces all accusations and inquisitions head on. She continually advances towards creating [a] world that works for everyone.

To keep with the religious tone, Good God! Those pesky scandals that just keep coming up, I wonder why? Perhaps because she hasn't yet been brought to justice?[697] I especially like, though, the Hillary Nixon touch of not so much denying the truth of any of this but rather insinuating that the falsity has been dealt with already elsewhere and anyway, as Madame Secretary has famously cried out in exasperation, "What does it matter now?"

The Rev. Sara[698] though makes some interesting points; like Bernie himself, there's a reasonable position here.

What if we embraced a politics that matched our spiritual conviction? What if we applied everything we know about feeling whole, perfect and complete to the world of effects writ large?

Fact: I am sick. Fact: I am poor. Fact: I am lonely. In our personal spiritual work, we know that conditions have no power over us. Hence, these "facts" under the lens of spiritual mind treatment give way to the *truth*, which is that I am whole, I am abundant, and I am loved. In spiritual science (the philosophy that I teach) we call that focusing on "First Cause." We are not interested in the conditions of the world, except as they point us to a new condition, a new thought, a new cause...

Well, if we embraced First Cause politics, it might look a lot like the current presidential political season. In it, the putative front-runner in the Democratic Party, Secretary of State Hillary

---

[697] "My record is clean ... thirty-eight arrests, no conviction!" – Big Julie, *Guys and Dolls*.

[698] I mean not offense; I assume she's the sort of clergy person who says "Just call me Fr. Joe!"

Clinton, is an expert on the politics of pragmaticism. She focuses on these *facts*: there is not enough money to provide cradle to grave health care coverage for every man, woman and child. Fact: There is not enough money to provide a four-year college education to every qualified student. Fact: we cannot convert to clean renewable energy overnight, and it takes money to do so. Fact: what's good for Wall Street is good for Main Street. Fact: even if there was enough money, Republicans would say no to it. Fact: these ideas are pie in the sky; they're not practical...

(Feel free, Dear Readers, to add your own "facts," perhaps enunciated in that hectoring school marm voice: "Demographic change is a fact." "Gay marriage is a fact." "Desegregation is a fact." "Millions of illegals is a fact, you can't just deport them.")

I support Sanders for President because to me he epitomizes a First Cause politics. He is calling us to get off the meditation mat and come out of our rooms to see what is happening in the world. He promises that we can, collectively, shift consciousness to demonstrate the true abundance that we are. He knows the truth of the matter: there is more than enough food, shelter, clean air, clean water and love for every man, woman and child in the world and it is simply a matter of changing the politics of pragmatism to a politics of possibility.

Sure, it's a little gooey, like Sanders himself, but like Sanders, there's some truth here. Clinton as the relentless, soul-less Fact Lady, grinding away at the supposed politics of the possible, like Maggie Thatcher—another hectoring schoolmarm—droning an about "there is no alternative;" while Sanders at least notices that if we didn't go to war with Iraq, fight spooks in the name of the Global War on Terror, and export jobs and import impoverished Mexicans (all Clinton policies), well, by golly we'd *have* 2 or 3 trillion to spend on, well, everything!

Our previous blogger, though, the one inspired by Trump, had a different opinion; along the way he drifts briefly into Trump's politics, as he understands them:

Furthermore I'll bet that with him as president, America will be taken well on its way to complete freedom and independence from debt. This is how Trump has navigated his own life, and he will take those same navigational s[k]ills into the presidency. *I am rooting for the guy, and it's a toss-up whether I would vote for him or Bernie.* Trump may be all the things everyone says he is. But unlike Obama, Trump knows money. To keep America out of another great depression, without causing the problems Obama did in his efforts to fix things, we need someone as intimate with money as Donald Trump, and that is why I would consider voting for him. The alternative is that America gets taken over by China and every other country we owe money to. I would prefer that America remain free and independent. I couldn't care less about a candidate's personal biases and opinions.

An anomaly? Is he just confused and in need of "re-education" by some kindly Unity minister? Not at all. I was glad to find that Mitch Horowitz, the aforementioned New Thought editor, [699] is pushing for a Big Tent approach to New Thought, as in this essay, "New Thought: Selfish or Socialist?" that also appears on Harv Bishop's website:

> Yes, New Thought has radical roots, which fit my personal ideals as a New Thought writer and seeker.
>
> But Harvey quoted a reader who rightly—and bluntly—articulated something that might appear diametrically opposed to the "social justice" model. This New Thought seeker wrote: "If I show up at a [New Thought church] I am there for one reason and one reason only – the advancement of my personal awareness. If some minister lectures me about some politically correct utopian fantasy (you call it a world that works) I am gone."
>
> I want that guy at my party, too. *The objectivist/ libertarian point of view is as legitimately grounded in the New Thought tradition as social radicalism.*

---

[699] And author of *One Simple Idea: How Positive Thinking Reshaped Modern Life* (Crown, 2014).

I liked the directness of that commentator's tone. Let's face it: we can get very squishy when talking about social justice. Especially when some of the loudest proponents of social justice in our communities can't be trusted to water a house plant...

Then, Mitch drops the bomb:

Seen in a certain light, the mystical teacher Neville Goddard— the New Thought figure whom I most admire—was a kind of spiritualized objectivist. [Mitch's italics} *Or perhaps I could say that Ayn Rand, the founder of philosophical objectivism, was a secularized Neville. Neville and Rand each believed, with uncompromising conviction, that the individual creates his own objective reality and circumstances. Rand saw this as a matter of personal will; Neville saw it as a matter of imagination. But both held, more or less, the same principle.*

Is there a dichotomy between Neville's radical individualism and the communal vision of *Science of Getting Rich* author Wallace D. Wattles, who saw New Thought as possessing an intrinsic ethic of societal betterment? Not for me. I'm skeptical toward language such as *inner/outer, essence/ego, spiritual/material*, which buzzes around many of our alternative spiritual communities. Not only do opposites attract, but paradoxes complete. It is in the nature of life.

And aren't those of us involved with New Thought striving to see life as "one thing"? That "one thing" can expand in infinite dimensions —but does my fellow seeker have to choose between a nice car and "awareness"? Do I have to choose between Marcus Garvey and Ayn Rand? Both were bold and beautiful and right in many ways.

Politically, my heart is with Canadian health care. But I stand with Chris: I refuse an *either/or* scenario, or a lame compromise. Good cannot be boxed in. Paradox is healthy. Reality has "many mansions." As my friend Erik Davis[700] says: "Keep it open."

---

[700] See my own appreciation of Erik in my review of his collection *Nomad Codes:*

No surprise that Bert Cooper, cranky but astute businessman and devotee of Ayn Rand,[701] should enunciate the New Thought credo (using a typical Oriental disguise) at a pivotal moment.[702] of *Mad Men*'s first season: faced with news that "Don Draper" is actually Dick Whitman, Korean War deserter and "who knows what else," Bert memorably intones:

> Cooper: Mr. Campbell, who cares?
>
> Pete: What?
>
> Cooper: Who cares?
>
> Pete: Mr. Cooper, he's a fraud and a liar. A criminal, even.
>
> Cooper: Even if this were true, who cares? This country was built and run by men with worse stories than whatever you've imagined here.
>
> Pete: *I'm not imagining anything.*
>
> Cooper: The Japanese have a saying: "A man is whatever room he is in," and right now Donald Draper is in this room. I assure you, there's more profit in forgetting this. I'd put your energy into bringing in accounts.

See what Pete does here? Bert has erroneously attributed Pete's information to his imagination, which Pete vociferously—and correctly—denies. Pete is the Fact Man par excellence, the man who trusts only his senses.[703] Bert responds with his (pseudo?) Japanese saying, which states the essential principle of Imagination: since we

---

Adventures in Modern Esoterica supra.

[701] "I'm going to introduce you to Miss Ayn Rand. I think she'll salivate. "(*Mad Men*, Episode 1.11)

[702] Appropriate for our subject today, the episode is "Nixon versus Kennedy" (1.12).

[703] He discovers Don's secret when a box of memorabilia is mis-delivered to him at the office. The box is from Don's half-brother, who hanged himself after Don refused to acknowledge him. For more on the hanged man motif in *Mad Men*, see my *End of an Era: Mad Men and the Ordeal of Civility* (San Francisco: Counter-Currents, 2015). As the Irish say, "You'll hang higher than Haman!" (Jon Hamm?)

are essentially imagination, wherever we imagine ourselves, is where we are.

Constant Readers will recall that I've previously analyzed this scene with an emphasis on the Judaic-Randian aspect of "Who cares?"[704] During another Counter-Currents meetup (such valuable gatherings!) I realized that Bert's Japanese saying actually references not "terrifying existential uncertainty," as Matt Weiner typically asserts on the DVD commentary track, but rather the liberating vision of Neville's method of Imagination:

> Humanity, understood psychologically, is an infinite series of levels of awareness, and you, individually, are what you are according to where you are in the series.
>
> Lose your soul on one level, and you will find it on a higher level, defined differently.
>
> Where you are psychologically is what you are in reality.
>
> Where you are psychologically is what you are; therefore, only associate with the feeling that leads you to the fulfillment of your dreams.
>
> Where "I" AM is always what "I" AM.
>
> The moment you look back at your former state, you re-enter it, as all states exist, preserved in your imagination and ready for occupancy.[705]

The "rooms" are of course the various intersection points on the x/y axes of the Tree of Manifestation, each of which determines a particular state of the being. "In my Father's house there are many mansions."[706] Reality, as Mitch says above, does indeed have many

---

[704] See *End of An Era, op. cit.*

[705] *The Power of Unlimited Imagination: A Collection of Neville's San Francisco Lectures*; transcribed by Margaret Ruth Broome (Camarillo, Ca.: Devorss & Co., 2015).

[706] See René Guénon, *The Multiple States of the Being* and *The Symbolism of the Cross*. Neville: "Think of the vertical line of the cross as the line of being upon which there are unnumbered levels of awareness" and "The Bible's teaching is one of rising higher and

mansions.

The attentive reader, of a certain sort, will no doubt have already noticed (or "noticed") that there is a lot of echoing in this essay. From Neville's Ethiopian rabbi, to Ayn Rand, to Mitch Horowitz to Ehud Sperling (publisher of Inner Traditions), to the authors of the *Post* article and the writers and producers of *Mad Men*. Even, it seems, Trump himself, who, despite all the cries of "anti-Semite" has married his daughters to members of the Tribe.[707]

As we've seen above, the relatively pro-Trump and pro-Rand students of Neville are wont to point out how similar his views are to the 70-year-old man in the race, and Pat Buchanan bluntly says "Trumps issues are Bernie's."[708] I guess it just depends what room you're in.

As Sailer points out, in the article we started from:

Part of the Ned Flanders nicey-niceness comes from positive thinking philosophy, whereby being effusively positive towards other people is believed to lead to positive outcomes, just as thinking and speaking positively about yourself is. *Trump's brashness and ego however adds a twist to this formula, and he won't speak positively to or about someone and will put someone down if it leads to himself thinking, feeling, and looking more positive.*

That's one aspect of Trump. But on the other hand, perhaps it's no surprise that Trump is something of a secret New Ager: he is, after

---

higher in consciousness until rebirth occurs. There is but one purpose in life, and that is to rise higher and higher on the vertical bar of the cross." (*op. cit.*) The Tree in the middle of the Garden is where Odin, Don's brother, and Lane Pryce are hanged; see *End of an Era* and Julius Evola, *The Hermetic Tradition*. See my discussion of the checkerboard floor in Henry James' "The Jolly Corner" in "The Corner at the Center of the World" in *The Eldritch Evola …& Others* (San Francisco: Counter-Currents, 2014) and the pigeon-holes in Fred Hoyle's *October the First is Too Late*. See my "Worlds Enough & Times: The Unintentionally Weird Fiction of Fred Hoyle," Counter-Currents, March 4, 2016.

[707] A reversal of the usual method, where daughters of the Tribe marry into the Gentile elite, thereby preserving the matrilineal bloodline.

[708] "The Trump Rebellion – Suicide of the GOP, or Rebirth?" Buchanan.org, March 17, 2016.

all, the Second Most Feminine-Sounding of the candidates (after Hillary),[709] which as Steve Sailer again points out, means that

[H]e Takes Everything Personally. Trump's is an extreme version of this trait that's *actually pretty common among Big Men, who, in contrast to Nerds, are very aware of their individual human relationships.*[710]

Unlike the Keyboard Kommandos of the Man-o-Sphere, real Big Men, as Evola points out, are not afraid to "get in touch with their feminine side," indeed becoming effectively androgynous, like the Original Man at the Center of the Garden, Adam Kadmon, as Neville would have learned from his Qabalistic rabbi.[711]

And what could be more New Age, or Traditional, than that?

Counter-Currents/*North American New Right*
March 21, 2016

---

[709] "Measuring Trump's Language: Bluster but Also Words That Appeal to Women," Claire Cain Miller, *New York Times*, March 14, 2016. For example, "He talks about himself more than any other candidate, using 'I' or 'we' 212 times per 1,000 words, and addresses voters directly less than anyone, 42 times per 1,000 words."

[710] "Trump is the second-most feminine-sounding candidate," Unz.com, March 15, 2016.

[711] "How disheartening to those who uphold the myth of manhood based on muscles and metallic strength: this [the Androgyne] alone is the TRUE man, the ABSOLUTE man. *He absorbs within himself the ambiguous virtue of the female...*" See "Serpentine Wisdom," in Julius Evola and the UR Group, *Introduction to Magic: Rituals and Practical Techniques for the Magus* (Rochester, Vt.: Inner Traditions, 2001). For more on the Androgyne, see his *The Hermetic Tradition: Symbols and Teachings of the Royal Art* (Rochester, Vt.: Inner Traditions, 1995). and my "Accommodate This! Bruce Jenner & the Hermetic *Rebis*," in the Embiggened Edition of *The Homo and the Negro* (San Francisco: Counter-Currents, 2017). Caitlin Jenner, one is inclined to say "of course," is a not only a Republican, but a supporter...of Trump; see "Caitlin Jenner Explains Why She's A Republican" by Gina Mei; *Cosmopolitan*, Feb 12, 2017. For example: "If we don't have a country, we don't have LGBT issues."

LORD KEK COMMANDS!
A LOOK AT THE ORIGINS OF MEME MAGIC

"Can a man decree a thing and have it come to pass? Most assuredly he can!" – Neville Goddard, *At Your Command*

"Trump's assault on truth and logic, far from hurting him, made him stronger." *Time*, "Man of the Year" cover story.

Readers are no doubt aware that even in these days of e-this and i-that, it can take at least a year or two to get a book from neat idea to bookstore shelves. So even though Mitch Horowitz is the editor at Tarcher/Penguin, it's not likely he planned to have this special edition of the first book (booklet, really) by 20th century New Thought lecturer Neville Goddard[712] out in time for the Trump victory.[713]

And yet, it's almost eerily appropriate.

---

[712] "Born to an English family in Barbados, Neville Goddard (1905-1972) moved to New York City at age seventeen to study theater. In 1932, he abandoned his work as a dancer and actor to fully devote himself to his career as a metaphysical writer and lecturer. Using the solitary pen name Neville, he became one of the twentieth century's most original and charismatic purveyors of the philosophy generally called New Thought. The awakened human imagination, Neville argued, is the God of Scripture, and each man and woman is a slumbering Christ awaiting resurrection. Neville wrote more than ten books and was a popular speaker on metaphysical themes from the late 1930s until his death. Possessed of a self-educated and eclectic intellect, Neville exerted an influence on a wide range of spiritual thinkers and writers, from Joseph Murphy to Carlos Castaneda. The impact of his ideas continues to be felt in some of today's bestselling works of practical spirituality." Penguin Random House website.

[713] According to the Amazon listing, it was released exactly on November 8, 2016 (the first day of Trump Year Zero).

There are almost as many explanations for Trump's victory as there are dumbfounded commentators.[714] Relatively little exploration of the role of the teachings of Trump's religious mentor, Norman Vincent Peale, has appeared, although his role in Trump's *Weltanschauung* would seem to be far more significant than, say, the influence of Jerimiah Wright on Barack Obama.

The possible role of Peale in the Trump ascendancy was explored in my essay "The Secret of Trump's A Peale: Traditionalism Triumphant! Or: He's Our Evola, Only Better," (*supra*) where it was suggested that Peale's "positive thinking" was what enabled him to ignore "what everyone knows" (e.g., Trump is a buffoon who will drop out after losing a couple primaries) and instead concentrate on remaking the future "in accordance with Will" (Crowley); in other words, "meme magick."

The key to that idea was to see Peale's ideas against the background of the more explicitly "magical" work of Neville Goddard. The relation between Peale and Neville, as far as I can tell, been never been determined or even studied at all.

In typically perverse fashion, I came to read the still well-known Peale after encountering the still hush-hush Neville. On that basis, I would say that Peale, always the subject of suspicion and mockery by the elites,[715] does give the impression of retailing the common ideas of New Thought[716] in a form that bourgeois Protestants would find comfortable;[717] proper and respectable, without either alarming secularism or the mysticism of those dirty Catholic immigrants.[718]

---

[714] See Charles Hugh Smith, "Six Narratives on the Ascendancy of Trump," Of Two Minds, November 30, 2016.

[715] "I find the teaching of Paul appealing, and the teaching of Peale appalling," sneered Adlai Stevenson, the original "egghead," before going down to humiliating, Clintonesque defeat before the amiable duffer Eisenhower. It seems likely to me he had never read either, of course.

[716] There are plenty of accounts of New Thought online but you might do well to read Mitch Horowitz's skeptical but enthusiastic *One Simple Idea: How Positive Thinking Reshaped Modern Life* (Crown, 2014).

[717] In particular, *Positive Imaging: The Powerful Way to Change Your Life* (1981) strikes me, from the title onward, as a fairly blatant attempt to ret-con his "power of positive thinking" system into something very much like Neville.

[718] On that basis, I recently tried to interest a troubled young woman of my acquaintance

While Peale is happy to throw around scripture quotes like any Congregationalist preacher would, Neville, on the other hand, is like one of those rabble-rousers such as Blake[719] who insist right from the start that there is no legitimate church hierarchy, nor any "history" in the Bible, which is rather a purely psychological document, whose hitherto secret meaning he will now disclose.[720]

In any event, that brings us to the book at hand: this is Neville's first attempt to present to the reading public his unique—yet entirely traditional—take on the power of imagination; what he ingenuously called "a simple method for changing the future," a kind of dream yoga, as he explained in a later work:

> Preparing to sleep, you feel yourself into the state of the answered wish, and then relax into unconsciousness...This is the way to discover and conduct your wishes into the subconscious. Feel yourself in the state of the realized wish and quietly drop off to sleep.
>
> Night after night you should assume the feeling of being, having and witnessing that which you seek to be, possess and see manifested. Never go to sleep feeling discouraged or dissatisfied. Never sleep in the consciousness of failure. Your subconscious, whose natural state is sleep, sees you as you believe yourself to be, and whether it be good, bad, or indifferent, the subconscious will faithfully embody your belief. As you feel so do you impress her; and she, the perfect lover, gives form to these impressions and out-pictures them as the children of her beloved. "Thou art

---

with Peale's work, as a substitute for recommending Neville, thinking that his churchiness would appeal (!) to her, since she still retained from childhood a love of the Episcopal church and its rituals. She handed the book back with some disgust: "No, he was satirized by Tom Lehrer." Those who doubt the power of cultural artifacts to control minds should reflect on the lingering power of one line in a satirical song from 50 years ago; "the most potent weapons known to mankind are satire and ridicule"– Saul Alinsky. See Lawrence Murray, "Saul Alinsky's *Rules for Radicals*," Counter-Currents, November 30, 2016

[719] See Neville's lecture "Blake and Religion" at RealNeville.com and on YouTube..

[720] "While Neville could quote from Scripture with photographic ease, one is left with the impression that he sometimes strained to fit all of it within a psychological formula." See Mitch Horowitz, "The Substance of Things Hoped For: Searching for Neville Goddard."

all fair, my love; there is no spot in thee," is the attitude of mind to adopt before dropping off to sleep. Disregard appearances and feel that things are as you wish them to be, for "He calleth things that are not seen as though they were, and the unseen becomes seen." To assume the feeling of satisfaction is to call conditions into being which will mirror satisfaction. "Signs follow, they do not precede." Proof that you are will follow the consciousness that you are; it will not precede it.[721]

Of course, this short booklet has been available for decades, and is now online everywhere. Why then this edition? Well, because it benefits from an afterword from TarcherPerigree editor Mitch Horowitz, consisting of his essay "Neville Goddard: A Cosmic Philosopher," which delves into many of the questions aroused by this little book: biographical, historical, scientific and metaphysical.

Horowitz summarizes Neville's "spiritual vision that was bold and total" though also "what many would find fantastical":

> Everything you see and experience, including other people, is the result of your own thoughts and emotional states. Each of us dreams into existence an infinitude of realities and outcomes. When you realize this, Neville taught, you will discover yourself to be a slumbering branch of the Creator clothed in human form, and at the helm of limitless possibilities.

Horowitz rehearses the facts of Neville's biography and his "extravagant claims" to have changed the course of reality by mental visualization, but what's uniquely valuable here is that he's done yeoman's work to actually track down what Jor-el might call "their basis in actual fact."

For example, in the post-Pearl Harbor panic, Neville—despite being 38 years old, married, with a son already in the Navy, and a British subject—was drafted into the Army "for the duration of the conflict" as they used to say (endless wars already being contemplated). Quickly deciding this was no life for him, but his

---

[721] *Feeling is the Secret* (1944).

request for a discharge being denied, he began to spend his nights visualizing his life as it would be if he were still in his apartment off Washington Square in Manhattan; within a few weeks, he was honorably discharged, in order to, as Army records show, "accept employment in an essential wartime industry."

The exact reasons for this are unknown, since according to the Army "Mr. Goddard's records were destroyed in the 1973 fire at the National Personnel Records Center." However, something mysterious must have been going on, since the "essential wartime industry" was: delivering metaphysical lectures in Greenwich Village.

One result of his servitude, however brief and unsought, was that Neville was awarded US citizenship. Yes, Neville was the original DREAMer![722]

But the real prize here is that Horowitz has amassed considerable evidence from public records in an attempt to document the probable identity of "Abdullah," the "black Ethiopian rabbi" with whom Neville claimed to have studied Hebrew, the Bible and the Qabalah. Horowitz has noticed that another immigrant New Thought teacher, Joseph Murphy, has recently described his own encounter with a "professor Abdullah, a Jewish man of black ancestry, a native of Israel, who knew, in every detail, all the symbolism of each of the verses of the Old and the New Testaments."

A check of historical accounts, census records and real estate listings reveals "a plausible candidate":

He is found in the figure of a 1920s and 30s-era black-nationalist mystic named Arnold Josiah Ford. Like Neville, Ford was born in Barbados, in 1877, the son of an itinerant preacher. Ford arrived in Harlem around 1910 and established himself as a leading voice in the Ethiopianism movement, a precursor to Jamaican Rastafarianism.

---

[722] Lehrer's aforementioned satirical reference to Peale—"Now Fred's an intellectual, brings a book to every meal. He likes the deep philosophers, like Norman Vincent Peale"— is from a song satirizing the pretensions of various men in his Army barracks; did the story of Neville's escape survive here in some twisted form, like one of the Gospel *pericopae*?

Ford's Ethiopianism also taught "mental metaphysics" and mind healing, as did another movement Ford belonged to, black nationalist Marcus Garvey's Negro Improvement Association.

Yes, Trump's meme magic, from Peale to Neville to Abdullah, is perhaps ultimately rooted in the black nationalist movement of the 1920s.

Unfortunately for the theory, as Horowitz admits, Abdullah left New York in 1931, responding to Haile Selassie's offer of land grants in rural Ethiopia for returnees from the black diaspora. This is a period "sparse of records," but ultimately "Ford died in Ethiopia in September 1935, a few weeks before Mussolini's troops crossed the border."

Since Neville claims to have met "Abdullah" in 1931 and then studied under him in New York for 5 years, it seems Ford can't be "Abdullah," although the latter may simply have been a handy "composite of several contemporaneous figures, perhaps including Ford."

Indeed, I would suggest that what Neville learned from Ford was the Hermetic tradition, and that the "Abdullah" character was an instance of a long-standing meme in which "ancient wisdom" is attributed to one or another exotic though conquered people.[723]

Guido von List gave an historical dimension to this meme when he claimed that the hermetic tradition was preserved from Christian heresy-hunters in the West only by being hidden among the Jews in the form of the Qabalah, re-emerging after the Renaissance. Neville combines both motifs by attributing his initiation to a black rabbi.

But by now the reader of Neville, or of this book, or of this essay, is likely saying "Come on, this stuff isn't real. Next you'll be telling me you can get a guy elected President by posting some frog cartoons on the Internet."

Horowitz addresses this concern as well, and brings in Quantum Physics.

---

[723] Many earlier New Thought writers adopted such pseudonyms as Swami Pachandasi or Yogi Ramacharaka (both William Walker Atkinson). We see another form of this today in "Magic Negro" who instructs clueless White consumers about insurance or banking in many commercials.

In essence, more than eighty years of laboratory experiments show that atomic-scale particles appear in a given place only when a measurement is made. Quantum theory holds that no measurement means no precise and localized object, at least on the atomic scale.

In a challenge to our deepest conceptions of reality, quantum data shows that a subatomic particle literally occupies an infinite number of places (a state called "superposition") until observation manifests it in one place. In quantum mechanics, an observer's conscious decision to look or not look actually determines what will be there.

To this, Horowitz adds:

Neville likewise taught that the mind creates multiple and coexistent realities. Everything already exists in potential, he said, and through our thoughts and feelings we select which outcome we ultimately experience. Indeed, Neville saw man as some quantum theorists see the observer taking measurements in the particle lab, effectively determining where a subatomic particle will actually appear as a localized object. Moreover, Neville wrote that everything and everyone that we experience is rooted in us, as we are ultimately rooted in God. Man exists in an infinite cosmic interweaving of endless dreams of reality – until the ultimate realization of one's identity as Christ.

In an almost prophetic observation in 1948, he told listeners: "Scientists will one day explain why there is a serial universe. But in practice, how you use this serial universe to change the future is more important." More than any other spiritual teacher, Neville created a mystical correlate to quantum physics.

Now, this is common enough in the "New Age" world, but analogies from QM tend to make me break out in hives. Like the apocryphal physicist who began to wear bunny slippers so as not to slip through the space between the atoms in the floor, I suspect the analogy is faulty; whatever happens on the quantum plane, things are fairly solid and deterministic up here, and visualization can't really cause millions of voters to pull the Trump lever. Or maybe it can; I just don't know.

But for now, perhaps we can get some advice from Scott Adams, the Dilbert cartoonist who has recently transformed himself into a pro-Trump blogger, offering political analysis based on his studies of hypnosis.

In between these activities, he published a book, *How to Fail at Almost Everything and Still Win Big: Kind of the Story of My Life*,[724] which may offer some assistance here. Adams points out that while we may not seem to control our physical surroundings, we do control our attitudes, which in turn can make it more likely we will have the enthusiasm and confidence to achieve our goals, thus, in effect, changing the future.

> If you could control your attitude directly, as opposed to letting the environment dictate how you feel on any given day, it would be like a minor superpower.[725]
>
> The best way to manage your attitude is by understanding your basic nature as a moist robot that can be programmed for happiness if you understand the user interface.
>
> A simple trick you might try involves increasing your ratio of happy thoughts to disturbing thoughts
>
> Your body and your mind will respond automatically to whatever images you spend the most time pondering.
>
> Imagination is the interface to your attitude. You can literally imagine yourself to higher levels of energy.

---

[724] *How to Fail at Almost Everything and Still Win Big: Kind of the Story of My Life* by Scott Adams (Portfolio, 2014).

[725] Or really, a pretty major one, compared to which Batman's skill set and even Superman are small beer. See my review of the Green Lantern movie, reprinted as the title essay of my *Green Nazis in Space!* (San Francisco: Counter-Currents, 2016), which also explores the Hermetic background of the Green Lantern's back-story.

My imagined future acts as a cue to keep my mood elevated today. Don't worry if your idea is a long shot. That's not what matters right now. Today you want to daydream of your idea being a huge success so you can enjoy the feeling. Let your ideas for the future fuel your energy today. No matter what you want to do in life, higher energy will help you get there.

As you can see, many of Neville's key words and concept recur here; "imagination is the interface to your attitude" even sounds like something Neville might say if he were lecturing in the post-PC (personal computer) world of today.

One of the things that holds us back the most, however, is our ideas about "what's real" and this is where Adams circles back to our last point. Rather than taking Horowitz's path of outsourcing the problem to QM, Adams addresses it directly:

> Reality is overrated and impossible to understand with any degree of certainty. What you do know for sure is that some ways of looking at the world work better than others. Pick the way that works best for you.
>
> Reality might be fixed and objective, at least according to most scientists. But how we think of our reality is clearly subject to regular changes.
>
> The external reality doesn't change, but your point of view does. In many cases, it's your point of view that influences your behavior, not the universe. And you can control your point of view even when you can't change the underlying reality.
>
> You shouldn't hesitate to modify your perceptions to whatever makes you happy, because you're probably wrong about the underlying nature of reality anyway.

Ironically, it's not reality itself (which is impossible to contact directly anyway) but our ideas about it, that stand in the way of imagining what we want. And in particular, one big idea: the egotistical idea that we have, in fact, figured out reality.

Every generation before us believed...that it had things figured out. We now know that every generation before us was wrong about a lot of it.[726]

This is another case where humility is your friend.

When you can release on your ego long enough to view your perceptions as incomplete or misleading, it gives you the freedom to imagine new and potentially more useful ways of looking at the world.[727]

I can't see the future, so I have the option of imagining it in whatever way gives me the greatest utility.

He also emphasizes that success in one or two areas tends to lead to more success in the future. Could this also be a factor? Trump is phenomenally successful in business and entertainment, while Hillary, despite her MSM-vaunted "experience" and resume, must have known herself that she was grossly incompetent. She might have run under the same slogan used to promote Richard Burton's legendary mega-bomb, *The Medusa Touch*: "The [Wo)man who can create catastrophe!"

Adams' talk of imagination and feeling (both are key terms for Neville) as well as enthusiasm bring us back to another criticism Horowitz addresses.

In a little-known book from 1946 [*The Romance of Metaphysics*], the occult philosopher Israel Regardie [Aleister Crowley's private secretary] took measure of the burgeoning creative-mind movements, including Unity, Christian Science, and Science of Mind. Regardie paid special attention to the case of Neville, whose teaching, he felt, reflected both the hopes and

---

[726] This is a version of what I believe Norman Malcolm called the Paradox of Induction: science is based on the principle of induction – the future will with some degree of probability be like the past. But, all past scientific theories have been shown to be wrong. Therefore, any given new theory is most likely to be false.

[727] Neville would point out that this is the meaning of Jesus' commands to "Put off the old man" and to "Let the dead bury their dead", and to not put new wine in old skins.

pitfalls of New Thought philosophy. Regardie believed that Neville possessed profound and truthful ideas; yet he felt these ideas were proffered without sufficient attention to training or practice. Could the everyday person really control his thoughts and moods in the way Neville prescribed?

Neville offered his listeners and readers simple meditative techniques, such as using the practice of visualization before going to sleep, or the repeat reenactment of a small, idealized imaginal drama symbolizing one's success, like receiving an award or a congratulatory handshake. But Regardie reasoned that, as a dancer and actor, Neville possessed a unique control over his mind and body which his audience did not share.[728]

This is an important point, and also the clue to answering a lesser but more pressing issue: if meme magic works, why didn't it work for Hillary & Co.? After all, there's as many if not more of them than us. The answer lies in their *divided attention*.

Scott Adams advises to ignore "the news," especially depressing news; but even generally:

> I don't read the news to find truth, as that would be a foolish waste of time.

Trump's supporters are the most likely group to ignore or despise the MSM. Hillary's supporters, with their complete control of the MSM echo-chamber, ironically sabotaged their own cause. Their minds were filled with not just images of the wondrous utopia Hillary would bring forth, but also with horrifying visions of the nightmare of Trump's victory. They effectively supplemented the Trump side's visualizations.

As Adams remarked after the election:

> As I often tell you, we all live in our own movies inside our heads. Humans did not evolve with the capability to understand their

---

[728] I've frequently pointed out the symbolism of the Dancer; see, for example, "Magick for Housewives," *supra*, and the literature cited there.

reality because it was not important to survival. Any illusion that keeps us alive long enough to procreate is good enough.

That's why the protesters live in a movie in which they are fighting against a monster called Trump and you live in a movie where you got the president you wanted for the changes you prefer. Same planet, different realities.[729]

As Gavin MacInnes writes:

> These people are not living among real Americans, and their theories about how everyone else should live are not rooted in fact. *They are floating in a magical never-never land and then scolding us when we say it isn't real.* This is why they are currently experiencing a national meltdown. They never considered it wasn't real. Well, dreamtime is over, kiddies. It's time to wake up and go to work.[730]

Ironically as well, despite the PC-hoopla occasioned by the failed remake of *Ghostbusters*, it seems that the original film is the best clue to what happened, as Steve Sailer notes that

> President Trump is like the emergence of the Stay-Puft Marshmallow Man as The Destroyer at the end of *Ghostbusters*, except [instead of] one guy conjuring up the thought in his head, *most of our cultural elite has been dreaming/dreading/exploiting the fear of the Coming of the Blond Beast for decades to justify their domination of power and thought.* The counter-revolution …has triumphed.[731]

Be careful what you dream of.

---

[729] "The Cognitive Dissonance Cluster Bomb," Blog.Dilbert.com, November 12, 2016; see also his "How to Break an Illusion," November 14, 2016, and "A Lesson in Cognitive Dissonance," November 23, 2016.

[730] "Reality Bites," TakiMag.com, December 1, 2016.

[731] "Trump As Haven Monahan's Dad," Unz.com, December 1, 2016,

To understand the Trump counter-revolution,[732] you need to read this book, preferably in this edition, as amplified with Mitch Horowitz's deep historical research and apt philosophical reflections. You will learn that

> You have become so enmeshed in the belief that you are man that you have forgotten the glorious being that you are. Now with your memory restored DECREE the unseen to appear and it SHALL appear, for all things are compelled to respond to the Voice of God, your awareness of being – the world is AT YOUR COMMAND![733]

Counter-Currents/North American New Right
December 30, 2016

---

[732] And how to handle the attempted counter-counter-revolution: "I think this is why he's been behaving extra-Presidential ever since he won. *In order to ensconce himself in the minds of many people as possible* as the incumbent, in order to deter game-playing with possible recounts, the Electoral College actual vote, and potential coups. In other words, *he's behaving like he's already President* to dare them to try any of those shenanigans." Commenter on "Maybe CIA/Washington Post Brainstorming About a Coup Needs a Rethink About Just Whom They Can Trust to Carry It Out?" by Steve Sailer at Unz.com, December 10, 2016.

[733] I can't help but recall here Thomas Mann's portrait of a deranged inter-war poet, a sort of Stefan George crossed with Ernst Jünger, whose sole work, self-published on fine paper and exquisitely bound, re-imagines Christ as a sort of Bismarck, issuing various orders of the day and ends thus: "Soldiers! I deliver to you to plunder – *the world!*"

INDEX

A

Abdullah 77, 84, 145, 243-244, 247-248, 252-253, 270, 318, 339, 340
Adi Da 12, 217, 271-272
Archdruid, The 179-180, 182-187, 191, 195-196

B

Burroughs, William S. 125-135, 137-140, 220, 231, 233, 286

C

Carpocrates 215, 217-223, 225-228

Crowley, Aleister 7, 84, 134, 138, 140-152, 185, 192-193, 195, 242, 250, 253, 281, 285, 304, 318, 320, 336, 344

D

Deck, John N., 14-15, 59-61, 97, 101-02, 115, 204, 251, 275, 311
Durden, Emericus 197-198, 200-214

E

Evola, Baron Julius 7, 12, 15-16, 24, 38, 45-48, 52, 57, 63, 79, 93, 119, 122, 134-137, 140, 146-147, 152-153, 155-162, 165-166, 168-180, 182, 184-189, 191, 193, 195, 199-200, 202-203, 208, 211, 213-214, 221, 224-228, 242, 250, 252-254, 256-257, 263-264, 266-267, 275, 306, 315, 320, 323-324, 332-333, 336

F

Ford, Arnold Josiah 77, 339-340

G

Goddard, Neville See Neville
Guénon, René 12, 14-15, 20, 24, 46, 66-67, 102, 119, 124, 135, 146, 186, 199, 203-206, 219, 226-227, 236, 252, 274-275, 323-324, 331
Greer, John Michael, 179; see also *The Archdruid*

H

Hesse, Hermann 38, 93, 153, 155-156, 158, 160-169, 171-176, 306

J

Johnson, Dr. Gregory R. 8, 13, 15, 17, 19, 28, 36, 39, 46, 48, 57, 63-64, 72, 97-98, 104, 113, 129, 172, 174, 176, 230, 236, 243, 288

K

Krishnamurti, U. G. 8
Krishnamurti, Jiddu 7, 77

M

McLuhan, Marshall 11, 38-39, 43
Mitrinovic, Dimitrije 39, 77

N

Neville 7, 75-77, 79, 80-91, 96, 115, 121, 123, 145-146, 151, 180-189, 193, 195-196, 209-210, 214, 223, 241-244, 248-255, 257, 259, 261, 263-264, 265, 267-281, 283, 286, 289, 291-294, 296, 298-299, 301-312, 318-322, 324, 329, 331-333, 335-341, 343-345

P

Peale, Norman Vincent 75, 102, 115, 180, 195, 241, 315-318, 320-321, 336-337, 339-340
Pieper, Joseph 14

S

Schuon, Frithjof 79, 83, 92, 252

W

Watts, Alan W. 7, 9, 11-13, 43-70, 72-110, 116-117, 120, 133, 147, 193, 206, 209, 220, 241-

243, 273-275, 278, 280-281, 286, 294-295, 318, 320, 324

Wilson, Colin 7, 11, 43, 45, 48, 81, 96, 113, 144-146, 151, 267, 281, 283, 285-299, 301-304, 306-309, 311-313

Wilson, Peter Lamborn 28, 230, 233-234, 239

Wilson, Robert Anton 142

www.ingramcontent.com/pod-product-compliance
Ingram Content Group UK Ltd.
Pitfield, Milton Keynes, MK11 3LW, UK
UKHW040635240325
5122UKWH00033B/301